FAR-FLUNG FAMILIES IN FILM

The Diasporic Family in Contemporary European Cinema

Daniela Berghahn

© Daniela Berghahn, 2013, 2014

First published in hardback in 2013

This paperback edition 2014

Edinburgh University Press Ltd
The Tun – Holyrood Road
12(2f) Jackson's Entry
Edinburgh EH8 8PJ
www.euppublishing.com

Typeset in 10/12.5 pt Sabon
by Servis Filmsetting Ltd, Stockport, Cheshire, and
printed and bound in Great Britain by
CPI Group (UK) Ltd, Croydon CR0 4YY

A CIP record for this book is available from the British Library

ISBN 978 0 7486 4290 8 (hardback)
ISBN 978 0 7486 9738 0 (paperback)
ISBN 978 0 7486 7785 6 (webready PDF)
ISBN 978 0 7486 7787 0 (epub)

The right of Daniela Berghahn
to be identified as author of this work
has been asserted in accordance with
the Copyright, Designs and Patents Act 1988,
and the Copyright and Related Rights
Regulations 2003 (SI No. 2498).

CONTENTS

List of Illustrations — iv
Acknowledgements — vi

Introduction — 1
1 Family Matters in Diaspora — 18
2 Families in Motion — 53
3 Family Memories, Family Secrets — 85
4 Gender, Generation and the Production of Locality in the Diasporic Family — 120
5 Romance and Weddings in Diaspora — 152

Bibliography — 186
Index — 216

LIST OF ILLUSTRATIONS

1.1	*Tea in the Harem* (Courtesy of the BFI)	35
1.2	*Pressure* (Courtesy of the BFI)	39
1.3	*America's First Family* (© Annie Leibovitz, courtesy of The Office of Public Engagement at The White House)	43
1.4	*Hidden* (© Wega Film, courtesy of Michael Haneke)	47
2.1	*The Edge of Heaven* (© corazón international Gmbh & Co KG)	55
2.2	*Immigrant Memories* (© Bandits. A film directed by Yamina Benguigui. DVD on sale at Editions MK2)	63
2.3	*Journey of Hope* (© Catpics, courtesy of the BFI)	68
2.4	*Almanya – Welcome to Germany* (© Roxy Film)	73
2.5	*Le Grand Voyage* (© Pyramide International, courtesy of Ismaël Ferroukhi)	77
2.6	*Le Grand Voyage* (© Pyramide International, courtesy of Ismaël Ferroukhi)	79
3.1	*Immigrant Memories* (© Bandits. A film directed by Yamina Benguigui. DVD on sale at Editions MK2)	92
3.2	*I for India* (Courtesy of Sandhya Suri)	96
3.3	*I for India* (Courtesy of Sandhya Suri)	98
3.4	*Lola and Bilidikid* (© zero fiction film)	107
3.5	*My Beautiful Laundrette* (© Film4)	111
3.6	*Nina's Heavenly Delights* (© Verve Pictures)	114
4.1	*Bend it Like Beckham* (Courtesy of Gurinder Chadha)	127
4.2	*When We Leave* (© Independent Artists Filmproduktion)	130
4.3	*When We Leave* (© Independent Artists Filmproduktion)	133
4.4	*East is East* (Courtesy of Film4)	137
4.5	*West is West* (© West is West Distribution Ltd.)	138
4.6	*Couscous* (© Pathé Production, courtesy of Abdellatif Kechiche)	145
5.1	*Evet, I Do!* (© Cinemendo GmbH, DVD ASIN: B003EGI61M, Blu-Ray ASIN: B003EGI61W)	166
5.2	*My Big Fat Greek Wedding* (© HBO/BFI)	168
5.3	*Monsoon Wedding* (© Delhi Dot/BFI)	175

| 5.4 | *Bride and Prejudice* (Courtesy of Gurinder Chadha) | 177 |
| 5.5 | *Bride and Prejudice* (Courtesy of Gurinder Chadha) | 178 |

ACKNOWLEDGEMENTS

I should like to thank my colleagues in the Department of Media Arts at Royal Holloway for their unwavering interest and support throughout this project, and to the Faculty of Arts and Social Sciences for granting me sabbatical leave during the early stages of writing this book. I am immensely grateful to the Arts and Humanities Research Council for awarding me a Research Fellowship that enabled me to devote myself entirely to the diasporic family in cinema for a sustained period of time.

Their generous funding has provided the necessary means to facilitate the exchange of ideas with other scholars, filmmakers and producers at an international conference on 'The Diasporic Family in Cinema', which I organised at the School of Oriental and African Studies (SOAS) in London in 2011, and on a Society for Cinema and Media Studies (SCMS) conference panel in New Orleans. I am also indebted to the Humanities and Arts Research Centre at Royal Holloway, University of London, for awarding me a Fellowship and funds to convene a conference entitled 'Welcoming Strangers' and several research seminars. I should like to extend warm thanks to everyone who contributed to these conferences, roundtable discussions, public film screenings with Q & As and to a panel on 'Hollywood Fathers and Bollywood Mothers' at the European Network for Cinema and Media Studies (NECS) conference in Istanbul in 2010: Feo Aladağ, Stella Bruzzi, Robin Cohen, Manishita Dass, Stephanie Hemelryk Donald, Rachel Dwyer, John Ellis, Mark Hobart, Marc Isaacs, Gareth Jones, Barry Langford, Yosefa Loshitzky, Sarita Malik, Barbara Mennel, Yasemin and Nesrin Samdereli, Claudia Sternberg, Sandhya Suri, Carrie Tarr, Rosie Thomas and Leslee Udwin. By generously giving of their time and sharing their professional and scholarly expertise they have offered me a wealth of insights, fresh ideas and complementary vantage points. I can only hope that *Far-Flung Families in Film* does justice to their intellectual input. I am grateful to the students on my Transnational Cinema course at Royal Holloway for making the first run such a rewarding and enjoyable experience. They have taught me that the notion of a 'diasporic optic' is not just an aesthetic strategy and a useful heuristic tool but also something that happens 'live' in the classroom while we are looking at diasporic family films through our own transnationally inflected lenses. I also owe a debt of gratitude to all of those colleagues whose suggestions and comments, via email or during long, inspirational conversations, have made a real difference to the progress of my research and have helped shape this book: Rob Burns, Paul Cooke, Richard Dyer, Thomas Elsaesser, Randall Halle, John Hill, Shirley Jordan, Mandy Merck, Hamid Naficy, Jonathan Powell, Karl Schoonover, Ayça Tunç and James Williams.

At a time when knowledge exchange and impact have become oft-invoked but also contentious buzzwords, no research project can be successfully conceived without a dissemination strategy in mind. Therefore, my sincere thanks go to those organisations and individuals who have enabled me to go public or virtual. Maren Hobein at the Goethe Institute and Charlotte Saluard at the Ciné Lumière lent me their efficient assistance with organising the screenings of *When We Leave* and *Almanya – Welcome to Germany*, both hosted at London's fantastic Ciné Lumière. Chris Jennings of PagetoScreen deserves full credit for developing and maintaining the website www.farflungfamilies.net, which combines beautiful design with functional interactivity and showcases all aspects of the project.

I should also like to thank the companies, filmmakers and producers who were so kind as to grant me permission to reproduce the images for which they hold the copyright and whose names are mentioned in the list of illustrations. Although every effort has been made to contact copyright holders and to obtain their permission for the use of images reproduced in this book, I have not always been successful. I apologise for any omissions and would be grateful to be notified of any additions that should be incorporated in future reprints or editions of this book.

Parts of Chapters 3 and 5 have appeared in the journal *Transnational Cinemas* (2:2, 2011) and in the anthology *Turkish German Cinema in the New Millennium: Sites, Sounds, and Screens* (2012). The feedback provided by the editors Deborah Shaw, Sabine Hake and Barbara Mennel on earlier versions of material that now forms part of this book has been most useful and brought some of the arguments into focus. My heartfelt thanks also go to Manishita Dass, who read Chapter 5 and kindly shared her knowledge of Indian cinema and culture with me. My biggest debt of gratitude is to Stella Bruzzi, whose enduring and enthusiastic interest in the project even extended to her reading an earlier draft of the entire manuscript. I have profited enormously from her intellectual generosity, her insightful comments and constructive feedback. However, I alone take full responsibility for any errors and oversights. At Edinburgh University Press, I should like to thank Esmé Watson for originally commissioning this volume and, above all, Gillian Leslie and Michelle Houston for seeing this project through to its completion with such expert guidance and tremendous dedication.

I could not have completed this book about families without the love and support of my own family. So finally, my deepest gratitude goes to my husband Chris and to my daughters Zoë and Hannah. Although they have kept me company in front of the big and the small screen over the past few years, I suspect that they will be relieved that, from now on, we can also watch films together that do not revolve around diasporic families.

This book is dedicated to my own far-flung family
in
Oxford
Germany
America
New Zealand
and in
Heaven

INTRODUCTION

In the popular Turkish German comedy, *Almanya – Willkommen in Deutschland* (*Almanya – Welcome to Germany*, Yasemin Samdereli, 2011), Cenk, the seven-year-old grandson of the Turkish family shown on the cover of this book, is rejected by both the German and the Turkish football teams at his school because, as the son of a Turkish German father and a German mother, he does not qualify for either side. He picks a fight, comes home bruised and beaten, and then, when the entire extended Yilmaz family are gathered round the dinner table, comes out with the all-important question: 'So what are we? Turks or Germans?'[1] Nobody knows for sure. Cenk's grandparents, who had left their Anatolian *Heimat* on the back of a sky-blue pick-up truck more than forty years before to go in search of a more prosperous life in Germany, have just acquired German citizenship and German passports but, paradoxically, also a home in their homeland. Cenk's father Ali speaks hardly any Turkish and is, in most respects, far more German than his blond and blue-eyed German wife. And so Cenk has to make do with the seemingly unsatisfactory answer: 'You can also be both'.

Cenk's innocent question raises the complex issue of belonging that, in some form or other, underpins all of the films about diasporic families in this book. As the heated debate that ensues amongst the Yilmaz family illustrates, memories of migration and an enduring attachment to the original homeland result in a diasporic consciousness, which feeds on nostalgic memories of the homeland and on 'the dream of a glorious home-coming' (Naficy 2001: 229). The vertical 'axis of origin and return' intersects with the lateral axis of dispersal, and both jointly constitute the diaspora experience (Clifford 1994: 322). Scattered across several countries or continents, diasporic communities are particularly reliant on modern transport and communication technologies to maintain social and familial networks transnationally, which has garnered them the accolade of being 'the exemplary communities of the transnational moment' (Tölölyan 1991: 5).

Khachig Tölölyan's much-cited remark in the inaugural issue of the journal *Diaspora* may help explain why diasporic family narratives proliferate in contemporary cinema. On account of their multi-locality, transnational mobility and local / global networking strategies, diasporas seem to epitomise what we commonly associate with the trendy catchphrase 'the age of globalisation' (although diasporas precede globalisation by some 2,500 years and the two concepts are not intrinsically related (see Cohen 2008: 154). Transnational mobility and migration are amongst the most powerful forces of social transformation in our contemporary world and are at the centre of public and political debates. Therefore, these agents of change evoke anxieties, with which mass migration and resettlement are charged, both for migrating and for receiving communities. Families, in particular, arouse a deep-rooted xenophobia, as testified by the headlines and news coverage they receive in the Western media.

The influx of immigrant families who, on the whole, tend to have more children than majority culture families engenders fears of 'being swamped' or 'outnumbered'. The inflammatory and hugely controversial bestseller *Deutschland schafft sich ab* (*Germany is Abolishing Itself*, 2010), written by former executive board member of the German Federal Bank, Thilo Sarrazin, expresses and mobilises such xenophobic sentiments. He argues that Turkish and Arab Muslim families in particular, who 'constantly produce little headscarf-wearing girls', are breeding grounds of alterity and that their growing numbers will eventually lead to the erosion of Germany's educational and cultural values and achievements.[2] The media, not just in Germany but also in Britain and France, regularly give sensationalist accounts of the oppression and victimisation of daughters or wives. Forced marriage and honour killings are cited as shocking evidence of an unbridgeable culture clash between 'immigrant', 'British Asian', 'Turkish German' or simply 'Muslim' families and dominant culture. The social and cultural values by which diasporic families (though this scholarly term is not used in the media) abide are stigmatised as archaic and incompatible with the enlightened and egalitarian values of Western liberal democracies. The family, as the smallest unit of society and as the prime site of socialisation and identity formation, plays a pivotal role in the provocative evocation of such culture clash scenarios, given that, in public discourse and political rhetoric, society's ills are regularly attributed to the decline or failure of the family. When, in the summer of 2011, rioters wreaked havoc in the streets of London and other major British cities, Prime Minister David Cameron (2011) put the blame on troubled families and admonished the nation to use some 'tough love' and 'do better at bringing up our children'. While these admonitions were not specifically directed at families with a migratory background (since, as was noted almost with surprise, black and Asian Britons were not over-represented amongst the alienated disaffected youth who were rioting and looting), in most other instances of civil unrest, delinquency and crime, ethnic minority youths are almost automatically identified as the prime suspects – and not just in the UK.[3]

Some films about diasporic family life, notably those that follow the conventions of 'the cinema of duty' (Malik 1996, see Chapter 1), a type of social problem film that engages with issues of race and ethnicity, reinforce these anxieties about excessive alterity presumed to jeopardise the social fabric and cohesion of the host societies. Others – and, indeed, the majority of the films made over the past twenty-five years – offer more nuanced family portraits or even project nostalgic fantasies of traditional families, imagined in terms of extended kinship networks and strong affective bonds. As sociologist Anthony Giddens notes, 'there is perhaps more nostalgia surrounding the lost haven of the family than for any other institution with its roots in the past' (2002: 53). Some idealised portrayals of happy and nurturing diasporic families satisfy this nostalgic fantasy and, in this way, intervene in debates about 'the myth of family decline' (Kain 1990) in the Western world by suggesting that diasporic families buck the trend on account of their superior family values. Imagined as a 'traditional' family as yet untroubled by fragmenting individualism and divorce, the diasporic family encapsulates the longing for the golden age of the family that, as Stephanie Coontz convincingly argues in *The Way We Never Were* (2000), never actually existed.

Whether filmic representations idealise or stigmatise diasporic families is, in large measure, determined by the ethnicity in question. In the essay 'Double occupancy and small adjustments', Thomas Elsaesser traces the ethnic fault lines between families 'from countries that have family values which make all the members economically productive and upwardly mobile, such as the Chinese and the Indians, and those that keep their women indoors and illiterate, and raise their male children in the patriarchal code of macho-masculinity' (2005: 122). We may want to add 'Hollywood Italians' to the positive end of the spectrum because, despite their machismo and excessive violence (in the gangster genre), they epitomise a people for whom *la famiglia* is the supreme value.[4] In the ethnic romantic comedy *Moonstruck* (Norman Jewison, 1987), to which I return briefly in the final chapter, *la famiglia* represents the integrative force that helps overcome marital infidelity and fraternal rivalry because the collective counts for more than individual desires, though the two are happily reconciled in the film's finale. The priority assigned to the collective (visually represented in large family gatherings and, in particular, the almost sacred ritual of family meals) makes idealised depictions of diasporic families an appealing counterfoil to the selfish pursuit of individual desire, which is often blamed for the alleged decline of the family in the West. In Francis Ford Coppola's trilogy *The Godfather* (1972, 1974, 1990), however, family values become perverted and what makes the Corleones arguably the most famous and most fascinating Italian American immigrant family is the schism between good family values and the 'amoral familism' (Bondanella 2006: 261) of the Mafia, structured like a family along generational lines and demanding uncompromising loyalty of its members. Whatever brutal murders Vito Corleone and his son Michael, who reluctantly inherits his father's mantle, commit, they do it in the name of the family – to protect their wives and children, to grant their sons a better life (Vito even aspires for Michael to become a Senator) and to honour the achievements of their fathers. Michael is such a compelling anti-hero precisely because of his ability 'to kill without blinking because of his love for the family' (Camon 2000: 65) – a perplexing moral ambiguity underscored in the parallel montage of his son's baptism with the mass killing of his enemies at the beginning of *The Godfather Part II*. The rift between violence and love cannot, however, ultimately be reconciled. Vendetta and brutal murders within the Corleone family lead to its moral and actual disintegration. Although *The Godfather Trilogy* charts the demise of a family dynasty (and one that Peter Bondanella (242), amongst others, has compared to America's First Family, the Kennedys), it nevertheless reflects a veneration of family values linked to another culture and another time: namely, Sicily's rural past.

As Thomas Elsaesser's observations and the considerations above suggest, a strong family orientation alone does not suffice for the valorisation of the ethnicised family on film. The will to integrate, to be upwardly mobile and to become somehow similar to the normative model of the white hegemonic family, yet without replicating its shortcomings and failures, are essential prerequisites for the positive endorsement of the Other – and for the cross-over appeal of diasporic family films. Consequently, families headed by single black mothers who are confined to a distinctly black urban culture – such as the aspiring music hall performer Anita in *Babymother* (Julien Henriques, 1998), or Ricky and Curtis's mother in *Bullet Boy* (Saul Dibb, 2004), who tries to protect her sons from falling victim to black-on-black gun crime on East London's 'Murder Mile' – do not qualify since they exhibit the problems that supposedly besiege the hegemonic white family in exponentially exaggerated form – and worse ones to boot.[5]

There also appears to be an implicit hierarchy of faiths that determines whether diasporic families in contemporary European and Hollywood cinema are valorised or vilified. Christians, whether Catholic, Protestant or Greek Orthodox, Jews, Hindus and Sikhs can all be assimilated into the secular and / or predominantly Christian host societies, whereas, in the wake of 9/11, in particular the Muslim patriarch and his sons have become almost irredeemable figures. All too readily associated with the lurking threat of Islamic fundamentalism and terrorism, young Muslim men are suspect as 'sleepers' (like, for example, Faysal, the titular heroine's Pakistan-born husband, in *Yasmin* (Kenneth Glenaan, 2004), or Nazneen's lover Karim in *Brick Lane* (Sarah Gavron, 2007)), whereas the Muslim patriarch is frequently typecast as the oppressor of womenfolk. As the narrative trajectories of *West is West* (Andy De Emmony, 2010) and *Mauvaise Foi* (*Bad Faith*, Roschdy Zem, 2006), discussed in Chapters 4 and 5, demonstrate, secularisation is the only path to the Muslim man's redemption and the precondition for his integration into the host society.

These preliminary observations suggest that the construction of the diasporic family between the poles of strangeness and familiarity reflects the ambivalence that, according to Homi Bhabha, makes the Other 'at once an object of desire and derision, an articulation of difference contained within the fantasy of origin and identity' (1994: 96). Stereotypes have the function of containing the powerful and unsettling threat of this ambivalent response by fixing it once and for all in a stable image and by repeating the stereotype, whose veracity can, of course, never be empirically proven, over and over again.[6] The threat of Otherness can be controlled, Bhabha suggests, glossing Edward Said's *Orientalism* (1978), by 'affixing the unfamiliar to something established, in a form that is repetitious' (105).

I would like to propose that diasporic family films, especially those that employ generic paradigms, succeed in muting the fear of the Other (often with laughter) in two ways. Family narratives are so ubiquitous in cinema because, in some form or other, all families are alike, or to be more precise, there is something universal about the family. Once we were all children, and many of us experience what being a mother or a father is like. That is why we can all relate to films about the family. In fact, many films about multi-ethnic and / or homosocial friendship groups (including *Métisse* (*Café au lait*, Mathieu Kassovitz, 1993), *La Haine* (*Hate*, Mathieu Kassovitz, 1995) and *Lola und Bilidikid* (*Lola and Bilidikid*, Kutluğ Ataman, 1999)) construct the close relationships between the protagonists as family narratives. Films about such alternative family arrangements promote social diversity and inclusivity by framing what may be deemed marginal or socially contested as familial and, therefore, familiar. Similarly, ethnic comedies, which often make the polarity of similarity and difference their key structuring device, invite audiences to recognise that families, whether they come from Pakistan, North Africa or some other far-flung place not charted on our Eurocentric maps (such as the Yilmaz family's ancestral Anatolian village in *Almanya – Welcome to Germany*, which cannot be marked with a flag because it literally falls off the European map in Cenk's classroom), have a great deal in common. The experience of family life is one that unites humanity and that, therefore, has the capacity to build bridges across borders and different cultures. The growing trend to narrate stories about diasporic family life within established genres reinforces this sense of familiarity, since, like stereotypes, genres rely on cumulative iteration. In this way, the 'genre film lures its audience into a seemingly familiar world' (Baudry 1985: 416). The formulaic narrative process of film genres, their well-rehearsed iconography and predictable conflict resolutions offer a sense of reassurance that, according to Thomas Schatz (1981: 31), stabilises ideological conflicts in society through dramatic closure.

By invoking the generic conventions of the road movie, the family melodrama and the romantic comedy, some diasporic filmmakers have succeeded in moving their films out of a narrow ethnic niche into the mainstream. Quite a few films about ethnic minority and diasporic experiences have achieved remarkable box office success and have promoted 'the emergence of a new mainstream cinema in the USA and Europe' by invigorating and rejuvenating the mainstream with 'a multiplex accent', Hamid Naficy proposes (2009: 3). In the essay 'From accented cinema to multiplex cinema', he uses 'multiplex' not to designate a particular site of film exhibition but rather to describe textual strategies that combine 'multiplicities of various sorts', such as 'multilingual dialogues, multicultural characters, and multisited diegeses', with media convergence and 'a consolidation of the global media' (3–5). Following on from his pioneering study *An Accented Cinema: Exilic and Diasporic Filmmaking* (2001), which paved the way for much of the transnational, postcolonial, migrant and diasporic film theory that was to follow, Naficy argues that many of the aesthetic strategies and thematic concerns which he identified as being distinctive in a cinema originating from the experience of displacement and dispersal through exile, migration, asylum and other forms of transnational mobility, have become more widely appropriated by filmmakers who themselves are neither mobile nor minoritarian. Moreover, multi-platforming, participatory media culture, multi-channel media, digitisation and the Internet have made accented cinema, which Naficy defined as an alternative niche cinema created by artisanal and collective modes of production, more widely accessible than it was in the past. Although I am less interested in the new distribution channels and the (often short-lived) cultural diversity agendas in the film and television industry that have benefited this kind of cinema than in issues of representation, I acknowledge that the shift from the margins to the centre (or at least closer to the centre) is of paramount importance for the films discussed in this book.

The attentive reader will have noticed by now that the book's subtitle, *The Diasporic Family in Contemporary European Cinema*, is somewhat disingenuous. In order not to put off potential readers by a double dose of 'diasporic', a term that has gained wide currency in academic discourse but that has been shunned by the media industry (which prefers the term 'World Cinema') and by most filmmakers (who prefer the flattering term 'cosmopolitan'), the subtitle does not spell out the fact that I am actually interested in a particular type of family in a particular type of cinema: namely, contemporary *diasporic* cinema in Europe.[7] Its recent emergence as a much-debated critical concept is inextricably linked to the postcolonial and labour migrations of the second half of the twentieth and the beginning of the twenty-first centuries that have 'dramatically changed the social and cultural composition of European [and other Western] societies' (Robins 2007: 152) and have led to the increased visibility of filmmakers with a migratory background and a growing interest in the representation of ethnic diversity and multi-culturalism on screen.[8] By foregrounding the experiences of diasporic subjects and by telling stories about the dynamics of cross-cultural encounters and postmodern multi-culturalism, diasporic filmmakers living and working in Europe have complicated our understanding of European cinema and what it means to be 'European'. European cinema is no longer just white, nor can it be adequately conceived of as an amalgamation of discrete national cinemas that coexist side by side, separated by geopolitical and linguistic borders.⁹ With its focus on Europe's most established diasporic film cultures, Maghrebi French, Black British, Asian British and Turkish German, the kind of European cinema at the centre of this book is emphatically transnational, trans-European and hybrid. It gained critical mass more or less simultaneously in these countries in the mid-1980s and has flourished ever since. Unlike the relatively isolated earlier attempts of diasporic filmmakers to capture their personal experiences or those of their ethnic constituencies on film, those filmmakers who have come to the fore since the mid-1980s in Britain, France and Germany have made mainly feature films, rather than shorts, television dramas and documentaries, thereby enhancing the visibility and cross-over appeal of their films.

As I illustrate in the first chapter, diasporic cinema in Europe and, especially, the rise to prominence of diasporic families on screen are linked to the social history of postwar immigration and European legislation on family reunification, which resulted in the transformation of temporary migrant into diasporic settler communities. The coming-of-age of the second generation that was born and / or raised in the host society has, in turn, led to the development of a vibrant diasporic film culture. Admittedly, the cinematic representation of diasporic subjects preceded the arrival of diasporic filmmakers on the scene, but these earlier films did not amount to a critical mass and, on the whole, took a totalising and homogenising approach to representing ethnic minorities. Only when the children of the postwar immigrants gained access to and control over their own images did they enter into the struggle over representing their identities by contesting negative and reductive images with positive or more complex and nuanced ones.

Although diasporic cinema has attracted scholarly attention only relatively recently,[10] partly in response to the boom in migration, diaspora and postcolonial studies, it is actually almost as old as cinema itself, yet previously different scholarly perspectives and terminologies have prevailed. For example, film historians usually do not conceptualise Jewish exile and émigré directors, actors and actresses, scriptwriters and producers, many of whom fled Germany when the National Socialists came to power in 1933, seeking refuge in Paris, London and eventually Hollywood, in relation to the Jewish diaspora.[11] Instead, these exiled Jewish filmmakers are generally referred to as 'European émigrés', a term that obliterates their Jewish ethnicity – and for good reason. As Thomas Elsaesser puts it, 'foreigners in Hollywood' had the choice between either 'disavowing their own homeland and heritage' and 'assimilate and become 110 per cent American or be European and exotic, but also 110 per cent!' (1999: 99). The point I am trying to make here is that these terminologies are not arbitrary but reflect different agendas: while émigré filmmakers in Hollywood had to calibrate carefully the images they projected, either through strategies of camouflage and assimilation or through promoting their alterity like a brand in order to succeed, for contemporary diasporic filmmakers – as the subsequent chapters will amply illustrate – a self-conscious engagement with difference is almost invariably the preferred and expected strategy.

In *The Postcolonial Exotic: Marketing the Margins*, Graham Huggan illustrates how cultural and ethnic Otherness has become part of a 'booming "alterity industry"', making 'marginality [. . .] a valuable intellectual commodity' (2001: vii–viii). Not unlike the celebrity postcolonial writers and critics whom Huggan discusses, diasporic filmmakers such as Mira Nair, Gurinder Chadha, Fatih Akın, Yamina Benguigui or Abdellatif Kechiche play an important role as brokers of cultural difference, trading the minoritarian experience as a prized commodity. On the international festival circuit, these transnational *auteurs* are now vying with their established European counterparts for attention and awards. Their 'double occupancy' as hyphenated identity subjects (Elsaesser 2005), their 'double consciousness' (Gilroy 1993a)[12] and 'diasporic optic' (Moorti 2003) can even give them a competitive advantage because they invigorate and renew the traditions of European cinema by drawing on multi-sited impulses and inspirations. Diasporic filmmakers have played a key role in making the boundaries between European and World Cinema more fluid, often juxtaposing and fusing stylistic templates, generic conventions, narrative and musical traditions, languages and performance styles from European and World Cinema, as well as from Hollywood, in their aesthetically hybrid and innovative films.

Diasporic cinema challenges and frequently disavows borders of all kinds. Its protagonists transcend the borders of the nation-state on account of their dual heritage and typically try to assert their place in the social fabric of the hegemonic host society. As such, it is a cinema of identity politics, probing 'difference along the multiple coordinates of race, colour, ethnicity, nationality, regionality, language, religion, generation, class, gender and sexuality' (Berghahn and Sternberg 2010a: 41). It is a cinema in which spatio-temporal and spatio-racial modalities coalesce and converge and whose strategic agenda is the relocation of the margins to the centre, the valorisation and, ultimately, 'the redemption of the marginal' (Stam 2003: 35). As an artistic practice that 'underscores the interstice, the spaces that are and fall between the cracks of the national and the transnational as well as other social formations' (Moorti 2003: 359), it is centrally concerned with hybrid identities. Thus, in diasporic family films we encounter racially mixed couples whose union does or does not get the blessing of their parents, multi-ethnic families and family-like formations involving surrogate father figures or queer lovers whose inclusion or exclusion in the family is being negotiated and that call the heteronormative model of the nuclear family into question.

Whereas most scholars conceive of diasporic cinema as linked to authorship, I regard this approach as problematic since it does not account for Avtar Brah's concept of the 'diaspora space' (1996: 209, see also Chapter 1), which constitutes an important critical intervention in diaspora scholarship. 'Diaspora space' (which is different from 'diaspora') challenges essentialist notions of origin as a prerequisite for partaking in the diasporic experience. It is a conceptual space in which forms of cross-pollination between the artistic sensibilities of the 'native' and the diasporian take place and which allows for the inclusion of films authored by non-diasporic filmmakers, provided they foreground the experiences and perspectives of diasporic subjects. Nevertheless, in *Far-flung Families in Film* I privilege films made by diasporic filmmakers with the intention to participate in the important project of moving productions that have until fairly recently been relegated to the margins of European film studies to the centre. Moreover, the majority of diasporic family films have actually been written and / or directed by second-generation immigrant filmmakers.

Much of the current scholarship in the burgeoning field of transnational, migrant and diasporic cinema seeks to map the still relatively new critical terrain; *Far-flung Families in Film* uses these important investigations as a springboard for providing the first sustained account of a particularly prominent theme – and one that has so far received scant scholarly attention. In the age of globalisation, diasporic and other types of transnational family are increasingly represented on film, yet they have been neglected in film studies. Except for Jigna Desai's study *Beyond Bollywood: The Cultural Politics of South Asian Diasporic Film* (2004), which addresses the centrality of family narratives in Indian and Non-Resident Indian (NRI) culture,[13] there is to date only one study that approaches the subject from a transnational perspective: *Shooting the Family: Transnational Media and Intercultural Values* (2005). Patricia Pisters and Wim Staat's edited collection, however, covers a more diverse terrain. The essays are concerned with the impact of globalisation, migration and intercultural encounters on the family and explore, for instance, the interrelationship between audio-visual technologies and the construction and mediation of family life in home videos, on Dutch television and in a range of family-centred films. The contributors' critical engagement with Michael Hardt and Antonio Negri's influential book *Empire* (2000) holds the anthology together and culminates in the overarching hypothesis that the upheaval of globalisation and the ensuing crisis of the nation-state have brought the ideological construct of the 'natural family' under scrutiny. In turn, this has led to a valorisation of immigrant families, whose interstitial position between nation-states, cultures and communities makes them the bearers of 'intercultural values' (Pisters and Staat 2005: 13).

Far-flung Families in Film takes a more focused approach and aims to complement existing scholarship on the family *in cinema*. It is based on the premise that kinship is an issue of universal significance but that the structures, value and belief systems are culturally specific. Although this warrants a comparative perspective, a systematic analysis of families on screen from a transnational angle has so far not been attempted. There is a significant body of work on the representation of the (predominantly white American) family in Hollywood cinema (Chopra-Gant 2006, Harwood 1997, Leibman 1995, Pomerance 2008, Traube 1992, Williams 1996) and on Indian families in popular Hindi cinema (Dwyer 2000a, Gopal 2011, Uberoi 2006). The cultural construction of motherhood and mothers in Hollywood cinema (Fischer 1996), and especially in (maternal) melodrama and the woman's film (Doane 1987, Gledhill 1987b, Kaplan 1992), has evidently held greater fascination for (feminist) film scholars than fathers. To date, *Bringing Up Daddy* (Bruzzi 2005) and *Fathers and Sons in Cinema* (Reiter 2008) remain the only systematic investigations of postwar Hollywood fathers, and this despite the fact that fatherhood narratives are a prominent theme in Hollywood, reflecting wider public debates about male parenting and changing family structures. Children, on the other hand, have triggered more interest over the past few years, as testified by three recently published books. Vicky Lebeau (2008) and Karen Lury (2010) are, however, less interested in the child in a family context than in its liminality and innocence in the encounter with war, death and sexual abuse. Alongside *Cinema's Missing Children* (Wilson 2003), which deals with the trauma inflicted by the loss of a child upon family members, these studies take scholarly discourse in the field beyond Hollywood by also covering examples from European and World Cinema.

A number of recently published essay collections, including *Family Affairs: Ansichten der Familie im Film* (Fröhlich and Visarius 2004), *Portraits de famille* (a special issue of *CinémAction*, Poirson-Dechonne 2009) and *Affaires de famille: The Family in Contemporary French Culture and Theory* (Barnet and Welch, 2007), bring family portraits in European cinema into view. *Affaires de famille* also takes immigrant families into account (Tarr 2007), as well as newly emerging family types in French cinema, which seem to testify to the decline of patriarchal authority and the growing significance of surrogate families (Powrie 2007). These, as well as Murray Pomerance's edited collection *A Family Affair: Cinema Calls Home* (2008), predominantly concerned with family portraits in contemporary Hollywood, attest to a growing fascination with the family at a time when it is deemed to be under threat. Family diversity is conceptualised primarily with reference to sexual orientation, whereas ethnic and racial diversity are all too often relegated to the margins. Perhaps Todd Haynes's *Far From Heaven* (2002) has attained canonical status as a modern-day Sirkian-style family melodrama (and as a widely discussed film in these anthologies), precisely because it probes how queer and interracial desire ruptures the fragile nuclear family and, thereby, problematises the hegemonic family along multiple axes of difference. In the main, however, one has to turn to studies on race and ethnicity, notably Linda Williams's *Playing the Race Card: Melodramas of Black and White from Uncle Tom to O. J. Simpson* (2001), which comprises discussions of racialised and, one might argue, diasporic families (though this theoretical framework is not applied), but inevitably critical attention lies elsewhere.

Finally, in my attempt to chart the scholarly fields with which *Far-flung Families* intersects, I also wish to acknowledge contributions from cultural studies: *Representing the Family* (Chambers 2001) and *Mediating the Family:*

Gender, Culture and Representation (Ticknell 2005) examine the discursive construction of the family in the media and in popular culture more generally, drawing on a range of conceptual frameworks and sources that have informed social, political and institutional debates surrounding the family in Western (predominantly Anglophone) societies since the postwar era. Deborah Chambers's understanding of 'the family as a site of cultural struggle', where 'the core values of civil society' and its 'deepest disputes and ruptures' are acted out (2001: 165, 176), is illustrated with reference only to a small number of mainstream films, which she reads as barometers of changing family values and structures.

Even though many film scholars might regard such an indexical reading of the family in cinema as somewhat reductive, there exists, nevertheless, an implicit consensus that the representation of the family in film reflects wider social and cultural trends, making the domestic sphere a symbolic stage or battleground on to which social conflicts are displaced. In *Far-Flung Families on Film* I propose that, as cinema tends to depict social struggles and historical transitions indirectly through affective relations in the family, the diasporic family crystallises the emotionally ambivalent response to growing ethnic diversity in Western societies. In this respect, the movies analysed here make important contributions to wider socio-political debates about immigration, ethnic diversity, the success or failure of multi-culturalism and even the rise of religious fundamentalism in Europe.

Although I bring to bear anthropological and socio-historical research on diasporic families (especially in Chapter 1), I do not use diasporic family films as social documents that give evidence of social trends. Instead, I conceive of these films as important discursive interventions that either resonate with prevailing cultural and social assumptions about 'immigrant', 'Muslim', 'black', 'Asian', 'Turkish', 'North African' or by whatever other name these families are marked as Other, or that, conversely, offer compelling counter-narratives and images. The significance of cinema as 'the most prominent medium of self-representation and symbolic action that the hyphenated citizens of Europe's nation states have made their own' (Elsaesser 2005: 119) in the struggle over cultural representation is not to be underestimated.

Historically, psychoanalytic and generic frameworks have dominated studies on the family in cinema, especially in Hollywood. Yet, more recently, there has been a greater diversity of approaches, perhaps fuelled by the growing scholarly attention given to families in European and World Cinema, which seems to call for greater historical and cultural acuity. In *Far-flung Families* I aim to develop a theoretical framework that is attuned to the specificities of the object of my investigation and that will facilitate further research in this area. I look at diasporic family films through the spatially inflected lens of diaspora criticism. Diaspora criticism is in dialogue with cultural and social anthropology, migration, memory, postcolonial and cultural studies, to mention but the most obvious related fields (see Chow 1993, 2010, Mishra 2006). It demonstrates the importance of place and displacement in relation to cultural identity, emphasising the fact that diasporic identities are, above all, spatially coded – hence the proliferation of border crossings, migratory journeys, the much-invoked opposition of roots versus routes (Clifford 1994, Gilroy 1993a) and the chronotope of the homeland. If displacement is, indeed, the most significant coordinate on which the diasporic family's putative Otherness can be plotted and from which racial, linguistic, religious and all other differences follow, then surely diaspora criticism promises to provide the most productive heuristic tool. Yet it is not the only one I engage when examining the thematic complex of diasporic families in film.

With the exception of the first chapter, in which I define the conjoined concepts of 'the family' and 'diaspora' and sketch the social–historical context that brought diasporic families to Europe and on to the silver screen, all subsequent ones take a theme-centred approach. The second chapter, 'Families in Motion', traces families' outbound and homebound journeys by drawing on Mikhail Bakhtin's influential concept of the chronotope that has been productively appropriated by Paul Gilroy and Hamid Naficy in relation to diaspora. My primary concern is how transnational mobility affects family structure. Does the family on the road (or on ships, trains or planes, for that matter) fall apart and disintegrate or does it forge new bonds within and beyond the family unit? Do the protagonists' itineraries confirm or challenge the myth of a glorious homecoming, regarded by many as fundamental to the diaspora experience? My secondary line of enquiry probes the films' generic and stylistic strategies and asks how *Reise der Hoffnung* (*Journey of Hope*, Xavier Koller, 1990), *Almanya – Welcome to Germany* and *Le Grand Voyage* (*The Grand Tour*, Ismaël Ferroukhi, 2004) inflect and modify the conventions of the road movie. And, finally, I examine how these films dislodge the Eurocentric notion of centre and periphery by projecting new and unfamiliar spatial geographies.

The third chapter, 'Family Memories, Family Secrets', takes Annette Kuhn's (2002) puzzling observation that families are held together as much by the memories they share as by the secrets they hide from each other as its starting point. Unlike the other chapters, this one attends to documentaries as well as feature films. I have included the postmemory documentaries *Mein Vater, der Gastarbeiter* (*My Father, The Guest Worker*, Yüksel Yavuz, 1994), *Mémoires d'immigrés – L'héritage maghrébin* (*Immigrant Memories*, 1997) and *I For India* (Sandhya Suri, 2005), amongst others, in which diasporic filmmakers excavate their parents' memories of migration, because these intensely personal explorations illustrate the autobiographical impetus behind much of diasporic cinema in exemplary fashion. Drawing on Pierre Nora (1989), Marianne Hirsch (1997) and Alison Landsberg's (2004) writings on memory, I interrogate how these documentaries triangulate the memory and postmemory within the family, the collective memory of diaspora and official accounts of immigration, written and preserved by the host societies. Family photos, home movies and other archival footage feature prominently and emphatically confirm John Akomfrah's observation that for the 'diasporic subject the archive acquires a special poignancy [...] because it is the space of the memorial. There are very few tangible memorials that say, "You have been here". And so, the archive is important because it is one of the spaces in which the memorial attests to your existence' (2010).

By going public with the audio-visual archives of family memories, diasporic filmmakers transgress the boundaries between the private and the public sphere and give private memories political resonance. I argue that both family memories and family secrets spin threads of continuity between the generations but do not always succeed in holding the family together. While memories are the family's public face, secrets are its dark underbelly, the shameful events that have been 'ruthlessly edited out' (Kuhn 2002: 2). Invoking Abraham and Torok's (1994) psychoanalytic model of the transgenerational transmission of undisclosed family secrets, I consider so-called 'phantoms' that haunt families, such as illegitimate birth and uncertain parentage, before investigating in detail the most prevalent secret and its revelation: the 'coming out' of queer sons and daughters in the diasporic family. I propose that in *Lola and Bilidikid*, *My Beautiful Laundrette* (Stephen Frears, 1985) and *Nina's Heavenly Delights* (Pratibha Parmar, 2006), queer diasporic identities function as a master trope of hybridity. 'Coming out' in the diasporic family critiques fantasies of purity, which simultaneously underpin the 'natural family', based on bloodline, heteronormativity and supposedly natural gender hierarchies, and nationalist ideologies, based on ethnic absolutism and other homogenising concepts.

Chapter 4 examines the dynamics of gender and generation in the diasporic family, broaching contested issues such as female dress codes (notably the headscarf) and honour killings in relation to the controversial figure of the (Muslim) patriarch. Rather than looking at these inflammatory themes through the critical lens of ethnic stereotyping, I approach them in relation to frameworks that emphasise the importance of place and the body, notably Arjun Appadurai's 'production of locality' (1996), Ulf Hannerz's 'habitats of meaning' (1996), Avtar Brah's 'homing desire' (1996) and Laura Marks's discussion of embodiment in intercultural cinema of the senses (2000). What these different theories suggest is that, in modern globalised societies, localised forms of belonging have become mobile and negotiable. As a consequence, locality – understood as a *'property of social life* [and] a structure of feeling' (Appadurai 1996: 182, italics in the original) – needs to be actively constructed and embodied through the material practices of everyday life. I argue that in diasporic family films, the production of locality is often imagined as a divisive cultural practice and as the cause of gender and generational conflict. Through adhering to the sartorial and culinary traditions, the language and rituals from the homeland, parents frequently profess their allegiances to a place and community far away. Their Westernised offspring, by contrast, typically engage in the production of culturally hybrid localities in the streets and playgrounds of urban youth culture and on their bodies. Close readings of *Die Fremde* (*When We Leave*, Feo Aladağ, 2010), *East is East* (Damien O'Donnell, 1999), its sequel *West is West* and *La Graine et le mulet* (*Couscous / The Secret of the Grain*, Abdellatif Kechiche, 2007) attend to the consumption of media and food and the performance of gendered and generational topographies. I try to establish how the protagonists' cultural attachments that are articulated in this way map on to the kinds of family structure that these films engender and endorse.

The final chapter, 'Romance and Weddings in Diaspora', asks why weddings proliferate in diasporic family films and what it is about the big fat diasporic wedding that captures the imagination of multiple and diverse audiences? After providing a succinct survey of the wedding theme in its many variations, ranging from films about arranged marriage, sham weddings and interethnic romance, I explore diasporic wedding films in terms of their generic characteristics. Wedding films emerged during the 1990s as an identifiable strand of the romantic comedy in mainstream cinema in the West and, as a variation of the romantic family drama, in Bollywood.[14] *Four Weddings and a Funeral* (Mike Newell, 1994) and *Hum Aapke Hain Koun* (*Can You Name Our Relationship?*, Sooraj Barjatya, 1994) are widely cited as the foundational texts, while *My Big Fat Greek Wedding* (Joel Zwick, 2002) established the generic paradigm of the diasporic wedding film. The overriding concern of this chapter is how *Evet, ich will!* (*Evet, I Do!*, Sinan Akkus, 2008), *Monsoon Wedding* (Mira Nair, 2001) and *Bride and Prejudice* (Gurinder Chadha, 2005) modify and invigorate the romcom / wedding film genre through a diasporic optic and the 'truly cross-cultural encounters' which Janet Staiger (2003: 196) has identified as a prerequisite of generic hybridity. I propose that diasporic wedding films fuse the conventions of romantic comedy with family melodrama, adding the allure of exotic wedding rituals, a heavy dose of heart-warming family feeling and some Bollywood-style song and dance numbers, thrown in for good measure.

Let me, then, conclude with the usual obligatory disclaimers. Although in each chapter I offer not only detailed discussions of three or four case studies but also a survey of additional, thematically relevant films, I do not purport to give an exhaustive account of Maghrebi French, Black and British Asian and Turkish German feature films about diasporic families released between 1985 and 2011, as I do not wish to sacrifice analytical depth for breadth. Crossing the borders of the national in more than just one way, I purposely avoid a question to which some readers may expect an answer: namely, how diasporic families in British cinema differ from those in German or French cinema. It seems to me that this line of enquiry would represent an undesirable relapse into the critical paradigm of national cinema. Most of the films I have chosen as case studies are available on DVD with English subtitles, which should make this book equally accessible to the polyglot and the monolingual reader. Furthermore, many of the films analysed in detail are in English in the first place, since for a Continental European like myself, British cinema is part and parcel of European cinema.

Finally, I should like to draw the reader's attention to the companion website of *Far-flung Families on Film*, which documents the Arts and Humanities Research Council-funded research project underpinning the genesis of this book. There you will find a wealth of additional material on the subject, including a searchable database of films, a blog and an archive of podcasts featuring conference presentations, roundtable discussions and interviews with filmmakers. The website offers much scope for interactivity and I hope that this book will inspire you to share your thoughts and ideas on www.farflungfamilies.net.

Notes

1. The English translation of this quotation and of all subsequent ones is taken, unless indicated otherwise, from the English subtitled version of the film.
2. The original German quotation from the interview with Sarrazin reads 'ständig neue kleine Kopftuchmädchen produziert', cited in dpa / Reuters 2009. Sarrazin's incendiary book sold over 1.5 million copies, making it the highest-selling political book in a decade. For an excellent survey on xenophobia and anti-immigration sentiments in Germany, see Göktürk, Gramling and Kaes (2007: 107–48).
3. The issue as to whether the London riots were related to race and racism in British society was widely debated in the British media. Peter Hitchens (2011) from the *Daily Mail* made the point that 'this is an equal-opportunity crime wave. The lawbreakers are not from any distinct ethnic group, and attempts to explain this behaviour on these grounds are baseless and poisonous'. Unlike in the French riots of autumn 2005 ('les émeutes des banlieues de 2005'), which involved a high proportion of youth of African or Maghrebi heritage, no such racial bias was evident in the London riots. Nevertheless, some journalists tried hard to construct a connection. Christina Odone, a columnist from the *Daily Telegraph*, blamed absent fathers and her blog, not coincidentally, featured the image of a black adolescent youth with the caption 'Children are lost without fathers' (2011). On the BBC's *Newsnight*, historian David Starkey provocatively equated black culture with gang culture and attributed the London riots to the influence of black 'destructive, nihilistic gangster culture' on white British youth who 'have become black' (Starkey 2011).
4. For further insightful discussions of Italian American immigrants in Hollywood, see Marx and Cohen (2010) and Bruzzi (2011).
5. Although I do not wish to be complicit in relegating alternative family structures to the margin, I have not selected these films for detailed case studies since their primary focus does not lie on the family. *Babymother*, though touching upon black single mothers and teenage pregnancy, is first and foremost about black music and dancehall culture (see Chapter 4 and Dudrah 2012b), while *Bullet Boy* centres on black gang culture. Representations of single black mothers struggling to protect their sons from drugs and gang crime are particularly prominent in American cinema. Perhaps the best-known example is John Singleton's critically acclaimed film *Boyz 'n the Hood* (1991). The protagonist's mother, Reva, hands over her son Tre to her former husband Furious in the full knowledge that she 'can't teach him to be a man'. Although Reva's decision, which allows her to pursue her career unhampered by maternal duties, may seem selfish at first, she is vindicated by the film's narrative trajectory. Furious, the idealised black father, is a perfect male role model and safely guides Tre to manhood, whereas Tre's friends Ricky and Doughboy from across the road, half-brothers who are brought up by their single black mother, become embroiled in crime and gang culture and are both murdered in a feud. See Bruzzi (2005) and Massood (2003) for insightful discussions of this film.

6. On (ethnic) stereotyping in cinema, I have found Dyer (1993), Friedman (1991), Rosello (1998), Shohat and Stam (1994), and Wiegman (1998) particularly inspiring.
7. For an exploration of the partially overlapping concepts 'transnational, 'diasporic', 'cosmopolitan' and 'World Cinema', see Berghahn and Sternberg (2010b), Durovicová and Newman (2010), Elsaesser (2005), and Nagib, Perriam and Dudrah (2012). For an industrial perspective on these categories, listen to interviews with John Akomfrah, Parminder Vir, Ralph Schwingel from Wüste Film Productions and Eve Gabereau from the distribution company Soda Pictures, available as podcasts on the website of my previous collaborative research project, Migrant and Diasporic Cinema in Contemporary Europe: http://www.migrantcinema.net/podcasts/
8. Following the collapse of communism and the fall of the Berlin Wall in 1989, migration from Eastern Europe to the politically more stable and prosperous old Europe has transformed Europe's geopolitical topography and has had a significant impact on European cinema. These changes do not, however, relate to the diasporic film cultures with which I am concerned here. They have been examined by Rosalind Galt (2006), who redraws the map of East and West European cinema at the historical juncture of the 1990s, and by Dina Iordanova (2003), who focuses on East Central European cinema.
9. Galt dates the emergence of a trans- or supranational European cinema to the 1990s. After the end of the Cold War and the expansion of the European Union, 'the idea of Europe [became] once again culturally and political central', as testified in a 'cinematic discourse on Europeanness' (2006: 105). Moreover, European co-productions had become common practice by then, making the search for a film's national specificity increasingly problematic.
10. A chronology of titles reflects the rapidly growing interest that diasporic cinema has enjoyed since the mid-1990s: *Cinemas of the Black Diaspora* (Martin 1995); *Women Filmmakers of the African and Asian Diaspora* (Foster 1997); *An Accented Cinema: Exilic and Diasporic Filmmaking* (Naficy 2001); *Floating Lives: The Media and Asian Diasporas* (Cunningham and Sinclair 2001); *Moving Pictures, Migrating Identities* (Rueschmann 2003b); *Bidding for the Mainstream: Black and Asian British Film since the 1990s* (Korte and Sternberg 2004); *Reframing Difference: Beur and Banlieue Filmmaking in France* (Tarr 2005); *Beyond Bollywood: The Cultural Politics of South Asian Diasporic Film* (Desai 2004); *From Tian'anmen to Times Square: Transnational China and the Chinese Diaspora on Global Screens, 1989–1997* (Marchetti 2006); *Contact Zones: Memory, Origin, and Discourses in Black Diasporic Cinema* (Petty 2008); *Diasporas of Australian Cinema* (Simpson, Murawska and Lambert 2009); *Screening Strangers: Migration and Diaspora in Contemporary European Cinema* (Loshitzky 2010); *European Cinema in Motion: Migrant and Diasporic Cinema in Contemporary Europe* (Berghahn and Sternberg 2010b); *Bollywood and Globalization: Indian Popular Cinema, Nation, and Diaspora* (Mehta and Panhariphande 2010); *Bollywood Travels: Culture, Diaspora and Border Crossings in Popular Hindi Cinema* (Dudrah 2012a); *The Chinese Diaspora on American Screens: Race, Sex, and Cinema* (Marchetti 2012) and *Turkish German Cinema in the New Millennium* (Hake and Mennel 2012). There are numerous other studies, including *The Skin of Film: Intercultural Cinema, Embodiment, and the Senses* (Marks 2000); *Black in the British Frame: The Black Experience in British Film and Television* (Bourne 2001) and *French Minority Cinema* (Johnston 2010) that also consider diasporic cinema but privilege other conceptual frameworks. The more encompassing concept of transnational cinema has received even more critical attention, so that I shall refrain from producing a comparable list here.
11. Naficy reminds us that 'the first generation of Jews and Jewish immigrants, primar-

ily from Eastern Europe and Russia, [were] dubbed the Hollywood "pioneers"' (2001: 7). Moreover, many German (Jewish) and other European émigrés went to Hollywood in the 1920, not as exiles or refugees but because they were attracted by the superior technology, resources and opportunities that Hollywood afforded them.

12. The term 'double consciousness' goes back to W. E. B. Du Bois's 'The Strivings of the Negro People' (1897), subsequently revised for *The Souls of Black Folk* (1903). Du Bois describes 'two warring ideals in one black body': that is, an internally divided diasporic self, resulting from conflicting cultural and ethnic affiliations. See Gilroy (1993a) for a discussion of 'double consciousness' in a contemporary context.

13. 'The term "Non-Resident Indian" generally refers to the post-1960s migrants from India to Australia, Britain, Canada, and the United States. The profile of the NRI changed since the 1990s, when a U.S. immigration reform act tripled the quotas for skilled immigrants, thereby producing a surge in migration from India to the United States. Unlike previous generations of Indians, particularly those who went to Britain in the 1960s and 1970s, this new group constitutes a transnational class that has the financial ability to live between their country of origin and place of residence' (Sharpe 2005: 77).

14. The term 'Bollywood cinema' has been widely adopted in the English-speaking world (and beyond) and is sometimes used imprecisely to refer to popular Hindi cinema or even Indian cinema generally. Prasad (2003), Desai (2004), Sharpe (2005) and Gopal (2011), amongst others, use 'Bollywood' to denote a globalised form of popular Hindi cinema that circulates transnationally, is watched by Indians at home and abroad, and has a following amongst Western audiences. In contrast to the more general term 'popular Hindi cinema', 'Bollywood cinema' refers specifically to films that have been made in the context of India's economic liberalisation and ensuing economic and cultural globalisation that has fundamentally transformed India – and commercial Indian cinema – since the early 1990s.

1. FAMILY MATTERS IN DIASPORA

What is a family and how is it defined? We tend to conceive of the 'family' as a self-explanatory concept, although its meaning is contested and perpetually shifting to reflect changing family structures over time and across different cultures. The focus of this book is on the *representation* of the diasporic family in contemporary European cinema, rather than on the social reality of this particular type of family. Nevertheless, in order to demarcate the boundaries of the present study, it will be necessary to clarify the conjoined concepts of 'diaspora' and the 'family', by drawing on disciplines such as sociology and anthropology, as well as on migration and diaspora studies, in order to provide some initial answers to the following key questions: What are the distinctive features of diasporic families and how are they constructed as different in relation to the normative model of the white nuclear family? What socio-historical factors have contributed to the growing prominence of diasporic families in European cinema over the past few decades?

The word 'family' is derived from Latin '*familia*', which is a derivative of '*famulus*' (servant). Originally, the term did not refer to what we commonly understand by it today but instead 'denoted all the slaves and servants living under one roof' (Zonabend 1996: 8), collectively called *famuli*. Subsequently, its meaning was extended to include 'the entire household, the master, on the one hand, and the wife, children and servants living under his control' (8). In other words, 'family' included the notion of kinship and shared residence. Over time, the word 'kin' (persons connected by blood relationship) has become less common and 'the one term "family" covers all the various groups of relatives denoted by words such as *household* (all the individuals living under one roof); *gens* (all those descended from a common ancestor), *agnati* (relatives on the father's side) and *cognati* (denoting relatives on the mother's side, and then, by extension, all blood relatives)' (8).[1] Thus, families are held together by ties of consanguinity or blood, as well as by conjugal ties between husband and wife, based on some form of social contract (normally marriage). Social scientists distinguish between the conjugal or nuclear family, defined as 'an intimate, closely organized group consisting of spouses and offspring', and the consanguine or extended family, defined as an 'almost unorganized group of blood relatives' (Linton 1959: 33) or kinship group.

According to the American anthropologist George Peter Murdock, who analysed around 250 small societies all over the world, the family 'is a universal human social grouping' (1949: 2). His definition, dating back to 1949, is still widely quoted. 'The family is a social group characterized by common residence, economic cooperation, and reproduction. It includes adults of both sexes, at least two of whom maintain a socially approved sexual relationship, and one or more children, own or adopted, of the sexually cohabiting adults' (1). Murdock uses the term 'family' synonymously with 'nuclear family', emphasising, however, that in most societies the nuclear family is part of larger composite family forms.[2] He explains the universality of the family by its social effectiveness, which he links to four key functions. Through marriage, the family controls sexuality in a socially acceptable form. The economic function, defined as the combination of sexual privileges, economic cooperation and cohabitation, serves as the basis for marriage and marriage as a precondition for the family. From the family's reproductive role follows its educational function, the nurture and socialisation of children, which ensures the transmission of culture, language and social norms across the generations. Murdock was convinced that no other societal institution could take over these four essential functions and that life, culture and society would cease to exist without the family: 'No society, in short, has succeeded in finding an adequate substitute for the nuclear family, to which it might transfer these functions. It is highly doubtful whether any society ever will succeed in such an attempt, utopian proposals for the abolition of the family to the contrary notwithstanding' (11).

Although the French anthropologist and ethnologist Claude Lévi-Strauss confirms the mutual dependency of the family and society when he writes that 'there would be no society without families, but equally, there would be no families if society did not already exist' (1996: 4), he nevertheless challenges the hypothesis that 'the family must be a universal presence, whatever the type of society' (5). Surveying information about some 4,000 to 5,000 human societies, past and present, he lists a number of counter-examples, including the matrilineal Nayar in southern India, among whom children traditionally belonged to the maternal line and the husband played virtually no role. He also cites alternative family arrangements in contemporary Western societies as evidence that the model of the *nuclear* family 'does not fulfil a universal need' (6).[3] In fact, Pierre Bourdieu reminds us that, nowadays, from a sociological standpoint, 'in most modern societies the nuclear family is a minority experience compared to the number of unmarried couples living together, single-parent families, married couples living apart, etc.' (1998: 64) and that the heterogeneous social groups called 'family' bear little resemblance to the dominant definition of the term. While we are led to regard the nuclear family as natural, it is actually 'a well-founded fiction', whose existence depends upon it being 'collectively recognised' (1998: 66).

The increasing diversity of family structures since the postwar era, in part triggered by second-wave feminism, the gay civil rights movement and rising divorce rates, cannot be reconciled with Murdock's influential definition, which tacitly conflates family with marriage and excludes single-parent families or gay and lesbian couples. The latter in particular have been campaigning to be recognised as families, arguing that families should not be confounded with genealogically defined relationships (Weston 1991). As Judith Stacey illustrates in her ethnographic study *Brave New Families*, advances in contraception and the legalisation of abortion during the 1960s and 1970s changed women's sexual behaviour and paved the way for 'the family revolution', during which 'the gap between dominant cultural ideology and discordant behaviours generated radical challenges to the modern family' (1990: 12).

The fundamental transformation of sexual mores and domestic arrangements that has occurred in Western societies since the 1960s has made a revision of the narrow and conservative definitions of 'the family' imperative. In 1965, the American sociologist and sexuality researcher Ira Reiss reduced the family's four functions to just one, which he believed to be of universal relevance. He defined the family as 'a small kinship structured group with the key function of nurturant socialization of the newborn' (cited in Ingoldsby 2006: 75). Meanwhile, family researcher Bron Ingoldsby (2006: 76) expands the concept further by including children of various ages, both natural and adopted ones.

In the wake of second-wave feminism, female participation in the workforce rose significantly, so that women became financially independent of a breadwinner-husband. Consequently, some social scientists propose that the chief function of the contemporary family (and of marriage, if no children are present) is to provide love and affection. The decreased relevance of the economic function gradually developed during the 1950s, identified by sociologist Anthony Giddens as 'the transitional phase of family development' (2002: 57). Although a gender-specific division of labour was still the norm, 'men and women by this time were more equal than they had been previously, both in fact and in law. The family had ceased to be an economic entity and the idea of romantic love as the basis for marriage had replaced marriage as an economic contract' (57). From there, it was only a small step for 'intimacy', understood primarily as 'emotional communication' (59), to become the core value of modern family life. Emotional communication is 'replacing the old ties that bind together people's lives – in sexual and love relationships, in parent–child relationships and in friendships' (61). In this 'emerging democracy of the emotions' (65), the feeling of love is even proclaimed to be *the* defining feature of the family. Such a dramatically revised conception of the family underpins the claims of 'families of choice'. During the Gay and Lesbian March on Washington in 1987, civil rights campaigners wrote on their banners: 'Love makes a family – nothing more, nothing less' (cited in Weston 1991: 107).

To what extent this famous rallying cry has become a socially accepted reality remains to be seen. Certainly, scholars appear hesitant to make the term 'family' a catch-all category and there is still widespread consensus that what makes a family is the presence of parents (or, in their stead, grandparents or aunts and uncles) and children, whose nurture and socialisation distinguishes a family from mere coupledom. In other words, while neither marriage nor heterosexuality is postulated as a necessary precondition for being classified as a family, couples without children do not normally count.

These considerations indicate that, ultimately, the ambiguity of the term 'family' revolves around the dialectical relationship of inclusion and exclusion. Consensus about who is in and who is out is perpetually shifting. Comparative research into families across different cultures undertaken by anthropologists shows that the family, for all its claims to universality and naturalness, is a highly heterogeneous and complex social construction.[4] Yet, instead of recognising family diversity, public discourse constructs a 'powerful myth within the collective imagination' which persistently privileges the white, heterosexual couple and their offspring as the norm and, thereby, naturalises and normalises the nuclear family 'as a regulatory ideal that inferiorises and discredits alternative' family structures and practices (Chambers 2001: 1, 3).[5] Moral panics about the crisis of the family make newspaper headlines and push controversial books such as Matthias Matussek's *Die vaterlose Gesellschaft: Eine Polemik gegen die Abschaffung der Familie* (*The Fatherless Society: A Polemic against the Abolition of the Family*, 2006) and Elisabeth Roudinesco's *La Famille en désordre* (*The Family in Disorder*, 2002) on to bestseller lists. Yet, rather than revealing an alarming increase in dysfunctional families or even the total demise of the social institution of the family, such books reflect a resistance to change and alternative family models – as well as a nostalgic longing for a family ideal that never really existed.[6] Representations of diasporic and ethnic minority families seem to encapsulate the emotionally ambivalent response to growing family diversity in Western societies. As will become apparent in the course of *Far-flung Families in Film*, their presence in our midst is charged with fear, fear of an 'excess of alterity' (Sartori cited in Grillo 2008: 17) that is perceived to pose a threat to our value and belief systems and to the social cohesion of Western societies. Yet, conversely, we project upon these 'Other' families our nostalgic longing for the traditional – and by implication happy – family which once was our own but from which the forces of progress and modernity have expelled us.

The Diasporic Family

In scholarly literature, the term 'diasporic family' is often used interchangeably with the 'transnational' and the 'immigrant family'. All three terms imply transnational mobility; however, in the case of transnational families, mobility can be individual or collective, whereas diasporic and immigrant families are inevitably linked to mass migration movements, whether forced or voluntary.

Migration can occur within the borders of nation-states, typically from rural areas to urban centres, or across national borders. Immigration and emigration both denote transnational mobility – with immigration foregrounding the arrival in the receiving country, whereas emigration connotes outbound direction, away from the homeland.⁷ Migration can be temporary or result in long-term settlement. Migration always precedes the formation of a diaspora, defined as a recognisable and minoritarian social group that preserves its 'ethnic, or ethnic-religious identity and communal solidarity' (Sheffer 1986: 9). But, as Richard Marienstras notes, 'time has to pass' before one can establish with certainty whether a community that has migrated 'is really a diaspora' (1989: 125). Though not all migrants eventually become long-term or permanent settlers in the destination country, the collective experience of migration is constitutive for the group identity of diasporic populations and, by implication, also for the diasporic family.

Etymologically, the term 'diaspora' is derived from the Greek verb 'speiro' (to sow or scatter seeds) and 'dia-' (over, across) (Cohen 2008: ix, Peters 1999: 23). Diasporic communities are, by definition, dispersed across two or more countries, though they do not necessarily have to be 'scattered to all lands', as the prophets claimed in the Bible of the Jews, whom many scholars still regard as the ideal or prototypical diaspora (Safran 1991; Cohen 2008). As the concept of diaspora remains inextricably linked to the plight of the Jews after the Babylonian and Roman conquests of Palestine between the eighth and sixth centuries BC and is closely associated with the African slave trade, as well as the genocide and deportation of Armenians and other so-called 'victim diasporas' (Cohen 2008), it 'invokes the imagery of traumas of separation and dislocation [. . .] but diasporas are also potentially the sites of home and new beginnings' (Brah 1996: 193) and, therefore, entail the positive affective component of hope.

In recent years, the concept of diaspora has become so fashionable and widely appropriated that theorists are struggling to achieve a consensus about its distinctive attributes and boundaries. In an attempt to contain the inflationary use of this prodigious term, Robin Cohen, building on William Safran's influential definition of diaspora (1991), proposes nine features constitutive of the classical notion of diaspora. These include 'dispersal from an original homeland [. . .] to two or more foreign regions; [. . . and] a collective memory and myth about the homeland' (2008: 17), which often manifests itself in a nostalgic longing to return. Diasporas are collectively committed to the 'maintenance, restoration, safety and prosperity' of their 'real or imagined ancestral home' (17). Diasporic communities are further characterised by 'a strong ethnic group consciousness [. . .] based on a sense of distinctiveness, a common history and the belief in a common fate' and they tend to have 'a sense of empathy and solidarity with co-ethnic members in other countries of settlement' (17). While their relationship with societies of settlement may be problematic in a number of ways (through marginalisation, as well as resistance to assimilation), diasporas also 'enrich life in host countries', contributing not just to the economy but also to creative and cultural pluralism and diversity (17). Paul Gilroy's seminal study *The Black Atlantic* (1993), which charts the transatlantic slave trade and subsequent voluntary migrations as the historical background for the emergence of a Black diasporic counter-culture of modernity, serves as a pertinent illustration.[8]

These considerations allow us to make some further distinctions between transnational and diasporic families in contemporary societies.[9] Both types of family are characterised by transnational mobility and multi-locality, which means that they live 'some or most of the time separated from each other' yet are held together by 'a feeling of collective welfare and unity, namely, "familyhood", even across national borders' (Bryceson and Vuorela 2002: 3). The geographical separation can run right through the nuclear family, as was common during postwar labour migration to the 'old Europe', when men left their wives and children in the country of origin, supporting their immediate and extended families by sending home remittances and visiting their families once a year, at the most. Sometimes, children are left behind or sent back to live with relatives in the country of origin (in the case of diasporic families) while both parents are working in another country. Alternatively, multi-locality may affect only the extended family, whereas the nuclear family lives in the same household. What distinguishes the diasporic family from other multi-local and transnational families is its pronounced orientation towards the 'axis of origin and return' (Clifford 1994: 321). This vertical axis between the country of origin and the destination country, the 'there' and the 'here', accounts for a particular diasporic consciousness. It finds its expression in a strong affective bond, a nostalgic longing to return (though this is rarely put into practice) to an idealised homeland. The myth of the home(land), based on the collective experience, memory or postmemory of migration, is an essential feature of the diasporic sensibility. In everyday family life, this is reflected in 'a strong retention of group ties sustained over an extended period (in respect of language, religion, endogamy and cultural norms)' (Cohen 2008: 61). Bryceson and Vuorela have coined the term 'relativising' for these 'modes of materializing the family as an imagined community with shared feelings and mutual obligations' (2002: 14), while cultural anthropologist Arjun Appadurai (1996) has theorised such practices as the 'production of locality' (see Chapter 4).

Whether out of a desire to be with their own people or as a result of social marginalisation, diasporic communities often reside in ethnic neighbourhoods, where families, torn apart in the process of migration and dispersal, are reconstituted or where migrants from the same village or country of origin develop family-like support networks. The Little Italies and Chinatowns in large cities all over the world illustrate this form of diasporic networking and the production of locality. Shops selling particular ethnic foods and clothing, or faith schools that complement or substitute the educational offerings of the host society create a sense of home elsewhere. Transnational elites, by contrast, frequently display 'reverse cultural alienation' by not wanting to mix and socialise with their less educated and less affluent compatriots, choosing instead to live in well-off majority neighbourhoods (Bryceson and Vuorela 2002: 21). More generally, transnational and diasporic families are distinguished by a markedly different sense of place. The anthropologist Ulf Hannerz associates transnational communities with particular occupations (diplomats, bureaucrats, foreign correspondents and so on) and describes their transnational hyper-mobility as making 'quick forays from a home base to many other places – for a few hours or days in a week, for a few weeks here and there in a year – and as they shift their bases for longer periods within their lives' (1996: 107). Such individuals and their families conduct their mobile lives from a base or from constantly shifting bases, following 'the siren call of opportunity wherever it leads' (Lasch 1995: 6).[10]

Bryceson and Vuorela draw attention to the class implications of 'transnational' and 'migrant / diasporic'. Families who came to Europe from the former colonies or as part of other labour migrations during the postwar era were predominantly low-skilled workers and belonged to the working class, at least the first generation. The term 'transnational family', by contrast, is commonly used with reference to social elites whose international careers make them 'mobile' rather than 'migrant'. They move out of choice rather than out of political or economic necessity and can freely negotiate their places of residence and, frequently, their nationalities too. Such highly skilled, multi-lingual transnationals are much sought after on the labour market and are welcome citizens who can cross borders freely and travel between their multiple homes. Still, without wanting to deny these class implications, it is worth noting that, by the second or third generation, many diasporic families have moved up the social hierarchy (often through considerable investment in the education of their children), so that the distinction becomes increasingly blurred. It would, therefore, be 'clearly a fallacy to identify the diasporic experience exclusively with the subaltern' (Cunningham and Sinclair 2001: 12).[11]

In their article 'The transnational family among urban diaspora populations', Rubel and Rosman conflate the two terms and illustrate how frequent inexpensive air travel and the use of email, particular internet sites and the exchange of home videos (especially of weddings and other family celebrations) have facilitated the transnationalisation of diasporic families. Hence, contemporary diasporic families can 'be in very frequent contact with their kinsmen back home, in contrast to an earlier period when this was not the case and ties would wither' (Rubel and Rosman 2009: 57). Accordingly, the transnational family would simply be a contemporary version of the diasporic family in the age of globalisation – and it is in this sense that recent studies such as *The Transnational Family: New European Frontiers and Global Networks* (Bryceson and Vuorela 2002) and *Transnational Families: Ethnicities, Identities and Social Capital* (Goulbourne, Reynolds, Solomos and Zontini 2010) use the concept.[12]

Nevertheless, I prefer to use the more narrowly defined term 'diasporic family' since, rather than being primarily concerned with what James Clifford (1994) describes as the decentred lateral axes – that is, the transnational connectedness of these families across several destination countries, I am first and foremost interested in the vertical axis, the shared experience and / or collective memory of migration from the homeland that has shaped the collective identity of diasporic communities. Most of the films about far-flung families that I analyse in this book privilege the vertical axis by linking the fictional lives they narrate to the postwar labour migrations from Europe's former colonies. This explains why, in Britain and France, in particular, the notion of diaspora is interlocked with ethnicity and race. In fact, Gabriel Sheffer defines 'modern diasporas [... as] ethnic minority groups of migrant origins' (1986: 3). Furthermore, black Britons of Afro-Caribbean descent, the South Asians from India, Pakistan or Bangladesh in Britain, and the Maghrebi diaspora (comprising people of Algerian, Tunisian and Moroccan heritage) are identified not only as ethnic minorities but also as people of colour. This distinguishes them, for instance, from Italian immigrants, referred to as 'white ethnics' in the US or as 'cultural minorities' in Canada (Fortier 2000: 20), and from the Turkish diaspora in Germany, whose status as an ethnic minority is based primarily on religious difference.[13]

How, then, is the diasporic family constructed as 'Other' in relation to the hypostatised norm of the white nuclear family, which 'remains a powerful ideological device for naturalising hierarchies of race, class, gender and sexuality' (Chambers 2001: 13)? Although race is a particularly important marker of difference, not least because it is immediately visible, value and belief systems that determine the dynamics within the family and its interaction with the host society emerge as the most controversial aspects of the diasporic family's perceived alterity. Ralph Grillo observes that social scientists increasingly contest the notion of the family as 'a "natural" form of human organisation', conceiving of it instead as a symbolic system governed by a culturally and historically specific ideology (2008: 16). It is 'a social construct which entails beliefs and values defining family members and relationships with them. It thus constitutes a moral order, albeit with widely diverse understandings of what that moral order should be' (16). By focusing on the most extreme deviations from the moral codes of the white hegemonic family, the yardstick against which other family models are measured, the mass media reinforce culturalist assumptions about the 'Otherness' of diasporic families.[14] Headlines display an almost voyeuristic fascination with honour killings, typically associated with traditional Muslim families and cited as evidence of an irreconcilable 'clash of civilisations' (Huntington 1997) between the Christian and the Muslim world. The headscarf and the *burqa* and other features of Islamic female dress codes are interpreted as visible symbols of gender inequality and female oppression and play an important part in vilifying the 'Otherness' of diasporic Muslim families (see Bowen 2007). The practice of arranged marriage conflicts with

Western values of individual self-determination and the ideal of romantic love. Yet those who condemn arranged marriage readily forget that love marriage is a fairly recent invention and by no means a guarantor of a happy and stable family life. Whereas the South Asian diasporic family, imagined 'as bounded by traditional and patriarchal frameworks', has emerged as 'one of the defining tropes' in the British media (Malik 2012), the African–Caribbean family is often type-cast as dysfunctional and, on account of absent fathers and matriarchal family structures, identified as the root cause of juvenile delinquency in the shape of drug and gun crime.[15] In other words, the cultural differences of diasporic families have given rise to some 'compelling myths proliferated around different ethnic minorities' (Malik 2012). By contrast, less spectacular examples of alternative family ideologies and practices rarely attract media attention.

Many aspects of these alternative family structures and values are classified as 'traditional' – a slippery term that means different things to different people and that has acquired predominantly pejorative connotations. Whereas, in feminist discourse, the traditional family is by and large co-terminous with the 1950s breadwinner–housewife model of the nuclear family, with reference to diasporic, ethnic minority families, 'traditional' is associated not only with patriarchy but also with pre-industrial family configurations. The premium placed on the family's economic function in pre-industrial societies meant that large households in which extended families, consisting of three or more generations and usually including aunts, uncles and other relatives as well, were more efficient as units of production than small nuclear families (see Goody 1983). Many immigrants come from poor, rural areas where such traditional family forms are deeply entrenched (see Lacoste-Dujardin 2000, Ewing 2008) and, therefore, transnational migration invariably involves a huge domestic upheaval. Families have to abandon their extended kinship networks and village communities and are expected to adjust to the Western model of the nuclear family. Disorientated and reluctant to let go of what they are accustomed to, many diasporic families cling to social practices and value systems that appear to be out of place in the host societies. For the first generation, in particular, economic and other utilitarian considerations frequently continue to take precedence over romantic love in the choice of spouse; patriarchal power structures and gendered division of labour prevail; female virtue, understood as virginity before marriage and fidelity afterwards, serves as the guarantor of family honour (see Ahmed 2003, Georgas 2006, Giddens 2002 and Chapter 4).

The enormous importance attached to family honour indicates that the traditional family places a much higher value on the group and its welfare than on the needs and desires of individual family members. 'Traditions are always properties of groups, communities or collectivities. Individuals may follow traditions and customs, but traditions are not a quality of individual behaviour' (Giddens 2002: 41). According to Anthony Giddens, the defining feature of tradition is not 'endurance over time' but 'ritual and repetition' (43). Nevertheless, tradition constitutes an important link to the past in so far as 'the past structures the present through shared collective beliefs and sentiments' (47). Through transnational migration – usually from rural areas to urban centres – traditional families find themselves catapulted into de-traditionalised societies with 'greater freedom of action' and 'emancipation from the constraints of the past' (47).

These considerations illustrate how, in discourses on the diasporic family, the notion of tradition is underpinned by the problematic 'racialized dichotomy of modernity versus tradition' (Erel 2002: 128). Yet, as already noted above, there is another side to the traditional family. Collectivism and continuity translate into the positive values of nurturing kinship networks and stability, which contrast with the fragmentation and alleged crisis of the hegemonic family. Thus, idealised representations of the diasporic family imagine it as 'the cradle of original, pristine forms of culture which remain uncontaminated by the "host" society's degenerate ways of life' (Fortier 2000: 61).

Whether or not 'traditional' is interpreted in positive or negative terms is determined by the family's ethnicity (see Introduction) and by the films' generic conventions. Put bluntly, while social realist dramas tend to emphasise what makes the diasporic family different from 'us', comedies explore what makes them similar. Yet, even if familiar binary structures such as tradition versus modernity, rural versus urban, the home versus host society, the periphery versus the centre and the West versus the rest continue to resonate in public discourse and in artistic representation, in the majority of more recent diasporic family films, they have been superseded by notions of flow and dialogism. Avtar Brah's discussion of the 'diaspora space' exemplifies such a dialogic perspective. She suggests that the diaspora space

> as opposed to that of diaspora [...] is 'inhabited', not only by those who have migrated and their descendants, but equally by those who are constructed and represented as indigenous. In other words, the concept of *diaspora space* [...] includes the entanglement, the intertwining of genealogies of dispersion with those of 'staying put'. (1996: 209)

Brah's radical critical intervention complicates the insistence upon boundaries between 'us' and 'them', foregrounding instead the social, cultural and creative dynamics of the encounter. Similarly, in their seminal book *Unthinking Eurocentrism*, Ella Shohat and Robert Stam (1994) propose a polycentric vision, which decentres a Eurocentric perspective by situating diasporic and minoritarian communities not on the margins of a pre-existing nucleus of society but instead at its very core, as active participants in the shaping of a shared – though often conflictual – past, present and future. Arjun Appadurai, too, disavows the notion of centre and periphery and replaces it with a model of disjunctive global flows. These transnational exchanges of people, finance, ideas and so on occur together but are not systematically related. Appadurai conceives of them in terms of fluid landscapes, which he terms 'ethnoscapes', 'mediascapes', 'technoscapes', 'financescapes' and 'ideoscapes'. Diasporic families form a vital part of such 'ethnoscapes', defined by Appadurai as 'landscape[s] of persons who constitute the shifting world in which we live: tourists, immigrants, refugees, exiles, guestworkers and other moving groups of individuals' (1996: 33). In such deterritorialised, mobile communities, affiliations between people are forged that transcend national belonging, race and religion. Whereas some critical frameworks conceptualise diasporic identities in terms of 'roots', emphasising the importance of origin, bloodline and descent, others prioritise the notion of 'routes' (see Gilroy 1993a; Clifford 1994) and conceive of diasporic identities as complex, hybrid and poised in transition, perpetually transforming and redefining themselves. For Stuart Hall, identity is 'not an essence but a *positioning*' ([1990] 2003: 237). Rather than proceeding 'in a straight unbroken line from some fixed origin', diasporic identities position themselves in relation to 'the vector of similarity and continuity; and the vector of difference and rupture' (237). Representing a fundamental departure from the more literal notion of diaspora outlined above, Hall's conceptualisation culminates in the following famous definition of diaspora and identity:

> Diaspora does not refer us to those scattered tribes whose identity can only be secured in relation to some sacred homeland to which they must at all costs return, even if it means pushing other people into the sea. This is the old, the imperializing, the hegemonizing, form of 'ethnicity'. [...] The diaspora experience as I intend it here is defined, not by essence or purity, but by the recognition of a necessary heterogeneity and diversity; by a conception of 'identity' which lives with and through, not despite, difference; by *hybridity*. Diaspora identities are those which are constantly producing and reproducing themselves anew, through transformation and difference. (244)

Hall's explicitly non-essentialist and non-dichotomous understanding of diaspora has proven enormously influential and resonates, amongst others, with Paul Gilroy's utopian vision of conviviality (2004), arising from the everyday interaction and cohabitation of many different racial and ethnic groups, which he regards as an ordinary feature of social life in postcolonial urban centres all over the world; with David Hollinger's idea of postethnicity (2000), which lays stress on voluntary affiliations and the formation of 'communities of consent', as opposed to involuntary affiliations based on descent; and with Cunningham and Sinclair's (2001) trope of 'floating lives'. All of these approaches propose ways of thinking about diasporic identities that eschew the divisive 'two worlds' paradigm. In relation to the diasporic family, they revalorise the notion of difference and conceive of its putative Otherness in positive terms. The ability to access multiple transnational networks, languages and cultures puts the diasporic family, at least potentially, in the privileged position of amassing more symbolic capital and transmitting it across the generations than those families who are staying put (see Bourdieu 1998: 23). In fact, it has been suggested that, as citizens of plural worlds, they occupy a pivotal position in processes of cultural hybridisation.

Family Reunion and the Formation of Diasporic Families

Without meaning to suggest that the diasporic family films analysed in this book reflect the history of immigration and settlement in Europe in a straightforward way, some socio-historical facts on the postwar mass migration movements that brought these families to Britain, France and Germany may prove useful. The years following World War Two were a period of restructuring and rapid economic growth in Western Europe.[16] When labour shortages jeopardised economic expansion, many west and north European nations actively recruited migrant workers, predominantly single men who were meant to stay for a number of years with a view to returning to their countries of origin. West Germany recruited *Gastarbeiter* (literally 'guest workers', a euphemistic term used in the early days of labour migration) from Italy, Spain, Greece, Turkey, Portugal and Yugoslavia, signing a series of intergovernmental agreements that regulated short-term labour recruitment between 1955 and 1968.[17] While the UK and France also actively recruited workers from southern Europe and elsewhere to combat labour shortages, the majority of immigrants came from former colonies. In the case of France, that included those from the Maghreb (Algeria, Tunisia and Morocco) and, in the case of the UK, from Jamaica and other Caribbean islands, as well as from India and Pakistan.[18] Not unlike the Turkish guest workers in Germany, these colonial migrants also sought to better their economic situation. Yet, in many respects, their situation was favourable compared to that of other labour migrants; not only had they developed a familiarity and cultural affinity with the metropolitan centres as a result of colonial rule, but they also enjoyed privileged access to certain civil and political rights and legal entitlements. For example, many colonial migrants brought their families with them from the outset and planned a medium- or long-term future in the destination country (Fielding 1993). The actual working and living conditions of colonial migrants in France and Britain and of guest workers in Germany were, however, not dissimilar. According to Castles and Miller, both colonial and guest workers

> became overwhelmingly concentrated in low-skilled manual work, mainly in industry and construction. Both tended to suffer substandard housing, poor social conditions and educational disadvantage. Over time, there was a convergence of legal situations, with family reunion and social rights for foreign workers improving, while colonial migrants lost many of their privileges. Finally, both groups were affected by similar

> processes of marginalization, leading to a degree of separation from the rest of the population and an ethnic minority position. (2009: 106)

Although it would go beyond the scope of this survey to trace the different histories of immigration in Britain, France and Germany and the many changes to the immigration legislation in detail, one salient point is worth bearing in mind: by the mid-1970s, primary migration in all three countries had come to a halt and family reunion (that is, chain migration of children, parents, spouses and sometimes other relatives, and marriage migration) has since been the most important form of legal immigration and the prerequisite for the formation of diasporas in these countries. Though the influx of refugees and asylum seekers has also contributed to rising immigration figures, statistically it has been less significant.[19] In Britain, immigration from the New Commonwealth countries was curtailed as early as 1962, when the Commonwealth Immigrants Act was passed. By that time, the presence of over half a million people of New Commonwealth origin led to strong anti-immigration sentiments and racial tensions. The situation was exacerbated by a much earlier onset of economic stagnation than in France and Germany. Nevertheless, the number of Commonwealth immigrants continued to grow, even after the Immigration Act of 1971 introduced further restrictions, including some on family reunification (see Hansen 2000, Castles and Miller 2009: 96–124). In France and Germany, immigration policies changed as a consequence of the sudden economic downturn caused by the Middle East War of 1973 and the sharp rise in oil prices ('the oil crisis'). Not only did the West German and French governments stop labour recruitment in November 1973 and July 1974 respectively, but over the next few years, they also devised various financial incentives to encourage migrants to return to their countries of origin. Yet, on the whole, voluntary repatriation schemes met with little success and, in particular, migrants from poor and less developed countries decided to stay. In order to prevent the long-term settlement of unwanted colonial migrants, the French government initially attempted to ban family reunification. However, this proved unworkable and was declared unlawful in 1978 (Hargreaves 2007: 23–7). In Germany, family reunification was contingent upon a very long list of conditions, including the resident sponsor's proof of work and of adequately sized accommodation, coupled with a four-year employment ban for any joining family members (Kolinsky 1996: 90). Although the West German and French governments discouraged family reunion by various means throughout the 1960s, not least by providing migrant workers with hostel accommodation unsuitable for families (as illustrated in the documentaries *My Father, the Guest Worker* and the narratives of 'The Fathers' in *Immigrant Memories*, both discussed in Chapter 3), these measures ultimately proved unsuccessful and family settlement had begun well before family reunion policies were officially instituted.

I would like to make a case for the crucial importance of family migration and reunion in relation to the formation of diasporic communities and even for the development of diasporic cinema in Britain, France and Germany. Family reunion changed not only the scale of migration (with more rather than fewer immigrants arriving since primary migration was no longer an option) but also its entire dynamics in relation to the host societies. The arrival of families meant that immigrants settled permanently (or at least aspired to do so) and gradually became embedded in the social fabric of the host societies. The needs and priorities of immigrant families were rather different from those of single labour migrants. They required proper housing and schools and worried about inculcating the right religious and cultural values in their children. Esther Ben-Davis (2009) explains Europe's shifting immigration dynamic with the arrival of families:

> Whereas single workers either isolated themselves or sought to experience the more liberal lifestyle of Europe, the arrival of families led immigrants to transport their honor culture and modesty standards to the West and to put into practice their attitudes towards women. [. . .] Immigrant parents brought their children to the West to give them new opportunities, but they did not want them to fall prey to Western temptations.

Yamina Benguigui's three-part documentary *Immigrant Memories* (see Chapter 3) and Yasemin Samdereli's *Almanya – Welcome to Germany* (see Chapter 2) trace in exemplary fashion this transformation from the segregated existence of male migrant workers, living in basic overcrowded hostels, to the arrival of their wives and children and the gradual embedding of these families.

Settlement and integration into a new culture take time and involve more than just one generation. For the generation of parents, arrival in the destination country was usually fraught with linguistic and cultural barriers and they needed to invest their energies primarily in the struggle for material survival, but their children and grandchildren were able to build on these achievements. Benefitting from better educational opportunities and from growing up bilingually, the second generation is well equipped to act as mediator between the majority culture and their parents. Yet, conversely, discrimination against and marginalisation of diasporic youth are widespread and, in some respects, this puts the second and subsequent generations at an even greater disadvantage than the first, who at least had employment. In terms of demographics, those migrants who moved to and settled in France, Britain and West Germany – the three countries with the largest diasporic ethnic minority populations in Europe – were generally young, healthy and of child-bearing age, and came from cultures with traditionally large families. Thus, over the next three decades, they grew to become sizeable diasporic communities, whose economic and social contributions benefit the host societies in numerous ways. Welcome or not, they continue to fill significant gaps in the labour market and, by bucking the trend of an ageing European population, even safeguard the retirement benefits of the majority culture population. In sum, family reunion has been the single most important prerequisite for the development of diaspora populations, whose presence is felt in all spheres of life. They have transformed the face of our cities, creating what Doreen Massey (1994) famously termed a 'global sense of place' in multi-ethnic urban neighbourhoods; they have enriched the material culture of our everyday lives by introducing ethnic food and fashion; and most importantly, in the context of this book, they have invigorated the arts, literature and film through a distinctive diasporic aesthetic that juxtaposes and fuses stylistic templates, generic conventions, narrative and musical traditions, languages and performance styles from more than one culture.

Bringing the Diasporic Family on to the Screen

Even a cursory glance at the biographies of some of Europe's most prominent diasporic filmmakers and scriptwriters, including Gurinder Chadha, Hanif Kureishi, Ayub Khan-Din, Mehdi Charef, Abdellatif Kechiche and Fatih Akın reveals that all of them are members of the second generation, born or raised in the country to which their parents migrated. Without family migration, the kind of diasporic film culture that emerged in Britain, France and Germany almost simultaneously from the mid-1980s onwards would never have come into existence. What is more, according to the scriptwriters' and directors' own testimonies, some of the films derive from their personal experience and thus reflect what Hamid Naficy has identified as a distinctive feature of 'accented cinema':[20] namely, the inscription of 'the biographical, social, and cinematic (dis)location of the filmmakers' (2001: 4).

Such a biographical impetus is particularly prominent in the work of Hanif Kureishi, who has written numerous screenplays, including that of the groundbreaking film *My Beautiful Laundrette*. He was born in Bromley in 1954, to a Muslim father from an affluent, upper-middle-class Madras family, who moved to Britain after the Partition of British India in 1947, and an English mother. His New Commonwealth origins are, however, complicated by his 'Anglo-Pakistani / Indian parentage, which makes him a minority within a minority', since, even amongst the growing number of mixed-race families in Britain at the time, 'Anglo-Caribbean children were much more common' (Moore-Gilbert 2001: 13). Kureishi enjoyed a comparatively privileged upbringing and, on occasion, explicitly dissociated himself from his compatriots: 'Most English don't realise that the immigrants who come here are the scum of Pakistan [. . .] I could not talk to them there, except give them orders. And won't be solid with them here' (Kureishi cited in Moore-Gilbert 2001: 20). An acute awareness of fully belonging neither to the Asian British community nor to the metropolitan majority culture underpins his work. 'I come from two worlds . . . There was my Pakistani family, my uncles, aunts and so on. Then there was my English family, who were lower-middle or working class. [. . .] And having an Indian father . . . So finding my way through all that . . . I wrote all those books to make sense of it' (Kureishi cited in Moore-Gilbert 2001:

14). The many mixed-race families in Kureishi's *œuvre*, as well as the culturally comparative treatment of them, gestures towards the autobiographical impetus of his writing. His narratives preclude any comfortable sense of superiority – be it on account of the more liberal values or on account of superior family values – amongst white majority culture or British Asians.

Actor, playwright and scriptwriter Ayub Khan-Din, who created one of the best-known British Asian families on screen, the Khan family in *East is East*, revealed in an interview: 'The parents are drawn directly from my own family. The youngest boy, Sajid, is me as a child' (Olden and Khan-Din 1999). Khan-Din was born in Salford in 1961 as one of ten children of a mixed-race marriage between a Pakistani father who, just like George Khan, owned a fish and chip shop, and an English mother. He started his career as an actor with a minor role in Hanif Kureishi and Stephen Frears's film *My Beautiful Laundrette* and played Sammy in their subsequent collaboration *Sammy and Rosie Get Laid* (1987), before moving on to playwriting. Khan-Din turned *East is East*, originally a critically acclaimed play written for the Royal Court Theatre in London, into the screenplay for what was to become one of the biggest British box office successes.[21]

Traces of the filmmakers' family histories can also be found in Meera Syal's autobiographical coming-of-age novel and screenplay *Anita and Me* (2002) and in Gurinder Chadha's girl-power movie *Bend It Like Beckham* (2002). The latter pays tribute to Chadha's father, who died in 1999 and who, like the turban-wearing Mr Bhamra, was of Sikh Punjabi origin and born in Kenya. The family moved from Nairobi to the London suburb of Southall in 1961, when Gurinder Chadha was one year old. Her contemporary, Meera Syal (who rose to prominence through her performance in the BBC comedy sketch series *Goodness Gracious Me*, 1998–2001), was born in Wolverhampton as the daughter of a Sikh Hindu couple from New Delhi. Syal and Chadha are high-profile British Asian media celebrities and, as such, were invited to appear on the popular BBC family history programme *Who Do You Think You Are?*, where they investigated the genealogies of their far-flung families by travelling to Kenya and India.

Motivated by the desire to record and preserve family memories of migration, a number of second-generation filmmakers, including the Kurdish German Yüksel Yavuz, the Turkish German Fatih Akın and Seyhan Derin, and the British Asian Sandhya Suri, made documentaries about their parents' memories of migration. In these postmemory films, considered in Chapter 3, the filmmakers trace their parents' histories, lest they be consigned to oblivion. Yet, interestingly, none of these Turkish German filmmakers nor their contemporaries, Aysun Bademsoy, Ayşe Polat, Züli Aladağ, Sinan Akkus and Yasemin and Nesrin Samdereli, have drawn as extensively on their own life stories for their feature films as the above-mentioned Asian British filmmakers or a number of Maghrebi French writers and directors have done.[22]

For instance, *Le Thé au harem d'Archimède* (*Tea in the Harem*, Mehdi

Charef, 1985), widely regarded as a landmark of *beur* cinema, is based on the writer–director's semi-autobiographical novel *Le Thé au harem d'Archi Ahmed*. Charef moved from Algeria to France when he was eleven years old and grew up amongst other immigrant families in a *bidonville* (shantytown) on the outskirts of Paris, until relocating to one of the working-class housing projects in the *banlieue*, which provides the setting of *Tea in the Harem*. Having received only an elementary education, he earned his living as a factory worker (Hargreaves 1997: 16, 33) until his life changed dramatically with the publication of his début novel in 1983. The book received good reviews. Media interest in immigration issues was rising and the filmmaker / producer couple, Constantin Costa-Gavras and his wife Michèle Ray-Gavras, were looking for a story about immigration for Costa-Gavras's next film. They invited Charef to write the screenplay but when they realised that he had a very clear vision of what the film should look like, they offered him vital production funding and the opportunity to make his first film (Hargreaves 1997: 33). *Tea in the Harem* won numerous prestigious prizes, including the Jean Vigo and César Awards, launching Charef as one of the foremost *beur* filmmakers in France. An enthusiastic review in *Cinématographe* describes it as one of the very first French films to show an Arab family (Durel 1985: 32). To be sure, the vantage point of Charef's début feature was markedly different from earlier depictions of North Africans in cinema, which foregrounded the experience of racism and constructed a 'militantly Manichaean universe' that pitted Arabs against the rest of French society (Bosséno 1992: 54). Earlier films, made by first-generation émigrés from North Africa, as well as by indigenous French filmmakers, had emphasised the alterity of North African immigrants and pursued an overtly political message in relation to immigration issues. This changed with the coming of age of a new generation of filmmakers of North African origin who were born and / or brought up in France and who were collectively referred to as '*beurs*'. In 1985, when the first two feature-length films by *beurs*, *Tea in the Harem* and *Baton Rouge* (Rachid Bourchareb), were released and when the film journal *Cinématographe* devoted a special issue to *cinéma beur*, the term gained currency. Over the next few years, films made by *beurs* about *beurs* steadily grew in number and gradually began to challenge a white-dominated monolithic representation of Frenchness. Carrie Tarr identifies the most significant contribution of *beur* filmmaking as lying 'in the shift it operates in the position of enunciation from which the dominant majority is addressed, focusing on minority perspectives which bring with them the potential for new strategies for identification and cultural contestation' (2005: 14–15).

Beur filmmakers, most of whom are French citizens, are intent on claiming their place in French society, complicating the significance of race in their films. The ubiquitous narratives about multi-ethnic male friendship groups are symptomatic in this respect. They make the point that social marginalisation affects disenfranchised white French men (almost) as much as it does *beurs*.

Figure 1.1 *Tea in the Harem* by Mehdi Charef marks the beginning of *beur* cinema in 1985

Banished to the *banlieue*, the working-class, multi-ethnic neighbourhoods on the urban periphery of France's big cities, white French and *beur* protagonists forge friendships based on the solidarity of the dispossessed. For filmmakers whose prime concern was to negotiate their own position in French society, their protagonists' relationships with their peers were far more important than the immigration histories of their families. Hence, it was not until the mid-1990s that stories about their parents and their families gained a more prominent place in French cinema. Seminal films include *Sous les pieds des femmes* (Rachida Krim, 1997), *Le Gone du Chaâba* (*The Kid from Chaaba*, based on an autobiographical novel by *beur* writer Azouz Begag, directed by Christophe Ruggia, 1998), *Immigrant Memories, Inch' Allah Dimanche* (Yamina Benguigui, 2001), *Vivre au paradis* (*Living in Paradise*, Bourlem Guerdjou, 1999) and *17, rue Bleue* (*17 Blue Street*, Chad Chenouga, 2001). *Couscous*, in which writer–director Abellatif Kechiche pays tribute to his own father, who migrated from Tunisia to Nice in 1966 (when Kechiche was six years old), is arguably the most significant portrait of a family of Maghrebi descent in French cinema to date. Unlike the majority of *beur*-authored films, which, as Carrie Tarr has convincingly argued (2005, 2007), feature socially disenfranchised *beurs* who are in no position to start a family of their own, *Couscous* shows a sprawling family with third-generation offspring, interethnic couples and a modern patchwork family structure instead of a traditional patriarchal family.[23]

Nowhere is the importance of generational change for the emergence of a new type of cinema made more explicit than in relation to *beur* cinema, yet, ironically, both the term '*beur*' and the concept of the 'second generation' have become highly contested. The neologism *beur* is 'derived from Parisian backslang (verlan) [. . . and] a playful inversion and truncation of the syllables of the word for "Arab"' (Tarr 2005: 3). Adopted as a self-ascription by young second-generation immigrants of Maghrebi descent during the 1980s, the term was subsequently appropriated by French majority culture, whereupon the *beurs* themselves rejected it as an expression of ghettoization and have, since the 1990s, referred to themselves 'according to their origins (as in "d'origine algérienne / marocaine / tunisienne") or more generally as "d'origine maghrébine" ("of Maghrebi origin")' (Tarr 2005: 4). In her study *Postcolonial Hospitality: The Immigrant as Guest*, Mireille Rosello draws attention to the problematic implications of the concept of the second generation, which never lets us forget the genealogy of immigration and which perpetually labels the descendants of 'a cheap and compliant labor force [recruited] to build cars or erect high-rises of future banlieues' (2001: 89) and impedes upward social mobility. That a certain social stigma is attached to the concept becomes evident, Rosello argues, if we consider that, paradoxically, not all immigrant groups are labelled 'first' and 'second generation'. The term '*séconde génération* started to be used with reference to the children of immigrants from the Maghreb toward the end of the 1970s and has gained cultural currency without being backed up by valid statistical data or solid "scientific research"'(Noriel cited in Rosello 2001: 90). Due to its inaccurate use, the term 'second generation' refers simultaneously to the children and grandchildren of first-generation immigrants.

Such ambiguities make the attempt to categorise migrant and diasporic filmmakers in terms of 'generation' problematic – and a transnational perspective throws up additional complexities.[24] Thus, celebrated *beur* filmmaker Mehdi Charef and first-generation Turkish German filmmaker Tevfik Başer were both born in the early 1950s. Their début features, *Tea in the Harem* and *Vierzig Quadratmeter Deutschland* (*Forty Square Metres of Germany*), premiered in 1985 and 1986 respectively. And yet, despite being contemporaries, Charef and Başer belong to different generations in terms of their migratory histories and in their approach to representing migrant and diasporic identities on screen. These inconsistencies can be explained by the fact that, in relation to immigrants, the concept of 'generation' refers to two different temporal coordinates that may or may not overlap. On the one hand, it designates different age groups that are separated from each other by some twenty to thirty years. On the other hand, it refers to the moment of arrival in the destination country. According to the sociologist Karl Mannheim, a generation is defined not just by being born roughly around the same time (biological generation) but, more importantly, by sharing 'a common location in the social and historical process' (1952: 291), which translates into shared experiences and sociocultural reference points. Accordingly, 'first generation' identifies the collective experience of migration and resettlement in another country as more decisive for constituting a sense of generational belonging than being born around the same time. This 'fresh contact' with a new 'social and cultural heritage' is 'in the literal sense beginning a "new life"', Mannheim notes (293). The second generation either was born or arrived during their early childhood and spent their formative years in the host country. However, if one 'first generation' arrived some fifteen or twenty years later than another, then the notion of immigrant generations gets very messy.[25] Such ambiguities can, perhaps, be partially resolved if, as Joachim Matthes proposes in his critique of Karl Mannheim, generation is reconceptualised and less importance is attached to temporal simultaneity (being born around the same year or arriving in the destination country during a particular time period) than to a shared world view, a shared response to a particular political or cultural event (1985: 368–9).[26]

Therefore, if the concept of generation is to be of any relevance in relation to migrant and diasporic cinema, which, as I argue, is a particular type of transnational cinema in which is inscribed the memory or postmemory of migration, then what matters are not temporal coordinates such as the filmmakers' year of birth or the date of their arrival in the destination country, but rather how their films reflect the experience or (post)memory of migration and settlement, thematically and aesthetically. There is, indeed, a considerable body of both filmic and critical evidence that suggests that the films made by *beur* and other second-generation scriptwriters and directors are recognisably different from those made by first-generation directors – and, indeed, from films made solely by majority culture directors. I write 'solely', since many diasporic films considered in this book are based on collaborations between minority and majority culture writer–director teams, usually adaptations of novels authored by diasporic writers.

To return to the example of *Tea in the Harem*, made by a second-generation Maghrebi immigrant director in France, and *Forty Square Metres of Germany*, made by Tevfik Başer just a few years after his arrival in Germany in 1980, different generational approaches to representing the lives of immigrants are discernible. Rob Burns cites Başer's film as a paradigmatic example of what he calls 'cinema of the affected', characterised by a documentary realist style and conveying a sense of authenticity and overwhelming miserableness. 'The perspective it brought to bear on the alien culture was one in which the focus was unremittingly on alterity as a seemingly insoluble problem, on conflict of either an intercultural or intracultural variety' (2006: 133). Narratives of victimhood about oppressed, abused and incarcerated Turkish guest workers' wives or daughters prevail and not only appeal to audiences' sense of compassion but also invite majority culture audiences to feel a sense of moral superiority. Whereas the cinema of the affected (also called 'Kino der Fremdheit' or 'cinema of alterity' by German film historian and critic Georg Seeßlen) produced well-intentioned depictions of the difficulties faced by migrants, *Tea in the Harem* and other films made by second-generation directors, whether of Turkish or Maghrebi origin, no longer portray migrant and diasporic characters as foreigners. Seeßlen (2000) links the different vantage point to the experience and new artistic impetus of second-generation filmmakers and calls it 'Kino der Métissage' (cinema of the *métissage*): 'The cinema of the métissage does not make a big deal of alterity',[27] focusing instead on the everyday experiences of migrant and diasporic protagonists and the irreversible hybridisation of cultures. What was once regarded as exceptional by the dominant culture is gradually being normalised.

Similar developments characterise the representation of migrant and diasporic families and communities in British cinema. British films made in the wake of the Notting Hill 'race riots' of 1958, such as *Sapphire* (Basil Dearden, 1959) and *Flame in the Streets* (Roy Baker, 1961), were made by white majority culture filmmakers and centre on a 'traumatised white family facing the reality of "race" in their lives' (Pines 2001: 179), frequently configured as interracial romance. According to Jim Pines, these so-called 'race relations' films voice 'liberal humanist pleas for racial tolerance' and black characters 'tend to function primarily as catalysts for the expression of white characters' anxieties' (179). This changed when migrant and diasporic filmmakers gained access to the means of film production and, thereby, self-representation.[28] *Pressure* (Horace Ové, 1975), the first British feature-length film made by a black director, places a black family from Trinidad firmly at the centre of the narrative.[29] It addresses issues still prevalent in more recent films about migrant and diasporic families, such as the children's conflicting cultural attachments and the parents' thwarted hopes of securing a more prosperous life and a better future for their offspring in the destination country. Although the depiction of a family life fraught with tensions is an important concern, the film's main theme is Tony's growing Black consciousness. Following the lead of his politically aware, older brother Colin, Tony challenges his mother's futile aspirations to integrate into white British society and aligns himself with the political cause of his Black Brothers and Sisters when he joins the Black Power Movement. The kinship terms used emphatically and repeatedly by Sister Louise, Brother John and the other black political activists suggest that *Pressure* validates a family based on racial solidarity and a shared political vision over the natural family in which a false – that is, assimilationist – consciousness prevails.

What sets *Pressure* apart, however, from more contemporary diasporic family films made by second-generation directors is its unequivocal political message coupled with the moral stance of the social problem film and a gritty documentary realist aesthetic. Like *Burning an Illusion* (Menelik Shabbazz, 1981) and other Black British films of the time, it bears all the hallmarks of 'the cinema of duty', defined by Sarita Malik as a social issue-based cinema that 'positions its subjects in direct relation to social crisis, and attempts to articulate "problems" and "solutions to problems" within a framework of centre and margin, white and non-white communities' (Bailey cited in Malik

Figure 1.2 Tony (Herbert Norville) and his brother Colin (Oscar James) enjoying a British and a Caribbean breakfast in *Pressure* (Horace Ové, 1975)

1996: 203–4). These early Black British films were 'important for the way in which they "answered back" to what Jim Pines has called the "official race relations narrative" [. . .] by offering an alternative view of the diasporic experience' (Malik 1996: 204) and exploring what it means to be black and British. Still, their ideological agenda was far from monolithic. In contrast to *Pressure*, *Majdhar* (1984), directed by Ahmed Alauddin Jamal, who was one of the founding members of the Retake Film and Video Collective, pursues an overtly assimilationist agenda, charting the progress of Fauzia from being a submissive Pakistani wife to a liberated British woman who wears Western-style clothes, has an abortion, earns her own living and has no intention of becoming reunited with her unfaithful Pakistani husband. What *Pressure* and *Majdhar* have in common is that they imagine the diasporic experience in black-and-white terms, as an unsettling experience that compels its protagonists to take sides either by asserting their racial Otherness and claiming a distinct Black British culture or by integrating into British majority culture and renouncing their origins.

The imperative to take sides and to use film as an expression of sociopolitical commitment changed in 1985 with the release of *My Beautiful Laundrette*, a landmark British Asian film and a marked departure from 'the cinema of duty' that had dominated British representations of ethnic minorities until then. As in France and Germany, this representational shift from social issue-based drama to a cinema that, in the words of Malik (1996), celebrates 'the pleasures of hybridity' in terms of both aesthetics and narrative treatment, only came to the fore with second-generation writers and directors. In contrast to their predecessors, they construct multi-dimensional and fluid identities on screen, challenging essentialising conceptualisations not only of race and ethnicity but frequently also of gender and sexuality. This explains the prevalence of queer diasporic identities that function as a master trope of hybridity in diasporic cinema; *My Beautiful Laundrette*, *Young Soul Rebels* (Isaac Julien, 1991), *A Touch of Pink* (Ian Iqbal Rashid, 2004) and *Nina's Heavenly Delights* (Pratibha Parmar, 2006) – to mention but a few British films about queer interracial romance – interrogate narrowly framed conceptions of heteronormativity and of racial and national belonging (see Chapter 3). These films promote fluid identities, while simultaneously juxtaposing different stylistic and generic templates in a bid to reach diverse audiences beyond the filmmakers' own ethnic constituencies.

Young Soul Rebels, written and directed by Black British filmmaker Isaac Julien, one of the co-founders of the Sankofa Film and Video Collective, blends generic features of the thriller, the music film, the urban youth film and queer cinema, and relies on the cross-cultural appeal of soul music. Amongst the film's range of different musical styles, soul is the most important. Whereas reggae, Julien explains, relates to the Caribbean and is 'tied up with black nationalism and certain rigidities of sex and race', soul 'takes one into the wider black diaspora' and 'allowed for inter-racial relationships and challenged some of the structures of black masculinity. It opened up a less fixed and more fluid space' (Julien cited in Korte and Sternberg 2004: 109–10). *Nina's Heavenly Delights* is a queer romantic comedy set in an Indian restaurant in Glasgow and spiced up with some Bollywood-style musical interludes and countless mouth-watering close-ups of food shots, perhaps capitalising on the current popularity of cookery programmes on British television in a bid for mainstream audiences. Meanwhile, Gurinder Chadha's international box office hit *Bend It Like Beckham* fuses the generic conventions of (romantic) comedy, sports film and coming-of-age film, a sub-genre of the youth film. As Barbara Korte and Claudia Sternberg convincingly argue in *Bidding for the Mainstream: Black and Asian British Film since the 1990s*, the shift from avant-garde shorts and documentaries (the kinds of film chiefly made by Sankofa, Retake and the Black Audio Film Collective) and from the social problem film to more genre-based formats has been a key trend in British Asian cinema since the 1990s as it attempted to escape its ethnic niche and cross over into the mainstream. Mainstream culture should, however, not be understood in negative terms 'as a "streamlining" of culture, as a subordination of cultural specificity to one hegemonic cultural strand', but instead as 'the integration of cultural diversity within the cultural assumptions and tastes of' a majority population (Korte and Sternberg 2004: 8).

Similar tendencies can be observed in Turkish German and Maghrebi French film over the past few decades, and comedies have been particularly successful in this respect, achieving remarkable box office figures. *Les Deux Papas et la Maman* (*The Two Dads and One Mom*, Smaïn and Jean-Marc Longval, 1996), *Le Ciel, les oiseaux . . . et ta mere* (*Boys on the Beach*, Djamel Bensalah, 1999) and *Le Raïd* (*The Race*, Djamel Bensalah, 2002) all attracted more than one million viewers in France, while Merzack Allouche's *Chouchou* (2003), about a cross-dressing Algerian immigrant involved in a queer interethnic romance, attracted more than three million. The feel-good integration comedy *Almanya – Welcome to Germany*, with 1.4 million admissions in Germany alone, is to date the commercially most successful Turkish German film, surpassing Fatih Akın's critically acclaimed *Gegen die Wand* (*Head-On*, 2004) and *Auf der anderen Seite* (*The Edge of Heaven*, 2007), which boasted audiences between half a million and 700,000. Meanwhile, *East is East* and *Bend It Like Beckham* are amongst the commercially most successful British films, grossing £7.2 and £11.5 million at the box office. They 'have been credited as significant examples of national, i.e. unprefixed British cinema', which is in itself evidence of the 'mainstreaming of a previously marginalised area of British cinema' (Malik 2010: 137).[30]

It is certainly no coincidence that several of these box office hits feature diasporic families. Gurinder Chadha explains the success of *Bend It Like Beckham* with its family theme:

> It's a family film, and most families have some kind of cultural definition, whereby parents have certain expectations of their children, and children want to do things that are perhaps not what their parents expect them to do. This is not an exclusively Indian phenomenon, it can be found in every culture – black, white, brown, whatever. (Cited in Korte and Sternberg 2004: 245)

These sentiments are echoed by Leslee Udwin, the producer of *East is East* and its sequel *West is West*, about a mixed-race British Pakistani family from Salford. She believes that even such politically innocuous feel-good movies fulfil an important mission and contribute to greater tolerance in multi-cultural societies: 'We are all people. We are all the same', and films about family life emphasise this common ground (Udwin 2011). Ethnic comedies revolve around the dialectical tension between similarity and difference and make a case for the *rapprochement* of ethnic minority and majority cultures, for tolerance and mutual understanding.

The Family as a Trope of Belonging

But there is more to films about the diasporic family than the implicit invitation to identify with and accept the Other. The narrative construction of the diasporic family also functions as a trope of postnational belonging. It builds on a long representational history that imagines the nation in terms of family structures and parental roles, thereby naturalising hierarchies of power, inclusion and exclusion. Familial tropes and the iconography of domesticity, Anne McClintock illustrates, proliferate in a wide range of discourses:

> The term nation derives from *natio*: to be born. We speak of nations as 'motherlands' and 'fatherlands'. Foreigners 'adopt' countries that are not their native homes and are naturalized into the national 'family'. We talk of the 'Family of Nations', of 'homelands' and 'native' lands. In Britain, immigration matters are dealt with at the Home Office; in the United States, the president and his wife are called the First Family. [. . .] In this way, despite their myriad differences, nations are symbolically figured as domestic genealogies. (1995: 357)

Since a patriarchal structure was regarded as the natural order, the trope of the family, when applied to nations or to the relationship between an imperial power and its colonies, would automatically sanction similar inequities of power by depicting them as familial and, therefore, natural. In colonial discourse the trope of the 'family of black children ruled over by a white father' (McClintock 1995: 358) infantilises the colonial subjects and legitimises their domestication and subordination. Drawing upon the scientific racism that mapped evolutionary progress and the Family Tree of Man 'as a series of anatomically distinct family types, organized into a linear progression, from the "childhood" of "primitive" races to the enlightened "adulthood" of European imperial nationalism' (Boehmer 1991: 359), the trope of the family served to legitimise the European colonisers' civilising mission and the domestication of the infantile races.[31]

Since the days of colonial rule, such inequalities along the colour line have, of course, been vehemently contested and fought over. But even so, when, forty years after the African American Civil Rights movement and the assassination of Martin Luther King Jr in 1968, Barack Obama was elected President of the United States on 4 November 2008 and he, together with his wife Michelle, their two daughters Malia and Sasha, and his mother-in-law, Marian Robinson, moved into the White House in January 2009, this historic event hailed the promise of change and the hope for a new beginning. For the first time in American history, America's First Family is black. While Barack Obama's racially mixed heritage (as the son of a black Kenyan father and a white mother from Kansas) was widely discussed in the press at the time, his wife Michelle, an Ivy League-educated lawyer from a humble family background, was described as 'the descendant of slaves and a daughter of the Great Migration, the mass movement of African-Americans northward in the first half of the 20th century' in *The New York Times* (Kantor 2009). In the same article, entitled 'Nation's many faces in extended first family: A portrait of change', the Obamas' move into the White House was celebrated as a pivotal

Figure 1.3 For the first time in history, America's First Family is black. President Barack Obama with his wife Michelle and their daughters Malia and Sasha

moment not solely for African Americans but for immigrants and ethnic minorities *tout court*. As President Obama's Indonesian American half-sister, Maya Soetoro-Ng, commented, at long last, the family living in the White House reflects 'the textures and flavors of this country' (cited in Kantor 2009).

The trope of the family in relation to the nation is coloured, as well as gendered. Whereas the concept of the fatherland invokes nationalist and even martial connotations (after all, we go to war and die for the fatherland), female representations of nation, such as the motherland, Mother India or the German concept of *Heimat*, conceive of her as the symbolic bearer and reproducer of national ideals and virtues (see Anthias and Yuval-Davis 1989; Fehrenbach 1995). The motherland is often depicted as the victim of male invasion and aggression, symbolically represented as sexual violation. However, the male / female binarism underlying the family–nation trope is ambivalent and contradictory if we consider the concept of the motherland alongside that of the mother country or 'metropole'. Metropole, from the Greek 'metropolis' – that is, mother city (where *polis* means 'city state') – denotes the colonising mother countries (Ashcroft, Griffiths and Tiffin 1998: 138–9). The metropolitan centre not only controls the colonies situated on the periphery of the British Empire but, as the trope of the mother country implies, also provides for and nurtures her colonial subjects.

These considerations draw attention to the multiple and conflicting allegiances of the postcolonial diasporas that migrated to and settled in the metropolitan centres of former empires after World War Two; their motherland, in the sense of their native or ancestral land, was violated and exploited by the imperial mother country to which they subsequently moved in search of labour and a better life. Where exactly is their place in these former colonial mother countries – if, indeed, in the age of globalisation and postnationalism, we can assume that the tropes of kinship still resonate? John Akomfrah's essayistic memory film *The Nine Muses* (2010), in which he uses Homer's *Odyssey* as a framework through which to explore postwar migration from the 'family of Commonwealth nations' to Britain, seems to suggest as much. 'I am in my mother's womb. It's I who live here now. I don't know how I got there. Perhaps in an ambulance', one of the film's disembodied voices, presumably that of a postcolonial migrant, repeats three times. The somewhat cryptic reference to the mother's womb, alongside Paul Robeson's rendition of the traditional Negro spiritual 'Sometimes I feel like a motherless child', encapsulates the postcolonial migrants' discordant attachments to the mother country and the motherland. *The Nine Muses* recasts the history of postcolonial migration as myth and lends the experience of an ethnic minority universal relevance by citing extensively from 'white' canonical literary texts, including James Joyce's *Finnegan's Wake*, Friedrich Nietzsche's *Thus Spake Zarathustra*, Dante Alighieri's *Divine Comedy* and the works of William Shakespeare.[32] Interweaving black-and-white archival footage of postwar migrants, arriving from the Caribbean and India and settling in Britain, with sequences (in colour) showing two solitary forlorn figures amidst a vast waste land of snow in Alaska, the film makes tangible how cold and monochrome Britain must have felt to immigrants who had left their warm climates and colourful cultures behind.

In 'It's a family affair: Black culture and the trope of kinship', Paul Gilroy argues that, although 'the discourse of family and the discourse of nation are very closely connected', for the black diaspora in Britain and America, the family–nation trope overlaps with the 'trope of race as family' and the 'discourse of racial siblinghood' (1993b: 201–3). In fact, 'family has come to stand for community, for race and for nation. It is a short-cut to solidarity' (1993b: 203). Similar intersections apply to other diasporas that may simultaneously belong to the 'Nation of Islam', the pan-ethnic South Asian diaspora or to other hyphenated national and ethnic communities. As transnational communities, their sense of belonging cannot be contained in the imagined community of the nation (Anderson [1983] 2006). Along which coordinates is their sense of belonging formed and their identity defined? To which family, to which imagined community do they belong? Khachig Tölölyan (1991) regards diasporas as the nation-state's 'Others', implying their marginalisation or exclusion, whereas Stuart Hall asserts their multiple belonging. He illustrates this with reference to Britons of Afro-Caribbean descent and argues that their cultural identities combine the *Présence africaine*, 'the site of the repressed [. . .] silenced beyond memory by the power of the experience of slavery' ([1990] 2003: 240); the *Présence européenne*, the site of colonialism, exclusion and expropriation; and the *Présence américaine*, the site 'where the fateful / fatal encounter was staged between Africa and the West' and 'the place of many, continuous displacements' (243), conquests and new beginnings. According to Hall, all diasporic identities are marked by heterogeneity, diversity and difference. It is precisely because of their plural heritage and multiple affiliations that diasporas cannot be comfortably accommodated within the nation as family with its inherent 'tendency to authorise homogenising perceptions and social structures and to suppress plurality. Nationalism, like patriarchy, favours singleness – one identity [...] one birth and blood for all' (Boehmer 1991: 6).

Michael Haneke's *Caché* (*Hidden*, 2005) serves as a perfect illustration of the family–nation trope, as the white, bourgeois family of Georges Laurent represents the French nation and the Algerian Majid the nation's victimised and excluded Other. In fact, the film stages 'a post-colonial re-run of the colonial encounter' (Silverman 2007: 245). Haneke's thriller cum family drama establishes a number of correspondences between France's colonial history at the time of the Algerian War and Georges's family history. The Paris massacre of 17 October 1961, during which hundreds of peaceful Algerian demonstrators were injured, killed and thrown into the Seine under the orders of the head of the Parisian police, was long suppressed in French collective memory. Georges suffers from a similar amnesia. It transpires that the now middle-aged Georges grew up together with Majid, the son of Algerian farm labourers, on his parents' country estate. When Majid's parents were killed during the Paris massacre, Georges's parents wanted to adopt the orphaned boy and provide a home and a good education for him. However, the jealous six-year-old Georges maligned Majid through a web of intrigues and lies, and thereby prevented his adoption and inclusion in the white hegemonic French family (of nation). And so Majid was sent to a state orphanage. *Hidden* maps France's collective amnesia for the Paris massacre, which was shrouded in silence for almost forty years, on to the repressed memory of Georges's betrayal of the Algerian boy Majid. When a series of mysterious videotapes and child-like drawings of someone spitting blood arrive on his doorstep, Georges is forced to confront the ghosts of the past and, suspecting Majid is the sender, tracks him down. That the trauma of the Franco-Algerian war lives on in the shape of the *fracture sociale* in contemporary France is reflected in Majid's social marginalisation and in Georges's refusal to learn from the past. Georges tries to have Majid, who supposedly terrorises him with the mysterious videotapes, arrested (having apparently forgotten the brutality Algerians suffered at the hands of the French police in 1961). When he subsequently witnesses Majid committing suicide by slitting his own throat (an eerie reminder of Majid's decapitation of the Laurent family's prized cockerel), Georges resorts to the familiar pattern of denial and silence. Rather than rushing home to confide in his wife Anne about the gruesome spectacle in which he has become embroiled, he goes to the cinema, where posters advertise a whole series of family-themed films whose symbolic meaning can hardly be missed. Elizabeth Ezra and Jane Sillars explain the relevance of the advertised films as follows:

> *Ma mere* (my mother – one of the adults responsible for sending Majid [...] away), *Deux frères* (two brothers, or Georges and Majid), *La*

> *mauvaise éducation* (bad education – what Majid's son informs Georges that Majid suffered as a result of being ejected from Georges's family home) and *Mariages* (marriages – the family melodrama hinted at when [Georges's son] Pierrot accuses his mother of having an affair with her colleague), which seem to spell out the various domestic and allegorical configurations in which Georges is implicated. (2007a: 217)

The parallels in Haneke's *Hidden* between the bourgeois French family and the postcolonial metropolitan, between Georges's repressed childhood memories and the collective amnesia for the anti-Algerian pogrom in 1961 underscore the allegorical dimension of this particular family narrative.[33] The Laurents' gated, fortress-like home in the affluent 13th *arrondissement* of the French capital aptly symbolises the hegemonic family's anxieties about protecting its social and economic privileges against invasion by undesirable intruders, specifically the postcolonial Other. Georges's deep-rooted paranoia about the Other, whom he invariably – and wrongly so – perceives as an assailant, manifests itself in the hostility he displays towards the black cyclist (with whom he nearly collides) and towards Majid and Majid's son. In his dreams, Georges is haunted by a gruesome scene he witnessed (or retrospectively imagined) as a young boy. It shows how Majid beheads a cockerel with a hatchet and how the headless animal flutters about in the courtyard of the Laurents' family estate. With the hatchet still in his hands and the cockerel's blood splattered all over his face, Majid approaches Georges. Then Georges wakes up from his nightmare. Given that the cockerel is a fairly overt reference to France's unofficial national symbol, the Gallic rooster, its killing gestures towards the perceived threat that the postcolonial Other poses for the French nation. And although, in Georges's dream, the positions of victim and perpetrator are evidently reversed (in relation to the massacre of Algerians in 1961), it nevertheless reinforces the narrative's allegorical impetus.

Pertinent as *Hidden* may be to the concerns of this study, at the film's centre is Georges's hegemonic family rather than Majid's diasporic one. Yet, similar conspicuous correspondences between familial and national belonging, between mechanisms of inclusion and exclusion, between family secrets and collective traumas can be discerned in numerous films about diasporic families, as the ensuing chapters will demonstrate. At the same time, it would be misleading to assume that, in all films, the diasporic family carries 'the burden of representation' (Mercer 1990) by metonymically representing its entire ethnic constituency in relation to the host nation. Nevertheless, the prevalence of certain recurrent themes, notably journeys in which the desire to be reunited with the mother and the ancestral homeland remains unfulfilled, the 'coming out' of queer sons and daughters in the diasporic family, and the trials and tribulations of interethnic romance, attest to the intertwining of the personal and the political, of the familial and the national.

Figure 1.4 Majid with the hatchet haunts Georges in *Hidden* (Michael Haneke, 2005)

CONCLUSION

The multi-faceted approach to the diasporic family taken in this chapter will, hopefully, provide a number of useful reference points for the exploration of diasporic family films, as well as a rationale for their selection. For the purposes of this study, 'family' is defined as 'a kinship group providing the nurturant socialization of its children (natural or adopted)' (Ingoldsby 2006: 76). As this definition implies the presence of at least two generations, it does not readily accommodate the 'surrogate families' consisting of close-knit multi-ethnic friendship groups that we encounter in *La Haine*, *Kurz und schmerzlos* (*Short Sharp Shock*, Fatih Akın, 1998) and numerous other films. Similarly, *Drôle de Félix* (*The Adventures of Felix*, Olivier Ducastel and Jacques Martineau, 2000), about a young, gay, HIV-positive man of mixed racial heritage, who travels through France hoping to be reunited with his biological Maghrebi father, is only tangentially relevant here. In the end, Félix abandons the quest for his 'real' father, and the film ultimately endorses the superiority of 'families of choice', culminating in the reunion with his white French boyfriend. Without wanting to suggest that these alternative family-like formations are of lesser significance – in reality or in fiction – I have decided to focus on films featuring two or more generations, because in diasporic family films the concept of generation is crucial for the films' narrative economy, being at the root of most of the tensions and conflicts and driving the plot.

Yet the notion of family underpinning this study neither is limited to the biological or 'natural' family nor is it complicit in promoting the normative model of the nuclear family. Thus, Ayşe Polat's coming-of-age-on-the-road movie *Auslandstournee* (*Tour Abroad*, 2000), about a gay transvestite performance artist who assumes the role of foster father for an orphaned Turkish German girl, qualifies, despite the potentially temporary nature of the father–daughter relationship and despite the absence of blood ties. In fact, the theme of voluntary affiliation, coupled with the motif of a 'home-bound' journey to Turkey in search of the protagonists' mothers, makes *Tour Abroad* a particularly pertinent *diasporic* family film. As I argue above, what distinguishes the diasporic family from other types of transnational family is the significance of the vertical axis, the connection between the ancestral homeland and the host country, which is based on the collective experience or (post)memory of migration. Whereas the lateral axis that connects dispersed diasporic communities trans-locally and transnationally hardly features in diasporic family films, a nostalgia for the homeland, real or imagined, is a pervasive theme.

The shift from primary migration to family reunion as the most important form of immigration that has facilitated the formation of diasporic families in Britain, France and West Germany since the 1970s, and the increased visibility of second-generation immigrant filmmakers since the 1980s demonstrate the close connection between the history of migration, the filmmakers' biographies and the appearance of diasporic families on screen in the mid- to late 1990s. Even so, I do not wish to imply that diasporic filmmakers can lay exclusive claim to telling 'authentic' stories about diasporic families. Although most of the films I examine in this book are actually authored by diasporic writers / directors, there are others, such as Xavier Koller's *Journey of Hope* or Feo Aladağ's *When We Leave*, that lack this kind of biographical legitimation.[34] Selecting films based on the filmmakers' biographical credentials would, in fact, be paradoxical, given that many diasporic family films challenge the primordial categories of bloodline and descent. However, it is worth bearing in mind that the modes via which diasporic and non-diasporic filmmakers access the collective memory of postwar migration differ. Diasporic filmmakers inscribe themselves in their family's history of migration, dispersal and resettlement through what Marianne Hirsch, in her influential study *Family Frames* (1997), theorises as postmemory, an imaginative reconstruction of the past drawing on kinship networks, oral history, family photos, home movies and similar personal memorabilia. Postmemory is essentially about the handing down of memories from generation to generation within the family. Alison Landsberg's (2004) closely related 'prosthetic memory', by contrast, is devoid of this personal connection. Instead, prosthetic memory enables alliances and forms of collective identification that transcend 'natural' belonging to a particular group, race, ethnicity or family.[35] Although films about the diasporic family made by majority culture filmmakers necessarily invoke a different memory frame, they are nevertheless included here. Such inclusion is not intended to diminish the important role diasporic filmmakers have played in bringing the diasporic family to the screen and challenging its previous invisibility and misrepresentation. At the same time, it is important to acknowledge that issues of migration and cultural diversity 'are so central to the European imaginary of the present moment that they occupy a prominent position in the work of film-makers of very different backgrounds' (Berghahn and Sternberg 2010a: 17). Purposely circumventing the biological and biographical fallacy, I propose that what constitutes a diasporic family film is, first and foremost, its subject matter rather than the filmmakers' migratory history or ethnicity.

On the whole, films analysed in the chapters that follow are 'contemporary European' in the sense that they have been made since the mid-1980s with European funding in Europe and tell stories centrally concerned with diasporic families that settled in West Germany, France or Britain. Admittedly, *Monsoon Wedding*, *My Big Fat Greek Wedding* and a few others fall outside these parameters but, since they have established the generic paradigm of the diasporic wedding film that has been copied and inflected by many less well-known European films, their inclusion is imperative. And would not too rigid an insistence on borders defeat the purpose of a book about transnational cinema and transnationally mobile families that is quintessentially concerned with the transgression of borders and boundaries of all kinds?

Notes

1. The term 'next of kin' denotes the 'most closely related [. . .] person (or persons) standing in the nearest degree of blood-relationship to another, and entitled to share in his personal estate in case of intestacy', *Oxford English Dictionary Online*, 2012. Under UK law, it has no legal definition and someone who is not related by blood, such as a spouse or civil partner, can be nominated 'next of kin'.
2. According to Murdock, composite family forms are more common than the isolated nuclear family prevalent in Western societies. He distinguishes between polygamous families, in which 'two or more nuclear families [are] affiliated by plural marriages, i.e. by having one married parent in common', and extended families, in which 'two or more nuclear families are affiliated through an extension of the parent–child relationship [. . .] i.e., by joining the nuclear family of a married adult to that of his parents' (1949: 2).
3. In addition to the Nayar, Ingoldsby and Smith (2006: 72–5) also discuss common-law unions amongst a high proportion of lower-class Jamaicans, in which fathers neither act as breadwinners nor participate in the socialisation of the children, and kibbutzim, as the 'self-contained communities based on communist ideals brought to Palestine in the 1920s by European Jews' (72) are called.
4. See the comprehensive anthologies by Burguière, Klapisch-Zuber, Segalen and Zonabend (1996), Ingoldsby and Smith (2006) and Georgas et al. (2006).
5. Grillo observes a widespread resistance 'to acknowledg[ing] alternative constructions of familial relations' (2008: 16) in European immigration legislation. This has important consequences for determining which relatives are regarded as 'family' and qualify for family reunion.
6. Gilroy explains the nostalgic yearning for the traditional family as a postfeminist phenomenon that reflects 'large dollops of masculinist nostalgia for simpler, ordered working-class existence [. . . and] the reconstitution of the bourgeois household' (2004: 130). On the issue of nostalgia for the traditional family, see also Coontz (2000), Kain (1990) and Van Every (1999).

7. See Pnina Werbner (2004) for the related concepts of 'transmigrants' or 'migrant transnationals'.
8. For a more detailed exploration of transnational migration and diaspora cultures in relation to cinema, see Berghahn and Sternberg (2010b).
9. Nicholas van Hear proposes only three criteria for disaporas: dispersal from the homeland to two or more other territories; an enduring, but not necessarily permanent, presence abroad; and some kind of exchange between the spatially separated diaspora population. He defines diasporas as a particular type of transnational community and, unlike Cohen (2008), includes in the concept 'also those populations that are contiguous rather than scattered and may straddle just one border' (1998: 6).
10. Ulf Hannerz's 'transnational elites' share many features with what Steven Vertovec and Robin Cohen (2002) call 'globally mobile cosmopolites' and which they distinguish from 'true cosmopolites', who possess the requisite cross-cultural competencies to interpret other cultures and can, therefore, feel at home anywhere in the world.
11. The artistic and political career of Yamina Benguigui, whose parents emigrated from Algeria to France in the 1950s, is a perfect (albeit still rare) example of such upward social mobility. Not only has she made numerous critically acclaimed films that attracted large audiences, but also, when François Hollande was elected President in May 2012, he appointed Yamina Benguigui to the post of Junior Minister for French Nationals Abroad and Relations with *la Francophonie* (French-speaking countries worldwide).
12. Goulbourne, Reynolds, Solomos and Zontini also include families that have not physically moved themselves but that have become transnational by virtue of 'social relations to people in distant and perhaps disparate locations' (2010: 12).
13. William Safran proposes that attitude is a key factor in determining whether an immigrant community qualifies as a diaspora. Those who emigrated with the intention to settle rather than return cannot be regarded as diasporas (1999: 262). Whereas African Americans, who are 'descendants of Africans sold into slavery and brought against their will to American colonies [. . .] wish to be fully integrated into American society' (262–3) and do not desire to return to Africa, black Britons from the West Indies 'who settled in Britain or the United States are a genuine diaspora; they regard Jamaica as their homeland, are imbued with its culture, and have an ongoing connection with it' (262).
14. For a discussion of representations of migrants in the media, see King and Wood (2001); Ewing (2008) offers a detailed analysis of the media image of Turkish Muslim men in Germany.
15. In the US, Daniel Patrick Moynihan's report *The Negro Family: The Case for National Action* (1965), better known as 'The Moynihan Report', commissioned by the United States Department of Labour, was particularly influential in crusading against black families.
16. Amongst the vast body of literature on postwar migration to Europe, I have found the following sources particularly useful: Castles and Miller (2009), Fielding (1993), Cohen (2008), Göktürk, Gramling and Kaes (2007), Hansen (2000), Hargreaves (2007), Horrocks and Kolinsky (1996), and King (1993).
17. The focus of this brief historical survey is on the Federal Republic, or West Germany, rather than on the German Democratic Republic (East Germany), where immigration patterns were different. In order to compensate for the mass exodus of its labour force to the West (an estimated 10,000 to 20,000 East German residents per month) prior to the erection of the Berlin Wall on 13 August 1961, the GDR recruited contract workers from its socialist brother countries, notably Poland, Hungary, Mozambique, Cuba, North Vietnam and Angola, amongst others. Immigration to the GDR was on a much smaller scale and, despite being celebrated

as 'socialist friends' and foreign guests in the press, in reality, contract workers lived segregated from GDR citizens in purpose-built, factory-owned accommodation. A three- to five-year rotation principle applied and family reunion was not envisaged by the GDR's immigration policy. After German reunification in 1990, the 'socialist friends' still living in the New Federal States were even less welcome, facing unemployment, premature discontinuation of their residence permits and violent xenophobia (see Göktürk, Gramling and Kaes 2007: 65–103; www.migration-online.de).

18. Algeria gained independence after the War of Independence in 1962 and, compared to immigrants from Morocco and Tunisia, which decolonised in the 1950s, Algerians were accorded a unique status with respect to immigration (see Hargreaves 2007, Castles and Miller 2009: 96–124). After the British government left British India in 1947, India was partitioned into the secular Republic of India and the Muslim state of Pakistan. Jamaica, Trinidad and Tobago achieved independence from the United Kingdom in 1962.
19. The military putsch in Turkey in 1980 led to a sharp rise in asylum applications from Turks and Kurds, and a second wave of immigration to Germany.
20. Hamid Naficy's concept of accented cinema comprises films made by exilic, diasporic and postcolonial ethnic minority filmmakers, whose experience of exile, migration, displacement and dispersal is reflected in distinctive aesthetic strategies that express the 'double consciousness' of their creators (2001: 22). Accented films are usually bi- or multi-lingual and blend aesthetic and stylistic impulses from the cinematic traditions of the filmmaker's home and adopted countries. Naficy uses the linguistic concept of accent as a trope to emphasise that this particular kind of cinema is different from dominant cinema, understood chiefly as mainstream Hollywood productions.
21. *East is East* topped the UK box office for UK feature films in 1999, grossing £7.25 million (BFI Information Services).
22. Except for Akın and the Samdereli sisters, these Turkish and Kurdish German filmmakers were born in Turkey between 1960 and 1970, and moved to Germany at a young age. Only Yüksel Yavuz was already sixteen when he joined his father, a guest worker in Hamburg in 1980.
23. The term 'patchwork family', not yet listed in the *Oxford English Dictionary*, has recently gained currency (especially in German-speaking countries) and refers to a type of family in which at least one partner brings a child from a previous relationship.
24. With respect to immigration from Turkey to Germany, the concept of generational belonging is further complicated by the fact that some immigrants, predominantly Turkish and Kurdish political dissidents and left-wing intellectuals who sought political asylum in West Germany following the military coup in Turkey, did not arrive until the 1980s – roughly twenty years later than the first wave of immigrants. Should they be classified as first- or second-generation immigrants?
25. Some social scientists distinguish between the 'second generation', which was born in the country of residence or arrived before starting primary school, and the '1.5' or 'in-between generation', which 'refers to children who migrated after starting their school careers' but spent a large part of their formative years there (King, Thomson, Fielding and Warnesl 2006: 256).
26. Neither Mannheim's nor Matthes's theories of generation, understood primarily as a socio-cultural phenomenon, engage specifically with generations of immigrants. Matthes's critique of Mannheim shares certain features with Sigrid Weigel's concept of 'generation as a symbolic form' (2002). See Ayça Tunç's as yet unpublished doctoral dissertation (2011) for an insightful discussion of generation in relation to Turkish German cinema.
27. 'Das Kino der Métissage kann [...] aus der Fremdheit selbst keine große Sache

mehr machen'. See James Williams (2011) for an excellent discussion of cultural *métissage* in the films of Abdellatif Kechiche.
28. See Naficy (2001, 2009) on the changing industrial contexts of accented cinema; and Korte and Sternberg (2004), Malik (1996, 2010), Tarr (2005), Halle (2008) and Jäckel (2010) for discussions of changes in the industrial contexts of British, French and German cinema that enabled migrant and diasporic filmmakers to gain access to the means of production and self-representation. I have explored issues of film funding, production and distribution in interviews and roundtable discussions with filmmakers, producers, diversity consultants, film festival directors, distributors and other industry professionals, and documented the findings in extensive podcasts on the research project websites, www.migrantcinema.net and www.farflungfamilies.net.
29. Horace Ové was born in Trinidad and came to Britain via Italy when he was twenty-one years old. *Pressure* is an important precursor of diasporic family films, albeit one made by a first-generation director.
30. For statistical information, see Tarr 2005; www.ffa.de; and BFI Information Services (n/d).
31. See Ella Shohat and Robert Stam's excellent discussion of the trope of infantilisation in the chapter 'Tropes of Empire' (1994: 137–77).
32. In *White*, Richard Dyer dislodges the tacit assumption that 'white' equals 'universal', suggesting that 'as long as white people are not racially seen and named, they / we function as a human norm. Other people are raced, we are just people' (1997: 1).
33. On the family as allegory of nation in *Hidden*, see Ezra and Sillars (2007b) and Wheatley (2009).
34. Feo Aladağ's Turkish surname is her married name. Her husband is the Turkish German filmmaker Züli Aladağ.
35. See Chapter 3, where I explore certain ambiguities inherent in the two types of memory.

2. FAMILIES IN MOTION

A group of villagers is sitting in a circle under the canopy of a large tree. They are washing their hands with water poured from a metal jug and invoke the names of Allah and Mohammed. A ram is being sacrificed. Singing and dancing accompany the communal meal. This rural idyll and the observance of the Muslim Festival of Sacrifice, or *Kurban Bayramı* in Turkish, are suddenly disrupted, as the camera pans to a group of young boys who are playing on the nearby railway tracks.[1] As a test of courage, they are lying on the tracks while a black steam engine with a grey plume of smoke is approaching rapidly. Who will hold out longest? The alarmed parents come to chase the boys off the tracks but a small boy stubbornly resists being picked up. The camera assumes his vantage point and, in a low-angle shot, captures the menacing approach of the train. He presses his body as flat as he can to the ground between the tracks and does not budge as the train thunders over him. Miraculously, he remains unharmed. The fast speed of the train along the long, straight tracks stands in stark contrast to the slow rhythm of village life, with its emphasis on circles and round objects that function as the visual correlative of the cyclical rhythm of the seasons and everyday life and the sense of stability and security they impart. The train, as an iconic symbol of modernity and modernisation, of displacement and emigration, cuts right through this rural idyll, puts the little boy's life under threat and signals danger.[2] Mobility – the opening sequence of Xavier Koller's film *Journey of Hope* seems to be saying – jeopardises a way of life that cannot get much better than this. And yet, the family of the seven-year-old Mehmet Ali, who risks his life to prove his courage, is lured away from a tranquil, albeit frugal, existence by a picture postcard with the snow-capped peaks of the Alps on the front and a tempting description of Switzerland as a land where milk and honey flow on the back. The promise of a more prosperous life results in the rupture of family ties. When Haydar and his reluctant wife Meryem embark on their journey of hope, they leave six of their children behind in the village, taking only their youngest son, Mehmet, who will die in the end.

Opening sequence two: as the tiny speck on the horizon moves closer, it is revealed to be a rickety old bus, camouflaged by the dust of the arid, desert-like landscape. The bus stops by a tree, also covered in dust. Three men and two women descend and roll out their prayer rugs. From the inside of the bus, a young woman with short-cropped hair, the only one not wearing a headscarf, observes the worshippers, while another woman, wearing a red-and-yellow headscarf, stares at her. Both are equally amazed at the strangeness they behold. The worshippers re-join the other passengers and the bus begins its slow and arduous ascent, following the unpaved serpentine road up and up until the driver alerts the woman with the short-cropped hair to the fact that she has reached her destination. She gets off in the middle of nowhere and continues on foot. Never-ending bus journeys like this one, at the beginning of *La Fille de Keltoum* (*Keltoum's Daughter*, Mehdi Charef, 2001), which takes the Swiss Algerian Railla back to her birthplace in Algeria, also feature in *Düğün – Die Heirat* (*Düğün – The Wedding* (Ismet Elçi, 1991), *When We Leave* and several other films. A series of long shots of a dusty old bus winding its way through an arid and inhospitable landscape, alternating with shots of passengers in Middle Eastern attire inside, convey a sense of remoteness and other-worldliness. Long before the films' narratives unfold, we can tell that, whatever these travellers hope to find at their journey's end, it will not bring them knowledge or insight compatible with their Westernised urban lives in Europe, where they are based and to where they eventually return.

Opening sequence three: the camera pans to the right, from a small white shed shown against the background of a bright blue sky and a shady tree in the centre of the frame, revealing a garage and then a red-and-white petrol station. A white car pulls up and the driver asks the attendant in Turkish to fill up. The mournful diegetic music on the soundtrack, a song by the popular Turkish singer Kazım Koyuncu,[3] and information conveyed in a casual exchange between the two men locate this place of transit as somewhere near the Black Sea. The young man's onward journey takes him across a sun-speckled country road, fringed by lush green trees and a series of tunnels that cut through mountains to a sudden fade to black – and to the German city of Bremen on the North Sea. The sudden spatial disjuncture, coupled with a flashback to the beginning of the narrative, underscores the transnational connectedness of events occurring in different locations. Towards the end of the film, the scene at the petrol station is repeated, only this time the driver of the white car, whom we now know to be Nejat, one of the six protagonists, reaches his final destination, a small town on the Black Sea, where he hopes to be reunited and reconciled with his father after years of separation.[4] In the last frame, Nejat is standing on a beautiful beach, a small wooden fishing boat beside him. He takes off his sunglasses and lets his eyes scan the horizon in search of his father, who has gone out fishing. Nejat, facing the sea with his back turned towards the camera, eventually sits down on the sand and awaits his father's return. The film's circular structure and its final frame arrest the breathless speed that propels the narrative of Fatih Akın's *Auf der anderen*

Figure 2.1 Nejat (Baki Davrak) is hoping to be reunited with his father in *The Edge of Heaven* (Fatih Akın, 2007)

Seite (*The Edge of Heaven*, 2007) forward. Its multiple strands trace the lives of three incomplete families, consisting of two mothers and two daughters and a father and his son, whose transnational itineraries and destinies intersect, as they move back and forth between Germany and Turkey. In the course of their frenzied mobility, their families become more fractured, as in each narrative segment someone dies: the Turkish German mother and prostitute Yeter in the first; the German student Lotte, who falls in love with Yeter's daughter Ayten and follows her to Turkey, in the second; and, so we surmise, Nejat's father, who will not return from his fishing expedition, in the third.[5]

The relationship between space and time in each of the three opening sequences carries a different emotional resonance: mobility as a sudden, threatening uprooting from a cyclical mode of existence; mobility as a slow and arduous journey to a remote place linked to the protagonists' past; and mobility as a quintessentially postmodern space–time compression that efficiently connects distant localities and people.[6] In each case, as will become apparent in the course of this chapter, mobility impacts upon family structure. In *An Accented Cinema* (2001), Hamid Naficy suggests that exile, displacement and dispersal result in loss of identity, separation, and the rupture of kinship ties. Yet his hypothesis needs to be carefully tested against a body of films that is, by and large, not concerned with forced migration and the trauma of displacement but with more voluntary forms of migration than those examined in his seminal book on exilic and diasporic cinema. There appears to be a dialectical tension between the family unit (typically imagined as bounded by the closed spaces of domestic life) and mobility. The family, which carefully guards its familial identity by controlling its lineage through marriage practices (such as endogamous and arranged marriage) and by discriminating against illegitimate offspring, feels the threat of disintegration when faced with the boundlessness of the open road or other wide-open spaces on its migratory journeys.

This idea is neatly expressed in an important precursor to the films considered in this chapter, the American Depression-era road movie *The Grapes of Wrath* (John Ford, 1940), based on John Steinbeck's novel of the same name. After being evicted from their farm in Oklahoma and travelling westwards along the famous Route 66 to California to look for work, the extended multi-generational Joad family is gradually decimated as family members die or leave, since they are unable to endure, physically or psychologically, the hardship of the road. As Mother Joad muses, back in Oklahoma

> we was on the land. There was a boundary to us then. Old folks died off and little fellows come. We was always one thing, we was a family. Kind of whole and clear. But now we ain't clear no more. They ain't nothing that keeps us clear no more [. . .] We're cracking up Tom. We ain't no family now.

The idea that the family is bound to the land and, once uprooted, in danger of disintegration seems old-fashioned but still resonates in the popular imagination, as testified by more recent films, including Luchino Visconti's *Rocco e i suoi fratelli* (*Rocco and his Brothers*, 1960), in which the family's move to Milan leads to fraternal rivalry and discord. In the similarly themed *Solino* (Fatih Akın, 2002), an Italian family leaves the idyllic, sun-drenched small town of Solino in search of an economically more prosperous life in the grey and dismal coal-mining town of Duisburg in Germany.[7] Though both films condense the migratory journeys to trains leaving or arriving at stations, they nevertheless suggest that the experience of deracination results in the families' disintegration, which can only be partially remedied by the mothers returning to where they came from, together with one of their sons.

The analysis of families in motion in this chapter engages Mikhail Bakhtin's influential concept of the chronotope (literally 'time-space'), which he defined as a spatiotemporal structure governing the relationship of narrative events in the novel (Bakhtin 1981: 250–1). According to Bakhtin, the chronotope 'provides the ground essential for [. . .] the representability of events' (250), because it materialises the passage of time through movement in space and vice versa. While his investigations centred on the novel, the concept of the chronotope has subsequently been productively applied to film and other cultural formations and, in the wake of Paul Gilroy's (1993a) discussion of the chronotope of the ship and the Black Atlantic, has had a significant impact on diaspora scholarship (see Peeren 2007). The chronotopes of the road and the ship, which drive journey narratives forward, as well the chronotope of the family idyll, deserve particular attention in relation to the transnational itineraries of diasporic families in film. As Avtar Brah reminds us, 'at the heart of the notion of diaspora is the image of a journey. Paradoxically, diasporic journeys are essentially about settling down, about putting roots "elsewhere"' (1996: 182). In closely examining films that make outbound and homebound journeys their central theme, I shall explore how the transnational itineraries they chart challenge the Eurocentric geography still prevalent in European cinema by shifting established notions of centre and periphery and, by implication, the place of diasporic families in our midst.

The experience of migration is fundamental to the collective memory and identity of diasporic families and communities: 'Diaspora consciousness lives loss and hope as a defining tension' (Clifford 1994: 312) and is, inevitably, marked by 'a dual or paradoxical nature' and 'decentred attachments' (Vertovec and Cohen 1999: xiii) to the 'here' of the place of residence and the 'there' of the real, imagined or putative home. Yet the number of diasporic family films actually charting these outbound journeys is relatively limited.[8] Instead of dramatising the families' emigration, most films reference it metonymically by showing a brief scene at a train station or an aeroplane taking off. This is particularly true of journeys between the Indian sub-continent and Great Britain or North America, presumably because, by the 1960s, air travel had replaced sea voyages – and neither would offer as much visual and narrative interest as overland journeys. *The Namesake* (Mira Nair, 2007) and *Brick Lane* (Sarah Gavron, 2007), for example, condense the protagonists' outbound migrations by cutting from a farewell scene at Calcutta airport to wintry New York City, and from the verdant rice paddies of Bangladesh to the bleak streets of London's East End with the protagonist's voice-over narration and extradiegetic music creating a sound bridge between places far removed from each other in terms of geography, culture and atmosphere. The same holds true for the journeys of remigration on which individual family members embark alone. In *Brick Lane*, Nazneen's husband returns to Bangladesh after his marriage and career have failed, while Nasneen and her two teenage daughters stay in London. The film's final shot shows them frolicking in the freshly fallen snow on the Brick Lane housing estate. An eye-line match cuts from a close-up of Nasneen's face to a tiny aeroplane high up in the sky that takes her husband back home. At the end of *The Namesake*, a rapid montage sequence connects Ashima, now back in Calcutta, her eldest son Gogol setting out on a train journey across America, and a flashback to his father's train journey in 1970s India, on which a fellow traveller encouraged him 'to go abroad and conquer the world. You will never regret it'. The cross-cutting between present and past, India and America, and a train passing by at high speed, conveys a postmodern temporality and spatiality that are markedly different from the slow-paced journey in *Keltoum's Daughter* and *Journey of Hope*. *The Namesake* and *The Edge of Heaven* celebrate mobility and literally shrink space to a global village, allowing far-flung families to bridge the gaps between different localities, the local and the global.

Yet few films seem to embrace the transformative effects of mobility on the family as enthusiastically as *The Namesake* and *The Edge of Heaven* do. More often than not, journeys of outbound migration, or 'journeys of escape, home seeking, and home founding', as Hamid Naficy labels this particular type (2001: 223), put the family under strain, whereas homebound journeys seldom offer the 'meliorative and redemptive experiences' (223) that Naficy was able to identify in an earlier corpus of exilic and diasporic films.

You Can't Go Home Again

A strong attachment to the homeland through the maintenance of cultural practices, language and kinship ties and through the preservation of memories of home as 'a mythic place of desire in the diasporic imagination' (Brah 1996: 192) is regarded as a distinctive feature of diasporic consciousness (see Chapter 1). However, the expression 'the myth of return' implies that the resolve to return to the homeland one day – for example, having saved enough money to afford a better life back home or on reaching retirement or however this vague notion of 'one day' may be defined – is actually a form of self-deception. First-generation migrants may never discard the suitcase in which they brought all their possessions when they first arrived, keeping it in plain sight on top of the wardrobe, from where they usually never take it down again. The resolve to return weakens from generation to generation and, as the children grow up and assimilate with the host society, their reluctance to return also tends to preclude the parents' return (Morely and Roberts 1996). Yet 'the dream of a glorious homecoming' (Naficy 2001: 229) remains an extremely powerful fantasy and one that runs through diasporic cinema as a dominant theme.

The dialectical tension between home and away, between displacement and a nostalgic longing for home, usually imagined or nostalgically remembered as the familiar haunts of one's childhood, is a phenomenon that emerges perhaps inevitably as a response to exile, displacement and increased transnational mobility. Bernhard Schlink (2000), David Morely and Kevin Roberts (1996), and Johannes von Moltke in his study of the German genre of *Heimatfilm*, *No Place Like Home* (2005), amongst others, examine the dialectical relationship between 'migration, displacement and other forms of unsettling mobility' and the notion of *Heimat*, understood as a 'personally lived space [and . . .] a spatially bound sense of belonging, settlement, and home' (von Moltke 2005: 230). *Heimat*, they agree, gains renewed currency at times when precisely those certainties and securities are threatened. As von Moltke observes with reference to the West German *Heimatfilm* of the 1950s and its subsequent reincarnations, 'increases in mobility and dislocation increase the currency of Heimat [. . .] The principal function of the Heimat genre, then, is both to *compensate* for the perceived loss of home and to *shape* the experience of that loss through representation' (230). The 1950s *Heimatfilm* offered millions of displaced people from the Eastern territories appealing picture-postcard projections of West German landscapes, notably the rural idylls of the Luneburg Heath, the Black Forest or the Alps, inviting them to accept these idealised locations and welcoming village communities as their new *Heimat* in the West. By contrast, the idealised homeland in diasporic cinema is not one to be appropriated in the present but one lost to the past. It therefore has a rather different temporality and emotional resonance, aptly summarised by the German filmmaker Edgar Reitz, whose tripartite television chronicle *Heimat* (1984, 1993, 2004) deftly illustrates von Moltke's observations about the many rebirths of the *Heimatfilm* genre.⁹ Reitz defines *Heimat* not just as a specific place, the small imaginary Hunsrück village of Schabbach and the geographical centre of his trilogy, but also as an elusive ideal, a nostalgic memory, a yearning for one's cultural and individual roots, one's childhood:

> The word is always linked to strong feeling, mostly remembrances and longing. 'Heimat' always evokes in me the feeling of something lost or very far away, something which one cannot easily find or find again. In this respect, it is also a German romantic word and a romantic feeling with a particular romantic dialectic. 'Heimat' is such that if one would go closer and closer to it, one would discover that at the moment of arrival it is gone, it has dissolved into nothingness. It seems to me that one has a more precise idea of 'Heimat' the further one is away from it. This for me is 'Heimat', it's fiction, and one can arrive there only in poetry, and I include film in poetry. (Reitz cited in Kaes 1989: 163)

Reitz's interpretation of *Heimat* is indebted to that of the philosopher Ernst Bloch, who, in the final sentence of his monumental treatise *Das Prinzip Hoffnung* (*The Principle of Hope*), defines *Heimat* as utopia – that is, in the literal sense of the word, 'utopia', a 'no place': 'There arises in the world something which appears to everyone in childhood and where no one has ever been: *Heimat*' ([1959] 1968: 1628).¹⁰ The connection between *Heimat* and childhood also explains the conflation of *Heimat* and the mother figure, discussed in Chapter 1 and asserted by Anton Kaes in relation to the iconic and aptly named mother figure Maria in Reitz's *Heimat* trilogy: 'wherever she is, there is Heimat' (1989: 168). Stuart Hall makes a similar observation about narratives 'of displacement', which typically reconstruct 'the endless desire to return to "lost origins", to be one again with the mother, to go back to the beginning' ([1990] 2003: 245). It is, thus, not coincidental that homebound journeys of quest often lead to the mother, the embodiment of origin and roots, concepts that are central and contested in diaspora scholarship.

Perhaps unsurprisingly, in view of diasporic cinema's scepticism about essentialist notions of identity defined in terms of biological origin, racial purity and, by extension, the notion of cultural homogeneity, homeward journeys of quest for mothers invariably end in disappointment. Railla, the protagonist of *Keltoum's Daughter*, learns that Keltoum, the woman whom she believed to be her mother, is in fact her aunt, who sold her as a baby, whereas her biological mother, Nedjma, lost her sanity over the trauma of separation. Railla's return to Algeria culminates in her profound disillusionment. The savage beauty of Algeria's arid and rugged mountain ranges marks it as an inhospitable and uncivilised place, where misogyny, rape and other forms of violence against women prevail. Alienated from her motherland, the protagonist's quest ends with her getting on the bus again, heading back to Europe.

Meanwhile, in the Turkish German road movie *Tour Abroad*, the recently orphaned eleven-year-old Senay and her deceased father's friend Zeki, a queer performer and singer,[11] embark on an odyssey that takes them across several European cities. One of the stopovers on the way to Istanbul is Wuppertal, a small German town well known to cinephiles as the end point of Philip Winter and Alice's journey in Wim Wenders's film *Alice in den Städten* (*Alice in the Cities*, 1974). The brief encounter between Senay and her mother, who abandoned her baby daughter immediately after her birth, does not end with a happy reunion but a rejection. Zeki experiences a similar rebuff when paying his cold and distant mother a visit. The only thing she cares about is whether he is married at all, ostensibly oblivious to her son's sexual orientation or simply unwilling to accept his homosexuality. Yet the fact that neither Zeki nor Senay is reunited with their mothers is not presented in altogether negative terms, since the film ends on an upbeat note. By the time they are heading for Atatürk airport to fly back to Germany, they have forged a strong familial attachment. Zeki's queer identity allows for the depiction of an intimacy between the forty-two-year-old man and the pubescent girl that never makes us suspect the purity of his affection, while at the same time equipping him perfectly to stand in for both Senay's unloving mother and her deceased father.[12] Mobility in *Tour Abroad* leads to the formation of an elective family, based neither on natural kinship ties nor on clearly demarcated gender and familial roles. In this repect, *Tour Abroad* represents a significant departure from Wenders's *Alice in the Cities*, to which it is unmistakeably indebted, but which culminates in the reconstitution of a 'natural' family (albeit one which remains off-screen). The film ends with Philip Winter and Alice on the train to Munich, where the nine-year-old girl will be reunited with her mother. *Tour Abroad*, by contrast, challenges any such secure sense of 'natural' belonging. Zeki and Senay's decision to return to Germany in the end, marking yet another circular itinerary, underscores the idea that 'you can't go home again', not just in the sense intended by Thomas Wolfe in his eponymous novel, but also more poignantly in the sense of being unable to recuperate one's roots.

In the aptly titled essay 'It's not where you're from, it's where you're at . . .', Paul Gilroy observes that 'dispersed people recognise how the effects of spatial dislocation render origin problematic, and embrace the possibility that they are no longer what they once were' ([1991] 1999: 297). Taking the idea further in *The Black Atlantic*, Gilroy critiques an understanding of identity reliant on roots and rootedness, and proposes that identity needs to be reconceptualised 'as a process of movement and mediation that is more appropriately approached via the homonym routes' (1993a: 19). He rejects the essentialist concept of roots because it echoes colonialist, nationalist and racist discourses and, instead, advocates the concept of transnational routes, thereby challenging the erroneous idea of the 'integrity and purity of cultures' (7).

Chronotopes of Diaspora

The most powerful image invoked by Gilroy to convey the idea that diaspora cultures, such as the African diaspora, are mobile and transcend national boundaries is that of the Black Atlantic, a transnational space historically demarcated by the triangular trade between Europe, Africa and, via the Middle Passage of the slave ships across the Atlantic to the Caribbean and the Americas, thence back to Europe. Building on the specific historical meaning of the slave trade, Gilroy conceives of the Black Atlantic in modern and contemporary culture as a space of transnational cultural exchange, in which the cultural practices of black people, dispersed across different nations and continents, circulate. 'The specificity of the modern political and cultural formations I want to call the black Atlantic can be defined, on one level, through the desire to transcend both the structures of the nation state and the constraints of ethnicity and national particularity' (1993a: 19). To evoke the sense of fluidity, exchange and mobility that Gilroy identifies as distinctive of black diaspora culture, he chooses, inspired by William Turner's painting *The Slave Ship* (1840),

> the image of ships in motion across the spaces between Europe, America, Africa, and the Caribbean as a central organising symbol [. . .] Ships immediately focus attention on the middle passage, on the various projects for redemptive return to an African homeland, on the circulation of ideas and activists as well as the movement of key cultural and political artefacts: tracts, books, gramophone records, and choirs. (4)

Although the chronotope of the ship is not particularly prominent in the films analysed in this chapter, it nevertheless features in succinct visual references to sea voyages that are not actually dramatised.[13] In *Little Senegal* by Maghrebi French director Rachid Bouchareb (2001), Alloune, an old Senegalese tour guide working in the History of Slavery Museum on the island of Goree on the coast of Senegal, travels to South Carolina and thence to the African American neighbourhood Little Senegal in New York, in order to trace his ancestors who were sold as slaves to plantation owners in the New World around 1800. The film remains vague as to whether Alloune actually travels across the Atlantic as his enslaved ancestors did, cutting instead from an eye-line match cut of Alloune with his eyes fixed on the endless horizon of the Atlantic Ocean, to him standing on a beach in South Carolina, now facing in the opposite direction. Alloune is saddened by the disintegration of African American family life that he observes amongst his remote relatives in New York. The negative portrayal of the African American family and African American culture more generally is interpreted as the long-term consequence of slavery. Several references to the heavy metal chains with which Africans were tied together on the slave ships and references to similar chains used in race crime on the streets of New York underscore the historical continuity of the African (American) experience. The film ends with Alloune's return to Goree Island, where he buries his nephew Hassan, the victim of Black gang crime in Harlem. The camera zooms in on Alloune's hands touching the red soil on Hassan's grave, thereby emphasising that Hassan has, at last, been returned to the soil where he belongs. The implied valorisation of roots contravenes precisely Gilroy's scepticism of the concept. At the same time, it resonates with the idea of a redemptive return to the homeland. In the film's concluding sequence, the slave ship is replaced by a little ferryboat that takes tourists back and forth between Goree Island and the Senegalese mainland. Through the 'door of no return' in the walls of the slavery museum, Alloune watches the ferryboat traversing the ocean, as the film cuts to Little Senegal in New York, where Ida, the family member with whom he developed the closest relationship, is opening her small kiosk at the start of the day. Both the ship and the metal chains function as chronotopes of the black diaspora experience, which resulted, as Bouchareb argues in *Little Senegal*, in an uprooting and a loss of African identity from which African Americans have never been able to recover. Yet the chronotope of the ship carries an emotional charge different from the chains. It invokes the memory of slavery and, simultaneously, validates the transnational familial and historical connections that Alloune, whose profession is not coincidentally linked to the preservation of the memory of slavery, has been able to establish through his journey.

The chronotope of the ship is also invoked in a number of French films about immigrants from the Maghreb, including Yamina Benguigui's documentary *Immigrant Memories*, and in her début feature, *Inch' Allah Dimanche* (*Inch' Allah Sunday*, also known as *Sunday God Willing*, 2001). In both films, the huge vessel that carries, first, immigrant labourers and, subsequently, their families from Algeria to France is linked to the pain of separation and loss. In *Inch' Allah Sunday*, Zouina, a young Algerian woman, is wrenched from the embrace of her mother, who is wailing in despair, before embarking upon the ship that will take her, together with her three small children and domineering mother-in-law, to France, where she will join her husband Ahmed after ten years of separation. The large metal bars separating Zouina from her mother and the mournful song 'Ageggig', performed by the popular Algerian musician Idir,[14] foreshadow her virtual imprisonment in her new French home, where she will suffer – and fight – the patriarchal rule of her husband.

Immigrant Memories, a documentary considered in more detail in the next chapter, includes a frame of a little girl in a yellow dress standing on a quayside with her back towards the camera. She is looking at a huge ship that is leaving the harbour. The image of the little girl with frizzy brown hair and face turned away from the camera invites multiple projections and identifications (see Hirsch 1999, Lury 2010).[15] Has she just bid farewell to her father, or even to both her parents, who are leaving Algeria on the big ship that will take them to France? Are tears streaming down the little girl's face because she has been left

Figure 2.2 The image of the little girl with the brown skin and frizzy hair in *Immigrant Memories* (Yamina Benguigui, 1997) invites us to empathise with her pain of separation

behind, not knowing when she will be reunited with her parents? The evocative and emotionally powerful image of the little girl and the huge vessel on the open sea crystallises how families are torn apart in the process of transnational migration and the pain of separation associated with it.

In the influential essay 'Forms of time and the chronotope', Mikhail Bakhtin defines the chronotope as 'the intrinsic connectedness of temporal and spatial relationships that are artistically expressed in literature' (1981: 84) and suggests that these concrete spatiotemporal structures 'are the organizing centres for the fundamental narrative events of the novel' (250). Elaborating upon 'the representational importance of the chronotope', Bakhtin explains:

> The chronotope is the place where the knots of narrative are tied and untied. [. . .] Time becomes, in effect, palpable and visible, the chronotope makes narrative events concrete, makes them take on flesh, causes blood to flow in their veins. [. . .] Thus the chronotope [functions] as the primary means for materializing time and space. (250)

Chronotopes such as that of the road, the threshold or the idyll are coloured by different 'chronotopic values' (243) or affective qualities. The road, for example, is the place of random encounters with strangers where 'human fates and lives combine with one another' and where 'social distances' collapse (243). The idyll, by contrast, imparts a sense of familiarity and stability.

Whereas Bakhtin explored the chronotope predominantly with reference to the novel and used it as a heuristic device that allowed him to distinguish between different novelistic genres, the concept has since gained far wider currency and has also been productively employed in the medium of film. Robert Stam argues that the concept of the chronotope is particularly appropriate for the medium of film, 'for whereas literature plays itself out within a virtual lexical space, the cinematic chronotope is quite literal, splayed out concretely across a screen with specific dimensions and unfolding in literal time (usually 24 frames a second)' (Stam 1989: 11). Meanwhile, Hamid Naficy (2001) adds to Bakhtin's inventory of chronotopes new ones that articulate the experience of exile and diaspora in cinematic texts, notably homeland chronotopes characterised by wide-open spaces that instil a sense of boundlessness and timelessness; exile chronotopes, such as prison cells, cramped living quarters and other claustrophobic interiors; and chronotopes of journeys and border crossings that correspond to the liminal and fluid identities with which much of exilic and diasporic cinema is concerned.

That the chronotope is a particularly productive analytical category in the context of diasporic cinema is further evidenced by the fact that the memory of migration can be regarded as the most important creative impetus underpinning this particular type of transnational cinema. In other words, it is a cinema whose genesis is chronotopically determined by the temporal component of memory and the spatial component of dislocation, both of which have been identified as constitutive of diaspora consciousness. Thematically, too, the dialectical tensions between two places, the 'here' and 'there', coalesce with the tensions between the present and the past. Diasporic family memories, examined in the following chapter, are invariably place-bound and the journeys undertaken by diasporic filmmakers in several of these semi-autobiographical documentaries are literally trips down memory lane. They lead as much to their parents' place of origin as to their past. While time and space are always inextricably intertwined, diasporic cinema emphatically foregrounds 'the principle of chronotopicity' (Bakhtin 1981: 251) by making it its principal concern. The chronotope provides a carefully calibrated instrument to assess the spatiotemporal dimension of migratory journeys and their affective qualities. As illustrated above, some far-flung places seem very far away because journey time 'drags itself slowly through space', is 'viscous and sticky' (Bakhtin 1981: 248), whereas on other journeys, time travels at the speed of light. Speed and duration of journeys say a great deal about the perceived alterity of the places and cultures connected.

Bakhtin devotes some attention to the family in his discussion of the family idyll and folkloric or cyclical time. The family idyll normally occurs in conjunction with the agricultural idyll, where people eat the fruit of their labour and where 'food and drink [...] partake of a nature that is social, or more often, family; all *generations* and *age-groups* come together around the table. For the idyll, the association of food and children is characteristic' (227), signifying the growth and renewal of life, which, just like the return of the seasons, encapsulate 'the cyclical rhythmicalness of time so characteristic of the idyll' (225). The family and rural idylls are marked by a unity of place,

> by the age-old rooting of the life of generations to a single place [...] which fuses the cradle and the grave (the same little corner, the same

earth), and brings together as well childhood and old age (the same grove, stream, the same lime trees, the same house), the life of the various generations who had also lived in that same place, under the same conditions, and who had seen the same things. (Bakhtin 1981: 225)

Bakhtin's observations on the rural and the family idyll identify the opening scene of *Journey of Hope* as such an idyllic chronotope – threatened by invasive, and ultimately destructive, mobility. They also explain why the image of a multi-generational family congregating in a circle for a meal functions as a powerful symbol of pre-lapsarian harmony. The almost sacred ritual of the family meal, which we find in many idealised depictions of diasporic domesticity, resonates with nostalgic fantasies of traditional family life.

If the chronotope of the family idyll is cyclical, characterised by the return of the same in 'a well-defined place and . . . the family circle' (132), and the chronotope of the road is linear, characterised by progress, random encounters with strangers and unexpected occurrences, then it is immediately apparent that the road is not the natural habitat of the family and that mobility seems to pose a threat to the family. This would also explain why, in the cinematic genre of the road movie, the successor of the picaresque novel and other types of journey literature, such as the *Bildungsroman* (novel of education) (Laderman 2002: 6–13), families are few and far between.[16] In fact, Timothy Corrigan reminds us that the emergence of the road movie in post-classical Hollywood cinema as a distinct genre coincides with the crisis of the family from the late 1950s onwards. 'More and more, the family unit, that oedipal centrepiece of classical narrative, begins to break apart, preserved only as a memory or desire with less substance' (1991: 145). What replaces idealised representations of the security of the family home and the formation of the heterosexual couple at the journey's end in antecedents of the road movie, which, according to Corrigan 'is very much a postwar phenomenon' (143), are the male buddies on the road. The 'male buddy group left over from the war', Corrigan suggests (147), resists re-integration into the family unit and escapes on to the American freeways in search of freedom of a particularly masculine kind.

The genre of the western, which pre-dates the 1950s, provides ample evidence that the search for a particularly masculine kind of freedom is by no means exclusively a postwar phenomenon. Moreover, some of Wim Wenders's films, widely regarded as an important European inflection of the road movie, seem to complicate the relationship between the lonesome kings of the road and the family that Corrigan outlines. In the above-mentioned *Alice in the Cities* and in *Paris, Texas* (1984), men travel in the company of children, not male buddies, and the purpose of their journeys is the reconstitution of the family unit. Admittedly, though, Philip Winter, as well as the traumatised Travis in *Paris, Texas*, realise with a sense of resignation that they remain excluded from the families they help to reconstruct. Unable to form lasting heterosexual and familial bonds, they cannot go home (again) and are condemned to a peripatetic life on the road.

Although these considerations and the evolution of the road movie beyond its heyday in the 1960s render Corrigan's apodictic assessment of the incompatibility of the road and the family somewhat problematic, the road movie's inherent 'hospitality [. . .] to the marginalized and alienated' (Cohan and Hark 1997: 12) points towards a certain affinity between the road movie and the diasporic family. This natural affinity extends to the genre's counter-cultural impetus and 'its obvious potential for romanticizing alienation as well as for problematizing the uniform identity of the nation's culture' (Cohan and Hark 1997: 1). Both the road movie and the diasporic family mount a critique of hegemonic and territorialised conceptions of identity and belonging. This is particularly evident in the European road movie, with its emphasis on borders and border crossings – political, cultural, social and linguistic – which not only makes the experience of being on the road rather different from the freewheeling mobility and promise of freedom of the American highways (see Mazierska and Rascaroli 2006), but also draws attention to the barriers that a territorialised understanding of nation and national belonging entails.

Clamouring at the Gates of Fortress Europe

Nowhere is the image of the border and the perils associated with border crossings more prominent than in *Journey of Hope*,[17] made by Swiss director Xavier Koller and winner of the Academy Award for Best Foreign Language Film in 1991. As Beverly Walker notes, 'the importance of borders, as geographical boundary and as metaphor, is the [film's] subtext [. . .]. Borders make the difference between dreams attained or shattered; between life and death' (1991: 2) and between haves and have-nots.

Tempted by the false promise of an affluent life in Switzerland, the Kurdish couple Haydar and Meryem, together with their youngest son, leave their Anatolian village that, as outlined above, bears all the hallmarks of the Bakhtinian chronotope of the family idyll. The small village community lives off the fruits of their land and labour, several generations live harmoniously together and the large group of children hail the promise of a happy future – that is, until the menacing image of the fast-moving train foreshadows the devastating impact that the arrival of modernity and mobility will have upon the family at the centre of the narrative. Foolishly, Haydar sells up his livestock and land to raise the funds for a journey that is orchestrated by unscrupulous traffickers. From Istanbul, Haydar's already fractured family travels as stowaway passengers on a freighter to Naples in Italy, where a Swiss truck driver gives them a lift to the Swiss border. But without the appropriate travel documents they cannot enter Switzerland. And so they re-join the group of illegal refugees and put their lives into the hands of a network of Swiss traffickers, who arrange the onward journey and squeeze the last penny out of the desperate migrants before showing them the path across the Alps.

The dramatic traversal of the snow-topped Alps, on foot, at night and left to their own devices without a guide to show them the way, confronts the desperate refugees with every imaginable hazard: separation, loss and even death. One of the film's ironies is that the illegal migrants aspire to a more prosperous life in Switzerland but, in order to get there, are gradually stripped of all their possessions. For each leg of their journey Haydar and his family have to part with more of their savings until all they have left is Meryem's wedding jewellery. This, too, is sold to satisfy the traffickers' greed. In order to make it to 'paradise beyond the mountains', the motley group of illegal immigrants need to discard their most treasured possessions since they are unable to carry their heavy suitcases across the mountain range.

Hamid Naficy regards the suitcase as a 'multilayered and contradictory key symbol of exilic subjectivity'. It 'contains souvenirs from the homeland' but also connotes 'wanderlust, freedom to roam, and a provisional life' and 'symbolizes profound deprivation and diminution of one's possibilities in the world' (2001: 261). In *Journey of Hope*, one of the traffickers asks a devout Muslim in the group: 'You are making a fresh start – why carry your suitcase with you?' But, like Haydar, who holds on to his suitcase because 'It's all we have', this refugee also clings to his prized possessions, only to lose them when his suitcase topples down a ravine and its contents, books and a prayer rug, spill out.[18] The loss of the suitcase signifies a loss of identity and cultural memory – the price these economic refugees pay for their dream of a more affluent life in Switzerland. Haydar does not relinquish his suitcase until, as in a pietà, he cradles his freezing and exhausted son Mehmet Ali, who eventually dies in the blizzard. As Yosefa Loshitzky observes, 'the shift from carrying the suitcase to carrying the dying child is an image of double loss, the loss of the past (whose metonymy is the suitcase) and the loss of the hope for a better future (the son)' (2010: 19).

If border crossing is associated with the trauma of loss, arrival in the Promised Land is represented as exclusion. Meryem, who has been separated from her husband and child during the treacherous trek across the wasteland of ice and snow, is amongst the first contingent of desperate refugees to reach a luxurious Swiss spa hotel. Yet here they encounter another border – the thick double-glazed windowpanes of a heated swimming pool, through which they can see the haven of comfort and prosperity inside but which they cannot access. No matter how forcefully they bang with their fists on the impenetrable wall of glass, they are left out in the cold – at least initially.

The glass barrier is a powerful symbol of the asymmetrical power structures that govern the relations between Fortress Europe and its neighbours on the periphery. The hotel owner, taking an early morning swim in the warm pool, sees the destitute refugees but keeps muttering, 'We're closed, we're closed'. Yosefa Loshitzky considers the encounter between the refugees and

Figure 2.3 Desperate refugees clamouring at one of the many gates of Fortress Europe in *Journey of Hope* (Xavier Koller, 1990)

the 'well-fed, overweight, white European "gatekeeper" [...] seemingly deaf to the plight of the underprivileged and to their desperation' as 'the ultimate iconic image of Fortress Europe, guarding its visible wealth and comfort against the dreams of non-Europeans in search of a better life. This image of "hospitality" denied is the image of the New Europe' (2010: 31).

Despite eventually receiving warm blankets and temporary shelter inside the hotel, ultimately the refugees will be deported to where they came from, neither having the required immigration documents nor being granted asylum. Worse still, Haydar is arrested by the Swiss police for crossing the border illegally and for causing his son's death through negligence. When the Swiss lorry driver, Ramser, visits Haydar in prison, another thick glass pane separates the two men, underscoring the impossibility of the friendship that might have developed had the borders not been as impenetrable as they are. 'I would have liked to be your friend', Haydar says to Ramser, who offers to pay for Mehmet Ali's funeral in Turkey. Although the film does not show the family's return to Turkey nor the repatriation of the son, the implied circular itinerary and the burial in the Turkish soil from which the family has voluntarily uprooted itself are reminiscent of the closure of *Little Senegal*. Both films are cautionary moralistic tales about the harmful and corrosive impact of migration, be it voluntary or involuntary, upon the family.

Journey of Hope deftly illustrates the aesthetic strategies and moral stance of what Sarita Malik has theorised as the 'cinema of duty' (1996) in relation to Black British film and Rob Burns as the 'cinema of the affected' (2006) in relation to Turkish German cinema (see Chapter 1). Like other early films about the plight of migrants and guest workers made by majority culture and first-generation immigrant filmmakers, Xavier Koller's film takes a 'social worker approach' (Göktürk 2000: 68) to ethnic relations and seeks to arouse the viewer's 'sense of moral indignation and compassion' (Fenner 2006: 25). Contrasting the naïve and innocent Turkish peasants with the corrupt traffickers from Istanbul and the even more unscrupulous Swiss ringleaders, Koller's film reprises the tropes of exploitation and victimhood (associated with guest workers and oppressed Turkish women in Turkish German cinema of the affected; see Chapter 1) and combines these with the motif of a hazardous journey, border crossings and trafficking.[19] Koller replaces the familiar iconography of claustrophobic interiors (such as the gloomy flat in *40 Square Metres of Germany* and the prison cell in *Abschied vom falschen Paradies* (*Farewell to a False Paradise,* Tevfik Başer, 1989) with the no less claustrophobic interior of a minibus, hurtling along winding back roads and negotiating borders of various kinds. The natural border of the inhospitable, snow-capped Alps, which claims lives as its toll, seems to reinforce and 'naturalise' the territorial borders of Switzerland – and, by extension, those of Fortress Europe. The topography of borders and barriers, coupled with the idyllic depiction of the Anatolian village, entails a rather problematic moral judgement on the clandestine refugees' ill-advised pursuit of a more prosperous life elsewhere. Moreover, the reference to the Festival of Sacrifice at the beginning of the film implicates Haydar in his son's death, whose life he unwittingly sacrifices on this journey of hope. Does this highly moralistic tale not ultimately assert existing geopolitical borders and condone the arbitrary division between the haves and the have-nots?

Welcoming Strangers in a Strange Land

The contrast between Koller's film of 1990 and *Almanya – Welcome to Germany*, which premiered at the Berlin International Film Festival in 2011, could not be more pronounced. This feel-good integration comedy (as the film has been dubbed in the German press) glosses over or even denies the existence of borders and boundaries. It purposely eschews the customary miserableness and the grim social realist aesthetics of the 'cinema of the affected' (Burns 2006) without being disingenuous. This kind of embellishment is achieved through a clever framing device, which allows for a child's expansive imagination to be the measure of reality and to enhance it with a magical realist touch.

That child is Cenk, the seven-year-old grandson of Hüseyin Yilmaz, who was amongst the first Turkish labour migrants to arrive in Germany in the 1960s. Cenk ponders his national identity after having been rejected by both the Turkish and the German football teams at his school. Is he Turkish or German or both? Even his extended, multi-generational family, consisting of his grandparents Hüseyin and Fatma Yilmaz, their four children and two grandchildren, are far from unanimous. And so, Cenk's cousin, the twenty-two-year-old Canan, tells him the story of how the Yilmaz family ended up in Germany.

From there on, the film's narrative bifurcates. One strand is set in the present and is, more or less, in keeping with the conventions of realism. The other strand is prompted by Canan's lessons in family history and consists of a series of extensive flashback sequences that take Cenk (and the viewer) back some fifty years to Hüseyin's natal village in Anatolia, his courtship of Fatma and his arrival in the Federal Republic of Germany in 1964. This strand, which is eventually conjoined with the first in the film's coda, follows the narrative logic and visual exuberance of magical realism. The magical realist perspective is psychologically motivated by being attributed to the little boy Cenk, in whose flights of fancy the mundane and difficult aspects of the migrant experience are commingled with the improbable and the fantastic. In contrast to fairy tales, which take place in their entirety on another plane of reality, magical realist narratives are grounded in reality but disrupt the real through momentary magic (Bowers 2004: 104).[20] In that sense, magical realism is an extension, rather than an outright rejection, of 'realism in its concern with the nature of reality and its representation' (Zamora and Faris 1995: 6). It is a mode that not only transgresses the boundaries of realism with its 'basic assumption of post-enlightenment rationalism' (8), but also challenges boundaries per se and therefore 'often facilitates the fusion, or coexistence, of possible worlds, spaces, systems that would be irreconcilable in other modes of fiction' (6). Magical realism has the propensity to assault binary structures, such as the real and the imaginary, the self and the other, and to advocate in-betweenness, plurality and hybridity instead. This explains why it is a representational mode privileged in postcolonial and diasporic texts, including Salman Rushdie's novel *Midnight's Children* (1995), to which *Almanya – Welcome to Germany* pays homage.

These cursory remarks about magical realism may explain why *Almanya* gets away with chronicling the history of Turkish labour migration to Germany as a family history in which national borders and cultural boundaries prove no obstacle, in which vast geographical distances can be overcome in a matter of seconds and in which the recruitment and real hardship and marginalisation of labour migrants are imagined as a cordial invitation and a warm welcome.[21] When Canan explains that Germany called Cenk's grandfather and other guest workers, he imagines the German state as a loud disembodied voice inviting able and willing workers from all over the world: 'Dear cosmopolitans, here speaks the Federal Republic of Germany. We are looking for a workforce. If you are young, strong and possess a good work ethic, then report immediately to the nearest recruitment office'.[22] A sound bridge links the voice, which sounds as if it emanated from a gigantic megaphone, to a series of snapshots in oversaturated colours, showing a group of Turkish men playing cards in Istanbul, an Italian father eating spaghetti in the family kitchen in Naples, a group of Greek men on the island of Rhodes and three Eskimos, huddling around a fire on a vast expanse of snow at the North Pole.

The film's chief premise, that Germany extended a warm welcome to all migrants, is developed further in a scene that intercuts the black-and-white documentary footage of the arrival of the one-millionth guest worker, Armando Rodrigues de Sá from Portugal, on 10 September 1964 with 'fake footage' in colour, showing Hüseyin Yilmaz arriving at the Cologne-Deutz train station at the same time. If Hüseyin had not kindly offered Rodrigues his place in the long queue of recently arrived guest workers, then he, rather than Rodrigues, would have made history and would have received the fashionable Zündapp moped, donated by the Federal Republic's Association of Employers as a welcome gift.[23] And so the story continues, juxtaposing what was and what would have been, and transforming the black and white of old documentaries and 'the faded greys of old family-album snapshots' into 'CinemaScope and glorious Technicolor' – as Salman Rushdie (1991: 10) has described the retrieval of the past through memory and its magical transformation when he wrote *Midnight's Children*.[24]

In keeping with magical realism's propensity to subvert and reposition existing structures of power, the relationship between German majority and Turkish German minority culture is turned upside down. Hence, in *Almanya – Welcome to Germany*, it is not the Turks but the Germans who are the 'Other' – and what peculiar habits they have! They put their dogs (which look like giant rats) on a leash and take them round the block for a walk. Their food, a diet consisting predominantly of potatoes and pork, is most unpalatable, not to mention their religious practices, which bear an eerie resemblance to cannibalistic rituals ... In this topsy-turvy world, a mirror is held up to German majority culture, inviting the 'natives' to marvel at their own 'Otherness'. In keeping with this inverted perspective, the Yilmazes speak accent-free German (which represents Turkish in the flashback scenes rendered from Cenk's perspective), whereas the Germans speak an invented language, reminiscent of the Heil-Hynkel German in Charlie Chaplin's *The Great Dictator* (1940), which neither the Yilmazes nor the audience can possibly understand. The film's humorous conflation of historical fact and fiction culminates in a public thanksgiving ceremony in Berlin, to which German Chancellor Angela Merkel invited two hundred migrants who had settled in Germany some fifty years ago, thereby officially acknowledging Germany's debt of gratitude. Hüseyin had even been asked to give a public address but, due to his sudden death, his grandson Cenk speaks on his behalf, simultaneously representing the first and third generations of Turkish Germans. 'I have been living here for forty-five years', he says, blurring generational boundaries and adding a considerable cuteness factor to the televised event and the film. As the sound fades and Cenk's words become inaudible, and the camera pans over the faces of the assembled Yilmaz family (including Hüseyin), showing how deeply moved they are by Cenk's speech, the film conveys an idealised image of a Turkish

German family, united by strong family feeling, intergenerational cohesion and a shared history.

If, in most films, transnational migration destabilises or even fractures the natural family, then *Almanya – Welcome to Germany* provides a pertinent counter-example. Mobility is conceived of as continuity and transformation rather than rupture. And yet, for a film centrally concerned with mobility, we see surprisingly little of it. This is because the magical touch of Cenk's imagination transcends borders and boundaries, and fuses what is separate in terms of time and space. For example, Hüseyin's outbound journey of migration is reduced to the moment of departure, when he gets on to a sky-blue pick-up truck and bids farewell to his beautiful young wife and three children in the remote Anatolian village, and the moment he arrives at the train station in Cologne-Deutz as guest worker number one-million-and-one. Scenes showing Hüseyin sending big bundles of bank notes, sealed with a kiss, from Germany are cross-cut with scenes showing Fatma with a big smile on her face, collecting the very same bundles at a post office in Turkey. Parallel editing conveys a sense of intimate connection that is ultimately unaffected by geographical distance. One minute, Hüseyin is reading a letter from back home in the guest workers' dormitory and, the very next minute, he arrives back home, welcomed by Fatma's warm embrace. Reinforced by the clichéd lyrics of a nostalgic 1960s-style pop song, 'Foreign People',[25] which speaks of the loneliness of foreigners on foreign streets and the prospect of an imminent homecoming, time and space are compressed and a seamless continuity between two localities, far apart from each other geographically and culturally, is constructed. When Hüseyin leaves the village again, it is together with his entire family, who gets on to the same sky-blue pick-up truck that came to collect Hüseyin several years ago. The villagers wave the same farewell as they did before. The repetition with a few variations creates the impression that time has stood still in the village.

The Yilmazes' next trip from Germany to Turkey, undertaken several years later in an old Mercedes-Benz (a status symbol for many Turkish families, intended to impress relatives back home), is rendered through a combination of archival footage and Canan's matter-of-fact voice-over commentary: 'The distance between the new and the old *Heimat* was 2,521 kilometres. And it took an entire three days and three nights to get there'. The grainy, faded colour footage of 1970s-style cars crawling bumper to bumper along the infamous '*Autoput*' or 'death route', as the transit route from Germany via Yugoslavia to Turkey was commonly known on account of the many fatal accidents, creates a documentary realist feel that functions as a sobering counterpoint to the magical aspects of the film.[26]

Almanya – Welcome to Germany offers a tongue-in-cheek take on the myth of a glorious homecoming. Hüseyin abandons his original plan to purchase a house in his 'old *Heimat*' when he realises that his family has become accustomed to the higher standards of living in their 'new *Heimat*'. Whereas the

Figure 2.4 Time may have stood still in the Turkish village but the Yilmaz family is on the move, off to Germany (*Almanya – Welcome to Germany*, Yasemin Samdereli, 2011)

ancestral village is depicted as a place where nothing ever changes (an important feature of Bakhtin's 'folkloric time'), the experience of living in diaspora has transformed the Yilmaz family and 'time could not be turned back', explains Canan. Instead of acquiring a dilapidated cottage in Turkey, Hüseyin buys a modern house in Germany that is large enough to accommodate the extended family, albeit in separate flats. As such, it symbolises the successful symbiosis between Turkish and German cultures. So when, several decades later, Hüseyin (who has just adopted German citizenship) proudly announces that he has purchased a house in the *Heimat*, his wife and children protest that they have no desire to 'go back home'. It transpires that the house is merely intended as a holiday home and, consequently, the film's third journey – and the only one dramatised in detail – charts the Yilmazes' trip by plane and minibus to the Anatolian village. As in Akın's *The Edge of Heaven*, the journey from Germany to Turkey is elided and transnational space is compressed, whereas the local journey in Turkey is depicted in considerable detail.

Almanya replaces the familiar iconography of a rickety bus on a dusty road with a modern minibus, travelling smoothly along a wide road embedded in sun-drenched fields and olive groves depicted in warm hues of verdant green and honey. The oversaturated chromatic of the road-trip sequences serves as yet another reminder of the transformative power of Cenk's imagination and recalls Rushdie's remarks about retrieving old family memories in 'glorious Technicolor' (1991: 10).[27] In contrast to the solitary Railla in *Keltoum's Daughter* and Haydar's family in *Journey of Hope*, travelling amidst strangers, the Yilmaz family's white-and-turquoise minibus is packed with a large and happy family. As the chronotope of the road functions as a metaphor for life, journey narratives and road movies often end with the protagonist's death. In *Almanya*, it is Hüseyin who dies unexpectedly on the way to Anatolia. Yet, in keeping with the film's comedic sensibility and its magical realist aesthetics, death is not interpreted as loss and separation, but as transformation. Thus, when Cenk asks his father, 'Where is Grandpa now?', Ali explains the relationship between life and death by using the water cycle as an analogy, leading Cenk to the logical conclusion: 'So Grandad has evaporated'. The idea that transformation constitutes an integral part of life is rendered through another magical realist device. When Hüseyin is buried in his natal village, all of the main characters are present twice – as children or young adults in their prime, as they appear in the flashback sequences, and as adults, as they appear in the scenes set in the present, played by different actors standing right next to one another. In the film's coda, Canan explains the magical conceit of doubling when she muses (adapting a quotation from Salman Rushdie's *Midnight's Children*):[28] 'We are the sum total of everything that went before us, of all we have been seen done, of everything done-to-us. We are everyone everything whose being-in-the-world affected was affected by us. We are anything that happens after we're gone which would not have happened if we had not come'.

Canan's voice-over accompanies a scene set in the grounds of the house that Hüseyin bought and that turned out to be merely a façade, a ruin rather than a habitable home. The ruin is an apt symbol of nostalgia and, as such, features prominently in the *œuvre* of the exilic filmmaker Andrei Tarkovsky. In his film *Nostalghia* (*Nostalgia*, 1983), the chronotope of the ruin encapsulates a deep yearning for one's childhood and the places associated with it that have become inaccessible due to exile or migration and the passage of time (see Naficy 2001: 173–8, see also Huyssen 2008). In her study *The Future of Nostalgia*, Svetlana Boym defines nostalgia in relation to exile and displacement:

> Nostalgia (from *nostos* – return home, and *algia* – longing) is a longing for a home that no longer exists or has never existed. Nostalgia is a sentiment of loss and displacement, but it is also a romance with one's own fantasy. [. . .] nostalgia is a longing for a place, but actually it is a yearning for a different time – the time of our childhood. (2001: viii, xv)

In that sense, nostalgia chronotopically 'charts time on space and space on time' (Boym 2001: xviii), intertwining the longing for home and longing for the past. Hüseyin's imaginary, uninhabitable home embodies this nostalgia but its painful emotional undertones are elided when Mustafa, one of his sons, decides to stay and rebuild the ruin. The scene recalls Boym's distinction between restorative and reflective nostalgia: the former 'stresses *nostos* and attempts a transhistorical reconstruction of the lost home', whereas the latter 'thrives in *algia*, the longing itself, and delays the homecoming' (xviii). While reflective nostalgia is satisfied with a fragmentary recollection and an idealised memory of an imaginary homeland, restorative nostalgia endeavours to patch up the gaps in time and memory and literally rebuild the lost home. Although both modes of nostalgia are present in *Almanya*, the film's prevailing sensibility is clearly that of reflective nostalgia inasmuch as it endorses multi-locality, 'inhabiting many places at once and imagining different time zones' (Boym 2001: xviii). Hence, the return to the imaginary idyllic home, in the film's coda, is only temporary.

The coda, a *tableau vivant* of a pre-lapsarian family idyll, shows the family re-assembled in the grounds of Hüseyin's imaginary home, overlooking a bucolic landscape drenched in golden sunlight. The scene pictures the Yilmazes (once again represented in their past and their present embodiments and performed by two sets of actors) sitting in a loosely arranged circle on the ground, eating the fruits of the land and enjoying each other's company. The presence of the deceased Hüseyin amidst his numerous children and the now visibly pregnant Canan identifies the scene as a magical realist variation of Bakhtin's family idyll with its emphasis on generational renewal. Still, with all its pre-modern pastoral iconography, this is a transnational and hybridised family idyll, touched but not destroyed by the forces of mobility and modernity. No longer rooted in just one place, the Yilmazes move freely between their old and their new *Heimat*. Included in the circle of the Turkish German family are Cenk's blond, blue-eyed German mother and the British father of Canan's baby. Whilst, in *Journey of Hope*, the family idyll is irretrievably lost once Haydar's family foolhardily succumbs to the temptations of modernity, in *Almanya – Welcome to Germany* the ease of modern transport makes it possible for the family to reclaim it momentarily, not just when on holiday in Turkey but also wherever they are, by harmoniously integrating culturally diverse influences and family members in the family circle.

Father and Son on the Grand Tour

Le Grand Voyage provides another example of transnational mobility conceived as an integrative experience. Yet, unlike *Almanya*, Ismaël Ferroukhi's feature-film début is a proper road movie that combines 'a plethora of road movie markers' (Corrigan 1991: 151) with the motif of a spiritual quest and an educational theme. An elderly Moroccan French father and his seventeen-year-old son substitute for the two male buddies of the classic American road movie. The film charts the 3,000–mile journey from Southern France to Mecca in Saudi Arabia, where the father (who remains nameless) wants to participate in the Hajj. Reda cannot comprehend why his father does not simply fly to Mecca, yet grudgingly succumbs to his father's request to drive him all the way. Their car, an old light-blue Peugeot with one bright orange replacement door, aptly symbolises the son's different worldview and his quiet rebellion against his father. The fact that they do not speak the same language (the father speaks Moroccan Arabic, his son replies in French) further underscores the estrangement between the two.

The film translates the generational and cultural divide that separates the Muslim father and his agnostic son into a series of real borders they need to cross en route to Saudi Arabia. Their journey takes them through Italy, Slovenia, Croatia, Serbia, Bulgaria, Turkey, Syria and Jordan. Border crossings are linked to passport controls and other formalities and especially to language barriers, confronting both father and son with shared communication problems. Linguistic barriers and the characters' idiosyncratic communicative behaviour function as key signifiers of cultural difference. In Serbia, father and son are joined by an old, slightly confused woman who would seem to be completely mute, were it not for the fact that she utters one word, 'delichi', which father and son (mis)interpret as the name of a town. Later on they ask for directions and barely manage to escape from the torrent of incomprehensible words in which a helpful stranger drowns them. At the Turkish border, a bilingual French-speaking Turk facilitates their crossing and joins them on their onward journey. Mustapha is an unstoppable, eloquent commentator on Turkish culture, Istanbul architecture and Sufism, who offers a more enlightened interpretation of Islamic scriptures than Reda's father approves of. The film's focus on family conflict represents a marked departure from the generic conventions of the road movie as sketched by Timothy Corrigan. This is further accentuated by the fact that the fellow travellers in *Le Grand Voyage* function as parental alter egos. Reda's father perceives Mustapha as a rival for his son's attention and affection – and gets rid of him. The mute Serbian woman is the alter ego of Reda's mother, whose brief appearance at the beginning of the film assigns her the role of an eloquent mediator between father and son.

The title *Le Grand Voyage* is reminiscent of *Le Grand Tour* and draws attention to the educational nature of this 3,000–mile journey. The purpose of the Grand Tour, which became a widely established social practice among the higher echelons of European society between the seventeenth and nineteenth centuries, was 'to round out the education of young men of the ruling classes by exposing them to the treasured artifacts and ennobling society of the Continent' (Buzard 2006: 38). It was an educational rite of passage extending over a period of one to five years, but unlike the Grand Tour in Ferroukhi's film, it was explicitly of a non-religious nature. Nor was it customary for the father to be the travel companion. The usual itinerary included cities such as Paris, Milan, Florence, Venice and Rome, so as to ensure that the young men of means were exposed to Renaissance art and the cultural legacy of classical antiquity. In *Le Grand Voyage*, however, the father makes sure they bypass Milan and Venice, despite Reda's eagerness to visit Europe's touristic highlights on the way to Mecca. By contrast, Mustapha takes Reda to the famous Blue Mosque in Istanbul and wants to show him other tourist attractions, thereby interfering with the purpose of the pilgrimage. Not only does Reda's

Figure 2.5 Father (Mohamed Majd) and son (Nicolas Cazalé) going east in *Le Grand Voyage* (Ismaël Ferroukhi, 2004)

father, a devout Muslim, want to make the Hajj and fulfil the fifth pillar of Islam before he dies, but he also hopes to impart some of his religious beliefs to his son, who knows very little about Islam. In order to achieve this, he needs time to extract Reda from the fast-paced secular lifestyle of the West.

The father throws away his son's mobile phone, thereby literally disconnecting him from his modern way of life (and his girlfriend) in France. He insists on leaving the busy motorways to travel along country lanes, lanes so small that they do not even appear on a road map. In any event, the father is unable to read road maps since, as Reda scornfully reminds him in one of their altercations, he is illiterate. The highways of super-modernity connect the far-flung corners of this world quickly and efficiently, whereas the small byways the pair actually take require a slower pace. 'Why did you not simply take the plane to Mecca?', Reda asks one day, whereupon his father explains, rather cryptically: 'When the waters of the oceans rise to heaven, they lose their bitterness and become pure again [. . . .] That's why it is better to go on pilgrimage on foot than on horseback, better on horseback than by car, better by car than by boat, better by boat than by plane'.

Inverting the road movie's fascination with speed, the father advocates slowness as a means of spiritual purification. He shares this view with Monsieur Ibrahim in the similar-themed French film *Monsieur Ibrahim ou les fleurs du Coran* (*Monsieur Ibrahim and the Flowers of Koran*, François Dupeyron, 2003), set in 1960s Paris. Ibrahim is an elderly Turkish Muslim man (mistakenly nicknamed 'the Arab' by his neighbours), who runs a grocery store in the Jewish quarter. The Jewish boy Moses from across the road is a regular customer (and shoplifter) there and, after his father's suicide, Monsieur Ibrahim adopts him, affectionately calling him 'Momo'.[29] Together they make Ibrahim's dream come true and travel via Switzerland, Albania and Greece to his native village in Eastern Turkey. Unbeknownst to Momo, Ibrahim pursues an educational mission with this Grand Tour: namely, to teach his adopted son 'all there is to know in my Koran'. He introduces Momo to Sufism, an esoteric form of Islamic mysticism, by acquainting him with particular devotional practices, such as the whirling dervishes, and guiding him to fathom the divine presence in the beauty of nature. Despite driving a flashy red sports car (a Simca Aronde Océane), Ibrahim prefers slowness to speed since, according to the precepts of Sufism, it is a means of finding happiness. At the same time, slowness is linked to old age and these fathers, both on the brink of death, may know full well that this is going to be their last journey and they had better spin it out for as long as possible.

If the road movie is about leaving the familiar behind and venturing forth into the unknown, if its route frequently leads from the strictures of civilisation to untamed nature, then Reda and his father's trajectory from the old Europe to the Middle East, from the centre to the periphery, is imagined as equally liberating. Once father and son leave the narrow undulating roads of Europe behind, the landscapes change and resemble those of the American road movie, in which the desert features as a privileged landscape. Yet, significantly, the Saudi Arabian desert is not some kind of empty wasteland but, because of its proximity to Mecca, a realm of love and spirituality.[30] The desert draws attention to the transcendental nature of the journey yet to come; the father prays, gives alms to a female beggar and eventually thanks his son for having made his pilgrimage possible. The reconciliation of father and son is underscored by the numerous shot-reverse-shot sequences that capture the sideways glances they cast at each other and the affectionate smiles that light up their faces. After many border crossings, father and son reach the final frontier, the main gate into the holy city of Mecca. It consists of two slightly curved posts that cross over in the middle and then diverge again, symbolising the momentary *rapprochement* of father and son – as well as their imminent separation.[31] As in the classic road movie that 'sets the liberation of the road against the oppression of hegemonic norms' (Cohan and Hark 1997: 2), here, too, the change of landscape underscores a growing sense of freedom that the father at least, a practising Muslim, is unable to experience in France.

The French Republican tradition of *laïcité*, the formal separation of church and state, affects Muslims considerably more than other faiths. As Alec Hargreaves argues in his study *Multi-Ethnic France*, headscarves are forbidden, whereas other religious insignia or items of dress, such as the crucifix or yarmulke, are not; there are many churches but few purpose-built mosques with minarets (2007: 106). The marginalisation of practising Muslims in France, coupled with high levels of illiteracy amongst first-generation Muslim immigrants, means that parents cannot offer any formal instruction about Islam to their children. This has resulted in 'the inter-generational erosion of Islam' (Hargreaves 2007: 104). These very real issues are alluded to in

Figure 2.6 The aerial shots of Mecca are a powerful reminder that millions of Muslims are not a minority (*Le Grand Voyage*, Ismaël Ferroukhi, 2004)

Ferroukhi's film and help explain the alienation of father and son at the beginning of their journey.

Against this socio-political background, their arrival in Mecca marks the father's liberation and homecoming. Fellow hajjis have 'reserved' a space to park his car, welcome him with a handshake or an embrace, and invite him and Reda to share a meal with them. At last, the father is amongst his kind – no longer part of a marginalised minority but part of the global *Ummah*. Here a common language, Arabic, and the shared knowledge of the holy rituals they have come to perform in Mecca unite hajjis from all over the world. In the words of the black American Muslim activist, Malcolm X, Mecca is 'the only place on earth where you can find every specimen of humanity – all cultures, all races ... all of everything' (cited in Coleman and Elsner 1995: 53). Ferroukhi is the first feature filmmaker to be allowed to film inside the holy city and, as Peter Bradshaw (2005) notes in a review, 'has his characters mingling with the pilgrims making the hajj – two million extras! It really is an incredible spectacle: an authentic religious phenomenon which is largely invisible and under-imagined in Western culture'. The aerial shots of millions of Muslims worshipping around the mosque are a powerful reminder that the notion of a Muslim minority reflects a skewed Eurocentric perspective. From a Muslim's point of view, Mecca is 'the centre in the desert' and a place where 'cultural diversity [is] submerged within a common religious identity' (Coleman and Elsner 1995: 52). The pilgrimage to Mecca charted in *Le Grand Voyage*, therefore, proposes a new spatial geography in which the 'uneven power geometry of West–Rest relations', resulting in the 'exclusion of racialized and ethnicized minorities' (McLoughlin 2010: 225) in the protagonists' host country, are inverted.

When the father leaves for the Kaaba amidst a large group of pilgrims, Reda stays behind. He later finds his father's body in a morgue, where he performs the required Islamic death rituals, thereby assisting his father to embark on what is another *grand voyage* as referenced in the title, the eternal journey to join Allah. This is not the only indication that his father's educational mission (not understood as proselytism but as respect for each other's belief system) has borne fruit. In the film's penultimate scene, Reda gives alms to a street beggar in reverence of his father, whose earlier practice of *zakat*, the third pillar of Islam, he criticised. The final shot shows Reda heading for the airport in a cab. With the warm desert wind tousling his hair, he casts his eyes up to heaven, a glance that underscores the mutual respect and affection that have developed between father and son.

The extra-diegetic song 'Ode d'Ibn Arabi', performed by the Moroccan vocalist Amina Alaoui, reiterates the film's reconciliatory message. As Thibaut Schilt argues, in tracing the numerous intertextual references of this song from Alaoui's album *Alcàntara*, or 'the bridge', 'the bewitching voice of the Arabo-Andalusian singer seems to evoke at once nostalgia for a time of vibrant Islamic intellectuals and contemporary, forward-looking optimism for a better understanding of an often highly misunderstood faith' (2010: 794). The lyrics are a plea for religious tolerance and the universal power of love ('Love is my religion and my faith' is the translation from Arabic cited in Schilt 2010: 797) that is capable of bridging the gap between father and son, as well as between Islam and Western secularism. 'I have learnt a lot on this journey', says the father to his son as they approach Mecca. Ferroukhi intended a similar learning experience for the audience. By showing the human face of Islam, he wanted to 'rehumanise a community whose reputation is smeared by an extreme minority using religion for political ends' (cited in Jaafar 2005: 66).

Whereas many road movies convey their protagonists' marginality and ultimate unassimilability through an open-ended narrative structure – these outsiders just carry on driving – the ending of *Le Grand Voyage* is less straightforward. The son embarks on his return journey 'home' to France. Meanwhile, for his father, Mecca signifies home, as well as the point of departure for an onward journey through which he will overcome the transcendental homelessness of modern life as such and, more specifically, of life in contemporary France. In keeping with the rebellious, counter-cultural impetus of the road movie, *Le Grand Voyage* critiques majority culture, with its insistence on cultural homogeneity, from the distant vantage point of the road and the wide-open spaces of the Middle East. Conversely, the familiar generic conventions of the road movie help to contain cultural difference and provide a strategy that enhances the cross-over appeal of a film about an ethno-religious minority in France, whose alterity is incompatible with the Republican tradition of French citizenship.

Conclusion

Transnational mobility in the films considered in this chapter is undeniably a force that transforms the structure and identity of the family, yet it does not necessarily result in its fragmentation and rupture. Even where journeys end in death and separation, as they often do, these experiences give rise to new beginnings and new alliances. The surrogate families in *Monsieur Ibrahim*, *Tour Abroad* and *The Edge of Heaven*, which are based on elective forms of kinship between Ibrahim and Momo, Senay and Zeki, and Susanne, a bereaved German mother, and Ayten, the Turkish lover of Susanne's deceased daughter, provide apt examples. In the process of personal reconciliation, these two women overcome generational, ethnic and political cleavages, intimating a desire for a cultural and political *rapprochement* on a larger scale.[32] The same agenda is discernible in narratives that chart the transformation of families through migration and living in diaspora. Interethnic marriages, professional success in *The Namesake* and an expanding three-generational family in *Almanya – Welcome to Germany* provide ample evidence that these diasporic families have found their place in the social fabric of the host society.

Nevertheless, what identifies these films and the families they portray as quintessentially diasporic is their persistent preoccupation with a mythical homeland, which lingers in the minds of some family members, even decades after they emigrated. Yet, with the exception of *Journey of Hope*, home is not simply the place of origin or the motherland, but a trope for other cultural attachments, such as belonging to the global *Ummah*. These films challenge the nostalgic fantasy of home, understood as 'a fixed origin to which we can make some final and absolute return' (Hall [1990] 2003: 237), and refute primordial notions of roots and 'natural' belonging – to one nation-state, to one natural family. Mobility is a means to express and engender new cultural and familial attachments. Hence, Susanne's decision to make Istanbul her new home (at least for the time being), Ashima's plan to spend half the year in India and the other half with her friends and grown-up children in America at the end of *The Namesake*, and Mustafa's intention to rebuild the dilapidated house his father bought in Turkey at the end of *Almanya* cannot be interpreted as a final homecoming but as the adoption of a multi-local lifestyle, 'criss-crossing in global space and time' (Mennel 2010), that privileges routes over roots.

Several of the films charting the transnational itineraries of families promote the project underlying much of diasporic cinema more generally: namely, in the words of Isaac Julien and Kobena Mercer, to interrogate critically the relationship between 'de margin and de centre' (2002: 355) by deconstructing prevalent binary oppositions and notions of race and ethnicity. In particular, *Le Grand Voyage* and *Almanya – Welcome to Germany* map new spatial geographies that call dominant Eurocentric assumptions about majority and minority cultures, Europe and its Others, into question. By filming a gigantic crowd of devout Muslims at the Hajj in Mecca, Ismaël Ferroukhi reminds Western audiences that diasporic Muslims may well be a minority in their European countries of residence but certainly not when seen in global perspective. Moreover, the aerial shots of an infinite number of hajjis worshipping peacefully around the Kaaba are a powerful visual counterpoint to prevalent media images of Islamist terrorism. In *Almanya*, the film's magical realist aesthetics invert the relationship between German majority and Turkish German minority cultures, thereby creating a similarly decentred perspective in some of the scenes. Arising from a position on the margins of hegemonic society, magical realism constitutes a strategy of subversion that engages with the real and reality but destabilises its structures of power and the implicit hierarchies between majority culture and its Others.

Notes

1. The Festival of Sacrifice or Greater Eid is celebrated by Muslims worldwide in commemoration of Abraham's (Ibrahim's) willingness to sacrifice his son Ishmael as proof of his obedience to God. But God intervenes and gives Abraham a ram to sacrifice instead. The story is referenced in a number of films, including *The Edge of Heaven*, where it serves as a reminder of the common ground shared by Islam and Christianity.
2. For Barbara Mennel, the train embodies 'the changing perception of time and space in modernity – space as urban versus rural and time as modern versus premodern' (2008: 8). In cinema and visual culture more generally, trains carry a whole range of predominantly negative connotations, including the 'taming' of the Wild West in the genre of the western, the 'civilising mission' of colonisers in India, Africa and elsewhere, and the deportation of Jews to Auschwitz and other concentration camps in Holocaust films.
3. The song by Kazım Koyuncu and the conversation about it introduce the theme of death. Koyuncu died of cancer at the age of thirty, presumably as a result of the long-term effects of the nuclear disaster at Chernobyl (see Göktürk 2010b).
4. Akın retraces the journey in his semi-autobiographical film *Wir haben vergessen zurückzukehren* (*We Have Forgotten to Return*, 2001), discussed in Chapter 3.
5. However, Mennel (2010) anticipates that the third chapter will conclude with the reconciliation of Nejat and his father.
6. David Harvey (1990: 240–323) identifies 'time-space compression' as a hallmark of postmodernity.
7. Solino is an imaginary place that shares a number of similarities with the Sicilian village where *Cinema Paradiso* (Giuseppe Tornatore, 1988) is set.
8. I do not mean to suggest that journeys are generally under-represented in diasporic cinema; in fact, the opposite appears to be the case. But the travellers in films such as *America, America* (Elia Kazan, 1963), *Winterblume* (*Winter Flowers*, Kadir Sözen, 1997), *Yara* (*The Wound*, Yılmaz Arslan, 1999), *The Adventures of Felix*, *Im Juli* (*In July*, Fatih Akın (2000), *Jeunesse dorée* (*Golden Youth*, Zaïda Ghorab-Volta, 2001) and *Exils* (*Exiles*, Tony Gatlif, 2004) tend to be solitary individuals, couples or groups of friends rather than families.
9. In 2009, the West German Broadcasting Corporation (WDR) programmed a series of feature films, documentaries and television dramas that examined *HeimatGefühle* (HeimatFeelings). Although advertised as a *Heimatfilm* programme, it included films such as *Solino* and *We Have Forgotten to Return*, about the experience of migration and diaspora. A public symposium and a documentary entitled *Suddenly So Much Heimat: Changing Identity in Film, Culture and Society* inaugurated a critical revision of what *Heimat* actually means in the age of transnational migration and cultural diversity; see Westdeutscher Rundfunk (2011).
10. '[. . .] so entsteht in der Welt etwas, das allen in der Kindheit scheint und worin noch niemand war: Heimat'; the English translation is that of the author.

11. For a discussion of Zeki's queer identity and the film's intertextual references to the Turkish drag artist Zeki Müren, see Kiliçbay (2006) and Berghahn (2009a).
12. With reference to Zeki's sexual orientation, Philip French's observations about *Alice in the Cities* ring true: 'This film could not be made now [...] because of our obsessive fear of anything that might be interpreted as paedophilia' (2008).
13. Ships feature more prominently in historical films about migration, notably *Nuovomondo* (*Golden Door*, Emanuele Crialese, 2006), about a Sicilian family's emigration to America at the turn of the twentieth century, and in films set in countries bordering the Mediterranean, including France and North Africa.
14. Idir is the stage name of Hamid Cheriet, an Algerian musician of Berber origin. Through popularising Kabyle music, he has become a cultural ambassador of the Kabyle people, an ethno-cultural and linguistic Berber community in northern Algeria.
15. Marianne Hirsch and Karen Lury offer compelling readings of the figure of the child in relation to trauma. Considering the preponderance of children in Holocaust narratives, Hirsch notes: 'Culturally, at the end of the twentieth century, the figure of the "child" is an adult construction, the site of adult fantasy, fear, and desire. [...] Less individualized, less marked by the particularities of identity, moreover, children invite multiple projections and identifications. Their photographic images elicit an affiliative and identificatory as well as a protective spectatorial look marked by these investments' (1999: 13). Lury suggests that the figure of the child, especially in films about war, is frequently deployed as a mere cipher and a 'vehicle for adult concerns', rather than being allowed to represent 'its own interests or desires' (2010: 109). The erasure of the child's individual identity is reflected in its impassive or inscrutable face.
16. Prominent examples of road movies with a family focus include *Raising Arizona* (Joel and Ethan Coen, 1987), *Paris, Texas* (Wim Wenders, 1984) and *Little Miss Sunshine* (Jonathan Dayton, Valerie Faris, 2006).
17. The film's title was inspired by an Italian film about the migration of Italian workers from Sicily to Milan, *Il cammino della speranza* (*The Road to Hope*, Pietro Germi, 1950).
18. Yosefa Loshitzky suggests that 'the images of the refugees, with their shabby and battered suitcases, invoke the iconography of the Holocaust. Implicitly, they conflate the memory of World War II's Jewish refugee with the contemporary Muslim refugee, creating [...] a "hybrid refugee"' (2010: 19).
19. These binarisms are not entirely based on nationality. Turkish traffickers are greedy and evil, too, while the Swiss are not all bad. See Brown, Iordanova and Torchin (2010) on films about trafficking, and Mazierska and Rascaroli (2006) on the European travel film, which they distinguish from the road movie.
20. Frederic Jameson (1986) examines magic realism as a particular mode of historical film and distinguishes it from the postmodern 'nostalgia film'.
21. West Germany and Turkey signed a bilateral labour recruitment agreement on 30 October 1961 and, by the end of 1961, 7,000 Turkish 'guest workers' had moved to Germany.
22. Significantly, the euphemism 'guest worker' (*Gastarbeiter*), which was commonly used for labour migrants in the early days of labour migration, is replaced by the flattering designation 'Weltenbürger' (meaning 'citizens of the world' or 'cosmopolitans'), which disavows the low social status and marginality commonly associated with the term 'guest worker'.
23. See http://www.angekommen.com/iberer/Mio/millionster.html and Göktürk, Gramling and Kaes (2007: 36–7) for news coverage of this historic event.
24. Rushdie's evocative account of memory work and the transformation from black and white to colour reads: 'An old photograph in a cheap frame hangs on a wall of the room where I work. It's a picture dating from 1946 of a house into which, at

the time of its taking, I had not yet been born. [. . .] Then I went to visit the house in the photograph and stood outside it, neither daring nor wishing to announce myself to its new owners. [. . .] I was overwhelmed. The photograph had naturally been taken in black and white; and my memory, feeding on such images as this, had begun to see my childhood in the same way, monochromatically. The colours of my history had seeped out of my mind's eye; now my other two eyes were assaulted by colours, by the vividness of the red tiles, the yellow-edged green cactus leaves, the brilliance of bougainvillea creeper. It's probably too romantic to say that that was when my novel *Midnight's Children* was really born; when I realized how much I wanted to restore the past to myself, not in the faded greys of old family-album snapshots, but whole, in CinemaScope and glorious Technicolour' (1991: 9–10).
25. 'Fremde Menschen' sounds like an authentic 1960s popular song but is simply a convincing fake, composed by Stefan Nölle and performed by Julia von Miller.
26. For an excellent documentation of this infamous transit route, see http://www.migration-boell.de/web/integration/47_3027.asp
27. *Le Havre* (Aki Kaurismäki, 2011), a whimsical film about France's attitude to illegal immigrants, uses a similar colour scheme (predominantly garish shades of blue and green) and magical realist elements (such as the sudden blossoming of the cherry tree in front of Marcel and Arletty's house in winter), thereby embellishing a touching tale about the miserable lives of its dispossessed protagonists with a sense of beauty and hope.
28. Mennel (2010) and Naficy (2010) identify 'doubling', whether of narrative structures, character constellations or particular scenes, as a distinctive feature of transnational cinema.
29. The similarity of the names Moses and Momo (short for Mohammed) reinforces the film's premise that Islam and Judaism are in many respects very similar.
30. In 'From pilgrim to tourist – or a short history of identity', Zygmunt Bauman observes that the boundlessness and emptiness of the desert promote the spiritual quest of the pilgrim (referring to the Christian pilgrim and hermit), allowing him to attain almost 'god-like' powers in this 'land of self-creation' (1996: 20).
31. The crossed gateposts in *Le Grand Voyage* correspond to the crossed flower stems that Momo finds on the very first page of the Koran that Monsieur Ibrahim has bequeathed to him. In both films, the cross-over expresses the idea that differences and divides can be overcome when love overrides religious dogma and intolerance. See also Chapter 4, where I discuss how Sufism is imagined as a worldly, non-dogmatic form of Islam in a number of films.
32. As Nezih Erdoğan (2009) and several contributors to Özkan Ezli's (2010) essay collection on *The Edge of Heaven* suggest, Fatih Akın is eager to assume the role of ambassador, promoting the political cause of Turkey's accession to the European union both in interviews and in some of his films.

3. FAMILY MEMORIES, FAMILY SECRETS

Based on the premise that families are held together by their shared remembering and their complicit forgetting, this chapter investigates the dialectical relationship between those past events that families wish to preserve and those moments that are forgotten and shrouded in silence and which, nevertheless, have a habit of coming out. While the first part of the chapter attends to what I shall call 'postmemory documentaries', in which second-generation diasporic filmmakers excavate and reconstruct the migratory histories of their parents, the second part examines fiction films about family secrets and identifies the 'coming out' of queer sons and daughters as the most prevalent one. The rationale for including documentaries in a book devoted to the representation of the family in fiction films is that they make the transmission of memories between the generations their chief concern, interweaving footage from old home movies, faded family photos and testimonial interviews with family members. They bring to the fore how generational belonging shapes the diaspora experience in markedly different ways. By interrogating acts of memory and performing their construction, these documentaries make explicit structures that also underpin feature films about diasporic families, but that are seldom narrativised. Moreover, the avowedly personal nature of these documentaries testifies to the autobiographical impetus that, as illustrated in Chapter 1, is deeply entrenched in much of diasporic cinema.

Both family memories and secrets spin a 'thread of continuity' (Fortier 2005: 184) between the past and present, the generation of the parents and that of their children and subsequent generations. Without the dynamic reconstitution and articulation of the past in acts of memory there would be no sense of continuity, community and identity. This holds particularly true for the cultural memory of diasporic families and communities because it is ruptured by displacement, submerged through trauma and amnesia, and silenced in the official accounts of migration in the hegemonic host society.[1] Diaspora studies privileges the spatial dimension of the diaspora experience, and the approach taken in this book, with its emphasis on journeys, mobility and the production of locality, is no exception. However, Anne-Marie Fortier contends that 'memory rather than territory is the principal ground of identity formation in diaspora cultures, where "territory" is de-centred and exploded into multiple settings' (2005: 184). When it comes to memory, the attempt to disaggregate time and space may be a futile endeavour, since these intrinsically interconnected categories coagulate in memory, as the discussion of certain chronotopes in the previous chapter and Pierre Nora's aptly named concept of *lieux de mémoires* illustrate. The emergence of such sites, 'where memory crystallizes and secretes itself' (1989: 7), is the result of the 'acceleration of history' in modernity and a loss of 'real' or 'lived memory' with its attendant ritual practices (8). This, Nora argues, has led to people's obsessive pursuit to record and preserve the material traces of the past in museums, monuments, commemorative practices, archives and collections, through which 'the responsibility of remembering' is delegated from individual and collective memory to the archive (13). In a socio-historical context in which '*milieux de mémoire*, real environments of memory' (7) no longer exist, individuals and social groups are called upon to act as custodians of their own memories. According to Nora, such 'commemorative vigilance' is vitally important for minorities because without it 'history would soon sweep them away' (12). Never before has there been such a keen interest in family genealogy, as the surge of websites and television programmes on family history indicates. Family photographs, home movies and the postmemory documentaries considered below are such *lieux de mémoires*, where records of a particular past are preserved and articulated. Situated at the interface of ethnographic and autobiographical documentary, these postmemory films fulfil precisely the function Nora ascribes to *lieux de mémoire*: not only do they 'block the work of forgetting' (19), but they also 'protect the trappings of identity' (16), charging, in particular, diasporic and minoritarian subjects, whose collective pasts have, in the main, been excluded from the official memory of the host societies, to reaffirm and proclaim publicly their collective identity and heritage.

Excavating the Parents' Stories in Postmemory Documentaries

One of my key concerns is how diasporic memory – that is, the memory of a particular collective – relates to individual and familial memory. How are memories transmitted across the generations and how is this process represented in cinema, which, as Isabelle McNeill outlines in *Memory and the Moving Image*, is a privileged medium for conceptualising 'the processes of memory, because of its potential to represent space and time, to juxtapose sonic and visual images and to mirror the associational movements of memory itself' (2010: 17–18)? And, finally, what role do diasporic filmmakers play in constructing counter-memories that cannot be readily reconciled with the hegemonic cultural memory of the host societies?

In her seminal study, *Family Frames: Photography, Narrative and Postmemory*, Marianne Hirsch provides a relevant critical framework of how memory is transmitted from one generation to the next.[2] Hirsch, who developed the concept of postmemory in relation to children of Holocaust survivors, distinguishes between memory based on events actually experienced by the remembering subject, and

> postmemory [which] is distinguished from memory by generational distance and from history by deep personal connection. Postmemory is a powerful and very particular form of memory precisely because its connection to its object or source is mediated not through recollection but through an imaginative investment and creation. [...] Postmemory characterizes the experience of those who grow up dominated by narratives that preceded their birth, whose own belated stories are evacuated by the stories of the previous generation. (1997: 22)

Whereas history may elide or even purposely obliterate memories that cannot be reconciled with official (often heroic) accounts of the past or that appear too insignificant to be recorded, the 'deep personal connection' that underpins postmemory accords a rather different meaning and affective value to events that would otherwise be forgotten or repressed.[3] Family archives reflect this personal connection since they contain what a particular group of people deems worth preserving and remembering. Therefore, family photos and family narratives, whether mediated through letters, diaries, oral history or home videos, are the sources through which memory is passed down from one generation to the next. For second or subsequent generations of diasporic subjects, who grow up far away from their ancestral homeland, grandparents and other relatives, this process of retrieval and reconstruction is often more complex. If parents are the sole or chief source of information about the past, their memories cannot be corrected and complemented by accounts from other relatives. Memory is always shaped by 'secondary revision. It is always already a text, a signifying system' (Kuhn 2002: 161), carefully edited in order to provide a plausible justification for migration, or fragmented and incoherent, the result of fading memory and amnesia. Memory transmitted from just one source therefore tends to be more skewed and incomplete. Such gaps of indeterminacy can be filled and adjusted by what Alison Landsberg has aptly termed 'prosthetic memory'. She identifies prosthetic memory, a type of memory that is as artificial and as useful as a prosthesis, as particularly relevant in the context of mass migration and diaspora, where generational ties have been ruptured and the 'traditional modes for transmitting cultural, ethnic and racial memory – both memories passed from parent to child and those disseminated through community life – [have become] increasingly inadequate' (2004: 2). The circulation of images and narratives about the past via film and television and other forms of commodified mass culture substitutes the more organic, hereditary forms of memory transmission unavailable to fractured and dispersed diasporic communities.

It is perhaps worth explaining that the distinction between Hirsch's 'postmemory' and Landsberg's 'prosthetic memory' is not always entirely consistent. In *Family Frames*, Hirsch stresses that postmemory is based on 'a deep personal connection' (1997: 22), which I interpret as belonging to the same family, kinship or other social or ethnic group. But in 'Surviving Images', Hirsch defines postmemory more loosely as a *'retrospective witnessing* by adoption', which allows for the inscription of 'traumatic experiences – and thus also the memories – of others' into one's own life story (2001: 10). Understood this way, postmemory would be interchangeable with prosthetic memory, which is not circumscribed by 'natural' belonging to a particular group or ethnicity, but instead has the ability to engender 'empathy and social responsibility as well as political alliances that transcend race, class and gender [and that serve as] the basis for mediated collective identification and the production of potentially counter-hegemonic public spheres' (Landsberg 2004: 21). While I concede that postmemory and prosthetic memory overlap in the sense that gaps in the process of transmission within the family may be filled by public accounts and mass media images, they vary in relation to their emotional intensity and structure. The 'deep personal connection' of postmemory would presumably make it more powerful in terms of affect than the bonds of empathy and social responsibility artificially constructed by prosthetic memory, no matter how socially desirable these allegiances may be.

The documentaries I consider below are therefore postmemory texts; they trace and perform the processes of memory within the family, availing themselves of a range of testimonial records. In the mid-1990s, Turkish German, Maghrebi French and Asian British filmmakers embarked on a shared yet independently pursued project. They recorded and preserved their parents' memories of migration to the old Europe, where their fathers, who were subsequently joined by their mothers, siblings and themselves, started new lives as factory or construction workers and ship builders, cleaners, teachers and doctors. What these films have in common is their intensely personal motivation, addressed explicitly in *We Have Forgotten To Return* by the Turkish German filmmaker Fatih Akın:

> I wanted to make a film about my family. I wanted to show how they came over to Germany and that they did not even have a loo in their flat. And now their children are working in a consulate and make films. Perhaps I wanted to make this film so that one day I can show to my own children who their grandparents were. Because my children are likely to be a lot more German than I am, if you know what I mean, supposing that they have a purely German mother. So that I can say to my children: 'Look, these are your grandparents, that's where they came from, that's how they spoke German and that's what made them tick'.[4]

But beyond the desire to document his Turkish heritage for the next generation, the film also reflects Akın's attempt to locate his own bicultural existence on the intersecting coordinates of memory and migration.

Meanwhile, Seyhan Derin's film *Ich bin Tochter meiner Mutter* (*I Am My Mother's Daughter*, 1996) pursues a different, though no less personal agenda. Inscribed in it is the desire to construct a feminist counter-narrative to Turkish patriarchal discourses on the family, in which the birth of a son is perceived as a far greater blessing than that of a daughter. The title obliquely refers to the saying 'You are the daughter of your father' but, by replacing 'father' with 'mother', challenges the model of the patrilineal and patriarchal family. In a letter Derin reads in the film's opening sequence, she accuses her father of having severed the father–daughter bond. The male counterpart to this 'daughter text' – a term Hamid Naficy (2001: 127) uses for such dialogic narratives – is Yüksel Yavuz's *My Father, the Guest Worker*. The film begins with a voice-over, spoken in accented German by the Kurdish German filmmaker, in which he recalls how he joined his father, who had been working in Germany since 1968 in a fish factory and later on a shipbuilding wharf, to ease his pain of solitude. Like the other postmemory films, this one, too, is motivated by an intensely personal agenda. It constitutes an attempt to preserve his father's efforts and achievements as a guest worker in Germany, achievements that have clearly not been recognised publicly: 'I saw that my father worked like crazy in order to leave some traces that would prove that he was esteemed and irreplaceable, traces that would compensate for the traces with which hard physical labour had scarred his body. The last and most durable trace was me. He had called upon me to be his successor' (Yavuz 1995).[5] *My Father, the Guest Worker* bears witness to the plight, the exploitation and the transitoriness of his father's sojourn in Germany and to that of other guest workers like him. The conjoining of the familial with the social role in the film title reflects the intertwining of individual, familial and collective memory. As Maurice Halbwachs (1985) and Jan Assmann (1995), amongst others, have argued, individual memories and self-images are inevitably composed in relation to the memories of the various social groups to which individuals belong and therefore mirror and refract long-standing inequalities of race, class, gender and ethnicity.[6] In this sense, the personal is always political too. That is why Yavuz's documentary is as much about family memories as it is about the collective memory of Turkish and Kurdish labour migrants in Germany.

Michael Renov refers to films such as these as 'domestic ethnography', which he defines as a documentary practice that

> engages in the documentation of family members, or less literally of people with whom the maker has maintained long-standing everyday relations and has thus achieved a level of casual intimacy. Because the lives of the artist and subject are interlaced through communal or blood ties, the documentation of the one tends to implicate the other in

complicated ways; indeed, consanguinity and co(i)mplication are domestic ethnography's defining features. (1999: 141)

Renov contends that, while ostensibly focusing on family members, especially mothers and fathers, domestic ethnography is actually a form of autobiographical practice 'that offers up the maker and his subject locked in a family embrace' (2008: 57). Though seemingly unearthing their parents' memories, in reality, the filmmakers seek 'to construct self-knowledge through recourse to the familial other [. . .] Familial investigation [. . .] is a kind of identity sleuthing in which family-bound figures – progenitors and progeny – are mined for clues' (141, 142) about the filmmaker's own identity and sensibility. Self-understanding, these films argue, is inextricably linked to an understanding of family history and ancestry. In diasporic families the desire for knowledge of the familial Other is particularly acute since it is charged with anxieties about losing access to the parents' past as a consequence of displacement and amnesia linked to trauma.

Yamina Benguigui was unable to access her own parents' memories of migration when making *Immigrant Memories* and her parents do not feature in the film. At the age of eighteen, she broke off contact with her father upon infringing his strict rules about marriage and sex (Durmelat 2000: 173). Meanwhile, her mother was never able to talk about the experience of leaving Algeria and starting a new life in France since she was utterly traumatised by it (McNeill 2010: 104). Hence, Benguigui relied on other fathers and mothers to reconstruct the memories of her 'family', understood as a trope of kinship and shared origins (see Gilroy 1993b, discussed in Chapter 1). Benguigui uses the familial roles of 'The Fathers', 'The Mothers' and 'The Children' as titles and structuring devices in this tripartite documentary in order to express her affiliation and solidarity with immigrants of Maghrebi descent, whose voices and memories she records in a series of interviews. In the eponymous book *Immigrant Memories*, the filmmaker, who is herself of Algerian descent, describes the project as 'the narrative of my journey at the heart of the Maghrebi immigration in France. The history of fathers, mothers, children, the history of my father, of my mother. My history' (cited in Ingram and Martin 2003: 113).

Immigrant Memories has been described as a 'commemorative monument' that shows 'the history of immigration as family history' and as 'THE document on immigration' (Durmelat 2000: 174, 175, 172). To construct this gigantic, 'collective narrative of an uprooted people' (Ingram and Martin 2003: 113), Yamina Benguigui conducted 350 interviews over two years and spent nine months editing 600 hours of rushes. Despite remaining silent and invisible in the documentary, Benguigui assumes an important place through the looks, smiles and tears that the Fathers, Mothers and Children share with her (and with us). The intensely emotional accounts of their individual memories add up to a 'polyphonic autobiographical documentary' (Ingram and Martin 2003: 112), albeit one in which the filmmaker has erased signs of her own presence, lending those who have been silenced for some forty years an even more powerful voice. Despite the intention to distance herself from her own story, Benguigui revealed, the process of making *Immigrant Memories* 'brought me back to it [. . . and] lent me an identity – as a director – so that I could reconstruct the one I was neglecting – as a daughter of immigrants' (cited in Durmelat 2000: 173).

The filmmaker's absence is very unusual for a postmemory film, yet it has the interesting effect of making the audience the immediate recipient of the testimonies, many of which are deeply moving self-revelations. In this way, *Immigrant Memories* reveals more explicitly than other postmemory films its underlying political intent. Yamina Benguigui is concerned not only with salvaging the first generation's memories for posterity but also with claiming a place in French society for her collective family of Maghrebi immigrants. In order not to jeopardise the project's reconciliatory and integrationist agenda, certain contentious issues (addressed in the eponymous novel), such as a young girl's decision to take the Islamic veil, are omitted. Such compromises paid off. When the French television station Canal Plus broadcast the three-part documentary in May 1997 (repeated in June 1997 and released in cinemas in 1998), it was celebrated as a major media event and garnered the accolade of 'memory entrepreneuse' for Benguigui (Durmelat 2000).

The documentary juxtaposes the collective memory of North African immigrants with that of state officials who devised or enforced immigration, labour and housing policies and thereby shaped the experiences of immigrants in France. Interspersed with these complementary accounts is archival news footage that shows immigrants arriving in France, male labour migrants learning the French language in a classroom, and President Giscard D'Estaing paying a visit to one of the *bidonvilles* where most of the first-generation immigrants lived until, following the Loi Debré in 1964, these muddy and desolate shantytowns were bulldozed down.[7]

In all of these postmemory films, family photographs function as mnemonic crutches, triggering recollections that unfold in the extended testimonial dialogues. Much has been written on the close connection between the institution of the family and photography. Susan Sontag describes family photography as a 'social rite' that goes 'with family life' (1979: 8) and that came into existence in America and Europe when 'that claustrophobic unit, the nuclear family, was being carved out of a much larger family aggregate' (9), the extended family. At that crucial moment of family change, 'photography came along to memorialize, to restate symbolically, the imperilled continuity and vanishing extendedness of family life' and to 'supply a token presence of the dispersed relatives' (9). Scholars like Sontag, Roland Barthes (1981), Pierre Bourdieu (1990), Marianne Hirsch (1997) and Annette Kuhn (2002) identify photography as 'the family's primary instrument of self-knowledge and representation' (Hirsch 1997: 6) and as a strategy to perpetuate family memory. When George Eastman invented the easy-to-use 'Kodak' in 1888, he had amateurs and,

Figure 3.1 Archival footage in *Immigrant Memories* (Yamina Benguigui, 1997) preserves childhood memories of growing up in a shantytown

especially, families in mind. 'She'll always be your little girl since you took a picture' (cited in Kuhn 2002: 23) was one of the company's advertising slogans in 1955, promising that photography would counteract forgetting. The insertion of photography in memory texts confers a seal of authenticity upon them and imbues subjective recollections with a sense of objective evidence: 'Look, this is how our family used to be', they seem to be saying. However, Sontag reminds us that photography merely gives us 'an imaginary possession of the past that is unreal' (9). Far from providing reliable evidence, Hirsch argues, family photographs immobilise 'the flow of family life into a series of snapshots' and thereby 'perpetuate [. . .] familial myths' (1997: 7).

Susan Sontag and Pierre Bourdieu both draw attention to the performative nature of family photography, which 'becomes a rite of family life' that constructs 'a portable kit of images that bears witness to its connectedness' (Sontag 1979: 8). Family photographs play a crucial rule in 'solemnizing and immortalizing the high points of family life [thereby] reinforcing the integration of the family group by reasserting the sense that it has both of itself and of its unity' (Bourdieu 1990: 19). The 'family function' of this photographic practice is reflected in the occasions that are captured: weddings, christenings, family holidays and other celebrations, showing the family group 'at a moment of its highest integration' (19). It is these moments that are preserved from the passing of time and forgetting in family photographs and family albums, the latter constituting yet another layer of constructedness, the result of further editorial decisions: who is included and excluded? At what point in time (wedding or birth of the first child) does the family (album) begin? By eliding the more mundane and difficult aspects of family life, family photography is a key instrument in the construction of familial mythology; it captures what families aspire to, rather than what they actually are.

Many of the photos with which the postmemory films are interlaced fulfil precisely this function, depicting in black and white or sepia, but rarely in colour, the happiest moments of family life, moments that are simultaneously universal and highly personal: wedding photos, mothers with their newborn babies or small children, a group of siblings, faded and creased portraits of family ancestors. 'We are who we are because of who *they* were' (Renov 2008: 55), these photos seem to assert, tracing the filmmakers' genealogy. The snapshots inserted in *Immigrant Memories*, especially in The Children's section, document the *beurs*' maturation from childhood through adolescence to adulthood, a development characterised by a gradual reduction or disappearance of the visible markers of their North African heritage. This is particularly evident in the series of photographs accompanying the story of Soraya Guezlane, an attractive female lawyer. Her once long, frizzy hair is now tamed in a sophisticated coiffure, the dress underneath the lawyer's robe is elegantly French, and the interview settings, a neo-classical law court and Guezlane's office, stacked with leather-bound law books, indicate that she has 'made it' in French society. Yet, in contradistinction to the observations made above, the photos that punctuate the narratives of The Children mostly show isolated individuals, the earlier selves of those giving testimony. This, coupled with the film's tripartite structure, which separates Fathers, Mothers and Children, presumably because gender and generation shape the experience of migration in distinct ways, suggests that displacement and dispersal have ruptured familial ties.

The photo in the opening sequence of *I Am My Mother's Daughter* conveys a similar idea. A full frame of an old passport cuts to a close-up of the passport photo, showing Derin's mother with her four daughters. Three of the faces are crossed out and a stamp marks the IDs as invalid. The annulled faces are perturbing, symbolising the father's rejection of these daughters because they did not comply with the return migration to Turkey he tried to impose upon his family. What has become invalid here is not just the photo on the identity card but also the sense of familial belonging and cohesion. Derin's film project constitutes an attempt to rebuild the family that her father destroyed through aligning herself with her mother's lineage and creating a female genealogy.

The project pursued by all of these postmemory documentaries is that of family reunion or reconciliation. The process of filmmaking reconstitutes families by bringing them together in a series of interviews, home movie footage and family photography – or, in the case of *Immigrant Memories*, reuniting the Fathers, Mothers and Children in one triptych. The dialogic stance of *My Father, the Guest Worker*, in which Yavuz addresses his father, and the letter to her mother, which Seyhan Derin reads out in a voice-over at the beginning of *I Am My Mother's Daughter*, proclaim the films' agenda: namely, to suture family ties that have been severed. But this is not the only sense in which these documentaries fulfil a performative function, similar to the 'performative utterances' theorised by J. L. Austin in *How to Do Things with Words* (1962). They are 'performative documentaries', as defined by Stella Bruzzi, in as much as they 'perform the actions they name' (2006: 197). They 'accentuate', rather than 'mask, the means of production' and, as self-reflexive documentaries, 'highlight the performative quality of documentary' by emphasising 'issues of authorship and construction' (187, 197). With the exception of *Immigrant Memories*, in which Benguigui decided to erase her voice and presence when editing the footage, these semi-autobiographical documentaries abundantly 'feature the intrusive presence of the filmmaker' (187) and, in the case of *I Am My Mother's Daughter*, even several versions of the filmmaker's self.

The final sequence shows a cameraman operating a Bolex 16 mm camera and then cuts to Seyhan Derin, who is being filmed amidst the verdant hills of her native village, Caycuma. She is directing a young girl to play what looks like a younger version of herself. Derin asks the girl, who is dressed in her Sunday best, to run down the hill and wave goodbye 'to her'. The goodbye is directed at a similar-looking little girl, presumably another alter ego of the filmmaker. The grainy black-and-white footage of this other girl, travelling all by herself on the fast-moving train, occurs three times in the film. It is a surreal and intensely haunting scene, not least because the girl tries to open the door of the train compartment in order to get out, only to discover that she has been locked in. Mine Eren interprets the scene as the 'melodrama of a girl who was forcefully separated from her Heimat' (2003: 47) – perhaps a guest worker's daughter en route to join her father, as insinuated by the archive footage of labour migrants arriving at a German train station, with which it is intercut the first time we see it. As implied by the shot-reverse-shot, in which the girl on the train smiles at the other girl, who waves goodbye, the re-enactment of the trauma of departure and separation brings about some form of reconciliation. 'It's a dream image', the director explains in the final frame to the little girl in the smart dress, thereby assigning a therapeutic function to this postmemory documentary; through the re-enactment of memories that haunted her she may have become reconciled with her past.

I FOR INDIA: PROJECTING TRANSNATIONAL MEMORY TRANSGENERATIONALLY

I for India furnishes another example of a documentary that performs the transmission of memories and, thereby, constructs family cohesion and continuity across different continents and generations. Sandhya Suri's film has been described as 'a chronicle of immigration in Britain, from the Sixties to the present day, as seen through the eyes of one Asian family and their movie camera' (Icarus Films 2007). That the personal experience of one particular family of immigrants can be regarded as representative of immigration in Britain per se is a bold assertion that disregards the specificities of ethnicity and class as regards the Suri family, whose lives are chronicled in this postmemory documentary. Still, the reviewer's claim cannot be completely dismissed. After all, the coalescence of the private and the public in memory work and memory texts is an issue that has been eloquently addressed by Marianne Hirsch in

Family Frames and Annette Kuhn in *Family Secrets*, among others. The fact that both take a feminist approach is not coincidental, given that 'the personal is political' was once the battle cry of the women's movement. In fact, Michael Renov explains the dramatic growth of personal and autobiographical documentary practice since the 1970s as a consequence of second-stage feminism, when 'the politics of social movements (e.g. antiwar, civil rights, the student movement)' were displaced 'by the politics of identity. [. . .] The women's movement ushered in an era in which a range of "personal" issues – race, sexuality, and ethnicity – became politicised' (Renov 2004: 176–7). He cites Annette Kuhn's *Family Secrets: Acts of Memory and Imagination*, a self-reflexive engagement with her own photographs and childhood memories, which offers ample evidence for his observation. Reflecting upon the public relevance of her ostensibly personal memory work, Kuhn proposes that, 'as far as memory [. . .] is concerned, private and public turn out in practice to be less readily separable than conventional wisdom would have us believe' (2002: 4). The memories of an individual can never be untangled from

> an extended network of meanings that bring together the personal with the familial, the cultural, the economic, the social, the historical. Memory work makes it possible to explore connections between public historical events, structures of feeling, family dramas, relations of class, national identity and gender, and 'personal' memory. (5)

But if, as Kuhn suggests, individual and collective memories inevitably coalesce, then the semi-autobiographical postmemory films emphatically foreground this process of convergence. Sandhya Suri's documentary *I for India* illustrates the intertwining of personal family memories with Britain's collective memory of immigration by relating the domestic to the wider social context of Britain's shifting – but, perhaps, ultimately unchanging – attitudes towards immigration. Like Benguigui's documentary trilogy, *I for India* is a polyphonic postmemory film, a compilation of home movie footage shot by Sandhya Suri's father and uncle over a period of forty years, interviews with family members, clips from BBC television documentaries relating to immigration (*Make Yourself at Home*, *The Dark Million*, *Immigrant Doctors* and *The End of the Line*) and other documents, including family photographs, which appear in a prominent place as the final credits roll.

When, in 1966, Sandhya Suri's father, Yash Pal Suri, emigrated with his wife and the first of their three daughters to England, where he took up a position as a doctor in a hospital in Middlesbrough, he wanted to share the experience of his new life with his brother and extended family back home. So he bought two Super 8 cameras, reel-to-reel tape recorders and projectors and sent one of each to his brother, keeping the other set of equipment for himself.[8] Over the next forty years, he and his brother exchanged what Sandhya Suri calls 'cine-letters'. Yash Suri's home movies capture the national idiosyncrasies, as

Figure 3.2 Photos in *I for India* (Sandhya Suri, 2005) capture the highlights of family life

well as the racism, of the British and, most importantly, the highlights of family life: children's birthday parties, the occasional trip to the seaside and the colourful lights of Blackpool. They also chart the family's settlement in England, marked by milestones such as Yash's promotion to more senior positions and the purchase of a house. This is perhaps the most significant milestone because it signifies permanence, despite Yash's emphatic protestations in one of the cine-letters that he could never call this house 'home', since a home anywhere else but in India would be inconceivable.

Meanwhile, his brother sends regular cine-letters from Meerut in the Indian state of Uttar Pradesh, featuring family get-togethers and festivities in the community. Some years down the line, the tone of the audiotapes changes, as Yash's parents put considerable emotional pressure on him, 'their favourite son', to return. Eventually, in 1982, triggered by Yash's intense remorse about his absence during his mother's fatal illness, the Suri family returns to Meerut. Since the family's reunion in Meerut makes the exchange of further cine-letters unnecessary, there is a gap in the home movie footage, which Sandhya Suri fills with a retrospective account of life back in Meerut. Shots of the buzzing, colourful street life in Meerut, as well as the squalor and poverty, are interspersed with the testimonies of family members, who recall, in the early 2000s, when *I for India* was shot, how they felt about their return to India, almost twenty years before. Yash describes how his heart was filled with an overwhelming sense of happiness at being reunited with 'the green, green grass of home'. But this did not last long. After only nine months, the Suris decide to go back to England. The film's final section offers a few glimpses of family life since then, including the wedding of the oldest daughter, the middle daughter's emigration to Australia and the parents' emotional struggle to come to terms with the fact that the family history of transnational dispersal is repeating itself – only this time, *they* are the ones left behind.

Although the film remains reticent about how family members in Meerut reacted towards Yash's decision to leave India for good, the absence of cine-letters arriving in neatly labelled cardboard boxes from India could be seen as an expression of resentment and estrangement – though Yash's attachment to his homeland apparently remains the same. The rhetoric of patriotism that informs the film throughout is emphatically reinforced at the end, as Yash's voice-over accompanies the close-up of a spinning audiotape: 'Please do not underestimate Y. P. Suri with regards to his patriotism, his loyalty ... no matter that he did not succeed in his own country ... to resettle. The love for my soil hasn't diminished ... I'm a true Indian'. This reaffirmation of being Indian at heart – a rhetorical strategy also in evidence in countless contemporary Bollywood films about Non-Resident Indians – gives away Yash's ambivalence. Symptomatically, he switches from Hindi to English, the language his relatives in India do not like to hear him use on the audiotapes, while the transition from the third to the first person reveals his ambivalent sense of identity and belonging. The final frame, a reprisal of the opening frame, captures the thirty-three-year-old Yash Suri against the backdrop of pure white snow. But whereas the opening frame is a moving image of the young man frolicking in the snow, the final sequence culminates in a freeze frame, signifying that his migratory quest came to a halt when he chose to settle in England – and this despite his nostalgic memory of India.

Dialectical tensions of this kind structure *I for India* throughout, reflecting, on the one hand, Yash's ambivalent sense of belonging and, on the other, the contradictions between familial memory and official discourse on immigration in Britain, included in the film as footage from the above-mentioned BBC programmes. In *Make Yourself at Home: A Weekly Programme for Indian and Pakistani Viewers* (1969), the presenter explains how to operate a light switch: 'If I press the switch on the wall, the light will come on'. Instantly and rather ironically, the screen goes dark before the film title *I for India* appears white on a black screen. Suri pokes fun at the programme's patronising attitude, which implies that migrants from the Indian sub-continent are unfamiliar with such sophisticated technology, by proving it wrong. Similarly, the commentator of the programme *The Dark Million* (1966) asserts that immigrants 'create an atmosphere of foreignness, very different from the sort of atmosphere British people are used to', by bringing their own food stuffs, films and languages to Britain. The black-and-white footage of turban-wearing Sikhs, ethnic food shops and a large Indian family performing a religious ceremony that involves an open fire (presumably posing a fire hazard) in the small garden of their terraced house gives way to colour footage of modern terraced houses in the Suris' neighbourhood and the no less strange customs of the British, such as their passion for gardening and their obsession with mowing their lawns.

Figure 3.3 Like father, like daughter . . . Yash Suri inspecting a film strip in *I for India* (Sandhya Suri, 2005)

Comparable to the decentred perspective of *Almanya – Welcome to Germany* discussed in the previous chapter, here, too, a mirror is held up to the 'natives', who are 'Othered' in the process. The contrapuntal relationship between the BBC programmes and the archive of home movies exposes the prejudices underpinning the official discourse on migration. The diasporic family, one of 'the dark million' that comes to light in this postmemory film, identifies the Suris as a paragon of successful integration rather than as importers of 'an island of their own culture', as suggested by the xenophobic programme *The Dark Million*.

What makes *I for India* a particularly interesting postmemory text is its complex layering and intertwining of different constructions of memory, coupled with its self-reflexive engagement with the medialisation of memories. The film draws attention to the important role played by advances in media technology in facilitating transnational communication between far-flung family members, as the exchange of cine-letters is superseded by the more instant communication via webcam with their daughter in Australia. *I for India* expresses a tender affection for the materiality that has made the transmission of memories across generations and across continents possible, as the camera lingers on the old Super 8 camera and on Yash's hands, threading the film into the old-fashioned projector, before he settles in a darkened room to relive the past by watching one of the home movies shot several decades before. Sandhya Suri appears to have inherited, along with her father's archive of home movies, a playful and self-reflexive approach to filmmaking that is also evident in her father's amateur films.

One of Yash's carefully crafted home movies from the 1960s is entitled

'East and West' and shows the English landscape, houses and railway tracks covered in thick snow. Commenting on the novel experience of ice and snow, 'East and West' uses the theme tune of one of the big box office hits at the time, David Lean's *Doctor Zhivago* (1965), remembered for its vast snow-covered landscapes and the magical frozen house with icicles. The director follows her father's cue by inserting similar intertextual references in *I for India*. For example, Yash's account of his childhood and education in India, commencing with the words, 'I was born, Yash Pal Suri, in Punjab, India in 1932', is illustrated not just by old family photos but also by references to Indian cinema. A song performed by Lata Mangeshkar, from the Hindi film *Shor* (Manoj Kumar, 1972), accompanies the black-and-white footage of rural India in the 1930s and creates a sound bridge to the preceding scene and another filmic reference. As Yash looks out from the kitchen window of his terraced house in Darlington, a superimposition transforms the view of a quintessentially British back garden, enclosed by a wood panel fence and adorned by a small statue of a female figure, into the wide-open space of the yellow mustard fields of Punjab, through which an Indian woman in a bright orange sari is walking. This particular image of an idealised rural India has been invoked in so many Bollywood films that it has crystallised into a visual cliché of a deep yearning for Mother India. The superimposition marks the convergence of Yash's individual memory and nostalgia for his native Punjab with prosthetic memory that is 'not premised on any claim of authenticity or "natural" ownership' (Landsberg 2004: 9). The clichéd image of the yellow fields of Punjab is indicative of a loss of authenticity that has affected both Yash, whose 'real' memories of India are fading and need to be complemented by mass-mediated memories, and the next generation. The assumption that the prosthetic memory corresponds with Sandhya Suri's vantage point is confirmed by the temporal disjuncture between the grainy footage of rural India in the 1930s, accompanied by a song from the 1970s *Shor*. The anachronism signals the impossibility of reclaiming an authentic past and underscores how memory is always filtered through (and distorted by) emotions. The montage of what looks like footage from Hindi cinema,[9] family photos, news coverage of the Indian brain drain (of which Yash Suri was part in the 1960s) and Yash's autobiographical narrative in the voice-over commentary makes explicit the multiple layering and complexity of postmemory processes. Similarly, the Suris' disillusionment with a much-changed India that does not live up to their fond recollections and their decision to leave Meerut for good, is accompanied by an old Hindi film song, 'Waqt ne Kiya Kya Haseen Situm', performed by Geeta Dutt in *Kaagaz Ke Phool* (*Paper Flowers*, Guru Dutt, 1959).[10] The intermeshing of personal memories with popular fantasies, as constructed in Indian cinema, emphasises yet again that the 'I' in *I for India* is as much individual as it is collective. The homophonic pun of 'I' and 'eye' and the superimposition of the mustard fields of Punjab on to the English back garden may also suggest that, despite having settled in Britain, Yash Suri's eyes are still fixed on

India, or rather on the nostalgic memories of an India that he was unable to retrieve.

I for India is a complex postmemory film with a palimpsest structure, which performs acts of memory and probes their effectiveness in spinning 'threads of continuity' that hold the family together. While the cine-letters were originally recorded in order to keep the dialogue with the extended family in India going, in the film's final sequence, Yash assigns a different purpose to his treasured archive. Using a combination of Hindi and English, he explains: 'The sketch I have given of this period of my life . . . I think our youngsters will gain a lot of insight about the early struggles'. By dedicating *I for India* 'To my parents', Sandhya Suri acknowledges that she is willing to take on her father's legacy and act as the custodian of her family's memories and to keep them alive. By 'going public' with the audio-visual archive, she transgresses the boundary between the private and the public sphere, thereby lending private family memories political significance.

Unspeakable Memories, Shameful Secrets and Revelations

Memory is not an archive of past events and facts but an intensely personal, emotional process that depends as much on remembering as it does on forgetting. Since it is constantly rewritten to suit the needs of the present, memory changes over time. In the essay 'Screen Memories', Sigmund Freud notes that 'our childhood memories show us our earliest years not as they were but as they appeared at the later periods when the memories were aroused. In these periods of arousal, the childhood memories did not, as people are accustomed to say, *emerge*; they were *formed* at that time' ([1899] 1995: 126). Such 'screen memories', which are not accurate recollections of past events, have the function of concealing experiences and desires occurring in the present (125). In family narratives in which memories provide the raw material such re-adjustments and revisions play a crucial role in the creation of family myths that allow us to imagine our family as a happy and socially acceptable unit. Annette Kuhn observes in *Family Secrets* that such

> narratives of identity are shaped as much by what is left out of the account – whether forgotten or repressed – as by what is actually told. Secrets haunt our memory-stories, giving them pattern and shape. Family secrets are the other side of the family's public face, of the stories families tell themselves, and the world, about themselves. Characters and happenings that do not slot neatly into the flow of the family narrative are ruthlessly edited out. (Kuhn 2002: 2)

How this editorial process, if we may call it that, actually works has been studied in particular in the context of the transgenerational transmission of traumatic or shameful family secrets. In their pioneering study *The Shell and the Kernel*, the psychoanalyst couple Nicolas Abraham and Maria Torok explore how family secrets, if undisclosed, become 'phantoms' that haunt subsequent generations: 'The phantom is the formation of the unconscious that has never been conscious – for good reason. It passes [. . .] from the parent's unconscious into the child's' (1994: 173). In folklore and literature (*Hamlet* functions as the paradigmatic text here), this psychological phenomenon is usually explained as the haunting of the dead 'who took unspeakable secrets to the grave' (171) and who return to haunt the living. But 'what haunts', Abraham explains, 'are not the dead, but the gaps left within us by the secrets of others'. Put differently, 'the phantom which returns to haunt bears witness to the existence of the dead buried within the other' (171, 175).[11] Shameful secrets, such as incest, child abuse, adultery, suicide, illegitimacy, bankruptcy, psychiatric internment and socially stigmatised illnesses, which are not talked about in the family and are therefore 'forgotten' instead of being mourned, may manifest themselves as a phantom in subsequent generations. A particular family member becomes the guardian of the unspoken family secret that escapes from a poorly shut family tomb, and 'keeps it locked up in his heart, in his body, as if in a coffin or "crypt" inside. And from time to time, this ghost seems to leave the crypt and manifest itself after one or two generations' (Schützenberger 1998: 44). The guardians of such family secrets, or phantoms, may have nightmares and obsessions that seem inexplicable and which cannot be overcome, or, as Anne Ancelin Schützenberger suggests in *The Ancestor Syndrome*, they feel compelled to repeat the shameful secret in their own lives.

Mira Nair's film *Mississippi Masala* (1991) illustrates how such an undisclosed family secret – and one that is neither fully revealed in the film nor widely addressed in critical discourse surrounding the film – is re-enacted in the next generation.[12] The film centres on the Lohas, an Indian family whose migratory trajectory takes them from Uganda – from where they are expelled under General Idi Amin's campaign to reclaim Africa for black Africans in 1972 – via the UK to America, where they settle in a small town in Mississippi. There, Mina, the only daughter of Jay and Kinnu Loha, falls in love with the African American Demetrius, an attractive and ambitious self-made man played by Denzel Washington. Whereas the South Asian family and community disapprove of the interracial romance, Demetrius's family and community show no signs of racial prejudice. The ostensible tolerance may actually reflect the internalisation of racial hierarchies based on lighter and darker shades of brown skin; amongst the black community, the dark-skinned Indian Mina is fair.

Yet, interestingly, the film offers another explanation: Mina describes herself as a 'masala', a mixture, a 'bunch of hot spices', and conceives of herself as the embodiment of hybridity, simultaneously African, Indian and American. A number of clues suggest that she is half-African not just by virtue of being born in Uganda but also in terms of bloodline and descent. A scene early on in the film shows the Loha family's expulsion from Uganda, bidding a hasty and tearful farewell to their African friends at the bus station. Perhaps the embrace between Kinnu and Okelo is more intimate than one would expect if he were merely her husband's best friend. Jay, who observes the farewell, looks distinctly uncomfortable, and the fact that Jay feels betrayed by Okelo (albeit on political grounds during Idi Amin's racial homogenisation campaign) reinforces the ambiguous undercurrent of the men's friendship. Amongst the few possessions Kinnu can salvage is a photograph of Mina and Okelo. Many years later, the same photograph is displayed on a shelf in the liquor store Kinnu runs in Greenwood, Mississippi. Yet the film remains reticent as to who Mina's real father is. The dark family secret of an adulterous liaison between Kinnu and Okelo that resulted in the illegitimate, racially mixed child, Mina, is never revealed. However, Mina's choice of the African American Demetrius as her lover is motivated by secret kinship ties with the 'other race' and represents the unconscious attempt to bring her mother's secret into the open. Demetrius and Mina's passionate love-making, which the film contrasts with the awkward and unsuccessful attempt of a South Asian couple to consummate their marriage, can be read as an unconscious repetition of her mother's undisclosed secret. In openly pursuing her interracial love affair with Demetrius, Mina takes a different path from that of her mother, a path that requires courage and sacrifice. Unable to overcome racial prejudice within the Asian family and community, Mina and Demetrius elope and their new life together begins at a petrol station on the open road. Although they pay the price of social exclusion, Mina's mixed racial origin and the re-enactment of her mother's secret are depicted in positive terms. What lies ahead of Mina and Demetrius is the prospect of 'unfettered, unlimited, and celebratory mobility' (Desai 2004: 95) and the possibilities of renewal and rebirth inherent in the notion of routes as opposed to roots (see Chapter 2 and Gilroy 1993a).

Typically, the secrets that come to light in diasporic family films challenge primordial notions of origin and fantasies of purity, be they racial or moral. For example, in *Keltoum's Daughter*, briefly considered in Chapter 2, the protagonist discovers a dark secret surrounding her birth and parentage that has devastated the entire family, leading to her grandfather's muteness (a highly symbolic somatisation), her grandmother's untimely death and her birth mother's insanity. The film imagines Railla's discovery of the family secret in terms of routes that take her from Europe to Algeria and back to Europe, whereby, as in *Mississippi Masala*, the itinerary valorises routes over roots. In *Babymother*, the titular black British heroine, Anita, also discovers that she is not her mother's daughter and that being a 'babymother' runs in the family. Whereas Anita, who is in her early twenties, is unemployed and struggling to raise two small children on her own while aspiring to become a reggae and dancehall performer, her own 'babymother' took a different course. When Anita's presumed mother, Edith, dies, it transpires that Anita's 'sister Rose', a successful career woman, is actually her birth mother. Rose, too, fell pregnant as a teenager and passed on her baby to her mother, Edith, so that she could fulfil her ambitions and succeed. Unlike the other films considered here, Julian Henriques's Black British musical cum social realist drama, set between the run-down housing estates and vibrant dancehalls in the black London neighbourhood of Harlesden, does not use the issue of mistaken descent to critique notions of racial purity. Instead, it lays bare the fact that absent fathers and gender inequalities place a dual burden on black women.

Paedophilia, a theme prominently addressed in recent books on the child in cinema (see Wilson 2003, Lury 2010), is another shameful family secret. In *Monsoon Wedding* (see Chapter 5), the disclosure of child abuse within the family fractures the ostensibly ideal and 'pure' Indian family on the wedding day, an occasion on which families solemnise their unity. However, by far the most common secret in diasporic family films is what Oscar Wilde euphemistically referred to as the 'love that dare not speak its name'.[13] What Omar and Johnny in *My Beautiful Laundrette*, Wei-Tung and Simon in *The Wedding Banquet* (Ang Lee, 1993), Murat, Lola and Bilidikid in *Lola and Bilidikid*, Alim and Giles in *Touch of Pink* (Ian Iqbal Rashid, 2004), Nina and Lisa in *Nina's Heavenly Delights* and Emrah and Tim in *Evet, I Do!* all have in common is that they are involved in a gay or lesbian relationship, in most cases with a partner who belongs to the white majority culture, and their families know nothing about it until their secret is revealed.[14]

What interests me in relation to this particular family secret is why the disclosure of same-sex desire is such a prevalent theme in diasporic family narratives, whereas, according to Harry Benshoff, 'queers and families are two concepts often diametrically opposed in our popular imagination' (2008: 223). Clearly, the opposite holds true for diasporic families in diasporic cinema. This may be due partly to diasporic cinema's avowed intention to shift the margin to the centre by privileging minority identities. Stella Bruzzi's observation that 'mainstream culture in general has not been historically hospitable to homosexuality, lesbianism or bisexuality (2009: 133) seems to confirm this *ex negativo*.

Because queer diasporic subjects are constructed as doubly marginal, they lend themselves particularly well to the identity discourses of diasporic cinema with its emphasis on marginality.[15] Still, the conjoining of these two particular identity categories is by no means coincidental; queerness and diaspora are both defined by a minority status and awareness, and one of the shared concerns of queer and ethnic minorities is the extent to which they enjoy full and equal citizenship (see Sinfield 2000, Williams 2010). Furthermore, the (often traumatic) experience of separation and loss of home and homeland, regarded by many scholars as constitutive of the diaspora experience, is shared by gays and lesbians who, when they 'come out', risk being 'cut off from the heterosexual culture of their childhood, which becomes the site of impossible return, the site of impossible memories' (Fortier 2002: 189). As David L. Eng (1997), Alan Sinfield (2000) and other scholars who examine the intersections between diaspora, ethnicity, sexuality and gender suggest, queer and diasporic subjects share a sense of loss and separation from an original place of belonging and the impetus to build a new home. Meanwhile, Avtar Brah identifies a 'homing desire . . . which is not the same thing as a desire for a "homeland"' (1996: 180) as a quintessential aspect of the diaspora experience.[16] Furthermore, the aforementioned notion of the 'diaspora space' (see Chapter 1) potentially functions as a site of liberation. Brah conceives of it as a conceptual space 'where multiple subject positions are juxtaposed, contested, proclaimed, disavowed; where the permitted and the prohibited perpetually interrogate [each other]; and where the accepted and the transgressive imperceptibly mingle even while [. . . being] disclaimed in the name of purity and tradition' (208).

In the context of diasporic family films, the diaspora space empowers the queer sons and daughters of migrants-turned-settlers to live or even declare their same-sex desire openly. Although the 'queer diaspora', understood as a minoritarian community of queers, and the 'queer spaces within ethnically defined diasporas' (Fortier 2002: 183) are not identical (despite overlapping partially), both constitute a challenge to essentialist notions of the nation and nationalist ideologies. Given that 'the heterosexual family is the essential building-block in the construction and elevation of the nation' and given that 'queer diasporas [. . .] decidedly "propagate" outside of the nation-building narrative' (189), the queer diaspora, as well as queer enclaves within ethnically defined diasporas, challenges nationalist ideologies based on ethnic and cultural homogeneity that have traditionally underpinned the idea of the nation-state. Diasporic citizenship transcends the borders of the nation-state and is characterised by multiple belongings and ambivalent attachments. In *Impossible Desires: Queer Diasporas and South Asian Public Cultures*, Gayatri Gopinath proposes an interesting equation: namely, that 'queerness is to heterosexuality as the diaspora is to the nation. If within heteronormative logic the queer is seen as the debased and inadequate copy of the heterosexual, so too is diaspora within nationalist logic positioned as the queer Other of the nation, its inauthentic imitation' (2005: 11).[17]

Drawing on Gopinath's observations, I propose that the preponderance of queer subjects in diasporic cinema and, in particular, in diasporic family films, is due to the fact that queer diasporic identity functions as a master trope of hybridity. 'The word "queer" means *across*' and is etymologically linked to 'the German *quer* (transverse), Latin *torquere* (to twist) [and] English *athwart*' (Sedgwick cited in Clark 2006: 557). Being queer is essentially about resisting containment within clearly demarcated borders and categories. Queer defines itself against the normal and the normative, of which the heterosexual is but one particular normative category (Eng 1997: 50). Queerness therefore implies transgression, subversion and dissent, and is often conceived of as a state of 'in-betweenness'. In discussing the cultural representation of gays, Richard Dyer notes that both the queen and the dyke 'are represented as if their sexuality means that they are in between the two genders of female and male. Thus dykes are mannish, queens effeminate' (1993: 30). Similarly, conceptualisations of diasporic identity revolve around the space of the 'in-between' that positions diasporic subjects at the interstice between the home and the host country, the culture of origin and the destination culture, national rootedness and transnational routes. The space of the in-between – if understood in negative terms as 'falling between two stools' – is imagined as a space of irreconcilable conflict between cultural and generational value systems, where the diasporic subject is caught in the middle, unable to choose between either. Yet, in-betweenness can also be understood in positive terms as 'having the best of both worlds'. This revalorisation is expressed in spatial metaphors of border crossing, third space (which resonates with Magnus Hirschfeld's designation of homosexuals as 'the third sex') and the concept of hybridity that has replaced previous dichotomous conceptualisations of diasporic subjectivity.

The widely used term 'hybridity' is generally understood to refer to a range of cultural phenomena that involve mixing, in particular in the context of metropolitan societies.[18] In this broad and fairly imprecise sense, hybridity represents the antithesis of purity. Discourses on nationalism, postnationalism and diaspora deploy hybridity as a 'a critique of the "Purities" around which minoritarian cultural nationalism mobilizes as much as those of the dominant "host" society', as both discourses stigmatise 'mergings between different cultures as undesirable, divisive and socially degenerative in tendency' (Moore-Gilbert 2001: 195). With regard to diasporic identities (which are inevitably hybrid), Stuart Hall ([1990] 2003) notes that they are never fixed and stable but, instead, fluid and poised in transition. Hybrid identities are complex and heterogeneous, characterised by cross-overs and mixes between different cultural traditions that are invoked and drawn upon simultaneously. Consequently, hybridity negates essentialist notions of ethnic absolutism, purity and the nostalgic fantasy of a fixed origin that can be fully recuperated. Queerness constitutes a further dimension of fluidity, gender ambivalence and boundary crossing, representing a vector of alterity that challenges dominant expectations of heteronormativity.

I would like to propose that queer diasporic identities function as a master trope of hybridity and that the revelation of queer desire in diasporic family films articulates a critique of fantasies of purity, which simultaneously underpin certain traditional models of the family and nationalist ideologies. As outlined in Chapter 1, the family functions as a trope for the nation and both mobilise discourses of inclusion and exclusion for their legitimation. In diasporic cinema, the family emerges as a privileged site, where the contested belonging of the over-determined Other (being simultaneously queer and diasporic) is negotiated. However, what marks the queer sons and daughters as Other in the context of the diasporic family, which is Other itself in relation to the majority culture, is not their ethnicity but their queerness.

Focusing on *Lola and Bilidikid*, *My Beautiful Laundrette* and *Nina's Heavenly Delights*, I shall examine how the revelation of same-sex desire is negotiated in the diasporic family. Are the queer sons and daughters expelled from the family? Can their Otherness be absorbed into a homogenising family of nation? Or are they able to build alternative structures of family and kinship and, in doing so, queer the family of nation?

The Phantom of Queer Desire and Homophobia in *Lola and Bilidikid*

Set in Berlin's Turkish gay and transvestite subculture, Kutluğ Ataman's *Lola and Bilidikid* illustrates how queer desire is employed as a critique of homogenising fantasies of purity and unity that lie at the heart of both minoritarian and hegemonic cultural nationalisms. The film shows how, in three very different cultural contexts (Turkish patriarchy, National Socialism and its neo-fascist legacy in contemporary Germany), queer identities have evoked extreme and violent homophobic responses, thereby drawing attention to the correspondences between belief systems that centre on fictions of purity, regardless of what their ideological underpinning is.

Homosexuals were one of the groups persecuted under National Socialism. Regarded as socially and morally aberrant, 'defilers of German blood', homosexual men challenged the ideal of the German heterosexual family, whose chief function it was to contribute to the creation of the Master Race. The National Socialists' idea of the Master Race – tall, blond, blue-eyed Nordic Aryans, deemed superior to all other peoples – encapsulates the obsessive pursuit of racial purity and of a racially homogeneous nation-state like no other ideology.

Lola and Bilidikid establishes continuities between the homophobic and racist ideology of German National Socialism and contemporary multi-cultural Berlin by situating scenes of xeno- and homophobic violence in locations such as the Olympic Stadium, 'a deserted master site of memory' (Webber 2008: 278), inextricably linked to Germany's legacy of the Nazi past. The Berlin Olympic Stadium was commissioned by Adolf Hitler for the summer Olympic Games of 1936 and has assumed a prominent place in cultural memory through Leni Riefenstahl's two-part documentary *Olympia: Festival of the Nations* and *Festival of Beauty* (1938). *Olympia* was not just a sports documentary but also a propagandist celebration of the beauty and perfection of the Aryan race. At the same time, the numerous scenes showing naked male athletes in the sauna or shower, massaging each other's perfect bodies in sporting camaraderie, oscillate between the homosocial and the homoerotic, therefore conflicting with the Nazis' persecution of homosexuals. It is, not coincidentally, in the underground public toilets of the Olympic Stadium that Murat, one of the Turkish German characters, has a sexual encounter with his classmate Walter, a German neo-Nazi, before being violently assaulted by Walter's homophobic neo-Nazi friends. Their provocative remark, 'The Turks are the Jews of today', establishes further historical continuities between Nazism and the queer-bashers' acts of violence.[19] Yet the film's narrative development reveals that a no less violent homophobia runs right through the Turkish German family whose dark secret propels the narrative forward.

Figure 3.4 Lola (Gandi Mukli) is the object of Bilidikid's (Erdal Yıldız) homoerotic desire and homophobic contempt (*Lola and Bilidikid*, Kutluğ Ataman, 1998)

The film's eponymous hero / heroine, Lola, is a Turkish German gay man, who performs as a drag queen in the cabaret show, *Die Gastarbeiterinnen* (*The Women Guest Workers*). The other Turkish German drag performers, Calypso and Shehrazade, and her macho boyfriend Bilidikid,[20] have become Lola's surrogate family after the disclosure of her sexual identity resulted in her being evicted from her Turkish birth family, also living in Berlin. Yet this is not the only family secret that comes to light and gradually tears the diasporic Turkish family apart. It transpires that the family's oldest son, Osman, is himself a closet queer, who raped his brother Lola and whose 'repressed same-sex desire returns in his homophobic violence' (Mennel 2004: 303), directed at Lola. A similar ambivalence is evident in Lola's hyper-masculine boyfriend Bili, who tries to talk Lola into having a sex change so that they can get married and live as 'a totally normal family' in Turkey. Bilidikid's attempt to convert his queer desire into a socially respectable straight relationship reflects the denial of his own sexual identity.

Despite working as a hustler and despite being in a same-sex relationship with Lola, Bili does not consider himself homosexual. In accordance with the Turkish conception of homosexuality, 'the label of *the homosexual* is attributed to any individual who is being penetrated or thought to be penetrated, whereas the other one remains free of this label regardless of the fact that he is engaged in homosexual sex as well' (Tapinc 1992: 42, emphasis in the original). The homosexual is regarded as a disgrace to manhood and exiled from the public sphere of Turkish men, which, according to Tapinc (45), explains why many homosexuals (in the Turkish sense of the term) identify themselves completely with women and often opt for a sex change. In line with this gender-stratified model of homosexuality, Bili tries to impose the same uneven power relationship that governs male and female gender roles in the patriarchal family upon Turkish German gay subculture. Bili's fear of gender ambivalence – another variant of both Osman's and the neo-Nazi closet queers' homophobia – is reflected, first, in his plan to turn his drag queen lover into a 'proper' woman and, second, in his violent revenge for Lola's murder. Presuming (wrongly as it turns out) that the neo-Nazi thugs have killed Lola before dumping her body in the River Spree, he castrates one of them and kills another, before being shot dead by his opponents in a harrowing blood bath. Via this violent act of castration, Bili subjects another man's body to the punishment he threatened Lola with, should she resist the sex change.

In *Lola and Bilidikid*, the disclosure of queer desire and homophobia is rendered as a narrative about the transgenerational transmission of shameful and traumatic family secrets.[21] Symptomatically, the same phantom that haunts the family also haunts the nation. Abraham and Torok, who examined such convergences between familial and collective memory in order to understand the psychological roots of ideological and political systems, argued that 'a phantom can help account for the periodic return of political ideologies rendered shameful' (cited in Rand 1994: 169), such as the return of Nazism in the shape of neo-Nazi movements in Germany and elsewhere. Considering that the persecution of homosexuals under National Socialism was largely excluded from public remembrance until 1985 and that Paragraph 175 of the Criminal Code, which outlawed homosexual acts under Nazi rule, remained in effect in West Germany until 1969, one could argue that the suffering of this particular group of victims of the Nazi regime has long been collectively 'forgotten'.[22] The periodic return of the Nazis' ideology of the Master Race, with its concomitant homophobia, manifests itself in the violent homophobia of the neo-fascist closet queers in *Lola and Bilidikid*. The phantom that haunts Murat and Lola's family, and which Murat, the guardian of the phantom, dutifully re-enacts, relates to a deep-rooted homophobia that is simultaneously personal and collective, national and transnational.

After Lola's death, Murat quite literally repeats her story, taking her place in the relationship with Bilidikid, 'sleeping in [her] bed, and even putting on the red wig, although he says to Bilidikid: "I am not Lola"' (Mennel 2004: 304). Still wearing Lola's red wig and women's clothes, which he donned in order to lure Lola's presumed killers to the dilapidated warehouse, where he discovers that the neo-Nazis are innocent of Lola's murder, he runs home. His 'coming out' in front of his mother and brother Osman in the kitchen requires few words of explanation, since by itself his resemblance to Lola in drag results in a *déjà vu*. The red wig serves as a startling reminder of Lola, who wore it in order to make her queerness visible and thereby deter Osman from further acts of incestuous rape. The unexpected apparition of what looks like Lola's ghost catches Osman off-guard and, bewildered, he shouts: 'They should have buried [the red wig] with him', thereby disclosing that he knows of Lola's death and is, in fact, guilty of murdering her. Murat breaks the vicious circle of silence and repetition by revealing what has been phantomised – his brother's violent homophobia and the heinous crime of fratricide.

By establishing analogies between the fictions of purity that govern fascist and patriarchal ideologies, *Lola and Bilidikid* condemns both, advocating instead fluidity and cross-over, not only in terms of gender and sexuality, but also in terms of transcultural encounters. Lola's performance of gender and ethnicity on stage, as well as in her personal life, in which she chooses the fluid identity of a gay transvestite over that of a male-to-female transsexual, embodies this notion of fluidity. She disproves Bili's dogmatic statement that 'A man is a man. A hole is a hole, it does not matter where you stick it in', by switching between being a man and being a woman, and she wants to keep it that way. It is therefore not coincidental that her death is associated with water; her red-bewigged body floats on the River Spree, where it is discovered by children, who believe it is a mermaid, a hybrid creature, half woman and half fish.[23] Lola's symbolically charged death validates the ideal of cross-over and hybridity along the multiple axes of gender, sexuality and ethnicity. It destabilises ontological conceptions of gender and sexuality and, by mapping them on to ethnicity in the form of a palimpsest, the film foregrounds the constructedness of all of these categories. In this sense, Lola represents the antipode of a unified, stable identity and purist fantasies of cultural and ethnic homogeneity that underpin nationalistic ideologies, which is why she must be destroyed by its proponents.

'COMING OUT' IN THE FAMILY OF NATION: *MY BEAUTIFUL LAUNDRETTE* AND *NINA'S HEAVENLY DELIGHTS*

My Beautiful Laundrette and *Nina's Heavenly Delights* are about queer interracial desire in the context of Asian British families. Dubbed 'My Beautiful Restaurant' (Wajid 2006) in a review in *The Guardian*, Pratibha Parmar's film evinces a number of conspicuous similarities with that of Stephen Frears. Like Omar and Johnny, Nina and Lisa are lovers as well as business partners; both films end with the dual promise of a lasting relationship and business success. Both films deploy the queer interracial couple to interrogate racial hierarchies, social divisions and the fantasy of an ethnically homogeneous nation. Frears and Parmar set out to normalise same-sex desire by refusing to stigmatise it as transgressive and, instead, celebrate the utopian potential of queer interracial desire as an agent to cross over barriers and 'power relations determined by race, class, gender, and sexuality' (Mercer 1993: 239).

The fragmented narrative of *My Beautiful Laundrette* centres on Omar, the son of a Pakistani father and British mother, who becomes an aspiring young entrepreneur when his wealthy Uncle Nasser asks him to manage one of his small businesses, a run-down laundry in south London. Omar employs his one-time schoolmate Johnny, who is white, British and unemployed, and hangs out with a group of xenophobic skinheads, to help him refurbish the laundrette. They become lovers, yet they never 'come out', and the film remains equivocal as to which members of Omar's extended family actually grasp the true nature of their relationship.

Filmmaker Julian Henriques has described *My Beautiful Laundrette* as a film about 'a love affair between two men, two races and two politics' (cited in Geraghty 2005: 22), while Christine Geraghty refers to it as a 'cross-over film' (5), paying particular attention to the cross-over appeal this landmark picture has had for both British Asian and white British audiences.[24] I would posit that *My Beautiful Laundrette* takes the idea of cross-over one step further not just by crossing over but also by *inverting* prevalent social class and power structures that testify to uncomfortable continuities of colonialism in Britain under Margaret Thatcher's rule and beyond. According to Bart Moore-Gilbert, Kureishi and Frears's film interrogates racially determined power relationships familiar from colonial discourse in as much as:

> Johnny's dependence on Omar plays off the colonialist trope of 'the faithful servant'; and in providing Johnny with work, Omar contributes to his friend's moral regeneration in a way that parodically recalls the colonialist project of 'civilising' the brutal natives. Instead of the white colonial male enjoying the native female [. . .] the non-white Omar enjoys the native British man. (2001: 73–4)

At the same time, Omar and Johnny's relationship inverts the widespread image of elite, white men 'pursuing working-class and / or Latin, Arab, Indian and Africano men', in which the 'the former [. . .] tend to be thought of as the queers, not the latter' (Dyer 2002: 6). In this sense, the character constellation 'queers' prevalent racial and class stereotypes and challenges binary oppositions that customarily serve 'as the basis of political cleavage and social division' (Brah 1996: 184). It thereby encapsulates Kureishi's utopian vision of a 'fluid, non-hierarchical society with free movement across classes' (cited in Korte and Sternberg 2004: 85). Imbued with a certain 'degree of old-fashioned sexual utopianism' (Hill 1999: 214), the film identifies sexual desire as the means through which barriers of race and class can be overcome; 'Much good can come from fucking', Omar remarks at a family get-together at Uncle Nasser's home, where he introduces Johnny as his business partner (though not as his lover), and where the socially disenfranchised Johnny is included in the circle of the prosperous Asian British family.

The pivotal scene capturing the utopian potential of queer desire is the gay couple's love-making in the back of the laundrette. As Johnny caresses Omar, Omar disentangles himself from Johnny's embrace and recalls how, several years ago, Johnny betrayed their friendship and that of Papa by joining

Figure 3.5 Omar (Gordon Warnecke) and Johnny's (Daniel Day-Lewis) queer desire is central to the utopian vision of *My Beautiful Laundrette* (Stephen Frears, 1985)

the National Front on their notorious anti-immigration marches through Lewisham. The moment of seduction crystallises into a moment during which Omar re-assesses his ethnic and familial loyalties. The chiaroscuro lighting, casting patches of light and shadow across his face, makes his inner conflict visible, as he remembers what he and his father witnessed: 'It was bricks and bottles and Union Jacks. It was immigrants out. It was kill us. People *we* knew. And it was you! He [Papa] saw you marching and you saw his face, watching you'. The fear of racial hatred and violence took its toll on Omar's family. Yet, despite implicating Johnny in his mother's tragic suicide and his father's steady decline since then, Omar succumbs to Johnny's tender caress and the two make love, allowing their desire – at least momentarily – to overcome the shadows of the past and whatever else may stand in their way.

Shortly after this symbolic 'act of racial reconciliation' (Bruzzi 2009: 139), they face one another on opposite sides of a one-way mirror, which separates the brightly lit public space of the laundrette at the front from the dark back room. Looking into each other's eyes, their faces are momentarily superimposed, blended into one unifying oval shape. Eva Rueschmann regards this superimposition as 'the most striking visual image of Kureishi's [and Frears's] filmic construction of a new British identity, one neither traditionally Pakistani nor exclusively white British but both, altered and transformed by the changes each character has wrought in each other' (2003a: xix).

The film's persistent preoccupation with social divisions and barriers is reflected in the *mise-en-scène*, with its conspicuous number of windows, mirrors and screens that 'both allow us to see the action and slightly obscure it' (Geraghty 2005: 57). In contrast to Omar and Johnny, who are frequently shot through windows and semi-transparent screens, the other interracial couple, Uncle Nasser and his white mistress Rachel, whose exuberant waltz and kiss in the laundrette's public space is synchronised with the gay couple's love-making and kissing in the office at the back, are on most other occasions shot through grids. Both the scene in which Rachel and Nasser make love and the one in which they break up are shot through a grille of black square bars that simultaneously imprisons and visually fragments the couple. These rigid rectangular bars stand in stark contrast to the permeable mirror, or 'liquid window' (Kaleta cited in Rueschmann 2003a: xix), in which Omar and Johnny's reflections merge.

Omar and his laundrette are persistently linked to fluidity and water. The sound of bubbling and gurgling water accompanies the title sequence and several subsequent scenes, especially those set at the Powders laundrette. Omar is introduced by a shot of his hands washing and wringing his father's clothes in a bathroom sink. Later the camera penetrates a windscreen covered in soap-suds to reveal Omar's hands and face, as he is washing a car at Nasser's garage. The film's final scene shows Omar, who has been tending the wounds Johnny incurred in a violent fight between 'his own people', the white supremacist gang, and Omar's cousin Salim, laughing and splashing each other with water in the laundrette's back room. The laundrette, decorated in pastel shades with stylised images of giant blue waves on the walls, reverberating with the sound of Strauss's *Blue Danube* waltz on its grand opening day and compared by Rachel to 'a wonderful ship', functions as a utopian space in which antagonisms of race and class dissolve. But, as Stella Bruzzi reminds us with reference to Omar and Johnny's playful water games, the laundrette 'is only the film's microcosm, the film's larger social concerns remain [. . .] unresolved' (2009: 140).

Kureishi and Frears do not naïvely propose that queer desire instantaneously creates social equality and harmony. The racial and ideological tensions that jeopardise Omar and Johnny's relationship resurface again and again. Yet, although *My Beautiful Laundrette* hardly disavows the social realities that put Omar and Johnny in the line of fire between warring sections of society, it nevertheless heralds the utopian vision that 'contemporary Britain has within its grasp the possibility of expanding traditional conceptions of national identity to create for the first time a genuine and revolutionary, though always *contradictory* rather than blandly harmonious, unity-in-diversity' (Moore-Gilbert 2001: 92).

Consistent with Kureishi's intention to depict homosexuality as normal, Omar and Johnny's queer romance does not constitute a dark secret and, arguably, *My Beautiful Laundrette* could hardly claim a legitimate place in this chapter if it were not for the fact that Omar and Johnny's relationship is deployed as a powerful critique of Thatcher's Britain, with its simultaneous emphasis on ethnic absolutism and family values. As Paul Gilroy argues in his aptly titled book *There Ain't No Black in the Union Jack* (1987), Thatcher's populist nationalism ultimately conceived of the British nation as white. Her vision of a regenerated British nation emphatically disavowed difference and extolled 'a political culture dominated by the notion that the family was the only social unit, as reflected in Thatcher's infamous statement, "There is no such thing as society: there are individual men and women, and there are families"' (cited in Tudor 2008: 145). Yet not any type of family would qualify. The Tory government discriminated as much against family diversity (in the shape of single mothers and other non-traditional family types) as it did against ethnic and sexual diversity. Sexual minorities were positioned alongside other 'enemies within' in Thatcherism's 'constant attempts to expel symbolically one sector of society after another from the imaginary community of the nation' (Hall cited in Waites 2000). Thatcher regarded immigrants from Britain's former colonies (also called the 'Commonwealth family' or 'family of nations') as a threat to the British nation and the values it stood for,[25] a point of view she expressed in her infamous 'getting swamped' interview on Granada Television in 1978 prior to becoming Prime Minister. *My Beautiful Laundrette* challenges this homogenising fantasy by making the point that there are no families that come even close to this ideal. Johnny has severed all bonds with his family; Omar's Papa has never recovered from his wife's suicide and is a bed-ridden alcoholic; and Uncle Nasser's 'traditional' Asian family, with a white mistress on the side, is barely holding up. If, as Margaret Thatcher pronounced, the moral integrity and stability of the traditional nuclear family were to be the chief guarantors of Britain's social stability and prosperity, then, according to Kureishi and Frears's ironic assessment, there was not much hope for Britain under Tory rule. Or, conversely, Thatcher's Britain had to open up to the reality of family diversity – and by implication – an ethnically diverse Britain.

Made twenty-one years after *My Beautiful Laundrette* and described by the Asian British director Pratibha Parmar as a film about the family, food and love (Parmar n/d), *Nina's Heavenly Delights* revolves around the Scottish Indian Nina and the white Scottish Lisa, who fall in love with each other while preparing for a cooking contest. Nina, who ran away from home after breaking off an engagement, returns to Glasgow to attend her father's funeral. Upon taking over her father's restaurant, the New Taj, she finds out that he has gambled half of it away and that the restaurant is co-owned by Lisa. She also learns that the New Taj has been shortlisted for the Best of the West curry competition, alongside the Jewel in the Crown, which boasts her ex-fiancé Sanjay as its master chef. Nina, who was initiated into the art of cooking by her father as a little girl, is confident she will win simply by following her father's advice: 'Taste it. Taste it in your heart, [. . .] no matter what the recipe says, always follow your heart. Best chicken chakuti this side of Maryhill!'. As David Martin-Jones observes, cooking 'is a way for Nina to recreate her father's presence from her childhood' (2009: 84) and to keep, via the family, the cultural memory alive. Significantly, though, this is not the memory of 'a homeland like India, but of a diasporic NRI childhood in Maryhill, Glasgow' (84). Exploring the sensuous delights of exotic food, Nina and Lisa grow ever more attracted to each other until, one day, they fall into each other's arms and passionately kiss – first amongst the sizzling pots and pans of the restaurant kitchen and then on national Korma TV, after winning the Best of the West curry competition.

Figure 3.6 Nina (Shelly Conn) and Lisa (Laura Fraser) 'come out' on national Korma TV in *Nina's Heavenly Delights* (Pratibha Parmar, 2006)

Nina's Heavenly Delights takes the sexual utopianism of *My Beautiful Laundrette* significantly further by resolving the narrative conflict between traditional Indian family values and queer interracial desire through a happy ending that affirms the lesbian couple's integration into the family circle and into the Scottish nation. The telling name of the curry competition and the victory of the racially mixed lesbian couple over what would have been a traditional heterosexual couple (if Nina had not broken off her engagement to Sanjay, the competing master chef), celebrates the mixed-race lesbian union as superior – simply the Best of the West.

Nina's Heavenly Delights normalises queerness by suggesting that Nina's secret is on a par with those harboured – and eventually revealed – by other family members: her little sister's innocent self-indulgence in traditional Scottish dancing, her brother's 'pure love' (an expression used several times) and clandestine marriage to a white Scottish woman, and her mother's secret love for the owner of the Jewel in the Crown. In a bid for mainstream audiences, Parmar's comedy remains coy about the depiction of same-sex desire, translating erotic into culinary delights, and foregrounding romantic love over lesbian desire. Whereas Omar and Johnny's love-making in the laundrette is charged with erotic frisson and sensuous physicality, the corresponding scene in *Nina's Heavenly Delights* is conventionally romantic. As Lisa enters Nina's bedroom, steeped in deep red light, Nina offers her an Indian-style dress similar to the purple one she is wearing, and holds it up against her body.

Lesbian desire is imagined as dressing up rather than undressing each other. The women's almost identical hairstyles in this scene, their similar height and body shapes, foreground similarity rather than difference and, thereby, tone down the transgressiveness of what was once tabooed as 'miscegenation'. The touching of white and brown skin is muted by the red lighting and limited to a close-up of intertwined arms. As soon as Lisa unzips her lover's dress, the screen fades to black.

The grand finale is a tongue-in-cheek endorsement of fluid identities, be they queer, diasporic or both. In this hybrid Bollywood-style song-and-dance number, the entire cast joins Nina's friend Bobbi, a gay drag queen who has come out, and the Chutney Queens in their celebratory performance of 'Love in a Wet Climate'. It is not just the Chutney Queens who are cross-dressing; everybody is wearing 'ethnic drag' (Sieg 2002) – some Scots are dressed in Indian saris while some diasporic Indians wear tartan. Parmar's romantic comedy presents the queer diasporic subject as fully integrated into the Scottish nation, represented through the same kind of clichéd nature imagery as used in the Scottish Tourist Board's advertising campaign 'VisitScotland'. Expansive, empty landscapes with high mountains and crystal-clear lochs conjure up visions of a pure Scotland and, by extension, pure Scottishness. In the film's final sequence, in which the performance of 'Love in a Wet Climate' gives way to the filming of the performance in the studio, this vision of 'pure Scotland' is revealed to be fake; it is a landscape that has been projected on to a green screen. This self-referential conceit underscores the fact that the ideal of purity – be it pure (i.e. heterosexual) love or a pure (i.e. racially homogeneous) Scotland – are nothing but pure fantasy.

Whereas *My Beautiful Laundrette* envisages the queering of the family of nation as an ongoing process in which new, fluid forms of kinship are established, only to disintegrate and be reconfigured again, the generic framework of the romantic comedy in *Nina's Heavenly Delights* provides the utopian space in which queer interracial desire can be fully accommodated in the diasporic family and in a culturally hybridised host nation. Just as Indian curries and Bollywood rhythms make the Scottish nation richer and more vibrant, Parmar's feel-good movie seems to be saying, so does diversity in love.

Conclusion

These documentaries about family memories and the feature films about family secrets represent counter-narratives aiming to lend a voice to those whose memories have been silenced and hidden from history and, by bringing them into representation, to empower them. The self-revelations that unfold in the semi-autobiographical documentaries examined in the first part of this chapter are conceived with a public in mind, even if the family members are ostensibly oblivious to the ultimate purpose of the footage in which they feature. Rather than inviting the audience to assume the vantage point of a voyeur who watches the lives of others without their explicit consent, these postmemory documentaries, John Ellis proposes (albeit with reference to other kinds of documentary), 'place the viewers in the position of the witness, as the persons to whom testimony is directed' (2012: 122). Put differently, the communicative intent of these films is simultaneously targeted at those inside and outside the family circle. Through the act of witnessing distant lives, we who do not belong to these diasporic families, are drawn into family (hi)stories that are not our own. As Ellis suggests, 'media witnessing' invites us to empathise with 'the virtual other' (127) and to recognise individuals who differ from us in terms of their ethnicity, language, social background and so forth as persons and 'to see them as "like us"' (129). Herein lies the implicit political relevance of these postmemory films, for the disclosure of familial memories in the public sphere is no longer just a family affair. Postmemory documentaries articulate the triangulated relationship between familial memories, the collective memory of diaspora, and official accounts of immigration written and preserved by the host societies. By privileging the memories of first-generation immigrant fathers and mothers, the films challenge inequities of power and visibility, and rescue hitherto untold stories from oblivion. The explicitly performative nature of most of these documentaries and the interplay between family photography, home movies, personal interviews and mass-mediated images lay bare the constructedness of acts of memory. Despite chronicling journeys that simultaneously lead back to the parents' past and to their place of origin, ultimately the documentaries assert that these diasporic families are here to stay in our midst. They make an impassioned plea for the inclusion of memories of the marginalised and the pluralisation of the cultural memory of the host nation.

The films about family secrets pursue a similar strategic agenda. Narrating what could, in the broadest sense, be described as revelations of impurity and hybridity, they promote the integration of the over-determined Other into the social fabric of the host society. The disclosure of queer desire (especially when interracial) in the diasporic family contests fantasies of racial and cultural homogeneity, ethnic absolutism and heteronormativity. These fantasies of purity underpin dominant social formations and imagined communities that rely on discourses of inclusion and exclusion for their legitimation. They determine who is in and who is out, who belongs to or who is expelled from the imagined community of nation, traditionally modelled on the family. However, the diasporic family, hybrid itself, problematises the notion of fixed and stable boundaries and functions as a site where the contested belonging of the Other is renegotiated. The representation of queer diasporic identities in these films challenges the hegemony of white heteronormativity and, by implication, the foundations of the family and the nation.

Notes

1. Baronian, Besser and Jansen (2007: 12) define memory as 'the complex relation of personal experiences, the shared histories of communities and their modes of transmission' and identify it as 'a privileged carrier of diasporic identity'. For extensive explorations of diaspora and memory, see Agnew (2005), Fortier (2000) and Petty (2008) in relation to black diasporic cinema.
2. Hirsch developed the concept of postmemory in relation to the children of Holocaust survivors but 'believes that it may usefully describe other second-generation memories of cultural or collective traumatic events and experiences' (1997: 22).
3. Nora suggests that, whereas 'memory is life, borne by living societies [... and] in permanent evolution, open to the dialectic of remembering and forgetting' (1989: 8), history is an incomplete reconstruction of the past that does not possess an immediate relevance for the present. Whereas 'history belongs to everyone and to no one, whence its claim to universal authority', memory 'is blind to all but the group it binds' (9).
4. The original German text was translated by the author: 'Ich wollte einen Film über meine family machen. Ich wollte zeigen, die Typen sind hier 'rübergegangen und hatten nicht mal ein Klo und jetzt haben sie halt – was weiß ich – Kinder, die im Konsulat arbeiten, die Filmemacher sind. Vielleicht wollte ich diesen Film machen, damit ich meinen Kindern irgendwann mal zeigen kann, guck mal hier: das sind Eure Großeltern. Weil meine Kinder werden wahrscheinlich viel deutscher sein als ich, angenommen sie haben eine rein deutsche Mutter oder so. Dann kann ich sagen, das sind Eure Großeltern, da kamen die her, die haben so und so Deutsch gesprochen, so waren die drauf.'
5. The original German text was translated by the author: 'Ich sah, dass mein Vater wie ein Wahnsinniger daran arbeitete, Spuren zu hinterlassen, geachtet und unersetzbar zu sein, Spuren, die die an seinem Körper ausgleichen sollten. Die letzte und sicherste Spur sollte ich sein, er hatte mich als seinen Nachfolger geholt'.
6. On the relationship between individual and group memory, see Halbwachs (1985), Connerton (1989), Assmann (1995) and Landsberg (2004).
7. Named after the French politician Michel Debré, the Loi Debré (14 December 1964) authorised local authorities to evacuate immigrants living in insalubrious and sub-standard housing in shantytowns on the outskirts of major French cities and to demolish these areas. Although it took several years for these measures to be put into place, residents of the *bidonvilles* were eventually rehoused in newly constructed housing projects. *Le Gone du Chaâba* (*Shantytown Kid*, *The Kid from Chaaba*, Christophe Ruggia, 1998) gives a vivid account of Azouz Begag's memories of growing up in such a shantytown.
8. See van Dijck (2005) on the use of 8 mm cameras for home movies and on the impact that changing technology has had on capturing family life.
9. The footage of the yellow fields was actually shot by Sandhya Suri herself. Email correspondence between Suri and the author, 22 November 2010.
10. In an email (22 November 2010), Sandhya Suri explained the song's relevance for her family: 'It fitted perfectly, for it was a love story between my father and India in some way. A sad one. Plus the actual scene in the film is one we used to watch often, being lovers of old Hindi films'.
11. See in particular, Abraham's essay 'Notes on the Phantom' in Abraham and Torok (1994) and, in relation to literature, Rashkin (1992) and Davis (2005).
12. To my knowledge, the only scholar who has suggested that Mina is likely to be the illegitimate daughter of Kinnu and Okelo is Erika Andersen (1993). Anne E. Kaplan (1997: 177) remains more cryptic, referring to Mina's unconscious affinity to 'the other race'.

13. The phrase, a euphemistic reference to homosexual love, was coined by Lord Alfred Douglas in his poem 'Two Loves' and cited by Oscar Wilde in a court trial in 1895, in which he was charged with indecency and sodomy.
14. See Chapter 5 for a discussion of *The Wedding Banquet* and *Evet, I Do!*.
15. See *inter alia* Mercer (1993), Parmar (1993), Provencher (2007), Williams (2010) and Johnston (2010), who examine the double marginalisation and oppression of queer diasporic subjects and the role of film in changing 'objects of oppression into subjects and agents busy making history in their own right' (Mercer 1993: 240).
16. Pratibha Parmar also conceives of the two identity categories as intertwined, stating that her aesthetic 'sensibility comes as much from my culture and race as from my queerness' (cited in MacKinnon 2006: 121).
17. Although European nation-states with sizeable diasporas are effectively hybridised nations, there is still a widespread reluctance to accept 'the Other' as 'one of us'. 'There Ain't No Black in the Union Jack', Paul Gilroy asserted in his seminal book of 1987, and, despite continuing to promote a postracial and postnational ecology of belonging in his more recent writings on diaspora and the nation, he remains sceptical about a widespread acceptance of alternative heterocultural and cosmopolitan conceptions of the nation-state.
18. Homi Bhabha is the most prominent interpreter of 'cultural hybridity' and has shaped the theoretical discourse on the subject in cultural studies; see Bhabha (1985, 1994, 1996). Rushdie (1991) identifies cultural hybridisation as a key factor in innovation and associates it with 'mélange' and 'impurity'. On diaspora and hybridity, see Kalra, Kaur and Hutnyk (2005); and for hybridity in relation to kindred concepts such as creolisation, *bricolage*, syncretism and cosmopolitanism, all of which evolve from cultural encounters and exchange, see Cohen and Toninato (2010: 243–305).
19. See Ruth Mandel (2008) for a fascinating ethnographic study of Turkish immigrants in Berlin in relation to Germany's legacy of the Holocaust; see Karin Hamm-Ehsani (2008: 374–9) on references to Germany's legacy of the Holocaust and Turkey's legacy of the Armenian genocide in *Lola and Bilidikid*.
20. Much has been written about the over-determined names in *Lola and Bilidikid*. Although this is not the place to unravel their complex intertextuality in detail, it is worth noting that Bilidikid 'references the legendary hero of the American West, Billy the Kid' – and a long list of Hollywood films about him – but 'the misspelling of the name as Bilidikid points to the gap between the American legend and the Turkish-German reception' (Mennel 2004: 298). The name Lola evokes the Marlene Dietrich character Lola-Lola in Josef von Sternberg's *The Blue Angel* (1939) and the eponymous heroine of Rainer Werner Fassbinder's film *Lola* (1981), in which he pays homage to Sternberg. The name is associated with seductiveness, spectacle and moral ambiguity. For a superb discussion of *Lola* in the context of Fassbinder's *BRD Trilogy*, see Elsaesser (1996: 97–128). On account of her red wig, Ataman's Lola also evokes the androgynous protagonist Lola in Tom Tykwer's *Lola rennt (Run, Lola Run*, 1998). To my knowledge, the most obvious reference to The Kinks's famous song 'Lola' (1970), the lyrics of which narrate how an innocent young man falls for a transvestite, has hitherto been neglected.
21. Admittedly, Abraham and Torok's theory of transgenerational phantoms does not map on to *Lola and Bilidikid* as neatly as it does on to Shakespeare's *Hamlet*. Being only seventeen years apart, Murat and Lola do not belong to different generations as such, but since Murat grew up without Lola, was conceived to replace her and did not even know of her existence, the brothers are separated by something that comes close to one generation, which is normally assumed to be roughly twenty to thirty years.
22. A memorial commemorating homosexual victims of the National Socialist regime was erected as late as 2008 in Berlin.

23. Mennel (2004) and Clark (2006) both explore the reference to Ophelia in Shakespeare's *Hamlet*.
24. *My Beautiful Laundrette* has received a considerable amount of scholarly attention. For diasporic subjectivities, see Desai (2004), Korte and Sternberg (2004); for production history and institutional context, see Hill (1999), Geraghty (2005) and Malik (2010).
25. Thatcher subsequently revised her views somewhat and, in particular, endorsed the entrepreneurship of Asian British shopkeepers and businessmen. In this sense, Uncle Nasser in *My Beautiful Laundrette* is very much a product of Thatcherism, as he himself acknowledges in the film.

4. GENDER, GENERATION AND THE PRODUCTION OF LOCALITY IN THE DIASPORIC FAMILY

In modern globalised societies, a world of places has been supplanted by a world of global flows. Whereas, in the past, cultural anthropologist Arjun Appadurai proposes, communities were bound to a specific territory that offered a sense of familiarity and belonging, accelerated transnational mobility and the conditions of contemporary urban living have created a disjuncture between territory and locality, understood as 'a property of social life' and 'a structure of feeling' (1996: 182). In a deterritorialised world, place-bound communities have become transformed into 'ethnoscapes', or shifting landscapes of transnationally mobile people, whose collective identities have assumed 'a slippery, nonlocalized quality' (48) and who, therefore, actively seek to produce locality elsewhere. Amongst the various strategies for the 'production of locality' discussed by Appadurai, the production of 'reliably local subjects as well as [. . .] reliably local neighborhoods, within which such subjects can be recognized and organized' (181) is of particular relevance in the present context. As localised forms of knowledge and belonging become increasingly negotiable and transnationally accessible through modern transport and communication technologies, a growing desire has arisen to 'embody locality as well as locate bodies in socially and spatially defined communities' (179). Rites of passage and other types of social ritual are important means through which locality can be embodied. Circumcision, ceremonies of naming and wedding rituals, as well as the material practices of everyday life, notably the adherence to culinary and sartorial traditions from the homeland, serve to profess allegiances and attachments to places and communities that are far away.

Appadurai's 'production of locality' is comparable to what Avtar Brah calls 'homing desire' (1996: 180, see Chapter 3), the desire to recreate home elsewhere, and to Ulf Hannerz's 'habitats of meaning' (1996: 23). All three concepts conceive of locality not so much as a physical space but rather as something that involves agency. Adapting Zygmunt Bauman's term 'habitat', defined as a 'setting in which both action and meaning-assignment are *possible*' (1992: 191, emphasis in the original), Hannerz proposes that transnational mobility has made the relationship between culture and territory more flexible in so far as habitats of meaning expand and contract and are as mobile as the people who inhabit, generate and carry them. Habitats of meaning are not just the places that we live in or travel to in a physical sense but also the virtual spaces that we access through zapping television channels or browsing the internet. The scope and size of these habitats depend, in large measure, upon our cultural competencies, 'the languages we understand, write, or speak, our levels of literacy with respect to other symbolic forms, and so on' (23).

In this chapter, I draw on these anthropological frameworks and argue that the production of locality in diasporic family films is imagined as a contested cultural practice that throws the fault lines between minority and majority cultures into stark relief, and that these fault lines are particularly visible in relation to gender and generation.[1] The social constructedness of these categories implies that the expectations attached to them are culturally specific and, in the films analysed here, they emerge as key sites of family conflict. The conditions of migration and translocality complicate and destabilise the transgenerational transmission of family structures, values and gender norms, as families and individuals are positioned 'in the course of their everyday lives within and across each of their places of attachment or localities of perceived belonging' (Vertovec 2009: 77). Men and women, parents and their children access habitats of meaning that only partially intersect. They participate differently in the public spheres of the country of residence, suffering from social marginalisation or availing themselves of opportunities to participate to varying degrees. Most diasporic family films imagine such a dynamisation of family structures as a widening generational gap. Whereas the parents' generation is usually eager to reconstruct the local practices of the homeland, their sons and daughters challenge parental authority by engaging in alternative locality-producing activities through which they align themselves with the value system and lifestyle of the Western majority culture or the icons of global youth culture. While generational conflict has been a prominent theme in cinema ever since the development of a distinctive youth culture in the 1950s (see Considine 1985; Doherty 2002), in diasporic family films it is compounded by the generations' cultural and emotional attachments to different localities and the ways in which they seek to produce them in the host society.

Nowhere is the generational segregation of place more evident than in *banlieue* cinema, a cycle of contemporary French films that is occasionally conflated with *beur* cinema, since many *beur*-authored films are set in the *banlieue*, while *beur* characters also feature prominently in *banlieue* cinema. Yet, strictly speaking, the former is defined by a distinctive topography, whereas the latter is linked to a specific ethnicity (see Chapter 1). '*Banlieue*' refers to the run-down, working-class housing estates on the urban periphery of Paris and other large French cities with a high concentration of immigrants. As a 'site of social struggle and [...] an emblematic space of marginality' (Higbee 2007: 41), the *banlieue* reflects France's *fracture sociale*, the increasing disparity between the haves and the have-nots, and the opposition between centre and periphery. While young, disenfranchised men roam the streets, playgrounds, cellars and stairways of these grim housing estates, their parents – to the extent that they feature at all in these films – are confined to the crammed kitchens or living rooms, where they recreate 'home abroad'. Here they speak Arabic, cook ethnic food, and roll out their prayer rugs in the privacy of their bedrooms or living rooms in order to preserve the cultural authenticity of their homeland through closure.

Additionally, and in keeping with conventional gendered topographies, the spaces of diasporic domesticity are marked as feminine; mothers cook, clean and nurture and sisters do their homework and help with domestic chores. If present at all, fathers are ineffectual. Following an accident at work, Majid's father, in the aforementioned foundational *beur* film *Tea in the Harem*, has lost his ability to speak and is entirely dependent upon his capable and nurturing wife Malika, who bathes and swaddles him like a baby. The disintegration of masculinity in *Tea in the Harem* and in other Maghrebi French films is implicitly attributed to exploitation at the workplace and social marginalisation encountered by first-generation immigrant men in France. The confinement of the father to the domestic sphere is symptomatic of the crisis of masculinity that has besieged the generation of the fathers and which their sons try to compensate for by hyper-macho posturing, which ultimately cannot mask their own powerlessness. With such weak father figures, generational conflict is displaced into the streets, where the protagonists rebel against racist and violent policemen who assume the role of symbolic fathers. Instead of supporting their sons' maturation and social integration, these bad and brutal fathers either arrest or accidentally kill them.

La Haine, Mathieu Kassovitz's stylish black-and-white *banlieue* film about a *black-blanc-beur* multi-ethnic male friendship group, and other diasporic youth films including the Turkish German *Short Sharp Shock*, *Chiko* (Özgür Yildirim, 2008) and the Black British film *Bullet Boy* (Saul Dibb, 2004), share the ghettocentric imagination of the 'hood film', which emerged as a new genre of African American cinema in the 1990s. *Boyz 'n the Hood* (John Singleton, 1991) and *Menace II Society* (Allan and Albert Hughes, 1993) are generally regarded as paradigmatic texts. Narratives about juvenile delinquency, the fatal consequences of guns, drugs, black-on-black violence and dysfunctional black families combine a moralising stance with rap music and the aesthetics of hip hop (see Bluher 2001, Massood 2003). The African American hood, and even more so the *banlieue* and comparable multi-ethnic neighbourhoods in London, Berlin or Hamburg, simultaneously function as symbolically over-determined sites of social disenfranchisement and as hothouses of cultural hybridisation. In contrast to the parents' generation, intent on preserving a sense of cultural authenticity, their offspring 'wrestle constantly to find an enabling interlocking of the different "cultures" in which they find themselves' (Massey 1998: 122) and readily buy into an eclectic mix of international cultural reference points, thereby producing hybrid cultures that assimilate global cultures into a specific locality. Amongst the most prominent cultural icons referenced in *La Haine* and *Short Sharp Shock* are boxing champion Muhammad Ali, the martial arts icon Bruce Lee, the psychotic Travis Bickle in *Taxi Driver* (Martin Scorsese, 1976), the boxer Jake La Motta in *Raging Bull* (Martin Scorsese, 1980) and Tony Montana / Al Pacino in *Scarface* (Brian De Palma, 1983). The physical prowess and hyper-masculinity of these 'emblematic embodiments of marginalized masculinity' compensate for their 'lacking access to material goods' (Mennel 2002: 135, 144). Similarly, hip hop, with its distinctive music (rap, reggae, DJing, human beat box), break-dancing, slang, fashion and graphics (graffiti and tagging), signifies cultural and generational rebellion in these films and serves as an important strategy of cultural hybridisation. Hip hop, though often misread as 'an expression of some authentic African-American essence', Paul Gilroy (1993a: 34) reminds us, is anything but authentic.

> The musical components of hip hop are a hybrid form nurtured by the social relations of the South Bronx where Jamaican sound system culture was transplanted during the 1970s and put down new roots. In conjunction with specific technological innovations, this routed and re-rooted Caribbean culture set in train a process that was to transform black America's sense of itself and a large portion of the popular music industry as well. (33)

Originally intended as a peaceful response to racism and violence that was to 'channel the anger of young people in the South Bronx away from gang fighting into music, dance, and graffiti' (Lipsitz 1994: 26), hip hop has since enjoyed enormous transnational and cross-over appeal and has become synonymous with global youth culture. In *La Haine*, break-dancing, Saïd's tagging and Cut Killer's DJing (he mixes NTM, Assassin and the iconic French singer Edith Piaf, and turns up the volume for the entire *banlieue* community to listen), appropriate hip hop culture to the specific context of French youth sub-culture (see Doughty and Griffiths 2006: 124). The production of culturally hybrid localities in *La Haine* reflects the protagonists' identification with the marginalised and dispossessed youth of black urban American culture and with the downtrodden transnational heroes of gangster and boxing movies, but includes remarkably few reference points to French majority culture. While Saïd alters the quotation 'The world is yours' from *Scarface* to 'The world is ours' on a large billboard,[2] he does not tag the oversize murals of the French poets Baudelaire and Rimbaud in Chanteloup-les-Vignes.[3] French high culture is so inaccessible that it goes unnoticed and is left untouched. By the same token, Saïd's engagement with his Maghrebi cultural heritage is minimal. He may well wear a Fatma's hand charm around his neck but he speaks French mixed with *verlan* (a particular form of back-slang associated with *banlieue* youth) rather than Arabic and is not shown once in his home environment.

Mathieu Kassovitz described the *banlieue* as a place 'where you don't mix genders' (cited in Vincendeau 2005: 66) and, indeed, with some notable exceptions, including *Raï* (Thomas Gilou, 1995), *La Squale* (*The Squale*, Fabrice Genestal, 2000), *L'Esquive* (*Games of Love and Chance*, Abdellatif Kechiche, 2003) and Benguigui's four-part television drama about Aïcha Bouamaza (2009–12), girls and women are under-represented or are the victims of misogyny, violence and even rape. Films about young *beurettes* typically pit the cool spaces of urban youth culture against the domestic sphere, which is charged with conflict as adolescent girls emulate the liberal lifestyles of their Western peers and rebel against the strictures imposed upon them at home. In *Samia* (Philippe Faucon, 2000), a film loosely based on Soraya Nini's autobiographical novel *Ils disent que je suis une beurette* (1993), this spatial dichotomy is memorably summed up by Samia's eldest brother, Yacine, who assumes the role of patriarch during his father's absence, as he reminds his sisters: 'This is not America. Outside is France, in here is Algeria'. The analogy between the domestic sphere and the Algerian nation-state is intended to legitimise power hierarchies in the Algerian French family against which the fifteen-year-old eponymous heroine and her sisters rebel. Samia's longing to break free is expressed not only in her many altercations with Yacine, a victim himself who is unable to find employment in a society in which *beurs* do not enjoy the same kind of opportunities as their white French peers, but also in the numerous shots that frame her perched on the balcony, a liminal space between the claustrophobic family flat on the outskirts of Marseille and the open space of a mountain range beckoning on the horizon. Samia's mother, by contrast, is consistently captured in the small, windowless kitchen, cooking traditional North African meals for her large family or doing other domestic chores – and putting pressure on her daughters to assist her and bow to male supremacy, even if violently enforced.

The family's media consumption illustrates how radio and television programmes are strategically deployed to support the production of Muslim culture in the home. As family members assemble for dinner during Ramadan, the broadcaster on Radio Soleil changes from Arabic to French, announcing: 'It is now 5.10 p.m. Time to pray and break the fast'.[4] In another dinner scene, Yacine acts as interpreter for his father, who is unable to understand the French news programme on television. Recalling Hannerz's argument that habitats of meaning are determined by cultural competencies, the father's monolingualism in *Samia* excludes him from the social and media spaces of majority culture. On another occasion, the family is watching a French programme featuring a sex scene. This is regarded as a morally corrupting intrusion into the domestic sphere, and the daughters are immediately asked to change the channel to one showing Muslim women wearing headscarves and speaking Arabic.

In contrast to the ghettocentric imagination of male-centred narratives that construct diasporic identities primarily with reference to distinctive urban topographies, in female-centred narratives locality is first and foremost produced on the female body. As Elleke Boehmer (1991), Anne McClintock (1995), Nira Yuval-Davis and Floya Anthias (1989), and other feminist scholars who have written on gender, nation and ethnicity in colonial and postcolonial cultures, have proposed, 'the woman's body is the site over which identity is asserted and culture is maintained. She, as the carrier and bearer of her ethnic group, has the obligation not to stray and disrupt the group's identity' (Meetoo and Mirza 2007: 191), by violating gendered codes of behaviour or by mixing with others outside the group. The desire to control women's behaviour, in particular their sexual behaviour, derives from the fact that, in patriarchal cultures, female modesty and 'the purity' of the woman are linked to the family's honour. Any violation of the family honour can be 'justifiably' punished by death. 'It's like erasing a dirty mark on the family' (Schreiber cited in Ewing 2008: no page).

The controversial film *Submission* (2004), based on the collaboration between the white Dutch filmmaker Theo van Gogh and Ayaan Hirsi Ali, a Somali-born, ex-Muslim feminist campaigner and former Member of the Dutch Parliament, provides a pertinent example. The eleven-minute short is a polemic indictment of the victimisation of women in Islamic cultures. It features an actress wearing the traditional *hijab* in combination with a transparent *chador* that reveals her breasts and other parts of her naked body, on which are inscribed verses from the Koran. The actress's voice-over in Arabic engages in a prayer-like dialogue with Allah, challenging the Islamic practices of arranged marriage, control over female sexuality and domestic violence, and even reveals that she has been raped by one of her uncles. Just as the voice-over is interspersed with the sound of whip lashings, the calligraphy on her body is overlaid with wheals, offering a compelling account of how locality is inscribed on to the female body.[5] *Submission* recalls Michel de Certeau's observation that 'the law "takes hold of bodies" in order to make them its text. Through all sorts of initiations [. . .] it transforms them into tables of the law, into living tableaux of rules and customs, into actors in the drama organized by social order' (1988: 139). Unsurprisingly, the film incensed large parts of the Muslim community and resulted in Theo van Gogh and Ayan Hirsi Ali receiving death threats after the film was aired on Dutch TV in August 2004. A Dutch Muslim fanatic subsequently assassinated Theo van Gogh.

There are countless less spectacular examples that demonstrate how women are expected to embody a locality from which they have been separated through geographical and generational distance. In cinematic and other popular representations of ethnicised women, different sartorial traditions and, in particular, the switching between Western and 'ethnic / traditional' clothes, serve as 'contested boundary markers between different group identities' (Dwyer 1998: 54) and as expressions of resistance, be it to the cultural values of the ethnic minority community or to those of the majority culture. For example, the heroines of the title in the Turkish German film *Yasemin* (Hark Bohm, 1988) and the British Asian film *Yasmin* both perform some form of masquerade as they leave or return to their family homes, lowering or lifting the hems of their skirts and wrapping or removing headscarves so as to conform to expectations of female modesty and avoid conflict. Yet, interestingly, in Glenaan's film, set in an ethnically mixed small town in northern England, Yasmin's attitude towards observing the *hijab* changes dramatically, as the demonisation of Muslims gathers pace in the aftermath of 9/11. After witnessing a racist attack on a *hijab*-wearing woman in the street and becoming the victim of racial prejudice herself, she decides to wear the headscarf outside her home and Pakistani neighbourhood to express her solidarity with the British Muslim community in a political climate of growing anti-Muslim racism.

In the light-hearted girl-power movie *Bend It Like Beckham*, featuring a Hounslow-based Sikh family of Punjabi origin, the female body and different dress codes also express cultural allegiances and give rise to intergenerational conflict. However, in contrast to films about Muslim families, which mostly centre on domineering patriarchs, in Chadha's comedy it is the mother who tries to ensure that her eighteen-year-old daughter Jess conforms to traditional notions of Indian femininity and heteronormativity. Much to her mother's dismay, Jess is not at all interested in learning how to cook *aloo gobi*, or any other Indian meal for that matter, but dreams of being able to bend the ball like British football star David Beckham, whose poster is pinned on her bedroom wall. Jess's predilection for football gear, masculine shoes and unisex tracksuits simultaneously transgresses ethnic and gender norms and mounts a challenge to her mother's reified notion of identity. As far as Mrs Bhamra is concerned, a girl with short hair (Jess's best friend Jules) is easily mistaken for a boy and Jess's football shorts indecently expose her legs and, what is more, a hideous scar on her thighs. Such imperfection is incommensurate with the ideal of a pristine (intact) female body. The scene in which the seamstress takes Jess and her sister Pinky's body measurements (breasts, waistline and hips) also draws attention to notions of gender normativity based on physical attributes.

By showing that Jess's best friend, the white British Jules, faces similar problems at home, *Bend It Like Beckham* mitigates the cultural dichotomies it sets up. Mrs Paxton also regards her daughter's passion for football as a threatening gender deviance and would rather buy Jules a sexy push-up than a sports bra. Both mothers are horrified when they begin to suspect that their daughters might be lesbians. The possibility is invoked on several occasions but, by foregrounding the budding heterosexual romance between Jess and the male football coach Joe, the film debunks the idea for the purposes of comedy.[6] By establishing correspondences between the Asian and white British domestic settings and parental attitudes towards female transgression of conventional

Figure 4.1 Jess (Parminder Nagra) demonstrates that hybrid identities live through transformation (*Bend It Like Beckham*, Gurinder Chadha, 2002)

gender roles, Chadha makes the point that the experience of growing up is essentially the same for a white and a brown British girl.

The overt signifying power attached to different dress styles in *Bend It Like Beckham* renders visible the multi-layered and transformative nature of diasporic identities in terms of the material practices of everyday life. It also recalls Stuart Hall's much-cited observation that diasporic identities are hybrid and poised in transition, 'constantly producing and reproducing themselves anew through transformation and difference' (Hall [1990] 2003: 244).

We can witness the performance of such a transformation in the memorable locker-room scene showing Jess surrounded by the all-women football team. Her team (predominantly white British girls) help her change from the red and white football gear (connoting masculinity and Western notions of gender equality) into her richly embroidered red and golden sari (connoting Indian femininity) to return to her sister's Indian wedding ceremony, which she temporarily left in order to play the all-important match.[7] The rapid cross-cutting between the locker room and the wedding location implies an easy and unproblematic switch between, or to be more precise, fusion of Jess's Indian and British identities. The dominance of the colour red in such disparate items of clothing emphasises sameness over difference and recasts the prevalent image of the diasporic heroine as torn between two cultures by asserting instead that she can have the best of both worlds.

In keeping with Chadha's ambition to reach South Asian as well as Western mainstream audiences, the film foregrounds the universality rather than the ethnic specificity of intergenerational conflicts in the family. An important factor, which reduces the 'Otherness' of the Bhamras, is the fact that they are

Sikhs rather than Muslims and middle- rather than working-class. But since Islam is the dominant faith in the Maghreb, Turkey and Pakistan (though not in India or the Caribbean), Muslim families feature prominently in the films analysed in this book. Moreover, as well-educated, middle-class families are under-represented, such positive portrayals of diasporic family life, as offered in *Bend It Like Beckham*, *I for India*, *Anita and Me* or *The Namesake*, remain notable exceptions.

Ethnicising Patriarchy

It is specifically the uneducated, working-class Muslim patriarch whose negative stereotype dominates the media, including cinema.[8] Widely debated by feminists of all factions in the 1960s and 1970s, the meaning of patriarchy has come to denote primarily 'male domination and the power relationship by which men dominate women', although the concept also refers to the rule of the father or oldest male over younger males in his family (Beechy 1979: 66, 68). Whereas Marxist feminists have linked the principles underlying female oppression to other forms of subordination, notably class exploitation resulting from the capitalist mode of production, the African American feminist bell hooks has emphasised the connections between 'a political system of imperialist, white supremacist, capitalist patriarchy' (2000: xiv) and other systems of unjust power distribution, notably those based on race. According to hooks, in the post-feminist era, 'radical feminist critique of patriarchy has practically been silenced in our culture' and 'using the word "patriarchy" is regarded as passé' (2004: 29), even though patriarchal structures have by no means been eradicated in the family or in society at large. The supposedly passé concept of patriarchy has recently risen to prominence again in the context of public debates about multi-culturalism and cultural diversity – yet, remarkably, the word itself hardly features. What make headlines are honour killings and the *hijab*, both pointing towards a problematic conflation of patriarchy and Islam.[9] In the wake of an intensified Islamophobia after the 9/11 terrorist attacks on the World Trade Centre in New York and subsequent acts of terrorism elsewhere, the Muslim man has become more suspect than ever before; as a possible 'sleeper', he poses a threat to security; as a Muslim patriarch, to the human rights of the women in his family and to fundamental principles of Western democracy (see Butterwegge 2007, Ewing 2008). The tacit equation between patriarchy, the Muslim man and the threat of terrorism has led to his unprecedented stigmatisation.

'When the talk is of honor, women become the symbols of honor' – not just in the context of family conflicts but also in relation to wars, Akbar Ahmed proposes in *Islam under Siege* (2003: 120). Thus, the mass rape of women in the Bosnian war was, above all, intended as a violation of honour and targeted the enemy where it was most vulnerable. Ahmed distinguishes between 'post-honour societies', such as America and most other Western societies in which traditional ideas of honour have become irrelevant, and others in which honour 'is still important and fiercely defended as in tribal Afghanistan. Other countries, like India, are somewhere in between, containing groups that aspire to be modern and also others that wish to emphasize tradition and honor' (55–6). As a result of globalisation and transnational mobility, such different attitudes towards honour have come into contact and have triggered fundamental controversies. While one camp understands honour 'as an idealistic and humanistic goal', the other conceives of it as an 'expression of group loyalty' (55) that can be legitimately defended through violence against those who violate it. The elusive and ambiguous idea of honour is deployed as much in wars of rhetoric, in which one individual, family or nation accuses the other of 'knowing no honour', as it is in the *jihad* and in America's 'war on terror' in the aftermath of 9/11.

Ahmed's discussion of the notion of honour illustrates yet again the pivotal role of women, who are called upon to act as the symbolic bearers of locally specific ideologies and value systems – in political as well as in familial conflicts. Yet there is another side to the controversial concept of female honour because it poses a considerable challenge to advocates of multi-culturalism. On the one hand, it violates the principles of equality and liberty, and calls for the 'saving of brown women from brown men' (Spivak cited in Meetoo and Mirza 2007: 195); on the other hand, tolerance demands that Western host societies grant diasporic communities the right to abide by social practices different from those of the majority culture, as long as they do not contravene the law. Yet the 'ban on the *burqa*' in France and the Netherlands, as the protracted controversies around Islamic female dress codes are succinctly referred to in the media, indicates that sartorial expressions of allegiance to Islam have emerged as symbolically over-determined and emotionally charged signifiers of Muslim patriarchy, which inscribe the religious and cultural practices of a locality regarded as remote and incompatible with Western secular society upon the female body.[10]

When We Leave – but Fail to Leave the Traditions of the Homeland Behind . . .

When We Leave, scripted and directed by the Austrian-born filmmaker Feo Aladağ, centres on the controversial issue of an honour killing in a Turkish German family. The film tells the story of Umay, who after a secret abortion and violent abuse by her husband, flees from him and his extended family in Istanbul, taking her young son Cem with her. When she turns up on her parents' doorstep in Berlin, Umay does not receive the warm welcome for which she had hoped. Her parents, Kader and Halyme, show little sympathy and insist that a wife belongs with her husband. 'Today he beats you, tomorrow he caresses you', says Umay's father. As for Cem, a son belongs to his father, no matter what! Nevertheless, Kader and Halyme are torn between

Figure 4.2 Umay (Sibel Kekilli) may kiss her father's hand but she will not bow to patriarchy in *When We Leave* (Feo Aladağ, 2010)

their love for Umay and the traditional honour code they fail to question fundamentally. Upon discovering that her parents plan to return Cem to his father in Turkey, Umay escapes the family home and seeks refuge in a woman's shelter. Gradually, she builds a new life, working in a canteen run by an open-minded, independent Turkish woman, attending evening classes and embarking upon a romantic relationship with a German man. But her brothers track her down and Kader tasks his youngest son Acar to execute the honour killing. When he fails to complete the mission, Mehmet takes over and accidentally stabs Cem instead of Umay.

The plot is loosely based on a real honour killing that made headlines in the German press in 2005, when Hatun Sürücü, a twenty-three-year-old Turkish woman living in Berlin, was shot dead by one of her brothers. Her desire for independence, her refusal to wear a headscarf and her alleged promiscuity were perceived as a violation of the Turkish German family's honour. 'From the beginning, even before Hatun's assailant had been identified, the tabloids marked her murder as [. . .] a "headscarf murder"' (Ewing 2008: 154). The reference to the headscarf implicated Islam in the practice of honour killings and the German tabloid *Bild* even reported 'She was killed for taking off her headscarf', whilst the Turkish paper *Zamam* quoted one of her brothers as saying, 'My sister had begun living like a foreigner' (cited in Ewing 2008: 155–6). The greatest furore, however, was caused when the German press quoted an adolescent boy from within the Turkish German community in Berlin, who had justified the honour killing in a casual remark to a news reporter, 'She had only herself to blame. The whore behaved like a German' (cited in Schiffauer 2005). Islamic groups in Germany stressed that Islam forbids murder in the name of honour and attributed the practice to rural customs and Anatolian family law.[11] The case of Hatun Sürücü was cited as evidence of the existence of a so-called 'parallel society' (*Parallelgesellschaft*) – a term widely used in the German media to describe the unwillingness of immigrants, in particular Turkish Muslims, to assimilate to German majority culture (*Leitkultur*).¹²

When We Leave reprises a theme that has dominated Turkish German cinema since the beginning – that of the victimised young Turkish woman. Despite some conspicuous similarities with *Yasemin* and, arguably, also Fatih Akın's *Head-On*, Feo Aladağ's family melodrama represents a marked departure in so far as it eschews the polarisation between the victimised daughter and the patriarchal perpetrator.¹³ In *Yasemin*, a Turkish greengrocer in Hamburg–Altona and father of two daughters turns from a loving and reasonably liberal father into a despotic patriarch when the family honour is violated because his elder daughter is unable to produce the bloodstained bridal sheet to prove her virginity after the wedding night. To protect his younger daughter, seventeen-year-old Yasemin, from the alleged moral depravity of 'a country of infidels', he deports her to Turkey to marry her off to a remote cousin in an even more remote village. At the eleventh hour, Yasemin's blond German boyfriend comes to her rescue and she elopes on the back of his motorbike. As Deniz Göktürk and other critics have noted, the film's stance vis-à-vis multi-culturalism is highly problematic, because it reinforces the dichotomy of a liberal and liberalising German culture that is contrasted with an oppressive and backward Turkish Muslim culture. It draws on the common fantasy of 'victimised Turkish women, who, especially when young and beautiful, need to be rescued from their patriarchal community' (2000: 69).

Even though *Head-On* (see Chapter 5) steers clear of this particular stereotype, featuring instead a heroine who is capable of rescuing herself, Akın's film is firmly focused on the various moral and emotional conflicts of Sibel, sparing neither thought nor sympathy for her father. By comparison, Aladağ's multi-award-winning feature film début conveys a rather more nuanced family portray, attending in particular to the problematic of gender stratification within the patriarchal family. Kader, who is faced with the moral dilemma of how to deal with Umay's 'dishonourable behaviour', fails to question fundamentally the inequality between men and women. 'I wish she was born a boy', he remarks. His inability to reject the archaic rituals that compel him to kill his only daughter and thereby change the course of events identifies Kader as an emotionally torn victim–perpetrator. Kader's dilemma is one that he shares with countless other protagonists in domestic melodrama, for whom moral imperatives translate into social pressures (see Elsaesser [1972] 1987, Gledhill 1987b). What is at stake is not so much morality as reputation. When his younger daughter falls pregnant and her fiancé refuses to marry into a family that has 'no honour', Kader sets things right by paying the fiancé's father a considerable sum as a means of compensation. Precisely because Kader is a pragmatist rather than a religious zealot, he does genuinely suffer from the ritualistic murder he feels impelled to instigate – and yet, he does not have the strength to break with the patriarchal honour code.

When We Leave links the inflammatory issue of female honour killings explicitly to the traditions of the Anatolian village while establishing connections with Islam more subliminally. Of particular significance in this respect is Kader's long journey across Turkey's vast expanses of barren, wide-open plains and rugged mountains to his final destination – his father's home in a village in the Kayseri province in Central Anatolia. The journey is reminiscent of those undertaken by Metin in *Düğün – The Wedding* and Keltoum in *Keltoum's Daughter*, discussed in Chapter 2. Here, too, the duration of the arduous overland journey translates spatial into cultural distance. The house of the family elder is spartan. Its claustrophobic interior is furnished with some rugs on the floor and a tapestry of Mecca on the wall. Not much light filters through the small window. When Kader arrives, his father is asleep, presumably not having been notified of his son's visit. There is no telephone, no television. The absence of any communication technology underscores the isolation and backwardness of the place, a significant detail, which reminds us of Ulf Hannerz's observation that 'habitats of meaning' are expanded (or not, as the case may be) through modern communication technologies and cultural competencies (1996: 22–3).

Kader has embarked upon the journey to seek his father's advice – or so we assume. Not a single word is spoken in this scene. The conversation between father and son, though absolutely crucial to the narrative development, is not dramatised. The camera leaves the room, as it were, contemplating the exterior of the primitive stone dwelling in this godforsaken place at the end of the world. When the camera re-enters the room, father and son are looking at each other in silence. The face of Kader's father, shot against the dim light that filters through the window, remains invisible. The patriarch is portrayed as a man without a voice and without a face – anonymous, yet enormously powerful. The expression on Kader's face, when he leaves his father's house, reveals that the advice he was given was not what he may have hoped for. When we leave one culture, how can we expect to be able to translate its traditions into another?

The English film title, *When We Leave*, draws attention to the conflicts arising from such dual and ambiguous attachments to two different localities. On one level, the title refers to the series of departures and goodbyes that propel the narrative forward: Umay and Cem's clandestine departure from Istanbul, their escape from her parents' home in Berlin, and their subsequent departure from the women's shelter after her brother has found her there. 'Each time we leave, we leave something of us behind', Umay explains to her little son, commenting as much upon her personal experience as on that of migrants more generally. Leave-taking is associated with the pain of separation and loss.

Conversely, the film advocates the necessity to leave certain cultural traditions behind, as they represent a form of baggage that precludes successful integration. Kader is burdened with baggage from back home. His return to the family elder in the Anatolian village makes palpable the spatiotemporal

Figure 4.3 Umay (Sibel Kekilli) and Cem (Nizam Schiller) running away from domestic violence and oppression in Istanbul in *When We Leave* (Feo Aladağ, 2010)

disjuncture that requires of him to come to terms, in just twenty-odd years, with a socio-cultural transformation so profound that it took Western societies at least four or five generations (see Seidel 2010). In fact, the moral dilemma Kader and his wife are faced with is reminiscent of that experienced by the parents of *Effi Briest* in Theodor Fontane's novel of 1894. Effi's parents also feel compelled by social convention to make a choice between their daughter and society when her adulterous liaison with the gallant and debonair Major Crampas is discovered, albeit many years after the end of the affair. Since public opprobrium has tarnished Effi's reputation, her parents ostracise her from the circle of family and friends. The separation from her child Annie, of whom her former husband is granted custody (a constellation comparable to the one envisaged in *When We Leave*), represents an additional punishment – and the cruellest – for Effi's moral trespass. There is also an honour killing in *Effi Briest*, though the practice of duels of honour in nineteenth-century Prussia (and elsewhere) put officers and gentlemen rather than women in the line of fire. The comparison with *Effi Briest*, far-fetched as it may seem, nevertheless reinforces the notion that the diasporic family portrayed in Aladağ's film abides by a system of values and social practices that is thoroughly outdated. By the same token, it could be argued that *When We Leave* adapts a theme that, in a different shape and form, played a significant role in German social history, making Umay's family not so alien after all.

Kader's cultural attachment to the traditions of his ancestral village is reflected in the claustrophobic interior of his flat in Berlin, which is as dark and sealed off from the outside world as that of his father's humble abode far, far away. The chiaroscuro lighting filtering through the shutters there, casts vertical grid-like shadows across the sleeping Umay here, making visible the fact that the family home is a prison from which she will have to escape. The painterly quality of the dark-hued colour scheme in both places, reminiscent of the genre paintings of the Dutch Masters, gestures towards Kader's efforts to reproduce the locality of Central Anatolia in his home in Berlin. In contrast to the similarly stifling bourgeois homes in the domestic melodramas of Douglas Sirk or Nicholas Ray, in which the moral pressures and social restrictions imposed upon the family by the local small-town community are palpable, the claustrophobic atmosphere in *When We Leave* stems from social pressures that wield their power trans-locally.

In keeping with Kader's endeavour to preserve the culture and mores of his homeland, the lingua franca of the domestic sphere is Turkish, although both Kader and Halyme are able to understand and speak German. Whereas in many other films, linguistic code switching is inflected schematically along generational divides, here it signals the cultural allegiance a character chooses to assert. For instance, when Umay gatecrashes her sister's wedding ceremony, she uses Turkish to plead publicly with her parents to welcome her back into the family. With tears streaming down her face, she then addresses her mother in German, reminding her of the blood ties that bind them. For Umay, German is coded as the language of the heart; she speaks it with Cem, with her Turkish German boss Gül and her friends. Turkish, on the other hand, is linked to patriarchy. Mehmet, the family's oldest son and the one who eventually executes the honour killing, speaks it more frequently than any of his siblings. Yet, ultimately, the language of patriarchy is silence.

It is not only the crucial conversation between Kader and his father that is shrouded in silence. The meeting in which Kader relays his own father's counsel, commanding his sons Acar and Mehmet to right the wrong by killing their sister, is also acted out in the absence of sound. In this way, *When We Leave* identifies the silence of patriarchal complicity surrounding honour killings – rather than Umay's 'improper' Western lifestyle – as the real violation of family honour. Like the family secrets discussed in the previous chapter, the barbaric practice of honour killings is an unspeakable family secret that is passed on not only transgenerationally (from the family elder to Kader and from Kader to his sons) but also trans-locally (from rural Anatolia to urban Berlin). The silence pervading the film's most crucial scenes also recalls Peter Brooks's characterisation of melodrama as 'the text of muteness'. To represent its most important meanings, melodrama relies on gesture, tableau and 'the mute role' that engenders meaning 'in the absence of the word' (1976: 62). The film's unexpected melodramatic twist at the end highlights the absurdity of honour killings. Intended to preserve the family lineage from suffering 'irreparable harm to its reputation' and restoring it 'to a place of respect in the community' (Laviosa 2010: 187), the accidental killing of Cem, the only male grandchild, actually curtails the male lineage. Patriarchy is devouring its own sons!

THE PRODUCTION OF LOCALITY IN A HYBRIDISED FAMILY:
THE KHANS IN *EAST IS EAST* AND *WEST IS WEST*

In *East is East* and its sequel, *West is West*, both based on semi-autobiographical screenplays by Ayub Khan-Din, the production of locality also coincides with the motif of the journey. In *East is East*, George Khan takes his sprawling family, consisting of his white British wife Ella and their seven children, on a day-trip to Bradford, known for its large Pakistani community, while in *West is West*, George and his youngest son Sajid embark on an educational expedition to his natal village in Pakistan. Both journeys constitute attempts to re-assert and legitimise his patriarchal authority, which has been severely undermined by his mixed-race family based in a white working-class neighbourhood in Salford.

The titles of both films draw attention to the importance of place and invoke a famous line from Rudyard Kipling's 'The Ballad of East and West': 'Oh, East is East, and West is West, and never the twain shall meet'. Yet the films prove Kipling's assertion of the cultural incompatibility of East and West wrong because they demonstrate that 'a meeting between East and West has taken place, [...] in the very heart of the former Empire, where mixed Muslim-English families like the Khans [...] have been created. At the same time', Barbara Korte and Claudia Sternberg propose with reference to *East is East*, 'the abridgement of Kipling's original phrase suggests that in that meeting of cultures, problems still exist – and that these problems are caused by an East which remains the East, rather than by the West' (2004: 156).

In *East is East*, George Khan represents 'the East' – and is both the ogre and the laughing stock, who tries to impose upon his English wife and mixed-race children the religious and cultural traditions of his native Pakistan, resulting in domestic conflicts and even violence. His struggle is intensified by the fact that he has minority status in his own family and neighbourhood. Except for his son Maneer, who is a practising Muslim, his children identify themselves as British and feel much closer to their mother. Tariq refuses to show the respect expected of a Pakistani son and provokes his father further by stating: 'Dad, I'm not Pakistani. I was born here. I speak English, not Urdu'.

Opening with an aerial shot of the rows of red-brick terraced houses, a setting instantly recognisable to a British audience from the long-running soap opera *Coronation Street*, the camera zooms in on a Whitsun Procession in which the Khan children (though secular) cheerfully participate, carrying a crucifix and other religious effigies amidst a crowd of white British Catholics. Ella, who is obviously in cahoots, alerts her children that their father has returned early from the mosque, whereupon, in another aerial shot, they are shown to separate from the procession, running along a parallel street that allows them to pass behind their father's back unnoticed. The sequence foreshadows the film's central themes: the importance of place, in which different constructions of locality compete with each other; the second generation's conflicting allegiances to two different cultures; and the mother's complicity in circumventing patriarchal authority.

George has not been left untouched either by the mutual entanglement and intertwining of cultures in the diaspora space. Having abandoned his first wife and daughters in Pakistan more than thirty years before and having subsequently married the white British Ella, George has embarked on an irreversible process of cultural assimilation. His business, a fish 'n' chip shop called 'George's English Chippie', is a quintessentially British institution; he 'forgot' to have his youngest son Sajid circumcised in time and, whenever Ella offers him a cup of tea, he, rather symbolically, asks for half a cup. Yet George is in denial about the contradictions and tensions within himself and obsessively pursues fantasies of cultural purity, which revolve around Islam on the one hand and the local traditions of the rural Pakistan of some thirty years ago on the other. Observing that their father does not live by what he preaches, his children question his moral integrity and boycott his attempts to subject them to the codes of Muslim patriarchy.

To buttress his authority, George relies on the advice of the local Mullah (who suggests various measures to Islamise the family) and on the empowerment that comes with a particular place and ethnic community: nearby Bradford, with its large Pakistani population. Talking to the Mullah about the shame his eldest son brought upon the family by running away from his wedding, George Khan muses: 'Maybe I should have taken them [his family] to Bradford long ago, more Pakistan, there, see?'. And so the Khans' trip to Bradford in *East is East* represents George's most successful attempt to produce the locality of his homeland in diaspora. A popular song from the Bollywood classic *Pakeezah* (Kamal Amrohi, 1971) provides the musical score for the journey in a brightly coloured van from Salford to 'Bradistan' (as Bradford is dubbed in graffiti on the road sign). Whereas the grey skies hanging over the Yorkshire countryside and the cheerful sounds of Bollywood music seem incongruous, music and setting are in harmony as soon as the van reaches Bradford. A series of tracking shots through the car window reveal street markets bustling with women dressed in colourful saris, conjuring up memories of Pakistan for George, who feels instantly at home in this 'town full of happy people', as he remarks to Ella. Even the large billboard, advertising OVO, which 'washes whiter than white', shows a dark-skinned, headscarf-wearing South Asian woman.[14]

The family outing to Bradford (which George uses to negotiate an arranged marriage surreptitiously behind his sons' back) ends with a visit to the local Indian cinema, the Moti Mahal, owned by a member of George's extended family. Ella announces, 'We've come to see *Chaudhvin Ka Chand*', a popular Hindi film from the early 1960s, starring Guru Dutt. Much to George and Ella's disappointment, a different film is showing. Yet to let down family would be unforgivable! And so the screening in front of a packed cinema is interrupted and the reels are changed. Amongst South Asians, this scene suggests, family takes precedence over business, highlighting one of the positive

Figure 4.4 A family trip to the Moti Mahal momentarily unites the fractured Khan family in *East is East* (Damien O'Donnell, 1999)

aspects of a culture (generally represented in negative terms) where family is everything. Ensconced in the dark cinema, for once, the Khan family are happily united through their shared enjoyment of Hindi cinema. As Claudia Sternberg observes with reference to *East is East* and other films featuring migrants at the movies, including *Brothers in Trouble* (Udayan Prasad, 1995) and *A Private Enterprise* (Peter Smith, 1974), 'in contrast to skin colour, dress codes and religious practice, cinema-going is perceived as "harmless" by the majority cultures, and popular productions have been embraced in a fashion similar to that of an exotic but ultimately unthreatening "ethnic cuisine"' (2010: 259).[15]

In contrast to George's media consumption, which consists of Hindi cinema and news coverage of the Indo-Pakistani war of 1971 on his small transistor radio, his children access more diverse 'mediascapes' – to return to Appadurai's concept of flows – all of which point toward their identification with British mainstream culture. Behind their father's back, they eat a dinner of bacon and sausages (identified as a form of culinary resistance as the camera zooms in to capture the plateful of forbidden food in a close-up) and watch a televised speech in which Enoch Powell advocates the assisted repatriation and resettlement of immigrants. The nonplussed Saleem cracks a joke about George's imminent repatriation, which indicates yet again that the adolescent Khans do not perceive themselves as immigrants and, therefore, not as the target of Powell's racist propaganda. On another occasion, they watch the animated children's television series *The Clangers*, featuring a happy family (rather different from the dysfunctional Khans) of alien creatures that look like the result of crossbreeding between mice and anteaters (perhaps a tongue-in-cheek reference to the racial hybridity of the Khan children), who live on a far-away blue planet.

Figure 4.5 'When Sajid looks at you, there is love in his eyes; if only he would look at me like that. Just once', George Khan (Om Puri) says to Pir Naseem (Nadim Sawalha) at the Kharee Sharif fair, while Sajid (Aqib Khan) sleeps on Pir's shoulder (*West is West*, Andy De Emmony, 2010)

The sequel *West is West* is set five years later in 1976. When the youngest son, Sajid, calls his father a 'Paki', George cannot but acknowledge that all of his attempts to instil a sense of Pakistani identity in his children have utterly failed. The only remedy left is an educational journey to his homeland. Predictably, after more than thirty years' absence, he finds his homeland and family much changed. *West is West*, just like the films discussed in Chapter 2, proves that you cannot go home again and that home is but 'a mythic place of desire in the diasporic imagination' and, ultimately, 'a place of no return even if it is possible to visit the geographical territory that is seen as the place of origin' (Brah 1996: 192). Although, upon his arrival, his first wife Basheera and his extended family show George the reverence he expected, it soon transpires that he has forfeited the love and respect he anticipated finding. Sending the occasional letter and remission payments from England hardly compensated Basheera and her two daughters for George's prolonged absence and neglect of familial duties.

The journey's educational mission is on the brink of failure – until, that is, Sajid meets Pir Naseem, a charismatic Sufi elder under whose gentle and loving tutelage he is transformed. Just as Reda in *Le Grand Voyage* is drawn to Mustapha, a rival father figure who is less dogmatic and more empathetic than his real father, Sajid too adopts the Sufi elder as his teacher and father of choice.

Where George is stern and authoritarian, Pir Naseem is gentle and tolerant, accepting of his own shortcomings and those of others. Rather than trying to exercise his power on those around him, he seeks to empower them. To be sure, Pir Naseem's spiritual guidance on the Sufi path by and large excludes devotional practices and centres instead on resolving Sajid's (and George's) conflicting allegiances to two different cultures and to each other. The most fundamental lesson he teaches Sajid is the need to assimilate to one's environment. First he coaxes Sajid into swopping his dark, ill-fitting suit, a garment entirely inappropriate for the heat and dust of Pakistan, for a light *shalwar kameez* that blends in with the golden hues of the scorched grass and dusty soil, and then he elaborates:

> Your father and many like him have made better lives for themselves abroad. But they fail to understand the consequences of their actions to themselves or their families. [. . .] Do you think you can move to another country and expect everything to be the same as the place you left? That your new world will have no effect on you or how you think? [. . .] We have to adapt to the situations and worlds we find ourselves in. It does not mean we have to lose any sense of where we're from. But it may give us a greater sense of who we are and what we can achieve.

Pir Naseem's words of wisdom neatly encapsulate the film's integrationist agenda. In contrast to *When We Leave*, which advocates a similar idea, *West is West* refrains from reiterating the facile opposition between a modern urban host society and a backward pastoral homeland. Admittedly, George's 'other' home is 'primitive' in the sense that it lacks all modern conveniences and even sanitation. There is no tractor and the fields are still ploughed with the help of two oxen (a skill which George no longer masters). The imputed backwardness of Pakistan provides a rich source of humour, which would be problematic if it were not for the fact that the ethnic stereotypes enlisted are promptly debunked. *West is West* makes the point that remoteness and poverty do not equal backwardness.[16] Thus, Pir Naseem, though not formally educated, is the best teacher Sajid could wish for and, compared with Mr Jordan, the headmaster at Sajid's school in Manchester, far more effective. Although it is Mr Jordan, a former colonial officer stationed in the Punjab, who gives Sajid a copy of the *National Geographic* on Pakistan and Kipling's novel *Kim* (1901), he fails to inspire Sajid. Yet when Pir Naseem reads the very same passage from *Kim* that Mr Jordan recited in the school office, Sajid and his friend Zaid listen attentively.

In a similar vein, the film compares and contrasts Mrs Khan No. 1 and No. 2. Basheera, though initially playing the demure and subservient wife, soon drops this traditionally female role. In openly castigating George for his unforgivable neglect, she reveals herself to be no less assertive than his English wife Ella. Thus the bond that Ella (who arrives unexpectedly in Pakistan with her best friend Annie in tow) and Basheera forge, despite not speaking the same language, is founded on female solidarity and the shared experience of loving their oppressor, rather than signifying compliance with the expectation that sisterly love should prevail between Muslim wives.

In a humorous reappraisal of stereotypes, the remote village in the Punjab reveals itself as a place that is more modern than it may seem and where the patriarch is divested of his prerogatives and his power is handed over to the women and the next generation. Whereas George's attempts to arrange his sons' marriages in *East is East* and *West is West* failed abysmally, Sajid instantly succeeds. The perfect bride he finds for his brother is a South Asian look-alike of Maneer's pop idol, the Greek singer Nana Mouskouri, complete with her trademark dark-rimmed glasses. The black spectacles also serve as a reminder of the unattractive brides-to-be from Bradford whom George introduces to Abdul and Tariq in one of the most memorable scenes from *East is East*. When Maneer first lays eyes upon Neelam, she performs (rather than produces) locality by masquerading as a traditional Punjabi woman, balancing not just one but three water pots on her head. 'He'll be more impressed with three', her mother remarks, whereupon Neelam replies in a broad Lancashire accent: 'He better be, 'cause I'm only gonna be turning the bleedin' tap on in England'. In a comic reversal of gender roles, the forthright and emancipated Neelam first chats up Maneer, dumbstruck by love at first sight, and later, when the Khans pay a formal visit to her family (significantly, a family without a father) to arrange the marriage, she runs the show. There is nothing left for George to do or say but to give his consent with a nod and a smile.

West is West confirms Hamid Naficy's (2001) observation that the homeland is often imagined as a place of redemption (see also Berghahn 2006, Burns 2009). In Ayub Khan-Din's narrative, redemption takes the form of an all-round family reconciliation. The mutual acceptance of one another culminates in a number of local Pakistani rituals in which all family members happily participate. For example, in preparation for Maneer and Neelam's wedding, Sajid and George share in the ritual of placing traditional headgear and garlands upon the groom. Meanwhile, Basheera applies henna decorations to Ella's hands, while her daughters Rehana and Raushana do the same to Auntie Annie. Ella has abandoned the 1970s-style purple crimplene trouser-suit for local silk garments that blend in with the colours around her. The exchange of glances and affectionate smiles between George's two families, captured in a montage of shot-reverse-shot sequences, conveys a sense of harmony and unity, strong enough to sustain the extended family's geographical separation.

The trans-local extended Khan family, which also includes Pir Naseem, Sajid's father of choice, and Auntie Annie (not a blood relative either), continues to profess its unity through reproducing aspects of the life they experienced in George's homeland, which has finally been accepted by everyone as part of the family heritage. The film's final sequence shows Sajid sitting on the annex roof of his Salford home (as he did on Basheera's roof), playing a melody on

Pir Naseem's flute, while Auntie Annie makes kebabs in George's English Chippie, following 'an old family recipe', as she proudly explains to one of the customers. Her tongue-in-cheek remark and one of the film's punch lines implies that Annie adopts both the extended Khan family and their cultural heritage as her own. By providing the white working-class neighbourhood of Salford with a welcome alternative to fish 'n' chips, she assumes an active part in the appropriation of the material culture of Pakistan and transforms it in the process; Basheera's home-cooked dinner becomes a take-away and the sharing of a meal in the circle of the extended family becomes a commodity. Annie's enthusiastic appropriation of the domestic – that is, feminine – aspects of George's cultural heritage illustrates what Appadurai (1988) refers to as 'the social life of things' and 'how things transport and transform cultural meaning, values and practices as they move in space and time' (Crang 2010: 140). It also demonstrates that the entanglement of the 'there' and the 'here' in the diaspora space is the necessary prerequisite for the hybridisation of culture.

Families who Eat Together . . . Family Cohesion and the Construction of Locality through the Senses in *Couscous*

As Laura Marks details in her inspiring study *Intercultural Cinema: Embodiment and the Senses*, the depiction of cooking and eating 'ethnic' food is a common strategy of representing the experiences of diasporic communities in cinema. Cinematic representations of ritual practices involving food articulate and invoke 'embodied memories and experiences' (2000: 200) and function as 'repositories of knowledge for people whose experience is not represented in the dominant society' (199). This would explain, Marks argues (albeit with reference to a corpus of non-mainstream, experimental films and videos), why ethnic cuisine features prominently in intercultural cinema, defined by her as a cinema that privileges the subjectivities of dislocated people living in diaspora. Examples are numerous, even in more mainstream films that do not conform to what Marks calls the aesthetics of 'haptic visuality' and which she identifies in films that, instead of privileging the optic sense, 'represent the "unrepresentable" senses, such as touch, smell, and taste' (xvi). Taste and smell, in particular, are closely linked to childhood memories but, for people who have been uprooted from the localities of their childhood (or even their ancestors' childhood), the memories encoded in these sensations are additionally important since they provide an 'important source of cultural knowledge' (199). The aesthetics of haptic visuality uses strategies that go far beyond 'appealing to the viewer's senses [. . .] through narrative identification' with characters who are shown to eat delicious food, but instead establishes 'intersensory' or 'synesthetic' links between colours, textures and sounds (213). Although only a few of the diasporic family films analysed in this book exploit these synaesthetic strategies to the same extent as the more avant-garde and experimental films that serve as case studies for Marks's arguments, there is abundant evidence that food, as well as the rituals surrounding its preparation and consumption, is fetishised. In *Nina's Heavenly Delights* (see Chapter 3), Nina honours the memory of her deceased father by cooking a prize-winning curry following a secret family recipe. Four immigrant families living in LA's Fairfax district in *What's Cooking?* (Gurinder Chadha, 2000) prepare an American Thanksgiving dinner inflecting the traditional roast turkey recipe in accordance with their particular ethnic cuisine. *West is West* locates the family's successful hybridisation in George's English Chippie, where kebabs are prepared alongside the quintessentially British fish 'n' chips. In the popular romantic comedy *My Big Fat Greek Wedding* (see Chapter 5), the food ways of Toula's extended Greek family, big eaters with big hearts, are contrasted with the culinary and emotional restraint of her fiancé's white Anglo-Saxon Protestant (WASP) family.[17]

Food is a conspicuously prominent theme in these films, functioning not only as an expression of cultural memory but also as a marker of ethnic identity and difference. In *We Are What We Eat: Ethnic Food and the Making of Americans*, Donna Gabaccia observes that food

> entwines intimately with much that makes a culture unique, binding taste and satiety to group loyalties. Eating habits both symbolise and mark the boundaries of cultures. Scholars and ordinary people alike have long seen food habits, both positively and negatively, as concrete symbols of human culture and identity. When we want to celebrate, or elevate, our own group, we usually praise its superior cuisine. And when we want to demean one another, often we turn to eating habits; in the United States we have labelled Germans as 'krauts', Italians as 'spaghetti-benders', Frenchmen as 'frogs', and British as 'limeys'. (1998: 8–9)

Gabaccia traces the culinary history of the bagel, the pizza, the taco and other ethnic foods in American culture and tells a fascinating tale of ethnic mingling and cultural hybridisation. Her observations are equally pertinent for European immigrant and diaspora cultures, as evidenced by the popularity of chicken tikka masala in the UK (which has replaced fish 'n' chips as the nation's favourite dish) and couscous in France, where it was elected the third favourite dish of the French in 2011.

The title of Abdellatif Kechiche's film *Couscous* uses this iconic North African dish as a trope for belonging and cultural hybridity. For the Franco-Tunisian family at the film's narrative centre, couscous embodies particular aspects of the cultural memory of the Maghreb. Extensive sequences dramatising the preparation and consumption of couscous underscore its symbolic significance for the maintenance of family ties. *Couscous* tells the story of Slimane Beji and his multi-generational and multi-cultural patchwork family, who live in the small port town of Sète on the French Mediterranean coast. After losing his job as a shipyard worker, the sixty-year-old Slimane is willing neither to return to 'the bled' (the Tunisian village he came from), as his sons suggest, nor to retire and be financially dependent upon his partner Latifa. Instead, he uses his redundancy payment to purchase an old barge, which he plans to convert into a floating couscous restaurant. Apart from having the skills to repair and refurbish the rusty old barge, Slimane is ill prepared for his new business venture and relies entirely on the support of the women in his life to make things happen. Rym, the adolescent daughter of his partner Latifa, develops and presents the business plan to the bank and municipal authorities, while the taciturn Slimane takes a back seat. For the restaurant's opening night, he depends on his ex-wife Souad, his daughters and his daughter-in-law to prepare huge quantities of couscous for more than one hundred invited guests. Their approval is vitally important in order for Slimane to obtain a loan and a licence. The one who lets him down is his eldest son, Majid, who disappears with the couscous in the boot of the car, thereby jeopardising the restaurant licence and causing Slimane's collapse and, presumably, his death.

The film was inspired by Abdellatif Kechiche's own family, who migrated from Tunisia to Nice when he was six years old, and is intended as a tribute to his father, whose self-sacrifice and inspiration the writer–director wanted to acknowledge.[18] Yet, unlike Ayub Khan-Din, Sandhya Suri, Yamina Benguigui, Yüksel Yavuz, Fatih Akın and many other second-generation filmmakers who aim to preserve the memory of their parents' migratory history, Kechiche (2008) refutes the centrality of this particular experience: 'I did not want to describe a family arriving from elsewhere, or a family of immigrants', he explained in an interview. The film addresses issues of social marginalisation only in passing and, rather than 'affirming the rightful place of North African immigrants and their descendants in France' (Higbee 2011: 217), as earlier *beur* films have done, it posits the integration of the Maghrebi French family as a *fait accompli*. It was Kechiche's (2008) avowed intention to portray 'an ordinary French family' amidst a social milieu of fishermen and shipyard workers. Nevertheless, his programmatic assertion that 'there is nothing exotic about' this family (Kechiche 2008) is difficult to verify, given the multi-cultural fabric of the Beji family (with Russian- and Spanish- or Portuguese-born in-laws) and the central importance assigned to the production of a distinctly North African locality. As the title makes abundantly clear, the film's centrepiece is the quintessentially North African dish of couscous. Long sequences are devoted to the family meal of couscous and to the preparation of huge quantities of the grain and the mullet for the restaurant's opening night. The camerawork fetishises the food in a series of close-ups of dinner plates laden with the saffron-coloured grain and the grey mullet. The camera traces Souad's hand, ladling sauce on to plates full to the brim, forks and fingers lifting the food from the plate to the lips, and even peers into mouths wide open with chatter and laughter, revealing the golden-hued grain on fleshy tongues, being chewed by pearl-white and gold-crowned teeth. These close-ups convey a raw and earthy sensuality that, combined with the jerky camera movements, lends the meal scenes a gritty documentary realist feel. They evoke sensuous pleasures by rendering visible the taste, texture and smell of the food – and provide an illustrative example of the multi-sensory aesthetics that Laura Marks has identified as a hallmark of intercultural / diasporic cinema.

The two ingredients, referenced in the original French title *La Graine et le mulet*, link the mother Souad to the grain, which she cooks better than anybody else, and the grey mullet to Slimane. Early on in the film, Slimane delivers some grey mullet to Souad (who accepts it with a dismissive remark), to Karima (who takes it for granted and puts it in the freezer) and then to Rym (who welcomes the gift of fresh fish enthusiastically). First and foremost, *la graine et le mulet* symbolise family cohesion that has survived despite Souad and Slimane's separation. Although Slimane is absent from the large Sunday lunch gathering round Souad's table, she puts a good helping of the couscous into a bowl, which Majid and Hamid take across to Slimane's humble room in the Hôtel de l'Orient. There, in the presence of his two sons, he shares the meal with Rym, who eats it with gusto, repeatedly professing that she has never eaten couscous that good before. The sharing of the couscous, prepared by Souad as a labour of love, effectively integrates Rym in the family circle. That circle extends further to include children, an elderly French neighbour and a homeless man, to whom Souad dispatches or delivers bowls of her treasured dish personally. The sharing of the couscous amongst the wider local community of Sète is indicative of the family's (desired though perhaps not actual) integration into French society.

Whereas in *Tea and the Harem* and the more recent *Samia*, the domestic and the public spaces are more or less clearly demarcated territories, in *Couscous* the boundaries between the two are permeable. Still, as William Higbee quite rightly observes, the floating restaurant is 'destined for, of all places, the Quai de la République [but . . .] never arrives at this prime tourist location due to problems with red tape, and is instead (symbolically) moored near the Hôtel de l'Orient' (2011: 223). These aptly named locations hint at different degrees of belonging to French culture, with the Quai de la République signifying white French majority culture and a Republican approach to integration that endorses assimilation to dominant culture, whereas the mooring place next to the Hôtel de l'Orient implicitly promotes the idea of a multi-cultural France. French film critic Serge Kaganski (2007), on the other hand, reads the French film title as an affirmation of cultural hybridisation, 'the inevitable and potentially fruitful mixing of the two shores of the Mediterranean, between couscous and bouillabaisse'.[19] Meanwhile, Stéphane Delorme in *Cahiers du cinéma* interprets '*la graine et le mulet*' as a reference to 'the most beautiful homage to filiation – a filiation which is chosen and not imposed' (2007: 11).[20]

Filiation, a term that normally denotes lines of descent, especially between fathers and sons and between the generation of the parents and that of their children, is employed by Delorme to describe the voluntary affiliation between Rym and Slimane. Rym actually refers to Slimane as her father. The affection-

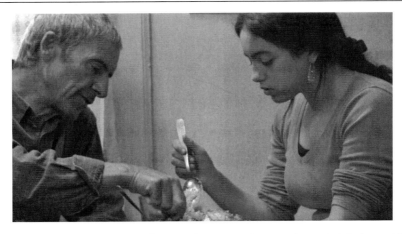

Figure 4.6 Slimane (Habib Boufares) and Rym (Hafsia Herzl) are tightly framed in a two-shot that emphasises the closeness of father and daughter of choice (*Couscous*, Abdellatif Kechiche, 2007))

ate bond between the two is underscored through the film's distinctive framing. Kechiche's documentary realist approach focuses on the minutiae of everyday life, people eating and talking with their mouths full, laughing and arguing, and throwing meaningful glances at each other. The film abounds with tightly framed headshots, typically of just one face or part of one face, arranged in a series of fast shot-reverse-shot sequences that capture small gestures and facial expressions, thereby conveying the emotional texture of family relations. Rym and Slimane, by contrast, are framed together on several occasions and, not coincidentally, when sharing the symbolically charged bowl of couscous.

Rym, whose natural father is absent, is also 'adopted' by the group of retired Maghrebi French men who live permanently in her mother's hotel. One of them, Saha, explains to Rym the implicit intergenerational contract and the spirit of self-sacrifice that motivated men of the first generation to emigrate to France and to keep 'slaving away' even now, not for their own good, but 'for you', for the sake of the next generation: 'When we see you happy and all that, we live again'.

Moreover, filiation refers to the film's cinematic lineage. French and British critics have compared *Couscous* with the humanist realism of Jean Renoir (whose film *Toni* (1935) is also set in Southern France and is concerned with an earlier phase of France's migration history), with Marcel Pagnol's 1930s Marseille trilogy (*Marius*, *Fanny* and *César*) and Maurice Pialat's *Loulou* (1980) (see Delorme 2007, Vincendeau 2008, Williams 2011). Meanwhile, in an essay entitled 'Family plots' written in 1992, Ginette Vincendeau identifies father–daughter plots as one of the master-narratives of French cinema. Second-generation immigrant filmmakers, however, she asserts at a time when Maghrebi French filmmaking was still in its infancy, challenge the familiar constellation of dominant father figures and women, young enough to be their daughters, by privileging strong mother figures and an imaginary relationship with the motherland instead.

Couscous unmistakeably invokes French cinema's master-narrative and its modification in *beur* and *banlieue* cinema; however, Kechiche's engagement with it is anything but straightforward. To be sure, Slimane is a gentle and kind *pater familias*, whose qualities as a father and provider are affectionately endorsed by his eldest daughter Karima at the Sunday lunch. He has little in common with the controlling, powerful father figures of dominant French cinema, let alone the oppressive Muslim patriarchs of Turkish German and Asian British film. At the same time, he differs from the absent, disenfranchised and debilitated fathers of the Maghrebi French cinema of the 1980s and early 1990s, and occupies the film's narrative and emotional centre. And yet, certain similarities between Slimane and his cinematic predecessors cannot be overlooked. Although he has not lost his ability to speak, as Majid's father in *Tea in the Harem* has, he is an exceptionally taciturn man; although he is not confined to the domestic (feminine) sphere, he, too, is portrayed as an increasingly disempowered man, who loses his job and then his potency, being unable to satisfy his much younger partner Latifa sexually. Embarrassed, he withdraws from her large bed and comfortably furnished flat to his own dingy room in Latifa's hotel, a pertinent reminder of Slimane and Latifa's unequal economic power. Slimane's agency is limited and he depends upon the strong and capable women who are rallying round him, helping him to make his dream of a floating couscous restaurant come true by negotiating with local authorities, cooking the food or offering their body as spectacle.

The film's optimistic assessment of intergenerational cohesion within the family contrasts with its portrayal of gender relations. Majid, Slimane's eldest son, is a notorious womaniser and, in keeping with a patriarchal value system, has been given licence to philander. Souad, typecast as the capacious and warm-hearted earth mother, has a darker side to her, in that she is complicit in her son's serial adultery. His sisters, too, appear to have internalised the double moral standards of patriarchy and collude with Souad and Majid.[21] The son may well be following in his father's footsteps, although the narrative remains reticent about the cause of Slimane and Souad's separation. The acceptance of double moral standards in the patriarchal family is further reflected in a few casual remarks over Sunday lunch, which imply that Souad has herself to blame for letting such a good husband as Slimane leave.

The problematic gender politics of *Couscous* are reinforced in the belly dance sequence, running for a full ten minutes. Admittedly, Rym's decision to don a revealing red costume and dance to the rhythms played by the musical ensemble of retired North African men, lodging at the Hôtel de l'Orient, reflects her devotion to Slimane, whose budding enterprise she tries to save through her alluring performance. While, on the one hand, the music and dance provide a further instance of the production of locality, intergenerational cohesion and communal solidarity, on the other hand, the sequence is uncomfortably complicit in its construction of Orientalising gender stereotypes. Rym's fuller figure functions as an important marker of ethnic difference and establishes a connection between the image of the curvaceous and voluptuous Arab woman, 'sexuality and nourishment, both emotional and physical' (Green 2011: 112), that invokes fantasies of the Orientalist woman's exotic sensuality and submissive subservience. This, according to Will Higbee, is the most troubling aspect of Rym's performance and rather undermines her 'presence as a forceful uncompromising and fiercely independent young female voice in the film (a sight that is all too rare in Maghrebi-French film-making)' (2011: 227). In a series of extreme close-ups, the camera both fetishises and fragments her body, culminating in an objectification of Rym's femininity and 'crude worship of female fecundity' (Vincendeau 2008). Rym's undulating belly, framed in a close-up together with the face of the old lodger and musician Saha, fundamentally transforms this symbolic father–daughter relationship into one redolent with a semi-incestuous desire. Once again, the film's sexual politics call into question the otherwise idealised portrait of a diasporic family and community, thereby complicating precisely the nostalgic fantasies it evokes.

Conclusion

The detailed exploration of how the production of locality is represented in diasporic family films has demonstrated that the maintenance of gendered topographies and of patriarchal values is a particularly prominent issue. Several of the films that serve as case studies portray the Muslim patriarch as an extremely controversial figure and pursue the project of his rehabilitation. The narrative strategies these films employ are not dissimilar to those discussed by Stella Bruzzi in relation to New Black Cinema, where the good black father comes deceptively close to 'the archetypal (White) Hollywood father' (2005: 166). Identifying Furious in *Boyz 'n' the Hood* as such an idealised black father, she notes: 'He is in a stable economic position, he is held in high regard by his community, he has gone beyond needing sex (sex in *Boyz* is associated with immaturity and irresponsibility) and views fatherhood as a vocation' (166–7). Although the parameters of what constitutes a 'good father' differ in New Black Cinema and in diasporic European cinema, they revolve around declining racial or ethno-religious Otherness:[22] on the one hand, the image of the testosterone-driven, promiscuous black male who fails to take care of or even abandons his family and, on the other, the Muslim patriarch who oppresses his wife, daughters and sons in the name of tradition. Thus the recuperation of the Muslim man necessitates that he is divested of the most conspicuous markers of his alterity – authoritarian power and religious dogmatism – so as to ensure his successful assimilation to Western culture, defined by gender equality and secularism. In order to become 'one of us', George Khan needs to hand over control to the women, as well as the next generation, while Slimane is already entirely reliant upon the strong women around him.

Given the demonisation of Islam, the most likeable and most powerless father of the three, Slimane, is portrayed as entirely secular while George, who visits the mosque and insists on having Sajid circumcised in *East is East*, is no longer identified as a practising Muslim in *West is West*.[23] It is perhaps no coincidence that in *West is West*, as well as in *Le Grand Voyage* and *Monsieur Ibrahim* (see Chapter 2), the 'fathers of choice' – Pir Naseem, Mustapha and Monsieur Ibrahim – are Sufis. This esoteric form of Islamic mysticism lays stress on emotion and imagination as a means of attaining divine knowledge, and privileges the close rapport between a Sufi teacher and his pupil over a legalistic interpretation of the Koran (see Esposito 2003). Sufi rituals, such as the trance-like dance of whirling dervishes, have long exercised a fascination over the Western popular imagination and add an element of exotic spectacle to *Monsieur Ibrahim* and *West is West*. Notwithstanding the trivialisation of Sufi religious practices and precepts, these films promote Sufism as a worldly, non-dogmatic form of humanist spirituality and the Sufi fathers of choice as the tolerant and gentle alter egos of the oppressive Muslim fathers.

These rival fathers, who are better than the biological fathers, mount an additional challenge to patriarchy by calling into question the significance of bloodline and patrilineal descent on which patriarchal family structures are based. Although the biological fathers, where present, are not replaced, idealised depictions of voluntary affiliations call the legitimacy of the traditional patriarchal family into question. The Maghrebi French family in *Couscous* combines certain features of the traditional extended family (solidarity and mutual support, three generations living in close quarters if not under one roof) with the modern-day patchwork family, consisting of Slimane, Rym and Latifa. The close friends who congregate round Souad's table for Sunday lunch and later help prepare the couscous, as well as the old Maghrebi men who regard Rym as their surrogate daughter, are also included in the circle of the family. James Williams considers it a trope of 'France at its most "*métissé*"' that 'operates beyond all essentialist notions of family or kinship' and that advocates the cultivation of 'new social and communal formations through decisive acts of solidarity' (2011: 411–12).

In a similar vein, George Khan's Salford-based nuclear family (entirely detached from George's Pakistan-based family in *East is East*) is transformed into an extended family when Ella and Basheera meet and bond in Pakistan in *West is West*. Yet, significantly, the extended Khan family differs from a traditional polygamous family in that it is created through the wives' reconciliation and not as a result of the Muslim patriarch's prerogative to take more than one wife. This, as well as the fact that the extended Khan family is dispersed across two continents and includes elective family members such as 'Auntie' Annie and Pir Naseem, makes it a transnational, postmodern family of choice.[24]

As Deborah Chambers reminds us, the 'idea of a "chosen" family based on negotiated modes of friendship, commitment and responsibility, rather than on biological kin relations, prioritises the assertion of personal values over biological ties and thereby has the potential to undermine claims to racial and ethnic purity' (2001: 117).

Chambers's reference to ethnic purity harks back to the fantasies of purity discussed in some detail in relation to queer-themed diasporic family films in the previous chapter. But whereas some of these films, especially *Nina's Heavenly Delights* with its exuberant celebration of cultural hybridity, make a genuine case for the inclusion of the over-determined Other in the family and the nation, the films closely analysed in this chapter are rather more hesitant and cautious. Ultimately, diversity translates into the diasporic family's adjustment to the value system and family structures of the European host society. Where the patriarch stubbornly resists the devolution of power and reproduces a locality that is clearly out of place, as Kader does in *When We Leave*, he is punished and has to learn the hard way that patriarchy is an ideology with no future. *Couscous* espouses a modern, hybridised variant of the extended family; however, the death of the sympathetic *pater familias* seems to call its viability into question. Except for *West is West*, which shares social comedy's utopian propensity with *Nina's Heavenly Delights*, films that genuinely affirm the superiority of non-Western family structures are few and far between. Once rigid gender and generational hierarchies have been successfully abolished, the diasporic family's Otherness is whittled down to such non-threatening features as ethnic food and clothing, Bollywood cinema, whirling dervishes, belly dancing and exotic weddings, all of which provide the common ground where minority and majority cultures can comfortably meet.

Notes

1. See Bertaux and Thompson (1993) and Grillo (2008) for anthropological accounts of gender and generation in immigrant and diasporic families, and Crul and Vermeulen (2003) on second-generation immigrants in Europe.
2. Vincendeau (2005: 73) identifies it as a reference to the poster of Howard Hawks's 1932 version of *Scarface*.
3. According to Vincendeau, Kassovitz claimed that he himself did not know whom the murals represented (2005: 75).
4. 'Radio Soleil caters mainly to listeners of Algerian, Moroccan and Tunisian origin whose first language is Arabic', whereas other radio stations, such as Beur FM, broadcast predominantly in French since they target second-generation Maghrebis who often do not understand Arabic or Berber (Hargreaves and McKinney 1997: 103).
5. The calligraphy on the woman's body in *Submission* also recalls Mona Hatoum's *Measures of Distance* (1988), discussed by Laura Marks (2000: 187–8) and Hamid Naficy (2001: 127–32), the latter regarding it as an example of a calligraphic, epistolary mother–daughter film.
6. Jigna Desai (2004: 214–16) suggests that Joe merely serves as a decoy in order to

dismiss any suspicion about the sexualised and queered nature of Jess and Jules's relationship.
7. See Rachel Dwyer's (2000b) excellent discussion of the sari and other Indian sartorial traditions.
8. To be sure, Bollywood films such as *Dilwale Dulhania Le Jayenge* (*The Brave Heart Will Take the Bride* or *DDLJ*, Aditya Chopra, 1995) or *Pardes* (*Another Land*, Subhash Ghai, 1997) feature similarly oppressive patriarchs who insist on marrying their daughters to unworthy husbands, but who are not identified as Muslims. In both films, Bollywood superstar Shah Rukh Khan intervenes and wins the bride but only after obtaining the family patriarch's consent. In contrast to the European films discussed here, *DDLJ* and *Pardes* ultimately endorse the inviolability of the patriarchal family structure (see Mishra 2002, Uberoi 2006).
9. See Muñoz (2006) on patriarchy and Islam; Meetoo and Mirza (2007) on honour killings in a wide range of cultural contexts; and Laviosa (2010) on their cinematic representation.
10. Farrokhzad (2006) notes that, after 9/11, the stereotype of the covered Muslim woman has changed, signifying solidarity with the Muslim community instead of patriarchal oppression.
11. See Mustafa Akyol (2011) on the controversy as to whether honour killings are primarily linked to Islam or to Anatolian village customs.
12. The term *Parallelgesellschaft* was coined by the German sociologist Wilhelm Heitmeyer (1996).
13. For detailed analyses of the landmark film *Yasemin*, see Kühn (1995), Göktürk (2000, 2002), Burns (2006), Schäffler (2007) and Berghahn (2009a). Sibel in *Head-On* and Umay in *When We Leave* are played by the same actress, Sibel Kekilli, a fact that seems to underscore the two film's thematic correspondences.
14. OVO stands in for OMO since, at the time of production, the rights for the Unilever brand OMO had not been cleared (email communication with Leslee Udwin, 7 September 2011).
15. See Marie Gillespie's (1995) groundbreaking study in which she examines how young Punjabis living in Southall, west London, negotiate their identities in relation to watching South Asian and British films and television. Their 'TV talk' demonstrates how they both reaffirm and rebel against their parents' cultural traditions.
16. *Bride and Prejudice*, discussed in the next chapter, also proposes that 'traditional' Indian brides are every bit as emancipated as their Western sisters.
17. See Roth (2005) for an exploration of food and ethnicity in *My Big Fat Greek Wedding* and other mainstream films.
18. Kechiche originally wanted his father to play the lead but decided to cast Habib Boufares, an old friend of his father's, after his father died.
19. The original French text was translated by the author: 'la mixité inévitable et potentiellement féconde entre les deux rives de la Méditerranée, entre couscous et bouillabaisse'.
20. The original French text was translated by the author: 'le plus beau des hommages à la filiation – filiation choisie et non subie'. See Johnston (2010: 89–90) on the concept of 'filiation' in French public discourse and cinema.
21. Similar forms of female complicity occur in *Inch' Allah Sunday*, featuring a domineering mother-in-law who makes her daughter-in-law's life hell, and in *When We Leave*, where Halyme fails to protect her daughter.
22. See Mireille Rosello (1998) for a thought-provoking discussion about the impossibility of declining stereotypes.
23. *West is West* was criticised in the British press for failing to address issues relating to Islam; however, this significant omission was part of a deliberate strategy to enhance the film's popular appeal (Udwin 2011).

24. As outlined in Chapter 1, the term 'families of choice' was coined by Weston (1991) in relation to gay and lesbian relationships, whereas I extend its meaning to include alternative family-like structures based on voluntary affiliation and comparable to David Hollinger's (2000) post-ethnic affiliations based on consent rather than descent.

5. ROMANCE AND WEDDINGS IN DIASPORA

At the end of *Moonstruck*, a romantic comedy set in Brooklyn, the lovers Loretta Castorini and Ronny Cammareri finally get together. Ronny's proposal of marriage takes place in the kitchen of the extended Italian American Castorini family, who have congregated around the breakfast table. Not only is a new couple created but also an old couple is reunited, as Loretta's mother insists that her husband Cosmo give up his mistress, reminding the self-pitying philanderer: 'Your life is not built on nothing. Te amo'. Cosmo confesses his love in return, lifts his glass and toasts, 'A la famiglia', thereby re-affirming that love is the foundation of the family. The camera pans away from the scene in the kitchen into the adjacent room, as if searching for material evidence of what actually constitutes a family. A slow tracking shot explores the family heirlooms, old china stored in glass vitrines, pieces of antique furniture and some paintings, a still life and a sepia-coloured picture of the Holy Family. Finally, the camera comes to rest on a collection of black-and-white family photos on a chest of drawers, which capture the memorable moments of family life: a small child, two little girls proudly holding their new dolls under a Christmas tree, a woman showing off an elegant dress and a man against the backdrop of what looks like an Italian landscape. Then it zooms in on a large hand-coloured photograph of an ancient couple, presumably the family matriarch and patriarch, looking straight into the camera. The camera lingers in a contemplative long take on their wrinkled and contented faces, while the cheerful banter and laughter and more toasts to the family reverberate around the room. As the credits roll, another photo replaces that of the old couple, showing Loretta and Ronny amidst the circle of their family on the day of their engagement.

This family portrait fulfils a function similar to that of wedding photographs, which became an established social practice at the beginning of the twentieth century and, according to Pierre Bourdieu (1990: 20), represent the earliest type of family photography. Wedding photos capture the two families that are 'implied within a ritual whose function is to consecrate, that is, to sanction and to sanctify the union of two groups effected through the union of two individuals' (21). They perform a vital role in a family's social memory and create a sense of lineage and family tradition across the generations (see Chapter 3). In an essay entitled 'The Family Spirit', Bourdieu describes weddings as 'rites of institution' that reinforce the institutional status of the family, 'establishing it as a united, integrated entity which is, therefore, stable, constant and indifferent to the fluctuations of individual feelings' (1998: 67–8). The performative act of naming, 'I declare you husband and wife' constructs 'an affective object and socializes the libido' by setting certain parameters for conjugal love. Rites of institution, Bourdieu notes, 'perpetuate structures of kinship and family [. . .] through a continuous creation of family feeling' (1998: 68). For diasporic families, such rites of institution play a particularly important role. They represent a key strategy for the 'production of locality' (Appadurai 1996, see Chapter 4) by sustaining affective and social obligations across long distances and in foreign lands, and thereby counteract the destabilising forces of transnational migration and diasporic dispersal.

This chapter is based on the premise that romance and weddings, though ostensibly concerned with the couple, have a legitimate place in a book about far-flung families since, in films set in a diasporic milieu, love cannot flourish without the family's approval, and weddings are, above all, a family affair. This holds true, in particular, for those ethnic communities that are imagined in terms of extended kinship networks and strong family values, notably Italians, South Asians, occasionally Turks and, since the box-office success of *My Big Fat Greek Wedding*, Greeks, too. I shall provide a brief overview of variations on this thematic complex, considering arranged marriages, sham weddings and interethnic romance, and then I focus on four films that make weddings their centrepiece: *My Big Fat Greek Wedding*, the first mainstream diasporic wedding film, *Evet, I Do!*, *Monsoon Wedding* and *Bride and Prejudice*. I aim to identify how these films draw on and inflect the conventions of romantic comedy, family melodrama and the wedding film, a strand of the romantic comedy that rose to prominence in the mid-1990s.[1] The inaugural film was *Four Weddings and a Funeral* and it took the box office in Britain, Europe and the US by storm in 1994.[2] It has been reworked many times since in films such as *My Best Friend's Wedding* (P. J. Hogan, 1997), *The Wedding Singer* (Frank Coraci, 1998), *Runaway Bride* (Gary Marshall, 1999), *The Wedding Planner* (Adam Shankman, 2001) and many more. These films usually bill in the title the dual attraction of a romantic happy ending, coupled with the visual spectacle of one or even several wedding celebrations (see Ingraham 1999, Otnes and Pleck 2003). What wedding films set in 'ethnic' milieus add to this tried and tested formula is the exotic allure of non-Western wedding rituals, dress codes, music and dance. Nowhere is this more apparent than in the Bollywood-inspired wedding films *Monsoon Wedding* and *Bride and Prejudice*. They take their cue from Indian wedding films of the 1990s, notably

Hum Aapke Hain Koun (*Can You Name Our Relationship?*, Sooraj Barjatya, 1994), usually cited as the first Bollywood wedding film and the first one to promote the apparently contradictory idea of an arranged love marriage. The overarching questions posed in this chapter, then, are why weddings (those that actually take place and those that are thwarted) proliferate in diasporic family films and how they enhance the films' ability to capture the interest and imagination of multiple and diverse audiences.

Variations on the Wedding Theme

Let me provide a tentative answer by proposing that the wedding practices of diasporic communities capture the popular imagination of majority culture audiences because they seem to crystallise the Otherness of diasporic cultures. As Homi Bhabha has argued in relation to colonial discourse, Otherness is invariably charged with ambivalence: that is, the attempt to position the Other simultaneously inside and outside Western knowledge (1994: 94–131). The Other is split between contradictory positions, with the negative pole connoting inferiority and the positive one fantasies of exotic allure. Stereotypes have the function of arresting the ambivalence, sliding between the polarities of similarity and difference in a fixed image that is repeated over and over again. The practice of arranged marriage, common amongst many of the cultures whose filmic representation I explore in this book, demarcates the negative pole and holds some kind of gruesome fascination for Western audiences, who tend to regard it as an atavistic social practice and evidence of the backwardness of those societies that abide by it.[3] From the destructive fantasy of a wedding that never takes place in *Shirin's Hochzeit* (*Shirin's Wedding*, Helma Sanders-Brahms, 1975) to the misery and even tragedy associated with arranged marriages in *Düğün – The Wedding* and *Aprilkinder* (*April Children*, Yüksel Yavuz, 1998), Turkish German cinema furnishes numerous examples. *Shirin's Wedding*, an early precursor made by Helma Sanders-Brahms, one of the *auteurs* of New German Cinema in the 1970s, centres on Shirin, a young woman from a poor family in rural Anatolia, who elopes from an arranged marriage. Despite its pertinent title, the film does not actually feature a wedding ceremony. Instead, it foregrounds the deal Shirin's paternal uncles strike with the groom: money and a piece of land are offered in exchange for Shirin. The wedding referenced in the title refers both to the arranged marriage and to Shirin's desire to marry Mahmud, a man from her village, to whom she was promised when she was still a child and long before Mahmud left to work in Germany. The wedding to her childhood betrothed remains a fantasy and the chief motivation for Shirin's migration to Germany in search of Mahmud. Gradual social decline and rape drive her into the arms of a pimp. Selling her body in the dorms of guest worker hostels, she chances upon Mahmud. The 'wedding night' she longed for turns out to be one both must pay for – Mahmud with money, Shirin with her life. *Shirin's Wedding* was made at a time when the women's liberation movement conceived of the institutions of marriage and the family as instruments of patriarchal oppression, and Sanders-Brahms seems less interested in the cultural specificities of Shirin's fate than in the wedding as a trope for the oppression of *all women* in patriarchal societies (see Brauerhoch 1995, Heberle 1978).

Düğün – The Wedding and *April Children* use the social practice of arranged marriage as evidence of an irreconcilable culture clash between liberal and enlightened German majority culture and Kurdish tradition. Unlike the earlier and widely discussed *Yasemin*, in which a young victimised Turkish German woman elicits our compassion (see Chapter 4), these films centre on young victimised men. In *Düğün*, Metin is lured from Germany, where he has a job and a German girlfriend, back to his native village in rural Anatolia under the pretence that his mother is dying. Upon his arrival, however, he is forced to marry Aygül, a girl from a nearby village. The wedding, with its numerous rituals, is presented in considerable detail, so that *Düğün*, at times, seems to border on ethnographic filmmaking. In contrast to South Asian diasporic wedding films, *Düğün* does not stage the celebrations as an alluring spectacle, foregrounding instead the other-worldliness of these ancient customs. When Metin abandons the bride on the wedding night without having consummated their marriage, he is evidently not aware of the consequences this will have for her. The dishonoured bride knows all too well and commits suicide, unbeknownst to Metin, who is already on his way back to Germany.

Yüksel Yavuz's *April Children*, about the everyday life of a Kurdish German family in Hamburg, ends with the arranged marriage of the family's oldest son, Cem, to one of his cousins from the family's natal village. Acting like a good Kurdish son at home while leading a Westernised life outside the domestic space, Cem earns his living in a non-halal slaughterhouse and is in love with Kim, a German prostitute. Nevertheless, he bows to family pressure and marries the bride brought to Germany from 'back home'. The wedding ceremony does not contain the promise of a happy ending. Even after lifting the bride's veil and discovering a very beautiful young woman, Cem looks miserable. Although Yavuz refrains from passing an explicit judgement, be it on Cem's parents or on Cem, the wedding scene conveys an overwhelming sense of resignation and claustrophobia. The newlyweds are at the centre of a circle formed by their families, who witness the unveiling of the bride and the kiss on her cheeks, and who clap to the rhythm of the music that accompanies the wedding ritual. But the approving smiles on their faces momentarily look like sarcastic grimaces – or so they may seem to Cem, from whose point of view the scene is shot. As the couple begins to dance, the camera swirls and swirls around in ever more rapid circles. The faces of the onlookers become more and more blurred and eventually disappear completely, reduced to an abstract, rapidly moving line that encircles the dancing couple, until Cem is completely caught in the circle of his family – and there is no escape from it.

In the British Asian culture clash comedy *East is East* (see Chapter 4), Tariq and Abdul subvert their father's plans to marry them to two Pakistani brides from Bradford, satirically portrayed as grotesquely unattractive, while George Khan's eldest son, Nazir, elopes from his wedding because he is gay. Nazir's rebellion against his father's authority is punished with his expulsion from the family, symbolised by the removal of his portrait from the gallery of family frames in the Kahns' living room. Though the ideological agenda of *East is East*, described by Sarita Malik as an 'intensely principled tale of freedom over oppression' (2010: 143), is similar to that of the Turkish German films in respect of arranged marriage, its irony, light-hearted humour and its (not entirely unproblematic) 'collusion with the ideologies of the mainstream' (143) set it apart from well-intentioned social problem films such as *Shirin's Wedding*, *April Children*, *Düğun* and the more recent British Asian film *Yasmin* (see Chapter 4). Despite having bowed to patriarchal pressure and married a remote cousin from rural Pakistan, Yasim refuses to consummate the marriage with a man who is depicted as utterly out of place in postindustrial northern England (he cooks on an open fire and keeps a goat for a companion in the back yard). Yasmin eventually insists upon divorce. To spare Faysal, who has become a terrorist suspect in the anti-Muslim climate after 9/11, from being deported to Pakistan, she proposes a divorce in accordance with Islamic family law rather than going through a British court. By demanding that the reluctant Faysal pronounces, 'I divorce you' three times, Yasmin inverts the patriarchal power imbalance underpinning *talaq*, the 'unilateral repudiation by the husband' (Yilmaz cited in Sternberg 2008: 87) and uses it to achieve her liberation.

The prominence of the marriage theme in Turkish German and Asian British films stands in stark contrast with its under-representation in Black British and Maghrebi French films.[4] This structured absence points towards the liminal status of *beurs* and blacks in French and British society, which makes it difficult for them to settle down. With regard to *beur* and *banlieue* cinema, Carrie Tarr explains the symptomatic blind spot by a dominant thematic focus on 'the multi-ethnic gang of unemployed youths' (2005: 79), whose social marginalisation and lack of work and money preclude them from forming lasting relationships that will lead to marriage. *Douce France* (Malik Chibane, 1995), *Chouchou* (Merzak Allouche, 2003), a comedy that ends with a fantasy white wedding of a gay, mixed-race couple, and *Bad Faith*, about a Muslim Jewish couple, are notable exceptions.

In *Douce France*, the *beur* protagonists Moussa and Jean-Luc have the good fortune to find a cache of stolen jewellery and thereby acquire the means to set themselves up in business. Their economic independence allows them to pursue serious relationships with two sisters, who represent different types of Maghrebi femininity: the independent, sophisticated Souad and the headscarf-wearing Farida. Moussa's romantic interest in Farida is threatened by an arranged marriage with a bride imported from Algeria. However, Myssad from 'back home' refuses to embark upon a marriage that is not based on love and runs away before the wedding. Significantly, it is the three young women (rather than the male protagonists) who function 'as agents of integration and change' (Tarr 2005: 79). Myssad defies the patriarchal practice of arranged marriage and Farida takes off her headscarf, at last – an over-determined gesture symbolising her liberation from patriarchal oppression and her integration into secular French society.[5]

Another variation on the wedding theme is that of the sham wedding, of which Ang Lee's *The Wedding Banquet* (1993) and Fatih Akın's *Gegen die Wand* (*Head-On*, 2004) are prominent examples. In both films, a son or daughter violates the sexual mores and family values that their parents try to uphold. In *The Wedding Banquet*, the Taiwanese American Wai-Tung lives with his American partner Simon in a gay relationship in a comfortable home in Manhattan. Ostensibly unaware of their son's sexual orientation, his Taiwan-based parents want him to marry a Chinese woman and produce an heir, so as to continue the family line. In the Turkish German film *Head-On*, Sibel flouts the normative codes of female chastity through her extreme promiscuity. In both films, the protagonists submit to parental pressure to get married but without actually relinquishing their Westernised liberal lifestyles by choosing spouses who are prepared to embark on an alibi marriage. Wai-Tung marries Wei-Wei, a penniless artist and illegal immigrant from Shanghai, who needs a Green Card. The lavish Chinese wedding celebrations, imposed upon the reluctant couple by Wai-Tung's parents Mr and Mrs Gao, culminate in Wei-Wei seducing the inebriated Wai-Tung and falling pregnant. As if 'the miracle of a woman made pregnant by a gay man and agreeing to marriage and motherhood' did not already strain credulity (Berry 2003: 185), Mr Gao's tacit acceptance of Simon as a member of the family, or perhaps even as the true bride who cooks elaborate Chinese meals and takes care of his son, adds a further melodramatic twist to the film's implausible conflict resolution. In the process, a new, hybrid family is created, in which the traditional Confucian family value of filial piety is preserved, albeit in the distinctly postmodern set-up of a *ménage à trois* involving a queer couple and a Green Card bride.

Head-On centres on a similarly unconventional marriage between twenty-year-old Sibel and forty-four-year-old Cahit, both of Turkish origin and living in Hamburg. They meet in a clinic after having attempted suicide: Sibel by slitting her wrists, Cahit by driving head-on against a brick wall with his car (hence the film's German title, *Gegen die Wand*). The beautiful and highly promiscuous Sibel proposes a marriage of convenience to the cocaine-sniffing Cahit because she hopes to escape her family's vigilant efforts to control her sexuality through an alibi marriage. 'I want to live, Cahit. I want to live, I want to dance, I want to fuck. And not just with one guy. Do you understand!?', she explains to Cahit, before grabbing and smashing a beer bottle and slitting her wrists with it. The dropout Cahit is the ideal husband in such a set-up. He has nothing to lose and is likely to give Sibel the freedom she desires, while his Turkish background makes him acceptable in the eyes of her parents. The traditional Turkish wedding is a sham and Sibel spends the wedding night with one of her lovers. All is well until Sibel and Cahit fall in love with each other, an unforeseen complication with disastrous consequences. Cahit accidentally kills one of Sibel's lovers and is sentenced to prison, while Sibel flees to Istanbul in order to escape her brothers' retribution (possibly an honour killing) for the shame she has brought upon the family. There, she gradually succumbs to the same self-destructive impulse that determined Cahit's actions in Hamburg. The dark back streets and opium dens of Istanbul's Beyoğlu district, where Sibel is raped and almost killed, function as the purgatory where the fallen woman's sins and guilt are atoned for and whence she emerges reformed. She trades the role of *femme fatale* for that of a mother, wearing androgynous clothes and short-cropped hair. Like the heroines of maternal melodrama, Sibel feels compelled to choose between desire and motherhood. After his release from prison, Cahit goes to find Sibel in Istanbul. She agrees to a few nights of clandestine passion but ultimately decides that her future lies with her four-year-old daughter and her new partner, presumably the child's father.[6]

Although the sham weddings, with their performance of the traditional rituals, appear to make a mockery of traditional family values and social norms, both the *Wedding Banquet* and *Head-On* raise the question as to who ends up being deceived in this masquerade. Though initially rebelling against their parents' value systems through their sexually transgressive behaviour, ultimately neither Sibel nor Wai-Tung is able to extract themselves fully from the powerful social norms they have internalised. Ironically, they end up fulfilling their parents' expectations, albeit on their own terms and in somewhat compromised ways: Wai-Tung produces the family heir and Sibel forsakes her hedonistic dissipations for the kind of stable and mediocre life her parents sought to impose upon her and which she abhorred.

Interracial and interethnic romance is a third and particularly significant thematic variant, since it functions as a kind of 'litmus test about racial attitudes' in society (Cowans 2010: 48). This is particularly true of love across racial divides, which instantly invokes the taboo of miscegenation, legally defined as the 'intermarrying, cohabiting, or inter-breeding of persons of different races' but, under the Hollywood Production Code, interpreted specifically as a '"sex relationship between the white and black races" alone' (Williams 2001: 180–1).[7] Whereas 'ethnicity' frames Otherness in terms of culture, 'race' emphasises nature. 'If race is always about bodies', as Richard Dyer suggests, 'it is also always about the reproduction of those bodies through heterosexuality. [. . .] The centrality of reproduction to heterosexuality can also be sensed in the extraordinary anxiety surrounding inter-racial sexuality, something explicit to the point of psychosis' (1997: 25). *Guess Who's Coming to Dinner* (Stanley Kramer, 1967), a seminal film about interracial romance, deftly illustrates these anxieties. The liberal attitudes of white, upper-middle-class American parents (played by Katherine Hepburn and Spencer Tracey) are put to the test when their daughter Johanna introduces her black fiancé, the African American doctor John Prentice (Sidney Poitier). Although the couple's romance is supposedly motivated by passion, the film eschews any visible evidence of the erotic energy between the white blonde woman and the handsome black man in order not to offend audiences' sense of propriety. The Motion Picture Production Code, which banned the representation of miscegenation on screen, was gradually falling into abeyance during the late 1960s. Nevertheless, the taboo-breaking image of John kissing Johanna is confined to a diminutive shot in the rear-view mirror of a cab. Although the couple's parents eventually give their consent, the wedding, signifying the ultimate affirmation of the family's and society's acceptance of interracial marriage, is not dramatised. *Guess Who's Coming to Dinner* is a paradigmatic film that mobilises interracial romance to support an integrationist agenda at a time when the Civil Rights Movement had raised a heightened awareness of racial discrimination and when, coinciding with the year of the film's release, the Supreme Court finally declared the anti-miscegenation legislation unlawful. Even though the fear of miscegenation is particularly prominent in American culture, presumably due to the long-term legacy of slavery (see Sollors 2000; Williams 2001), myths about the degenerative results of racial hybridisation, dangerous intermarriage and doomed offspring still resonate in most cultures to a greater or lesser extent (see Sollors 1986: 224).

In the films examined in this book, the depiction of interracial romance tends to foreground ethno-cultural and religious markers of difference over physical features, such as skin colour. Still, interethnic romance is no less contested and often doomed. *Pierre et Djemila* (*Pierre and Djemila*, Gérard Blain, 1987), telling the story of a teenage romance between a white French boy and a Maghrebi French girl, ends with Djemila being sacrificed by her Islamist brother in the name of religion and tradition. In *Love + Hate* (Dominic Savage, 2005), religious differences coupled with racial prejudice get in the way of love, forcing the British Asian Muslim girl and her white British boyfriend to elope together. Whereas these films, from the social realist tradition of the 'cinema of duty', espouse greater tolerance by appealing to audience's sense of moral indignation and empathy with the victims of racism, romantic comedies such as *Café au lait*,[8] as well as the diasporic wedding films discussed below, invite audiences to picture a world in which love triumphs over ethnic divides.

Featuring a multi-ethnic trio similar to that in Mathieu Kassovitz's subsequent film *La Haine*, *Café au lait* centres on Lola, a beautiful Christian *métisse* (racially mixed female) of Caribbean descent, and her two lovers, Jamal, an African diplomat's son and a Muslim, and Félix, a white, working-class Jew. She is expecting a baby but is unsure which of her two lovers fathered the child, and enlists the support of both throughout the pregnancy. The film remains equivocal about the issue of paternity since the baby and his skin colour are not shown. The final tableau frames the two proud fathers bending over Lola and their son, suggesting the formation of yet another unconventional *ménage-à-trois*-type family. Kassovitz is less interested in resolving the family plot than in challenging the racial thinking he deliberately invokes through the original French title *Métisse*. Jamal may well be the descendant of African slaves, as he points out, but he is a wealthy, well-educated diplomat's son and hopeless at playing basketball (a sport at which blacks are supposed to excel), while Félix, the white Jew, comes from a poor, working-class background and plays rap music (linked to black urban culture) in the flat that the trio shares. *Café au lait* makes a powerful plea for what Paul Gilroy, in the context of Black British culture, has called postcolonial urban conviviality. As the antipode to race thinking with its insistence on racial purity, postcolonial urban conviviality finds its expression in the spontaneous cohabitation and interaction of different races and ethnicities that have made 'multiculture an ordinary feature of social life' in urban centres and postcolonial cities in Europe and elsewhere (2004: xi).[9]

Probing the limits of Gilroy's utopian vision, *Ae Fond Kiss . . .* (Ken Loach, 2004) and *Bad Faith* dramatise how ethnic minority couples try to negotiate religious difference and family expectations. Set in contemporary Glasgow, Ken Loach's social realist drama tells the story of Casim, a second-generation Pakistani Muslim, and Roisin, a Roman Catholic of Irish extraction. By making Roisin Irish rather than Scottish, the film alludes to the shared 'colonial legacy of partition and historic patterns of emigration' (Hill 2009: 100) that have shaped the histories of Ireland and Pakistan. Scriptwriter Paul Laverty, himself raised as a Catholic, explains that he tried to establish parallels between the demonisation of Muslims post 9/11 and Catholics: 'When Catholics first came to Scotland 150 years ago they were seen as aliens with a loyalty to something foreign to the indigenous population. Drunken Protestants would go and beat them up' (cited in Mottram 2004). Casim is expected to marry a cousin from Pakistan and, despite being passionately in love with Roisin, feels initially unable to renege on the arrangement his parents made out of loyalty to his family. Family ties represent a double bind, with parents who care deeply about their son and two daughters but who, bound to tradition, limit their children's freedom of choice and autonomy. The film assesses both value systems even-handedly, conceding that arranged marriage may offer greater stability than the fleeting passion of a Western-style romance, while, at the same time, validating the powerful bond created by love and erotic passion, captured in some fairly explicit sex scenes. Yet neither the Muslim family nor the Catholic priest (a substitute father figure), whose interventions lead to Roisin's dismissal from the Catholic school where she teaches, approves of Casim and Roisin's romance, let alone of them living together out of wedlock. The priest raises moral objections to Roisin living in sin while Casim's family regards his relationship as a violation of the family's honour.[10] Despite its sympathetic depiction of interethnic romance, the film remains sceptical about its viability. Even if the promise of commitment, sealed with a kiss, in the concluding scene were to signify a happy ending, what are we to make of the film's title? The reference to Robert Burns's song about lovers parting, 'Ae fond kiss, and then we sever! / A farewell, and then forever', appears to anticipate the eventual breakdown of Casim and Roisin's relationship.

The Maghrebi French counterpart, *Bad Faith*, featuring the Jewish Clara and her Arab Muslim boyfriend Ismaël, offers a more optimistic prognosis for the couple's tumultuous romance across ethno-religious and political divides, to which televised news footage of the Israeli–Palestinian conflict alludes.[11] Similar conflicts surface in the domestic sphere as Clara and Ismaël, initially both secular-minded, begin to assert their different religious allegiances when Clara becomes pregnant. Ismaël decides to observe Ramadan (or at least pretends to) and Clara hangs a Mezuzah on the door of their shared flat. The sudden prospect of parenthood requires the couple to reveal their hitherto clandestine relationship to their respective parents. Although *Bad Faith* does not culminate in a wedding, the film's coda, taking place a few years later, proves that the couple have overcome the familial and religious obstacles that stood in their way. They now live in an elegant, upmarket apartment and have started a family. As they are about to leave for work, dressed in smart professional clothes, their mothers arrive on the doorstep, both eager to take care of the two utterly adorable little grandchildren that this interethnic union has produced. In fact, the smart setting and the young couple's social status (she is a physiotherapist, he a teacher of classical music) challenge the audience to revise their preconceived ideas about ethnic minority families. Starring the attractive Roschdy Zem, one of the most bankable Maghrebi French actors, Zem's directorial début offers a broadly appealing image of the Republican model of integration, proposing that vanquishing one's 'bad faith' will be rewarded in the end. *Bad Faith* espouses the model of a secular, hybridised family and even holds out the promise of an affluent middle-class lifestyle, attainable for anyone who tries to live like the French do.

Notwithstanding the happy ending of *Bad Faith*, in the main, interethnic romance is portrayed as fragile and fraught with conflict; promises of commitment remain tenuous and, in the films surveyed so far, weddings – signifying the integration of the couple within existing familial and societal structures – remain the exception. But, conversely, there are a growing number of films that indulge in the visual spectacle of weddings, often celebrating with much pomp and circumstance the union of a minority culture bride and a majority culture groom. The emphasis these films place on ritual practices and traditions from 'the homeland' testifies to the ability of diasporic families to maintain a deep connection with their culture of origin. At the same time, weddings in a diasporic setting assign the newlyweds a place in society, symbolically represented by the family, which, especially in melodrama, functions as 'a "natural" as well as a social collective, a self-contained society in and of itself' (Schatz 1981: 227).

The centrality of the family, constructed as a social and moral institution, underscores the generic affinity of diasporic wedding films with the family melodrama. The family focus distinguishes wedding films set in a diasporic milieu from contemporary mainstream wedding films with white dresses and white, middle-class protagonists. Whereas the latter portray the romantic couple amidst their circle of friends, ex-lovers and amorous rivals, the former invariably depict the couple in the circle of the family.[12] The snapshots of newlyweds at the end of *Four Weddings and a Funeral* show isolated hetero- and homosexual couples (all of whom are friends of Charles and Carrie, the central romantic couple) on their wedding days.[13] The absence of the family in these freeze frames, accompanied by Elton John's song 'In the Chapel of Love' and the whirring sound of a camera shutter closing, reflects the different narrative trajectories of romantic comedies, set in a milieu in which race and ethnicity are normalised, presumably being of no importance, and diasporic wedding films, which combine the generic conventions of romantic comedy and family melodrama and which are usually punctuated by wedding photos of the couple surrounded by their extended family.[14]

As noted above, the wedding film emerged as an identifiable strand of the romantic comedy, and particularly the chick flick, during the mid-1990s (Otnes and Pleck 2003: 165), roughly simultaneously in mainstream cinema in the West and in Bollywood cinema.[15] Usually classified as 'romantic family drama' (Uberoi 2006: 138), 'domestic drama' (Gopal 2011: 62, Malhotra and Alagh 2010) or 'family romance' (Dwyer 2011), the Indian wedding film has risen to prominence in association with the forces of economic globalisation, the emergence of a wealthy middle-class elite and the increased importance of the Indian diaspora, better known as Non-Resident Indians or NRIs.[16] According to Sangita Gopal, *Hum Aapke Hain Koun*, *Dilwale Dulhaniya Le Jayenge* and the cross-over hit *Monsoon Wedding* marked a new departure in popular Hindi cinema and revitalised India's ailing film industry. 'These films present the trials and triumphs of family life in India and the diaspora through melodramatic narratives and spectacular song sequences that celebrate the rites and rituals of Hindu marriage' (2011: 62), offering a number of enticing fantasies to Indian and NRI audiences and, as was the case with *DDLJ* and *Monsoon Wedding*, crossing over into the global mainstream. The 'increasingly mythical status' that these films bestow upon the traditional joint family is a response to growing anxieties about its actual demise among the new, urban middle classes in India (Dwyer 2000a: 49).[17] Bollywood's 'recuperation of the family' actively solicits NRI audiences by suggesting 'that "family values" neutralise the threat of globalization' by linking the diaspora to the nation (Gopal 2011: 67).

Whether red (the predominant colour of the Hindu wedding) or white, lavish wedding films celebrate the pleasures of conspicuous consumption and are tied in with a booming wedding industry, in India and America in particular. 'The allure of the lavish wedding', Cele Otnes and Elizabeth Pleck propose, 'marries two of the most sacred tenets of American culture – romantic love and excessive consumption' and developed into 'the most important cultural ritual in contemporary consumer culture' (2003: n/p). In India, these material pleasures have only recently become available to a small upper-class urban elite as a result of economic globalisation during the 1990s. The ostentatious display of wealth at a wedding marks 'an unabashed departure from an earlier Gandhian–Nehruvian embarrassment around conspicuous consumption in a predominantly poor nation' (Kapur 2009: 226). Bollywood wedding films have been a key force in validating this shift by making affluence look as if it were a traditional family or even spiritual value.

The emphasis on the spectacle of these nuptial extravaganzas, often including a detailed account of the planning and preparations leading up to the big day, distinguishes the wedding film from other genres revolving around the formation of the couple (see Wexman 1993). Wedding films indulge in the display of affluence and / or in the culturally specific rituals and material practices that elicit a cosmopolitan curiosity across diverse transnational audiences. What the diasporic wedding film (and I include Bollywood films about NRIs in this category) adds to this formula for success is the celebration of family values and the promise that they will be perpetuated through the formation of the new conjugal family.

HYBRIDISING THE GENERIC CONVENTIONS OF THE ROMCOM: *MY BIG FAT GREEK WEDDING* AND *EVET, I DO!*

Nowhere is the perpetuation of family values and traditions in the diaspora more apparent than in the coda to *My Big Fat Greek Wedding*, which takes place six years after the Greek American Toula and her WASP husband Ian got married. Not only do they live in a suburban house right next to Toula's parents, a domestic arrangement comparable to that of the modern extended Turkish German family in *Almanya – Welcome to Germany* (see Chapter 2), but they also send their daughter off to Greek school. This rather significant plot detail seems to provide the comforting reassurance to Greek (and other diasporic) audiences that outmarriage does not entail betrayal of one's cultural roots.

I contend that *My Big Fat Greek Wedding* has hybridised the conventions of the romcom and established the generic paradigm of the diasporic wedding film in the West. It has served as the blueprint for similar feel-good movies set in an ethnic minority milieu, notably the Turkish German *Evet, I Do!*, *Meine verrückte türkische Hochzeit* (*My Crazy Turkish Wedding / Kiss Me Kismet*, Stefan Holtz, 2006) and *Suzie Gold* (Ric Cantor, 2004), set in north London's Jewish community. In order for the couple, usually configured as a minority culture bride and a majority culture groom, to get together in the final reel, they need to obtain the consent of the bride's parents, whose ethnic minority background automatically implies that they are the last bastions of traditional family values. According to the romcom's narrative formula, 'boy meets, loses, regains girl', the couple have to overcome a major obstacle before they can tie the knot. Since the happy ending and the formation of the couple constitute the moment when desire is satisfied and when romance turns into matrimony, romcoms delay this moment, thereby heightening desire through a series of obstructions that need to be overcome (Shumway 2003: 400). In romcoms set in a majority culture milieu, typical obstacles are a romantic rival (whose unsuitability serves to prove the rightness of the central couple's romance), fear of commitment, intrigues, misunderstandings, false consciousness and differences of social class and education. In romantic comedies in which the couple has to overcome racial or ethnic divides, such as *My Big Fat Greek Wedding* and *Evet, I Do!*, the chief obstacle is the parents' anticipated or actual disapproval. The parents perceive outmarriage as a threat to the ethnic homogeneity and lineage of the diasporic family. They also worry that a partner from Western majority culture will fall short of the superior family values on which diasporic families pride themselves.

Ethnic romantic comedies are 'unlikely couple films', as defined by Thomas Wartenberg. They trace 'the difficult course of a romance between two individuals', whose different ethnicities make 'their involvement problematic. The source of this difficulty is the couple's transgressive makeup, its violation of a hierarchic social norm regulating the composition of romantic couples' (1999: 7). Unlikely couple films, such as *It Happened One Night* (Frank Capra, 1934) and *Pretty Woman* (Gary Marshall, 1990), mount critiques of existing social norms and power structures by mobilising sympathy for the transgressive couple, whose love represents a higher value than the socio-cultural differences and prejudices it needs to overcome. In this way, the unlikely couple film potentially challenges social hierarchies and ethnic or class stereotypes.

The surprise box office success of *My Big Fat Greek Wedding*, an American 'indie' with a modest production budget and a skilful marketing and release strategy (Perren 2004), partly stems from its effective use of ethnic stereotypes and a clever reworking of familiar generic conventions. The film centres on Toula Portokalos (played by the Greek American actress Nia Vardalos, who also wrote the screenplay), a second-generation Greek American woman in her early thirties, and Ian Miller, a shy American high-school teacher. The Portokalos family embody a nostalgic dream of family life in a bygone era that supposedly still exists in American immigrant culture but has become extinct almost anywhere else in Western societies (see Chapter 1). They are emotionally very close, live in each other's pockets and maintain an extended kinship network. The Millers, by contrast, are emotionally reserved, only have one son and, ostensibly, no other relatives at all.

Family structure and food habits are deployed as the chief markers of difference. When the Millers are invited to one of the Portokalos family feasts, they bring a modestly sized, dry Bundt cake as a gift, whilst the Portokalos family provides an abundance of Greek culinary delights, including a whole spit-roasted pig; the Millers try to abstain from alcohol, whereas the Portokalos family drink gallons of *ouzo* and spontaneously break into Zorba-the-Greek-style *bouzouki* dance. Although the patriarchal family structure and the emphasis placed on communal family values restrict Toula's personal freedom, the film leaves us in no doubt as to whose family has more fun and more love, and to whose family we would rather belong. Thus, not surprisingly, Ian and even his parents 'go Greek' in the end.

Evet, I Do! borrows a number of plot elements from Joel Zwick's Greek wedding film and combines these with the multi-stranded narrative structure of *Four Weddings and a Funeral*. Akkus's wedding film intertwines four narrative strands about Turkish German, Kurdish German, Turkish, gay and heterosexual couples.[18] The central couple are the Turkish German Özlem and her German boyfriend Dirk, both university students in their early twenties. He is shy and under his mother's thumb (an inversion of the stereotype of the oppressive Turkish patriarch), while she is beautiful, confident and a far cry from the stereotype of the victimised Turkish woman. Dirk and Özlem would make an unlikely couple in the above sense, whose romantic fulfilment is potentially thwarted by social expectations and norms, were it not for the fact that the generic conventions of the romantic comedy open up a utopian space for the realisation of romantic love. 'Particular films may toy with the progress towards a happy ending, but it remains a firm structural expectation, which the path of courtship leads towards' (Neale and Krutnik 1990: 139). The couple in romantic comedies can scoff at social decorum and social conventions and find happiness in 'a self-sufficient marital unit distinct from their social milieu' – a path not open to couples in family melodrama, who have to resign themselves to the 'strictures of social and familial tradition' or else suffer exclusion (Schatz 1981: 222). Ethnic romantic comedies conjoin the narrative conventions of the romcom and family melodrama, in as much as a happy ending *without* the family's approval would be inconceivable. The transgressive couple cannot find happiness in isolation but need to be reconciled with and reintegrated into their families (or at least into the bride's diasporic family). The ethnic romcom achieves this through reappraising cultural traditions and norms hitherto regarded as incontestable truth.[19]

Romcoms typically narrate and visualise this process of negotiation as the crossing of borders.

> Validating love as a traversing of borders, romantic comedy moves each partner from the territory of the known to the sexual and emotional space of the other. On occasions, the motif of boundary crossing is directly visualised. The *locus classicus* is found in *It Happened One Night* where the unmarried protagonists, forced to share a bedroom, erect a rope-and-blanket partition to demarcate their respective spaces. (Krutnik 1998: 26)

In order to overcome the symbolic partition referred to as the 'Walls of Jericho' in *It Happened One Night*, at least one partner has to undergo a fundamental transformation. More often than not, it is the woman who needs to be taught the correct values and demeanour by the man.[20] By contrast, in the

Figure 5.1 'Only Muslims living here!', Dirk's father (Heinrich Schafmeister) observes as he is about to cross over into alien territory (*Evet, I Do!*, Sinan Akkus, 2008)

ethnic romcoms under consideration here, the majority culture male needs to be educated in the customs and traditions of the minority culture bride before he can marry her. *Evet, I Do!* imagines the crossing of borders in both spatial and ritualistic terms. Turkish tradition prescribes that a proper marriage proposal requires not just the man to elicit the magical words, 'Evet, I do' from the woman he loves, but also that the father of the bride gives his consent. Therefore, the film's most important scene, repeated with variations in all four narrative strands, is the meeting between the bride and groom's families. Dirk and his parents are required to enter 'alien territory', a high-rise building inhabited almost exclusively by Muslims, as Dirk's father notes when he reads the foreign-sounding names next to the doorbells.

The décor of the living room marks Özlem's home as equally alien territory: the settee in shades of beige and brown is old-fashioned, the wallpaper dazzlingly patterned, and the room stuffed with laced table mats and quaint objects, the most peculiar item being a mosque-shaped alarm clock that goes off to remind the parents to roll out their carpets, turn towards Mecca and say their prayers. The scene makes much of the two families' inability to understand each other without the help of Özlem and her sister, who happily translate or mistranslate, as they see fit. Dirk's parents bend over backwards to demonstrate their open-mindedness regarding Turkish customs and traditions. Dirk's mother has donned a headscarf, since she assumes that this is the appropriate dress code for such an important occasion, but Özlem's mother seems bewildered by Helga's strange attire. Dirk's father has learned a few words from the Koran but mispronounces them so that Özlem's parents are unable to understand him. He has also carefully considered whether he should begin proceedings by saying, 'In the name of Allah and *our* Prophet', or '*your* prophet', and eventually stutters 'In the name of Allah and *a* Prophet'.

Evet, I Do! translates inverse class snobbery, a plot device common in screwball comedy and still to be found in post-classical romcoms, into inverse ethnic snobbery, whereby the ethnic minority family considers the majority culture groom unacceptable. Dirk's amorous pursuit of Özlem can only be accomplished if he is prepared to assimilate to Turkish culture. Turkish identity post 9/11 is defined, first and foremost, in terms of religion. The shift in conceptualisations of Turkish identity, from exploited guest workers to oppressed Turkish women, through drug-pushing and otherwise delinquent young men to Muslims, indicates that religion has become central to discussions about identity, difference and belonging. Yet, in the popular imagination, Islam has all too readily become associated with Islamic fundamentalism, which explains its negative image. *Evet, I Do!* makes this form of negative ethnic stereotyping explicit, thereby voicing fears prevalent in German majority culture.

The generic conventions of comedy allow for the containment and domesticisation of ethnic and religious difference by incorporating 'alien' elements within normal, everyday life (see Neale and Krutnik 1990: 244). The formation of the couple deflates the perceived threat of Muslim Otherness and its exaggeration in the spectre of Islamic fundamentalism by incorporating difference into the family unit through the conjugal bond between a German man and a Turkish German woman and through the groom's conversion to Islam. In an attempt to de-demonise Islam, the film stages Dirk's conversion as the performance of its allegedly most alien or embarrassing ritual practice – circumcision – and dissociates it from its religious significance. Dirk, who is terribly scared of the surgical procedure, initially provides fake photographic evidence of a circumcised penis (though not his own). When he finally succumbs to the operation, his father joins him – but for all the wrong reasons, since he believes that circumcised men make better lovers. An Islamic cultural and religious practice is translated into a secular Western system of values by associating it with improved sexual performance. In this way, the supposedly irreconcilable differences between the Islamic world and Western secularism, as delineated by Samuel Huntington (1997) in his controversial study about the clash of civilisations, are literally reduced to the existence or non-existence of a tiny piece of skin. For the German male, the removal of the foreskin is loaded with fear – a fear that proves entirely unjustified – as unjustified, the film seems to suggest, as the fear of Islam and its association with Islamic fundamentalism and the threat of terrorism. *Evet, I Do!* uses humour to trivialise ethnic difference and thereby makes a case for the *rapprochement* of Turkish Muslim and German secular cultures.

Sexual innuendo is also deployed as a strategy to normalise 'alien' cultural

Figure 5.2 Ian (John Corbett), who has hardly any relatives, marries into Toula's (Nia Vardalos) big family in *My Big Fat Greek Wedding* (Joel Zwick, 2002)

and religious practices in *My Big Fat Greek Wedding*. Here, the WASP groom, Ian Miller, needs to be baptised and become a member of the Greek Orthodox Church before he can marry Toula. His sexy and voluptuous sister-in-law sensuously anoints Ian's muscular body, whereupon the priest dunks Ian three times into an inflatable paddling pool, which serves as the super-size baptismal font required for the christening of a fully-grown man. This rather grotesque rite of passage integrates the majority culture groom into the ethnic minority community and even transforms him from a high-school teacher with an unsuccessful track record in dating into a desirable Greek man, as testified by Ian's proud proclamation, 'I am Greek now!'. But interethnic romance has hybridised not only Ian's identity; Toula, too, has been transformed from an ugly duckling, waitressing in her father's restaurant, to a beautiful and confident bride who has finally learnt to accept her Greek American identity with its emphasis on a vast kinship network, consisting of her twenty-seven first cousins, uncles and aunts, parents and brothers, and all-embracing family love.

In *Evet, I Do!*, the groom's integration into the Turkish German family fulfils a similar function, in that it facilitates a return to old-fashioned matrimony. In fact, Dirk's choice of a Turkish German bride and a big Turkish wedding represents an act of rebellion against his parents, who, as members of the so-called '68 generation, rejected marriage as a capitalist bourgeois institution. In both films, inverse cultural assimilation reflects a nostalgic longing for more traditional forms of family life and the invigorating encounter with the exotic Other. After some initial reluctance, Dirk's parents also embrace Turkish culture with proverbial German thoroughness. At her son's wedding, Helga performs a Turkish belly dance in which everything moves except for her belly, while her husband Lüder happily mingles with his new in-laws. These well-meaning German parents, at whom the film pokes as much fun as it does at the Turkish German families, do not get it quite right. Nor should they have to try so hard to demonstrate their acceptance of Turkish culture, for Germany is already 'Turkified', as the film's playful engagement with notions of cultural hybridity suggests.

The final frame captures the Berlin cathedral and the television tower at night. The juxtaposition of these two architectural landmarks of Berlin's cityscape creates a vista that looks like a mosque with a minaret. The Orientalised architecture epitomises what Doreen Massey has theorised as 'a global sense of place' (1994: 146–56), which reflects the time–space compression of the postmodern era, a progressive sense of place characterised by the continuous crossing of social and ethnic boundaries and a positive integration of the local and the global. The fusion of the Berlin cathedral and the television tower in the image of a mosque and a minaret translates the notion of hybridity from the domestic sphere of the family into the public sphere, thereby reinforcing the symbolic function of the family as a microcosm of society.

As Ella Shohat and Robert Stam (1994: 43) quite rightly remind us, any celebration of hybridity needs to be attentive to the asymmetrical power relations implied. Not dissimilar to some of the films discussed in the previous chapter, *Evet, I Do!* valorises Turkish Muslim identity only up to a point. While at face value endorsing the assimilation of Germans into Turkish Muslim culture, ultimately the film promotes an assimilation into a moral universe in which Western values of romantic love, premarital sex, gender equality and individual self-determination are prioritised over Turkish Muslim value and belief systems. Furthermore, just as the unlikely couple does not mount challenges to the social norms and hierarchies of the dominant culture, so the film's aesthetic strategies conform to mainstream Western generic templates instead of embracing a 'diasporic optic'. Sujata Moorti defines it as a 'visual grammar that seeks to capture the dislocation, disruption and ambivalence' of diasporic subjects (2003: 359). Its cultural reference points are eclectic and it appropriates generic conventions, narrative and musical traditions, languages and performance styles from more than one (film) culture. We can observe the 'sideways look [. . .] that does not reside in one place, but in several locales simultaneously' (359) and that Moorti identifies as characteristic of the diasporic optic, in *Monsoon Wedding* and *Bride and Prejudice*.

Hosting an Indian Wedding for a Western Audience? Mira Nair's *Monsoon Wedding*

Mira Nair, a transnationally mobile NRI filmmaker who has shot and produced internationally successful films such as *Salaam Bombay* (1988), *Mississippi Masala*, *Vanity Fair* (2004) and *The Namesake* in North America as well as in India, described *Monsoon Wedding* as a Bollywood film made on her own terms (cited in Sharpe 2005: 70).[21] Inspired by the Bollywood blockbuster *HAKH*, which Nair remembers as 'a family wedding film with 21 songs that was four hours long', she and scriptwriter Sabrina Dhawan decided to 'make a realistic family movie, one that actually shows you what it is really like' (cited in Bowen 2002: 78).

Monsoon Wedding appropriates the generic conventions of Bollywood family melodrama, characterised by an explicitly Manichean moral universe in which kinship ties and familial obligations function as the cornerstone of morality (Thomas 1996), and inflects them with a Western feminist perspective. Nair also tones down the high gloss and unimaginable affluence that has become a common feature of contemporary Bollywood (especially of the films of Karan Johar) since the mid-1990s and intersperses what is, none the less, a fantasy of globalised affluent India with some *cinéma vérité* scenes, paying homage to John Cassavetes and D. A. Pennebaker (see Bowen 2002: 80). Despite intertwining the main wedding theme with a number of sub-plots, the narrative structure is not as loose and meandering as in popular Hindi melodrama; nor does the movie run a full three hours. Nair, who is also influenced by the strong realist impulse of Indian New Wave Cinema of the 1970s and 1980s, privileges realism and psychological complexity over the pleasures of self-indulgent spectacle. She cuts down the excessive number of song-and-dance sequences, a staple of Bollywood cinema, to just one at Aditi's pre-wedding celebration, where acclaimed folksinger Madhorama Pencha sings traditional Punjabi wedding songs. Pencha's performance, as well as the re-enactment of romantic songs from film classics such as *Samadhi* (*Memorial*, Ramesh Saigal, 1950) and *C. I. D.* (Raj Khosla, 1955) by family and friends, are fully integrated into the wedding extravaganza rather than being non-diegetic spectacles in their own right.[22] They affirm the far-flung family's shared sense of belonging, whether they live at home or abroad. Unlike in some popular Hindi films, these songs do not function as coy substitutes for on-screen kisses; nor is a rain dance and wet sari number required to stand in for more explicit representations of eroticism and sexuality.[23] As a diasporic filmmaker operating outside the mainstream Hindi film industry, Nair is at liberty to ignore Bollywood's carefully circumscribed rules of decorum and propriety. In fact, she has been blamed by some critics (Cooper 2007, Geetha 2002) for playing or even pandering to Western and NRI audiences, assuming an Orientalist perspective in the guise of Indian authenticity. According to Nair herself, it was her intention to educate Westerners who 'don't have a clear picture of contemporary India' in a film where 'East meets West' (cited in Bowen 2002: 80).

Monsoon Wedding is set not in the diaspora but in an affluent suburb of New Delhi. Nevertheless, its central concern is the relationship between the diaspora and the homeland, rendered through the microcosm of the extended Verma family, most of whose numerous members are NRIs who fly in from Houston, Sydney, London, Muscat and Dubai to attend the wedding. The inclusion of this film may require further justification since *Monsoon Wedding*, though an international co-production between the USA, Germany, Italy, France and India, is regarded by many critics as a hybrid between Bollywood and independent American cinema, and appears to have no obvious place in a book devoted to contemporary European cinema. To be sure, though, there are other critics who cite *Monsoon Wedding*, with its juxtaposition of three languages (English, Punjabi and Hindi) and its stylistic and musical mélange, as a film that defies 'the conventions of any specific national cinema' and that embodies the 'pan-cultural eclecticism' (Bowen 2002: 78) so distinctive of the hybrid aesthetics of contemporary diasporic cinema. As outlined in Chapter 1, conceiving of South Asian diasporic film culture in nationally territorialised terms would miss precisely its transnational dimension, and this chapter would not be complete without this landmark diasporic wedding film.

Monsoon Wedding charts the preparations for a traditional Punjabi wedding between Aditi, daughter of wealthy Indian textile trader Lalit Verma, and Hemant, a handsome computer engineer of Indian descent, based in Houston, Texas. When the groom arrives for the engagement and prenuptial festivities, Aditi is still in love with a sleazy talk-show host and married man, whom she meets for one last clandestine rendezvous. Eager to enter into marriage with a clean slate, she confesses her affair to Hemant. He is angry and shocked at first but then confides that he, too, has had a premarital relationship; he decides to marry Aditi anyway, musing: 'What marriage isn't a risk? Whether our parents introduce us or we meet in a club, what difference does it make?' A scene showing Aditi and Hemant kissing passionately prior to their wedding suggests that this arranged marriage will not be devoid of love and passion. In this way, the film vindicates the parental choice of husband as superior to Aditi's own ill-advised choice of lover. The couple's 'arranged love marriage' also invalidates Western viewers' prejudices that such marriages are based on principles in conflict with the values of modern Western societies. As the trailer for *Monsoon Wedding* states, this is 'the story of a modern family'.

How, then, does the film negotiate the contested relationship between tradition and modernity that, according to Rosie Thomas, also constitutes the central dichotomy underpinning mainstream Hindi melodrama? In a straightforward equation, the traditional 'becomes subtly conflated with [. . .] that which is Indian' and therefore good, whereas modernity is associated with 'the nontraditional and the "non-Indian"' (1996: 160), imagined as evil. As Thomas illustrates, popular Hindi cinema articulates 'notions of "tradition", "modernity" and "Indianness"' (157) in the context of the family, imagined as the centre of the film's moral universe and as a trope of the Indian nation. That is why 'ideas about kinship and sexuality feed directly into notions about national identity' (160). *Monsoon Wedding* complicates these familiar dichotomies in several ways: Aditi, the bride, with her short bob of henna-dyed hair and her premarital affair, is anything but 'the receptacle of traditional Indian values' (Sharpe 2005: 70), a role usually ascribed to heroines in popular Hindi melodrama. India's new transnational mediascapes in the form of satellite television, imported porn films and Aditi's liaison with the TV talk-show host, her reading of the sexually frank *Cosmopolitan* magazine and her effeminate brother's interest in televised cookery programmes have left their indelible marks on the Indian family and eroded traditional gender roles.

But even Alice, the family's beautiful and innocent maid, whose romance and impromptu wedding to wedding planner P. K. Dubey serves as a narrative and visual counterpoint to the big affluent wedding, does not promote an unambiguously nostalgic fantasy of a pre-modern and, by implication, pure India either. Alice's virginal purity, subservience and passive devotion seem to make her the traditional Indian bride, were it not for the fact that she is Christian. As Jenny Sharpe points out, 'having a Christian occupy the position of the pure Indian woman undermines the Hindutva identification of the nation with the chaste, upper-caste Hindu woman and a Bollywood stereotyping of Indian Christians as mini-skirted, sexually loose women' (2005: 74). Similarly, Dubey represents the new upward social mobility of India's lower middle class in the wake of India's recent dot-com boom.[24] Formerly a traditional wedding decorator, he now runs a professional event management operation, aptly named YK2. Moreover, their marriage transgresses boundaries of faith (he is Hindu) and class. Yet, for all its modernity, the Alice–Dubey sub-plot, with its intertextual references to classic Hindi films of the 1950s, *Awaara (The Vagabond*, 1951) and *Pyaasa (Thirst*, 1957), invites the fantasy of an old India that can be salvaged from the morally corrupting forces of globalisation and, consequently, satisfies NRI audiences' nostalgic yearnings for a mythic Mother India, always there and immutable, to be reclaimed.[25]

Monsoon Wedding plays on these fantasies by invoking the familiar stereotype of the decadent, debauched NRI that has dominated mainstream Hindi cinema until the mid-1990s, since when it has been substantially modified. Idealised depictions of NRI heroes, including Raj in *DDLJ* and Arjun in *Pardes (Another Land*, Subhash Ghai, 1997), both played by Bollywood's superstar Shah Rukh Khan, indicate such a re-appraisal. Raj may well be wearing a black leather jacket, the sartorial marker of villains in popular Hindi cinema, but he has remained Indian at heart, prepared to forsake the bride he loves rather than taking her without her father's consent. Mira Nair also reworks the NRI stereotype by imbuing the Westernised villain with greater moral complexity and by linking him to paedophilia. The US-based Uncle Tej is exposed as having molested Aditi's adopted sister, Ria, when she was still a child and is about to do the same to one of his little nieces during the wedding festivities. After painful deliberations, Lalit expels Tej not just from the wedding celebrations, but also from the family for good. The association of the NRI man with an act of sexual transgression echoes mainstream Hindi cinema's construction of the villain as a morally depraved Westernised outsider who returns to Mother India to exploit and pollute her (see Thomas 1996: 169). But Uncle Tej is neither an outsider nor merely a villain. He is the much loved and highly respected family patriarch, who bailed out Lalit's financially struggling family after the turmoil and hardship of Partition and who offers to contribute to the costs of the wedding and to Ria's education in America. Thus, the values at stake in the pivotal scene in which Lalit confronts Tej in the presence of the extended family and in front of the ancestral shrine of his deceased brother, are not only the traditional Indian values of female purity, controlled male sexuality and kinship obligations but also money, the key value of contemporary India. Lalit decides against money and in favour of tradition and, thereby, retrospectively recuperates Ria's honour.

As Jigna Desai convincingly demonstrates, this narrative trajectory overrides the conventions of popular Hindi cinema, which depicts the sexually violated girl or woman as an 'abject undesiring and undesirable victim', whose honour cannot be recuperated and who must die (2004: 226).[26] Pursuing a similar line of argument, Darius Cooper criticises *Monsoon Wedding* for its lack of cultural authenticity, for what is actually at stake is not Ria's fate, 'but the *izzat* or *honor* of this entire joint family! Traditionally, Ria would have been asked in stern tones to "keep quiet" and Tej's lapses would have been conveniently "covered up and silenced" for the sake of this wedding and this family's reputation' (2007: 260). In Nair's 'westernized feminist fantasy' (Cooper 2007: 260), Ria is saved from being an undesirable victim and transformed into a bride-to-be, as the exchange of flirtatious glances between her and a cousin, who has arrived late for the wedding from London, suggests. The conjoining of the wedding theme with that of child molestation marks a significant deviation from the conventions of Bollywood melodrama, where it is still a taboo. In fact, the Indian film critic Geetha asserts (and thereby reinforces the fantasy of a pure India) that paedophilia is 'more of a reality, almost a phobia, in the West' (2002: 69) than in India and therefore a clear indication that Nair, alongside other feminist NRI filmmakers and writers, is pandering to Western audiences.[27]

Just as Alice serves as the pure alter ego of Aditi, so does Hemant recuperate the tainted image of the NRI. He is the perfect husband-to-be and his broadmindedness and tolerance of Aditi's premarital affair result from his experience of greater gender equality and liberal mores in America. Moreover, all eligible women in the film direct their attention to NRI men: so much so, in fact, that some Indian critics were offended by the implication that India's own men were made to look less worthy and desirable. In the film's narrative economy, of course, the still-to-be-forged nuptial bonds between Indian brides and NRI grooms serve to suture the diaspora to the homeland. It is, thus, no coincidence that Aditi and Hemant's wedding takes place in India – and only after the monsoon has brought about catharsis – not so much from the heat of the Indian summer as from the sexual transgressions and moral trespasses that have compromised the purity of the Verma family.

In keeping with the generic conventions of the wedding film, the preparations, spanning four days, are charted in considerable detail. The emphasis is very much on the preservation of Punjabi wedding rituals, as these are closely associated with the institution of the traditional Indian family. The *mandap*, the tent-like structure under which Hindus marry, is red and saffron, the traditional Punjabi wedding colours, rather than the increasingly fashionable white, which signifies the influence of Western white weddings.[28] The film shows the engagement ceremony, with bride and groom exchanging rings and feeding each other sweets; the traditional *mehndi* party, where women gather to have their hands and feet decorated with intricate henna designs before the wedding and where bawdy songs are performed; the *baraat*, the marriage procession in which the groom arrives on a horse, accompanied by the members of his family; and the exchange of marigold garlands between bride and groom (*jaimala*). The religious aspects of the Hindu ceremony, including the seven steps with which the couple circle the holy fire (*saptapadi*), are intercut with the film's final credit sequence, a position that seems to downplay the religious aspects of the wedding.

Above all, the wedding provides a social occasion that reinforces Indian (defined as Punjabi Hindi) identity, especially that of those living abroad, and that reunites the far-flung family. 'We finally made an Indian out of you', says one of Aditi's female cousins flirtatiously to Rahul, her male cousin from Sydney, while they are dancing together at the end of the film. Similarly, the taking of the wedding picture ostensibly celebrates the unity of the extended Verma family. 'Smile ... beautiful ... what a lovely family!', comments the wedding photographer. Meanwhile, the audience is poignantly aware of the dissemblance created in the family photograph, showing the family patriarch Uncle Tej at the centre with Ria by his feet, shortly before his shameful expulsion. The family portrait, like the film as a whole, resonates with the ever-present dialectical tension between the ideal and the reality of the Indian family.

In the film's moral universe, belonging (to the family and to India) is determined not so much by ties of consanguinity and conjugal affiliation through marriage than by the ability to negotiate the values of the past and the present successfully. Whereas Uncle Tej, who has violated the traditional values of female purity and the sanctity of the family, is ostracised, Alice and P. K. Dubey, whose wedding symbolises the union between rural India (Alice is from the rural province of Bihar) and urban dot.com India, can justifiably claim their place in the modern Indian family. Hence, Lalit invites the newlyweds to join in the celebration of his daughter's wedding at the end of the film. As everyone is dancing exuberantly to the same *bhangra* rhythms, the film constructs the extended Verma family as a microcosm of India in which divisions of class, caste and religion have been overcome.

Extensive parallel montage that cuts from the domestic space of the family home to the hustle and bustle of Delhi's streets, shot in *cinéma vérité* style with fast-paced tracking shots, reinforces this integrative vision. The juxtaposition of domestic and public spaces articulates the idea that the affluent, upper-middle-class Verma family is part and parcel of the diverse social fabric of contemporary India. As Patricia Uberoi notes, 'the family remains, and not merely by default, the sole institution which can signify the unity, the uniqueness, and the moral superiority of Indian culture in a time of change, uncertainty and crisis'

ROMANCE AND WEDDINGS IN DIASPORA

Figure 5.3 Aditi (Vasundhara Das), the bride, in the circle of her family with her father (Naseeruddin Shah) behind her and Uncle Tej (Rajaat Kapoor) by her side (*Monsoon Wedding*, Mira Nair, 2001)

(2006: 170). Through its focus on the family, *Monsoon Wedding* participates in the project of global Bollywood and sutures the diaspora to the motherland.

Although Mira Nair's film does not purport to be a genuine Bollywood film, it nevertheless offers sufficient familiar reference points to be appreciated in terms of Bollywood cinema. It has, in the words of Sujat Moorti, the capacity 'to construct a community of sentiment that is articulated in the domestic idiom, one that emphasizes kinship and affective relations based on shared affiliations and identifications' (2003: 256). Moorti identifies such strategies of dual or multiple address as a distinctive feature of diasporic aesthetics that reflects the filmmaker's double consciousness, born out of the experience of dislocation and cross-cultural encounters in the diaspora space. Janet Staiger has theorised such cinematic cross-cultural encounters from the vantage point of genre criticism. She suggests that certain 'films created by minority or subordinated groups' are truly 'hybrid genres' (as opposed to 'inbred genres'), in so far as they 'use genre mixing or genre parody to dialogue with or criticize the dominant' (2003: 196, 197).[29]

Bride and Prejudice: 'Bollywood meets Hollywood ... and it's a perfect match'

Bride and Prejudice serves as a perfect case study to illustrate how a diasporic optic and a dialogic imagination interact with and hybridise mainstream cinema. British Asian filmmaker Gurinder Chadha taps 'into the warehouse of cultural images that western and Indian popular culture have on offer' (Moorti 2003: 359), targeting mainstream audiences in the West and in India, as stated in the film's tagline: 'Bollywood meets Hollywood ... And it's a perfect match!'. However, as I will demonstrate below, its appeal to Indian audiences did not compare to that of *Monsoon Wedding*.

Bride and Prejudice transposes to India the courtship and marriage theme of Jane Austen's novel *Pride and Prejudice* (1813), a canonical literary text adapted for the screen many times before. Shots of an aeroplane in the opening sequence mark the arrival of the UK-based NRI Balraj and his American friend Darcy, two single men in possession of a good fortune and in want of a wife, to Amritsar. Like Austen's Mr and Mrs Bennet, Chadha's Mr and Mrs Bakshi are looking for eligible suitors for their four (rather than five) daughters, Jaya, Lalita, Maya and Lakhi. An Indian wedding provides the social setting where the romantic couples Lalita and Darcy, Jaya and Balraj first meet. In keeping with the source novel and the generic conventions of the romantic comedy, the paths of their courtship are rocky. The chief obstacle standing in the central couple's way is Darcy's cultural snobbery vis-à-vis 'Hicksville, India', as he derogatively calls Amritsar. Before he is worthy of the beautiful bride Lalita, he has to be educated in all things Indian – be it dancing, drumming or even keeping his Indian-style trousers from falling down. In all other respects, *Bride and Prejudice* downplays cultural difference, emphasising the commonalities between Indian and Western cultures instead. Lalita is every bit as independent and assertive as any Western woman and, except for the fact that she wears stunning saris (as well as Western clothes), has little in common with idealised notions of traditional Indian femininity portrayed in popular Hindi cinema. Played by Indian superstar, model and former Miss World, Aishwarya Rai, Lalita is exceptionally fair and represents a universal ideal of beauty. Meanwhile, Darcy, except for the fact that he is not Indian, comes close to 'the consumable hero of globalised India'. This new type of Bollywood hero is the 'creation of the liberalised market' (Deshpande 2005: 202), and his jet-setting lifestyle and extreme affluence reflect the neo-conservative consumerist ideology that has seized India – and Bollywood – since the 1990s. The pleasures of conspicuous consumption are depicted as the great equaliser that transcends boundaries of race, culture and ethnicity. Whether it is called arranged marriage or not, *Bride and Prejudice* argues, the criteria for the choice of spouse are pretty much the same the world over. Nor have they changed much over time: '200 years ago, England was no different than Amritsar today', Chadha explained her choice of source novel in an interview (cited in Jha 2004). This is not to say that India is backward but rather that marriage has always been a form of exchange and that the choice of husband amongst the middle classes in the West is no different from the practice of arranged marriage in India. Thus, Mrs Bakshi attempts to set up a lucrative match between Lalita and the wealthy Los Angeles-based NRI Mr Kohli (the counterpart of William Collins), while Mrs Darcy, the American owner of a luxury hotel empire, would like her son to tie the knot with a rich American woman. By the same token, the Bakshis raise no objection to Darcy since he is super-wealthy, making him an extremely good catch by any standards.

Figure 5.4 Bollywood-style song-and-dance sequences add some exotic spectacle to the wedding celebrations in *Bride and Prejudice* (Gurinder Chadha, 2004)

Despite adhering to the conventions of romantic comedy by following the well-worn narrative formula of love at first sight, the lovers' separation, an amorous rival (globetrotting backpacker Wickham) who is clearly inferior to 'Mr Right' in terms of both his morality and his financial means, the film makes the point that marriage is not so much about love as it is about money. The connection is established on multiple levels throughout the film. The first sentence of Jane Austen's novel, one of the most famous lines of English literature, 'It is a truth universally acknowledged, that a single man in possession of a good fortune must be in want of a wife', is translated into a more contemporary idiom in Lalita's observation: 'Anyone who's got big bucks is shopping for a wife'. The film's four weddings – three in Amritsar and one in Los Angeles – are all closely linked to the pleasures of consumption. As in *Monsoon Wedding*, the women go shopping in the local stores before the wedding day, accompanied by one of the film's title songs, 'A marriage has come to town / laughter, colour, light and sound / life is great, let's celebrate / the sacred union two souls have found', which is performed in the style of Bollywood song and dance interludes (arranged by Saroj Khan, one of the most famous choreographers of Hindi cinema) by a crowd of people in the streets.

Ironically, however, there is little evidence of the 'sacred union' mentioned in the song. Though the first wedding provides a glimpse of a traditional Punjabi-style ceremony, it is relatively brief, while the double wedding at the end elides the wedding rituals altogether. Instead, accompanied by a reprise of 'A marriage has come to town', it shows Lalita and Darcy and Jaya and Balraj in red-and-gold Indian wedding attire on the backs of two festively decorated elephants. The several-day-long wedding ceremony is condensed, as it were, to a sign 'Just Married' attached to the rear of the elephant, a playful reference to the Western custom of mounting such signs on wedding limousines. The narrow streets of Amritsar are packed not only with crowds celebrating but also with billboards for global and local brands that have also 'come to town'. These icons of global consumer culture foreground the fact

Figure 5.5 Bollywood and Hollywood are a perfect match – and so are Lalita (Aishwarya Rai) and Darcy (Martin Henderson) (*Bride and Prejudice*, Gurinder Chadha, 2004)

that the institution of bourgeois marriage – be it in Jane Austen's time or in contemporary India – has always been about economic and sexual exchange, even though it has been mythologised as romantic love. Rachel Dwyer refers to this idea in the felicitously chosen title of her book *All You Want is Money, All You Need is Love: Sexuality and Romance in Modern India* (2000a). With the rise of the new middle classes in globalised India, Dwyer suggests, notions of self-realisation through romantic love and intimacy are becoming more accepted but continue to compete with the supreme value of familial love with its emphasis on duty and sacrifice, while the new value of material affluence adds further complexity.

For all the playful references to Western prejudices towards an allegedly backward India, Gurinder Chadha is not genuinely interested in weighing the pros and cons of Indian and Western approaches to marriage. Rather, her chief ambition has been to create a crowd-pleaser capable of simultaneously appealing to mainstream audiences in Britain, America, India and the Indian diaspora – an ambition she was ultimately not able to realise fully. Her attempt to bring together Hollywood and Bollywood, or, to be more precise, to bend the generic conventions of Bollywood melodrama, mainstream romantic comedy and European heritage film, failed at the Indian box office, where *Bride and Prejudice* played for less than two weeks and was dismissed as a 'fake' and a 'bogus wannabe' that lacked the emotional authenticity of real Bollywood cinema (Samant 2005: 83, 84). In a scathing review entitled 'Appropriating Bombay cinema: Why the Western world gets Bollywood so wrong', the NRI critic Sapna Samant refers to Chadha as 'an imposter', whose film reflects the 'present-day love affair of the West with anything Indian' but who fails to understand Indian sensibilities and how Indian popular culture 'works for Indians' (2005: 83). That is why Indians and NRIs 'gave it the cold shoulder [...] a unanimous rejection from one billion, twenty million inhabitants of this earth'. By contrast, Indian audiences could not get enough of the real thing,

DDLJ, which ran for 500 consecutive weeks at the Maratha Mandir theatre in Bombay (Samant 2005: 83, 86).[30]

Meanwhile, critics and audiences in the West were also somewhat puzzled by this filmic mélange, consisting of Punjabi- and English-language song-and-dance sequences and references to an eclectic mix of high and popular culture sources, including Austen's canonical novel and its numerous previous adaptations, musicals such as *West Side Story* (Jerome Robbins, Robert Wise, 1961), *Oliver* (Carol Reed, 1968) and *Grease* (Randal Kleiser, 1978), and ethnic stereotypes of the Indian family familiar from the British television comedy *Goodness Gracious Me* (1998–2000), alongside affectionate tributes to iconic scenes from Bollywood films such as *Barsaat* (*Monsoon*, Raj Kapoor, 1949), *Purab Aur Pachhim* (*East and West*, Manoj Kumar, 1970) and *DDLJ*.[31] The British film critic Philip French (2004) admires the ingenuity with which Chadha transposes certain characters and scenes from Austen's novel to what he calls 'the global village of the Indian diaspora', but wonders whether 'we are watching a parody of a Bollywood musical, or a pastiche' and concludes that 'in simultaneously sending up and celebrating Bombay cinema, Chadha is trying to have her chapatti and eat it'.

I would like to propose that Gurinder Chadha uses pastiche as an integral part of the diasporic optic of *Bride and Prejudice* in order to celebrate cultural diversity and the hybridisation of cinematic genres in the age of transnational cultural flows. Rather than pursuing a strategy of subversion and destabilisation of the centre from the margins through parody, she deploys pastiche, defined by Richard Dyer as 'a textually signalled imitation' (2007: 23). Whereas parody implies a negative or critical attitude towards the work of art it references, pastiche is 'evaluatively open' (24). Unlike parody, pastiche does not imply the vantage point of an outsider who possesses superior knowledge or better judgement (46–7). Frederic Jameson has famously characterised pastiche as 'blank parody', as imitation 'without any of parody's ulterior motives, amputated of its satirical impulse, devoid of laughter and of any conviction that [. . .] normality still exists' (1991: 17). In this sense, pastiche could be said to be egalitarian and to foreground commonalities between cultural and artistic conventions. At the same time, pastiche may seem elitist in so far as it requires certain cultural competencies for it to be 'understood as pastiche by those who read, see or hear it. For it to work, it needs to be "got" as pastiche' (Dyer 2007: 3). The above-cited scathing Indian reviewer clearly did *not* 'get' the point of *Bride and Prejudice*, missing out on its self-reflexivity and chiding Chadha for failing to make an authentic Bollywood film.

Dyer distinguishes between two types of pastiche: pastiche as combination, which he calls 'pasticcio', using the original Italian culinary term from which the English word is derived, and pastiche as imitation. He suggests that its inherent multi-vocality and heterogeneity make pasticcio an apt aesthetic strategy for expressing 'the new hybrid identities forged in an era of multiple migrations and interacting heterogeneous populations' (20).[32] While pasticcio involves some element of imitation (quoting, referencing, reproducing and copying), it differs from pastiche as a textually signalled imitation, which can take many different forms, depending on how the signalled imitation copies, deforms or otherwise interacts with the original (see Dyer 2007: 138). Given that pastiche imitates art (as opposed to life), it is a particularly appropriate representational mode for a diasporic filmmaker like Chadha, whose familiarity with Indian culture is, to a large extent, mediated (and in this respect differs from Nair, who grew up in Delhi). She was born and grew up in the London suburb of Southall, and Hindi films in local cinemas provided a formative contact with Indian culture for her (Jha 2004).

In *Bride and Prejudice*, she employs pastiche both as combination and as imitation in order to make a case for the transcultural and historical affinities between Western and Indian cultures, which she conceives of not in oppositional but rather in relational terms. The film translates European high culture via its popular inflections in the shape of screen adaptations of Austen's canonical novel into the idiom of Indian popular culture, notably Bollywood cinema. Chadha's tongue-in-cheek wedding film 'Bollywoodises' certain stylistic conventions that have become associated with British and European heritage cinema and in which Jane Austen film and television adaptations assume a prominent place (see Galt 2006, Geraghty 2006, 2008, Higson 2003, Monk and Sargeant 2002). The film's opening scene, a shot of the Golden Temple in Amritsar that cuts to the green fields of the Punjab, evokes the distinctive iconography of heritage cinema with its emphasis on stately homes and pastoral idylls. The tourist's gaze of India, offered in *Bride and Prejudice*, recalls the picture-postcard impressions of a picturesque, middle-class England that prevail in heritage cinema (under which I subsume the 1995 BBC television adaptation of *Pride and Prejudice*). John Urry (2002) defines 'the tourist's gaze' as a particular way of experiencing and viewing landscapes, monuments, cities and so forth that emphasises the extraordinary and the exotic. In the age of mass tourism, it has become closely linked to the pleasures of consumption. Far from showing the 'real India' – with which Lalita ostensibly wants to acquaint Darcy – India is rendered as a theme park featuring Amritsar's Golden Temple, colourful markets and the beaches of Goa as its main attractions. The same applies to the tourist impressions of the film's other locations where Lalita and her family stop over in pursuit of love and money, including the London Eye, the LA Biltmore Hotel, Santa Monica Beach, the Grand Canyon and other iconic landmarks.

It is hard to determine what is being imitated here, since the tourist's gaze is not only a feature of European heritage film but also of numerous Bollywood films whose protagonists embark on a Grand Tour of Europe's top tourist destinations. Thus, the green fields of the Punjab in the opening sequence could be seen either as a reference to the green meadows of British heritage film or as a reference to the opening sequence of the Bollywood blockbuster *DDLJ*, in which the fields of the Punjab epitomise a nostalgic fantasy of an uncontaminated India. And what are we to make of Lalita's dream – the fantasy of a white wedding to Wickham, set in a quaint English village, complete with Morris dancers, a maypole and a country church but oddly also a windmill, an architectural feature more commonly associated with the Dutch than the English countryside? When this bucolic scene is suddenly transformed into a Gothic setting with thunder and lightning and Wickham turns into Darcy, who tries (but fails) to kiss Lalita in the monsoon-like rain, there is no doubt that a slippage from pastiche to parody has occurred.

The reprise of the song 'My Lips are Waiting' and 'Take Me to Love', first performed by the African American singer Ashanti on Goa Beach, mixing contemporary R 'n' B vocals (in English and Hindi) with Indian instrumentation and *bhangra*-style backing, and subsequently rendered by a blue-robed gospel choir, surfers and scantily-clad lifeguards on Santa Monica Beach, is another instance of such slippage. Chadha has described this 'hyperstylised version of a Bollywood musical number' as 'the epitome of the Bollywoodizing of LA' (Chadha cited in Wilson 2006: 328). But what American culture is actually Bollywoodised here? White or African American culture? Or is it perhaps the global tourist industry? For an aerial shot of the gospel choir (in blue) and the lifeguards (in red), who move like tiny ants across the white sand, eventually to form an eye with Darcy and Lalita as the pupil in the middle, references Saatchi & Saatchi's classic television commercial 'Face' for British Airways. Pastiche in *Bride and Prejudice* draws attention to the global circulation of cinematic and other media images and, at times, remains equivocal as to what is the original and what its imitation.

Yet how exactly does pastiche relate to the theme of romance and weddings? *Bride and Prejudice* makes the point that the different aesthetic traditions it imitates and juxtaposes are equally profound or trivial, imaginative or clichéd. Pastiche, which, according to Frederic Jameson, is a quintessentially postmodern phenomenon, negates the notion of normalcy, understood as a dominant or guiding culture (1991: 17). Chadha's playful use of pastiche in *Bride and Prejudice* disavows ready-made hierarchies of high and low cultural forms, of ostensibly sophisticated Western art and allegedly lowbrow Indian entertainment, and, in so doing, promotes an egalitarian approach to cultural diversity. In this sense, Bollywood and Hollywood – and, I wish to add, European heritage film – are a perfect match. And so are Lalita and Darcy. In today's globalised world, thus the film's premise, the commonalities between cultures far outweigh their differences. Matchmaking, whether it is called arranged marriage or romantic love, is a universal game that families play. It follows the same rules all over the world – and has done so for the past 200 years or more.

Conclusion

The advent of the wedding film in the mid-1990s, which occurred simultaneously in mainstream cinema in the West and in Bollywood, and its successful hybridisation in diasporic wedding films herald a remarkable convergence of mainstream and diasporic cinema, which was relegated to an ethnic niche until not so long ago. The big fat diasporic wedding film, with its emphasis on spectacle, exoticism and / or excess (strange rituals, an onslaught of vibrant colours and sounds that mesmerises our senses, numerous weddings in one film and nuptial extravaganzas lasting for several days), has the capacity to unite multiple audiences by simultaneously inviting different viewing positions. Amongst Indians and NRIs, 'the big fat Bollywood wedding has become a trademark attraction of contemporary Indian culture' and has sparked a 'Bollywood culture industry' that markets 'a cultural style [. . .] to an entire range of cultural production', including television, fashion, food, décor and design (Kapur 2009: 221, 222). As Kavita Ramdya illustrates in her anthropological study *Bollywood Weddings: Dating, Engagement, and Marriage in Hindu America* (2010), *Monsoon Wedding* – though not a Bollywood film as such – has become the yardstick by which the Hindu American diaspora measures the authenticity of a traditional Hindu wedding, indicating that wedding films fulfil an educational function for diasporic audiences who are gradually losing touch with their ancestral culture. Redolent with nostalgia, diasporic wedding films offer the comforting reassurance that cultural traditions and family values can and do live on and that kinship networks remain intact despite the family's dispersal, often across several continents.

To Western majority audiences, Jigna Desai proposes, wedding films provide 'a nonthreatening spectacle of otherness that at the same time can be absorbed into the narrative of universal heterosexuality' (2004: 222) and family. Their 'cross-cultural consumption [. . .] relies on the rejuvenation of an anthropological desire for knowledge of and intimacy with the other. Weddings have been a site of fascination in anthropology and the ethnographic film' (222). Paradoxically, the allure of the exotic may appear strangely familiar. For example, the Hindu wedding procession in *Monsoon Wedding*, led by the groom on a white horse, resonates with the popular image of the knight in shining armour in chivalric romance and therefore lends itself to be readily appropriated by Western culture.

Those films that frame diasporic romance as comedy open up a utopian space in which the interethnic or otherwise transgressive couple can find romantic fulfilment and secure their place in the family and, by extension, in society. Whereas, in the romcom, such a happy ending is (almost) mandatory, the narrative openness or pessimistic conclusions of the social problem film preclude it. This indicates that the diasporic wedding film's use of familiar generic formats resonates with an ideological agenda that disavows the divisiveness of racial, cultural and religious difference. What *My Big Fat Greek Wedding, Evet, I Do!, Monsoon Wedding* and *Bride and Prejudice* have in common is that they promote integration rather than segregation by emphasising cultural affinities rather than alterity.

Nobody expresses the dramatic and narrative tensions between similarity and difference more memorably than the father of the bride at the end of *My Big Fat Greek Wedding*. Having welcomed both the Portokalos family and the Miller family, who have come together for Toula and Ian's big day, Mr Portokalos invents yet another one of his funny, far-fetched etymologies. He explains in broken, heavily accented English that 'the root of the word Miller is a Greek word. Miller come from the Greek word milo, which is apple', and Portokalo 'come from the Greek word portokali, which is orange', which leads him to conclude triumphantly: 'So here tonight we have apple and orange. We all different, but in the end, we all fruit'.

Notes

1. Romance and weddings have, of course, been a staple of cinema long before the 1990s. As Virginia Wright Wexman details in *Creating the Couple: Love, Marriage, and Hollywood Performance*, romantic love is the major concern of Hollywood cinema and '85 per cent of all Hollywood films made before the 1960s, have romance as their main plot, and 95 percent have romance as either their main or a secondary plot' (1993: 3). Since, in mainstream Hollywood cinema, romance tends to culminate in marriage, weddings have always formed an integral part. But what makes the wedding films of the 1990s different is that they are more interested in the spectacle of the opulent wedding and the pleasures of conspicuous consumption than in the couple getting together (see Otnes and Pleck 2003: 164–96).
2. *Four Weddings and a Funeral* grossed over £27 million in the UK and over £52 million in the US (BFI Film Stats 1990–2003).
3. Anthropological studies document that arranged marriage fulfils many vital functions for diasporic families (Rubel and Rosman 2009) and that it is perceived as safeguarding against the 'lack of "family" in the host society' (Palriwala and Uberoi 2008: 42).
4. According to Penn and Lambert (2003), arranged marriage is on the decline amongst second- and third-generation Maghrebi French immigrants but remains central to South Asians in Britain, albeit in a modified form that grants sons and daughters the right to veto their parents' choice of spouse.
5. In *Lola and Bilidikid* (see Chapter 3), Murat's mother removes her headscarf and throws it on the street after she and her son have abandoned the oppressive patriarch Osman.
6. See Göktürk (2010a) for an excellent discussion of *Head-On* as ironic melodrama.
7. Although often used interchangeably, 'interracial' and 'interethnic' romance are not equivalent. Ethnicity is a more encompassing term that has been used increasingly since the 1960s to replace 'the discredited generalizations of race with its assumption of humanity divided into fixed, genetically determined biological types' (Ashcroft, Griffiths and Tiffin 1998: 80). Though also comprising the notion of race (especially in the context of 'ethnic minority'; see Sollors 1986: 36, Friedman 1991), ethnicity 'refers to a fusion of many traits that belong to the nature of any ethnic group: a composite of shared values, beliefs, norms, tastes, behaviours, experiences, consciousness of kind, memories and loyalties' (Ashcroft, Griffiths and Tiffin 1998: 80).
8. See Sherzer (1999), Sadock (2004) and Higbee (2005) on interethnic relationships in *Café au lait*.
9. *Wondrous Oblivion* (Paul Morrison, 2003), about two families – one Jewish, the other Afro-Caribbean – who live next door to each other in 1960s north London, is an apt example of Gilroy's 'postcolonial urban conviviality'. This heart-warming

coming-of-age cum cricket film also declines a number of stereotypes about black families (the Samuels are not dysfunctional but nurturing) and black masculinity (Dennis Samuel is not a testosterone-driven male, but resists his neighbour's sexual advances).
10. It transpires that Roisin is married but separated, which makes her living with Casim even more sinful in the eyes of the priest.
11. See Cowans (2010) on interethnic romance in American and French cinema, including discussions of *Pierre et Djemila, Romuald et Juliette (Mama, There's a Man in Your Bed*, Coline Serreau, 1989) and *Bad Faith*; and Tarr (2011) on Muslim–Jewish relations in *Bad Faith*.
12. Some notable exceptions of white wedding films focusing on the family, rather than only on the couple, include *Father of the Bride* (Vincente Minelli, 1950; Charles Shyer, 1991), *The Graduate* (Mike Nichols, 1967) and *A Wedding* (Robert Altman, 1978).
13. Although the central couple, Charles and Carrie, renounce the institution of marriage in which they have lost faith, their solemn promise of a life-long commitment in the film's final scene effectively amounts to marriage.
14. Katherine Rowe suggests that the emphasis placed on the mother–daughter relationship and the mother's story in *Moonstruck* displaces 'romantic comedy's traditional focus on the isolated heterosexual couple', contributing to the film's melodramatic modality (1995: 204).
15. See Introduction, note 14, for a discussion of the term 'Bollywood cinema'. To distinguish it from pre-1990s mainstream Hindi cinema, Gopal refers to it as 'New Bollywood cinema'. She identifies a number of features, including 'the growth of the diasporic market as a major source of revenue for the Hindi film industry; the emergence of NRI films featuring characters located in London or New York; the tie-ins between film and other entertainment industries; the dissemination of Bollywood as a global brand; genre formation; the rise of multiplex exhibition; and the blurring of lines between popular and parallel cinema' (2011: 14) as distinctive attributes of global or New Bollywood.
16. See Introduction, note 13, for an explanation of the term 'Non-Resident Indian'.
17. The Indian joint family is a particular type of extended family in which male family members live together under one roof with their wives and children. However, the term is often used in a less literal sense, whereby rather than designating a 'joint household', the term refers to the joint family as 'a moral institution [. . .] in which the claims of individual members, the sexual relation of husband and wife, and the biological relation of parent and child are subordinated to the larger interests of the family collectivity' (Uberoi 2006: 156).
18. The inclusion of gay characters or couples has become a common feature since *Four Weddings and a Funeral*. Yet, although Gareth and Matthew validate gay love by depicting the couple's deep commitment as on par with, if not 'better' than, that of heterosexual couples, the film ultimately denies its vitality and long-term future by linking it with Gareth's funeral rather than a wedding.
19. The widely held belief that marriage outside one's own ethno-religious community or social class involves high risk, jeopardising family lineage, cultural traditions and the prospect of a long happy marriage, exemplifies such an 'incontestable truth'.
20. George Bernard Shaw's *Pygmalion* (1916) is the archetypal text and has been adapted many times, for instance in *My Fair Lady* (George Cukor, 1964), *Educating Rita* (Lewis Gilbert, 1983) and *Pretty Woman*.
21. Mira Nair grew up in India and moved to the USA when she was nineteen to study at Harvard University; see Foster (1997) and Muir (2006) for biographical details.
22. For an excellent discussion of the hybrid musical styles in *Monsoon Wedding*, see Gopal (2011: 47–50).

23. As Dwyer (2000b) outlines, in popular Hindi cinema, rain is often associated with love, sensuality and sexuality.
24. Dubey represents what is often referred to as the 'aspirational India', a sector of urban or urbanising India which is different from the upper-class, Anglicised social strata to which Aditi's family belongs. But this social group also participates in the fantasies of consumerism and mobility unleashed by liberalisation in the 1990s.
25. For a discussion of these filmic references, see the bonus material on the Film Four DVD release of *Monsoon Wedding* and Sharpe (2005: 75). Interestingly, the fantasy of an 'old' India was once the vision of a 'new' India. Many of these 1950s films (which were inflected by the aspirations and frustrations of India's first decade of independence) reworked the idea of India, creating a fantasy of a secular, more democratic India. These films emphasise the plight and hopes of the disenfranchised, and question some, if not all, aspects of tradition, rather than focusing on the affluent and embracing the 'traditional' as wholeheartedly as some of the more recent Bollywood family films of the 1990s and onwards have done.
26. In mainstream Hindi film, rape and other forms of sexual violation are 'seen to be as much a contamination of the woman as a crime of the rapist' and, ultimately, the raped girl or woman can only be exonerated if she dies (Thomas 1996: 167, 176).
27. Geetha's position is either strategic or naïve, given that the realities of paedophilia in India (and the conspiracy of silence shrouding the crime) have been well documented in recent times.
28. In Hinduism, white is associated with funerals and mourning, as well as with purity; see Dwyer (2000b).
29. Staiger uses the term 'inbred' to refer to 'the mixing of genres in post-Fordian Hollywood cinema' (2003: 196) that involves only Hollywood genres and that is, therefore, aesthetically less innovative.
30. Chopra (2002: 8) notes that *DDLJ* has been 'the longest running film in the history of Indian cinema' but mentions a slightly lower figure, namely six consecutive years. *DDLJ* was a huge hit in India and among diasporic audiences but has also been severely criticised by Indian scholars, critics and some Indian viewers for its apparent endorsement of regressive patriarchal values.
31. See Geraghty (2006, 2008), Jivani (2004), McFarlane (2005) and Ramachandran (2004) on the film's rich intertextuality.
32. Although Richard Dyer devotes most of his book to pastiche as imitation, he briefly comments on pasticcio and suggests that the original ingredients 'typically retain their identities' (2007: 21) rather than becoming entirely amalgamated. These observations are not easy to reconcile with the notion of cultural hybridity, arguably the most distinctive feature of postcolonial and diaspora cultures, which are characterised precisely as 'mélange and hotchpotch' and 'change-by-fusion', as Salman Rushdie famously remarked in *Imaginary Homelands* (1991: 394).

BIBLIOGRAPHY

Abbott, Stacey and Deborah Jermyn (eds) (2009), *Falling in Love Again: Romantic Comedy in Contemporary Cinema*, London: I. B. Tauris.
Abraham, Nicolas and Maria Torok (1994), *The Shell and the Kernel: Renewals of Psychoanalysis* (ed. and trans. Nicholas T. Rand), Chicago and London: University of Chicago Press.
Agnew, Vijay (ed.) (2005), *Diaspora, Memory and Identity: A Search for Home*, Toronto: University of Toronto Press.
Ahmed, Akbar S. (2003), *Islam under Siege: Living Dangerously in a Post-Honor World*, Cambridge: Polity.
Akomfrah, John (2010), 'Chiasmus. An interview with John Akomfrah', bonus material on the DVD release of *The Nine Muses*, New Wave Films.
Akyol, Mustafa (2011), 'Islam and liberty', TED Talk delivered at Warwick (5 March 2011), http://www.youtube.com/watch?v=Gk6–TWX-jk0 (accessed 7 September 2011).
Albers, Thies and Matthias Grundmann (2007), 'Familie im Film: Die Familie im filmischen Wandel', in: Markus Schroer (ed.), *Gesellschaft im Film*, Constance: UVK, pp. 87–110.
Andersen, Erika Surat (1993), '*Mississippi Masala*', *Film Quarterly*, 46:4, pp. 23–6.
Anderson, Benedict ([1983] 2006), *Imagined Communities: Reflections on the Origin and Spread of Nationalism*, London: Verso.
Anthias, Floya and Nira Yuval-Davis (eds) (1989), *Woman – Nation – State*, Basingstoke: Macmillan.
Appadurai, Arjun (1988), 'Introduction: Commodities and the politics of value', in: Arjun Appadurai (ed.), *The Social Life of Things: Commodities in Cultural Perspective*, Cambridge: Cambridge University Press, pp. 3–63.
— (1996), *Modernity at Large: Cultural Dimensions of Globalization*, Minneapolis and London: University of Minnesota Press.
Ashcroft, Bill, Gareth Griffiths and Helen Tiffin (1998), *Post-Colonial Studies: The Key Concepts*, London and New York: Routledge.

Assmann, Jan (1995), 'Collective memory and cultural identity', *New German Critique*, 65, pp. 125–33.
Austen, Jane ([1813] 2010), *Pride and Prejudice*, Oxford: Oxford University Press.
Austin, John Langshaw (1962), *How to Do Things with Words*, Oxford: Clarendon.
Azoury, Philippe (2002), 'Charef charge son Algérie', *Libération*, 10 April.
Bä, Saër Maty and Will Higbee (2010), 'Re-presenting diasporas in cinema and new digital media: Introduction', *Journal of Media Practice*, 11:1, pp. 3–9.
Bakhtin, Mikhail (1981), *The Dialogic Imagination: Four Essays*, ed. and trans. Michael Holquist, Austin: University of Texas Press.
Bal, Mieke, Jonathan Crew and Leo Spitzer (eds), *Acts of Memory: Cultural Recall in the Present*, Hanover, NH, and London: University Press of New England.
Balibar, Étienne (1991), 'Racism and nationalism', in: Étienne Balibar and Immanuel Wallerstein (eds), *Race, Nation, Class: Ambiguous Identities*, London and New York: Verso, pp. 37–67.
Barnet, Marie-Claire and Edward Welch (eds) (2007), *Affaires de famille: The Family in Contemporary French Culture and Theory*, Amsterdam: Rodopi.
Baronian, Marie-Aude, Stephen Besser and Yolande Jansen (2007), 'Introduction', in: Marie-Aude Baronian, Stephen Besser and Yolande Jansen (eds), *Diaspora and Memory: Figures of Displacement in Contemporary Literature, Arts and Politics*, Amsterdam: Rodopi, pp. 9–16.
Barthes, Roland (1981), *Camera Lucida: Reflections on Photography*, trans. Richard Howard, New York: Hill & Wang.
Batra, Kanika and Rich Rice (2012), 'Mira Nair's *Monsoon Wedding* and the transcoded audiologic of postcolonial transvergence', in: Sandra Ponzanesi and Marguerite Waller (eds), *Postcolonial Cinema Studies*, London and New York: Routledge, pp. 205–17.
Baudry, Leo ([1976] 1985), 'Genre: The conventions of connection', in: Gerald Mast and Marshall Cohen (eds), *Film Theory and Criticism* (3rd edn), Oxford: Oxford University Press, pp. 411–33.
Bauman, Zygmunt (1992), *Intimations of Postmodernity*, London and New York: Routledge.
— (1996), 'From pilgrim to tourist – or a short history of identity', in: Stuart Hall and Paul du Gay (eds), *Questions of Cultural Identity*, London: Sage, pp. 18–36.
Beechy, Veronica (1979), 'On patriarchy', *Feminist Review*, 3, pp. 66–82.
Bekkar, Rabia, Nadir Boumaza and Daniel Pinson (1999), *Familles maghrébines en France, l'épreuve de la ville*, Paris: Presses Universitaires de France.
Ben-Davis, Esther (2009), 'Europe's shifting immigration dynamic', *Middle East Quarterly*, 16:2, pp. 15–24, http://www.meforum.org/2107/europe-shifting-immigration-dynamic (accessed 20 December 2011).

Bennet, Andy (1999), 'Hip hop am Main: The localization of rap music and hip hop culture', *Media Culture Society*, 21, pp. 77–91

Benshoff, Harry (2008), 'Queers and families in film: From problems to parents', in: Murray Pomerance (ed.), *A Family Affair: Cinema Calls Home*, London and New York: Wallflower, pp. 223–33.

Bergfelder, Tim (2005), 'National, transnational or supranational cinema? Rethinking European film studies', *Media, Culture and Society*, 27.3, pp. 315–31.

Berghahn, Daniela (2006), 'No place like home? Or impossible homecomings in the films of Fatih Akın', *New Cinemas: Journal of Contemporary Film*, 4:3, pp. 141–57.

— (2009a), 'From Turkish greengrocer to drag queen: Reassessing patriarchy in recent Turkish–German coming-of-age films', *New Cinemas: Journal of Contemporary Film*, 7:1, pp. 55–69.

— (ed.) (2009b), *Turkish German Dialogues on Screen*, special guest-edited issue of *New Cinemas: Journal of Contemporary Film*, 7:1.

— (2011), 'Queering the family of nation: Reassessing fantasies of purity, celebrating hybridity in diasporic cinema', *Transnational Cinemas*, 2:2, pp. 129–46.

— (2012), 'My big fat Turkish wedding: From culture clash to romcom', in: Sabine Hake and Barbara Mennel (eds), *Turkish German Cinema in the New Millennium: Sites, Sounds, and Screens*, Oxford and New York: Berghahn, pp. 19–31.

Berghahn, Daniela and Claudia Sternberg (2010a), 'Locating migrant and diasporic cinema in contemporary Europe', in: Daniela Berghahn and Claudia Sternberg (eds), *European Cinema in Motion: Migrant and Diasporic Film in Contemporary Europe*, Basingstoke: Palgrave Macmillan, pp. 12–49.

— (eds) (2010b), *European Cinema in Motion: Migrant and Diasporic Film in Contemporary Europe*, Basingstoke: Palgrave Macmillan.

Berry, Chris (2003), '*Wedding Banquet*: A family (melodrama) affair', in: Chris Berry (ed.), *Chinese Films in Focus: 25 New Takes*, London: BFI, pp. 183–90.

Bertaux, Daniel and Thompson, Paul (eds) (1993), *Between Generations: Family Models, Myths and Memories*, Oxford: Oxford University Press.

Betz, Mark (2009), *Beyond the Subtitle: Remapping European Art Cinema*, Minneapolis: University of Minnesota Press.

BFI Information Services (n/d), *The Stats: An Overview of the Film, Television, Video and DVD Industries in the UK 1990–2003*, London: BFI National Library.

Bhabha, Homi K. (1985), 'Signs taken for wonders: Questions of ambivalence and authority under a tree outside Delhi, May 1817', *Critical Inquiry*, 12:1, pp. 144–65.

— (1994), *The Location of Culture*, London and New York: Routledge.

— (1996), 'Cultures in-between', in: Stuart Hall and Paul du Gay (eds), *Questions of Cultural Identity*, London: Sage, pp. 53–60.
Bloch, Ernst ([1959] 1968), *Das Prinzip Hoffnung*, Frankfurt am Main: Suhrkamp.
Bluher, Dominique (2001), 'Hip-hop cinema in France', *Camera Obscura*, special issue on *Marginality and Alterity in Contemporary European Cinema*, ed. Randall Halle and Sharon Willis, 46: 16, pp. 77–97.
Boehmer, Elleke (1991), 'Stories of women and mothers: Gender and nationalism in the early fiction of Flora Nwapa', in: Susheila Nasta (ed.), *Motherlands: Black Women's Writing from Africa, the Caribbean and South Asia*, London: Women's Press, pp. 3–23.
Bondanella, Peter (2006), *Hollywood Italians: Dagos, Palookas, Romeos, Wise Guys, and Sopranos*, London and New York: Continuum.
Bosséno, Christian (1992), 'Immigrant cinema: national cinema. The case of *beur* film', in: Richard Dyer and Ginette Vincendeau (eds), *Popular European Cinema*, London: Routledge, pp. 47–57.
Bourdieu, Pierre (1990), 'The Cult of unity and cultivated differences', in: Pierre Bourdieu (ed.), *Photography: A Middlebrow Art*, Stanford: Stanford University Press, pp. 13–72.
— (1998), *Practical Reason: On the Theory of Action*, Cambridge: Polity.
Bourne, Stephen (2001), *Black in the British Frame: The Black Experience in British Film and Television*, London: Continuum.
Bowen, John Richard (2007), *Why the French Don't Like Headscarves: Islam, the State, and Public Space*, Princeton: Princeton University Press.
Bowen, Peter (2002), 'Hello, Bolly', *Filmmaker* (Los Angeles), 10:2, pp. 78–80.
Bowers, Maggie Ann (2004), *Magic(al) Realism: The New Critical Idiom*, London and New York: Routledge.
Boym, Svetlana (2001), *The Future of Nostalgia*, New York: Basic.
Bradshaw, Peter (2005), '*Le Grand Voyage*', *The Guardian*, 14 October, http://www.guardian.co.uk/culture/2005/oct/14/3 (accessed 1 February 2011).
Brah, Avtar (1996), *Cartographies of Diaspora: Contesting Identities*, London and New York: Routledge.
Brandt, Kim (2007), *Weiblichkeitsentwürfe und Kulturkonflikte im deutschtürkischen Film: Zur integrativen Wirkung von Filmen*, Saarbrücken: VDM.
Brauerhoch, Annette (1995), 'Die Heimat des Geschlechts – oder mit der fremden Geschichte die eigene erzählen: Zu "Shirins Hochzeit" von Helma Sanders-Brahms', in: Ernst Karpf, Doren Kiesel and Karsten Visarius (eds), *Getürkte Bilder: Zur Inszenierung von Fremden im Film*, Marburg: Schüren, pp. 108–15.
Braziel, Jana Evans and Anita Mannur (eds) (2003), *Theorizing Diaspora: A Reader*, Oxford: Blackwell.
Brooks, Peter (1976), *The Melodramatic Imagination: Balzac, Henry James, Melodrama and the Mode of Excess*, New Haven and London: Yale University Press.

Brown, William, Dina Iordanova and Leshu Torchin (2010), *Moving People, Moving Images: Cinema and Trafficking in the New Europe*, St Andrews: St Andrews University Press.

Brunow, Dagmar (forthcoming), 'Amateur home movies and the archive of migration: Sandhya Suri's *I for India* (UK, 2005)', in: Sonja Kmec and Viviane Thill (eds), *Tourists and Nomads: Amateur Images of Migration*, Marburg: Jonas.

Bruzzi, Stella (2005), *Bringing Up Daddy: Fatherhood and Masculinity in Post-War Hollywood*, London: BFI.

— (2006), *New Documentary* (2nd edn), London and New York: Routledge.

— (2009), 'Where are those buggers? Aspects of homosexuality in mainstream British cinema', in: Robert Murphy (ed.), *The British Cinema Book* (3rd edn), London: BFI, pp. 133–41.

— (2011), 'Macho Italiano: Hollywood's Italian American fathers. Why are they so awful?', podcast of a keynote address presented at The Diasporic Family in Cinema Conference in London on 21 May, http://www.farflung families.net/podcasts/item/macho_italiano_hollywoods_italian_american_fa thers_why_are_they_so_awful (accessed 7 July 2011).

Bryceson, Deborah Fahy and Ulla Vuorela (2002), 'Transnational families in the twenty-first century', in: Bryceson, Deborah and Ulla Vuorela (eds), *The Transnational Family: New European Frontiers and Global Networks*, Oxford: Berg, pp. 3–30.

Burgière, André, Christiane Klapisch-Zuber, Martine Segalen, Françoise Zonabend (eds) (1996), *A History of the Family: The Impact of Modernity* (vol. 2), trans. Sarah Hanbury Tenison, Cambridge: Polity.

Burns, Rob (2006), 'Turkish–German cinema: From cultural resistance to transnationalism?', in: David Clarke (ed.), *German Cinema since Unification*, London: Continuum, pp. 127–49.

— (2007), 'Towards a cinema of cultural hybridity: Turkish–German filmmakers and the representation of alterity', *Debatte*, 15:1, pp. 3–24.

— (2009), 'On the streets and on the road: Identity in transit in Turkish German travelogues on screen', *New Cinemas*, 7:1, pp. 11–26.

Butterwegge, Christoph (2007), 'Benehmt euch. Ihr seid hier nicht zu Hause', *Die Zeit Online*, 45, p. 57, http://www.zeit.de/2007/45/Migranten-in-Medien (accessed 10 September 2010).

Buzard, James (2006), 'The Grand Tour and after (1660–1840)', in: Peter Hulme and Tim Youngs (eds), *The Cambridge Companion to Travel Writing*, Cambridge: Cambridge University Press, Cambridge Collections Online, pp. 37–52. http://cco.cambridge.org/extract?id=ccol052178140x_ CCOL052178140XA005 (accessed 15 March 2011).

Cameron, David (2011), 'Rioters need tough love, says David Cameron', BBC News, 2 September, http://www.bbc.co.uk/news/uk-politics-14760686 (accessed 10 September 2011).

Camon, Alessandro (2000), '*The Godfather* and the mythology of Mafia',

in: Nick Brown (ed.), *Francis Ford Coppola's The Godfather Trilogy*, Cambridge: Cambridge University Press, pp. 57–75.
Campt, Tina (2009), 'Family matters: Diaspora, difference, and the visual archive', *Social Text*, 98:27, pp. 83–114.
Castles, Stephen (2000), *Ethnicity and Globalization: From Migrant Worker to Transnational Citizen*, London: Sage.
Castles, Stephen and Mark J. Miller (2009), *The Age of Migration: International Population Movements in the Modern World* (4th edn), Basingstoke: Palgrave Macmillan.
Certeau, Michel de (1988), *The Practice of Everyday Life*, trans. Steven Rendell, Berkeley and Los Angeles: University of California Press.
Chamberlain, Mary (2006), *Family Love in the Diaspora: Migration and the Anglo-Caribbean Experience*, New Brunswick, NJ: Transaction.
Chambers, Deborah (2001), *Representing the Family*, London: Sage.
Chambers, Iain (1994), *Migrancy, Culture, Identity*, London and New York: Routledge.
Chiang, Mark (2002), 'Coming out into the global system: Postmodern patriarchies and transnational sexualities in *The Wedding Banquet*', in: Peter X. Feng (ed.), *Screening Asian Americans*, New Brunswick, NJ, and London: Rutgers University Press, pp. 273–91.
Chopra, Anupama (2002), *Dilwale Dulhania Le Jayenge*, London: BFI.
Chopra-Gant, Mike (2006), *Hollywood Genres and Post-war America: Masculinity, Family, and Nation in Popular Movies and Film Noir*, London: I. B. Tauris.
Chow, Rey (1993), *Writing Diaspora: Tactics of Intervention in Contemporary Cultural Studies*, Bloomington: Indiana University Press.
— (2010), *The Rey Chow Reader*, ed. Paul Bowman, New York: Columbia University Press.
Clark, Christopher (2006), 'Transculturation, transe sexuality, and Turkish Germany: Kutluğ Ataman's *Lola und Bilidikid*', *German Life and Letters*, 59:4, pp. 555–72.
Clifford, James (1994), 'Diasporas', *Cultural Anthropology*, 9:3, pp. 302–38.
Cohan, Steven and Ina Rae Hark (1997), 'Introduction', in: Steven Cohan and Ina Rae Hark (eds), *The Road Movie Book*, London and New York: Routledge, pp. 1–14.
Cohen, Robin (2006), *Migration and its Enemies: Global Capital, Migrant Labour, and the Nation-State*, Burlington, VT, and Aldershot: Ashgate.
— (2008), *Global Diasporas: An Introduction* (2nd edn), London and New York: Routledge.
Cohen, Robin and Gunvor Jónsson (eds) (2011), *Migration and Culture*, Cheltenham and Northampton, MA: Edward Elgar.
Cohen, Robin and Paola Toninato (eds) (2010), *The Creolization Reader: Studies in Mixed Identities and Cultures*, London and New York: Routledge.

Coleman, Simon and John Elsner (1995), *Pilgrimage Past and Present: Sacred Travel and Sacred Space in World Religions*, London: British Museum.
Connerton, Paul (1989), *How Societies Remember*, Cambridge: Cambridge University Press.
Considine, David M. (1985), *The Cinema of Adolescence*, Jefferson, NC: McFarland.
Coontz, Stephanie (2000), *The Way We Never Were: American Families and the Nostalgia Trap*, New York: Basic.
Cooper, Darius (2007), 'The "Baimaan" or "betrayed vision" of Mira Nair's *Monsoon Wedding*', *Asian Cinema*, 18, pp. 253–61.
Copier, Laura (2005), 'Radicalism begins at home: Fundamentalism and the family in *My Son the Fanatic*', in: Patricia Pisters and Wim Staat (eds), *Shooting the Family: Transnational Media and Intercultural Values*, Amsterdam: Amsterdam University Press, pp. 89–101.
Corrigan, Timothy (1991), *A Cinema without Walls: Movies and Culture after Vietnam*, London: Routlege.
Cowans, Jon (2010), 'Black and white on the silver screen: Views of interracial romance in French films and reviews since the 1980s', *French Politics, Culture and Society*, 28:3, pp. 46–65.
Crang, Philip (2010), 'Diasporas and material culture', in: Kim Knott and Seán McLoughlin (eds), *Diasporas: Concepts, Intersections, Identities*, London and New York: Zed, pp. 139–44.
Crul, Maurice and Hans Vermeulen (2003), 'The second generation in Europe: Introduction', *International Migration Review*, 37, pp. 965–86.
Cunningham, Stuart and John Sinclair (eds) (2001), *Floating Lives: The Media and Asian Diasporas*, London and Boulder: Rowman & Littlefield.
Davis, Colin (2005), 'État présent: Hauntology, spectres and phantoms', *French Studies*, 59:3, pp. 373–9.
Delorme, Stéphane (2007), 'Bateau ivre: *La Graine et le mulet* d'Abellatif Kechiche', *Cahiers du cinéma*, December, pp. 11–13.
Dengel-Janic, Ellen and Lars Eckstein (2008), 'Bridehood revisited: Disarming concepts of gender and culture in recent Asian British film', in: Lars Eckstein, Barbara Korte, Eva Ulrike Pirker and Christoph Reinfandt (eds), *Multi-Ethnic Britain 2000+: New Perspectives in Literature, Film and the Arts*, Amsterdam and New York: Rodopi, pp. 45–63.
Desai, Jigna (2004), *Beyond Bollywood: The Cultural Politics of South Asian Diasporic Film*, London and New York: Routledge.
Deshpande, Sudhanva (2005), 'The consumable hero of globalised India', in: Raminder Kaur and Ajay J. Sinha (eds), *Bollyworld: Popular Indian Cinema through a Transnational Lens*, New Delhi and London: Sage, pp. 186–203.
Doane, Mary Ann (1987), *The Desire to Desire: The Woman's Film of the 1940s*, Bloomington: Indiana University Press.
Doherty, Timothy (2002), *Teenagers and Teenpics: The Juvenilization of*

American Movies in the 1950s (2nd rev. edn), Philadelphia: Temple University Press.

Doughty, Ruth and Kate Griffiths (2006), 'La Haine and the art of borrowing', *Studies in European Cinema*, 3:2, pp. 117–27.

dpa / Reuters (2009), 'Sarrazin muss sich entschuldigen', *Die Zeit Online*, 1 October, http://www.zeit.de/politik/deutschland/2009-10/sarrazin-aeusserung-integration (accessed 8 December 2009).

Du Bois, W. E. B. ([1903] 1990), *The Souls of Black Folk*, New York: Vintage.

Dudrah, Rajinder (2012a), *Bollywood Travels: Culture, Diaspora and Border Crossings in Popular Hindi Cinema*, London and New York: Routledge.

— (2012b), 'Beyond World Cinema? The dialectics of Black British diasporic cinema', in: Lúcia Nagib, Chris Perriam and Rajinder Dudrah (eds), *Theorizing World Cinema*, London and New York: I. B. Tauris, pp. 113–27.

Duits, Linda and Liesbet von Zoonen (2006), 'Headscarves and porno-chic: Disciplining girls' bodies in the European multicultural society', *European Journal of Women's Studies*, 13:2, pp. 103–17.

Durel, Michel (1985), 'Le Thé au harem d'Archimède', *Cinématographe*, 110, pp. 32–3.

Durmelat, Sylvie (2000), 'Transmission and mourning in *Mémoires d'immigrés: l'héritage maghrébin*: Yamina Benguigui as "memory entrepreneuse"', in: Jane Freeman and Carrie Tarr (eds), *Women, Immigration and Identities in France*, Oxford: Berg, pp. 171–88.

Durovicová, Natasa and Kathleen E. Newman (2010), *World Cinemas, Transnational Perspectives*, New York and London: AFI / Routledge.

Dwyer, Claire (1998), 'Contested identities: challenging dominant representations of young British Muslim women', in: Tracey Sketon and Gill Valentine (eds), *Cool Places: Geographies of Youth Cultures*, London: Routledge, pp. 51–65.

Dwyer, Rachel (2000a), *All You Want is Money, All You Need is Love: Sexuality and Romance in Modern India*, London and New York: Cassell.

— (2000b), 'The erotics of the wet sari in Hindi films', *South Asia: Journal of South Asian Studies*, 23:2, pp. 143–60.

— (2000c), 'Bombay Ishtyle', in: Stella Bruzzi and Pamela Church Gibson (eds), *Fashion Cultures: Theories, Explorations and Analyses*, London and New York: Routledge, pp. 178–90.

— (2011), 'Innocents abroad: The diaspora in the shaping of the imagined Indian family', podcast of a paper presented at The Diasporic Family in Cinema Conference in London on 21 May, http://www.farflungfamilies.net/podcasts/item/innocents_abroad_the_diaspora_in_the_shaping_of_the_imagined_indian_family (accessed 1 July 2011)

Dyer, Richard (1993), *The Matter of Images: Essays on Representation*, London and New York: Routledge.

— (1997), *White*, London and New York: Routledge

— (2002), *The Culture of Queers*, London and New York: Routledge.
— (2007), *Pastiche*, London and New York: Routledge.
Eckstein, Lars, Barbara Korte, Eva Ulrike Pirker and Christoph Reinfandt (eds), *Multi-Ethnic Britain 2000+: New Perspectives in Literature, Film and the Arts*, Amsterdam: Rodopi.
Eleftheriotis, Dimitris (2010), *Cinematic Journeys: Film and Movement*, Edinburgh University Press.
Ellis, John (2012), *Documentary: Witness and Self-revelation*, London and New York: Routledge.
Elsaesser, Thomas ([1972] 1987), 'Tales of sound and fury: Observations on the family melodrama', in: Christine Gledhill (ed.), *Home is Where the Heart Is: Studies in Melodrama and the Woman's Film*, London: BFI, pp. 43–69.
— (1996), *Fassbinder's Germany: History Identity Subject*, Amsterdam: Amsterdam University Press.
— (1999), 'Ethnicity, authenticity and exile: a counterfeit trade?', in: Hamid Naficy (ed.), *Home, Exile, Homeland: Film, Media, and the Politics of Place*, New York and London: AFI / Routledge, pp. 97–123.
— (2005), *European Cinema: Face to Face with Hollywood*, Amsterdam: Amsterdam University Press.
Eng, David L. (1997), 'Out here and over there: Queerness and diaspora in Asian American Studies', *Social Text*, 15: 3–4, pp. 31–52.
Erdoğan, Nezih (2009), 'Star director as symptom: Reflections on the reception of Fatih Akın in the Turkish media', *New Cinemas: Journal of Contemporary Film*, 7:1, pp. 27–38.
Erel, Umut (2002), 'Reconceptualizing motherhood: Experiences of migrant women from Turkey living in Germany', in: Deborah Bryceson and Ulla Vuorela (eds), *The Transnational Family: New European Frontiers and Global Networks*, Oxford: Berg, pp. 63–82.
Eren, Mine (2003), 'Travelling pictures from a Turkish daughter: Seyhan Derin's *Ben annemin kiziyim – I'm My Mother's Daughter*', in: Eva Rueschmann (ed.), *Moving Pictures, Migrating Identities*, Jackson: University of Mississippi Press, pp. 39–54.
Esposito, John L. (ed.) (2003), *Oxford Dictionary of Islam. Oxford Reference Online*, Oxford: Oxford University Press, http://www.oxfordreference.com/views/ENTRY.html?subview=Main&entry=t125.e2260 (accessed 10 December 2011).
Evans, Nicola (2002), 'The family changes colour: Interracial families in contemporary Hollywood cinema', *Screen*, 43:3, pp. 271–92.
Everett, Wendy E. (2005), *European Identity in Cinema* (2nd edn), Bristol: Intellect.
— (2009), 'Lost in transition? The European road movie, or a genre "adrift in the cosmos"', *Literature Film Quarterly*, 37:3, pp. 165–75.
Ewing, Katherine Pratt (2008), *Stolen Honor: Stigmatizing Muslim Men in Berlin*, Stanford: Stanford University Press.

Ezli, Özkan (ed.) (2010), *Kultur als Ereignis: Fatih Akıns Film "Auf der anderen Seite" als transkulturelle Narration*, Bielefeld: Transcript.
Ezra, Elizabeth (ed.) (2003), *European Cinema*, Oxford: Oxford University Press.
Ezra, Elizabeth and Terry Rowden (eds) (2006), *Transnational Cinema: The Film Reader*, London and New York: The Film Reader.
Ezra, Elizabeth and Jane Sillars (2007a), 'Hidden in plain sight: bringing terror home', *The Caché Dossier, Screen*, 48:2, pp. 215–21.
— (eds) (2007b), *The Caché Dossier, Screen*, 48:2, pp. 211–49.
Farrokhzad, Schahrzad (2006), 'Exotin, Unterdrückte und Fundamentalistin. Konstruktionen der "fremden Frau" in deutschen Medien', in Christoph Butterwegge and Gudrun Hentges (eds), *Massenmedien, Migration und Integration*, Wiesbaden: VS, pp. 53–84.
Fehrenbach, Heide (1995), *Cinema in Democratizing Germany: Reconstructing National Identity after Hitler*, Chapel Hill and London: University of North Carolina Press.
Fenner, Angelica (2006), 'Traversing the screen politics of migration: Xavier Koller's *Journey of Hope*', in: Eva Rueschmann (ed.), *Moving Pictures, Migrating Identities*, Jackson: University of Mississippi Press, pp. 18–38.
Ferriss, Suzanne and Mallory Young (2007), 'Chick flicks and chick culture', *Post-Script: Essays in Film and the Humanities*, 27:1, pp. 32–49.
Ferry, Jane F. (2003), *Food in Film: A Culinary Performance of Communication*, New York and London: Routledge.
Fielding, Anthony (1993), 'Migrations, institutions and politics: the evolution of European migration policies', in: Russell King (ed.), *Mass Migrations in Europe: The Legacy and the Future*, London: Belhaven, pp. 40–62.
Fincham, Victoria (2008), 'Violence, sexuality and the family: Identity "within and beyond Turkish–German parameters" in Fatih Akın's *Gegen die Wand*, Kutluğ Ataman's *Lola + Bilidikid* and Anno Saul's *Kebab Connection*', *German as a Foreign Language*, pp. 40–72.
Fischer, Lucy (1996), *Cinematernity: Film, Motherhood, Genre*, Princeton: Princeton University Press.
Fontane, Theodor ([1894] 1968), *Effi Briest*, Munich: Nymphenburger Verlagshandlung.
Fortier, Anne-Marie (2000), *Migrant Belongings: Memory, Space, Identity*, Oxford: Berg.
— (2002), 'Queer diaspora', in: Diane Richardson and Steven Seidman (eds), *Handbook of Lesbian and Gay Studies*, London and Thousand Oaks: Sage, pp. 183–97.
— (2005), 'Diaspora', in: David Atkinson, Peter Jackson, David Sibley and Neil Washbourne et al. (eds), *Cultural Geography: A Critical Dictionary of Key Concepts*, London and New York: I. B. Tauris, pp. 182–93.
Foster, Audrey Gwendolyn (1997), *Women Filmmakers of the African and*

Asian Diaspora: Decolonizing the Gaze, Locating Subjectivity, Carbondale, IL: Southern Illinois University Press.

French, Philip (2004), 'Bride and Prejudice', *The Observer*, 10 October.

— (2008), 'Alice in the Cities', *The Observer*, 6 January.

Freud, Sigmund ([1899] 1995), 'Screen memories', in: Peter Gay (ed.), *The Freud Reader*, London: Vintage, pp. 117–26.

— ([1908] 2001), 'Family romances', in: James Strachey (ed. and trans.), *The Standard Edition of the Complete Psychoanalytical Works of Sigmund Freud*, vol. 9, London: Vintage / Hogarth, pp. 237–41.

Friedman, Lester D. (1991), 'Celluloid palimpsests: An overview of ethnicity and the American film', in: Lester D. Friedman (ed.), *Unspeakable Images: Ethnicity and the American Cinema*, Urbana and Chicago: University of Illinois Press, pp. 11–35.

— (ed.) (2008), *Fires Were Started: British Cinema and Thatcherism* (2nd edn), London and New York: Wallflower.

Fröhlich, Margit, Reinhard Middel and Karsten Visarius (eds) (2004), *Family Affairs: Ansichten der Familie im Film*, Marburg: Schüren.

Gabaccia, Donna R. (1998), *We Are What We Eat: Ethnic Food and the Making of Americans*, Cambridge, MA: Harvard University Press.

Galt, Rosalind (2006), *The New European Cinema: Redrawing the Map*, New York: Columbia University Press.

Galt, Rosalind and Karl Schoonover (eds) (2010), *Global Art Cinema: New Theories and Histories*, New York: Oxford University Press.

Geetha, J. (2002), '"Don't mind": A take-off on *The Monsoon Wedding*', *Deep Focus: A Film Quarterly*, March, pp. 68–72.

Georgas, James (2006), 'Families and family change', in: James Georgas, John W. Berry, Fons J. R. van de Vijver, Çigdem Kagitçibasi and Ype H. Poortinga (eds), *Families Across Cultures: A 30–Nation Psychological Study*, Cambridge: Cambridge University Press, pp. 3–50.

Georgas, James, John W. Berry, Fons J. R. van de Vijver, Çigdem Kagitçibasi and Ype H. Poortinga (eds) (2006), *Families Across Cultures: A 30–Nation Psychological Study*, Cambridge: Cambridge University Press.

Geraghty, Christine (2005), *My Beautiful Laundrette*, London and New York: I. B. Tauris.

— (2006), 'Jane Austen meets Gurinder Chadha: Hybridity and intertextuality in *Bride and Prejudice*', *South Asian Popular Culture*, 4:2, pp. 163–8.

— (2008), *Now a Major Motion Picture: Film Adaptations of Literature and Drama*, Lanham, MD, and Plymouth, UK: Rowman & Littlefield.

Giddens, Anthony (1992), *The Transformation of Intimacy: Sexuality, Love and Eroticism in Modern Societies*, Cambridge: Polity.

— (2002), *Runaway World: How Globalisation is Reshaping Our Lives* (2nd edn), London: Profile.

Gillespie, Marie (1995), *Television, Ethnicity and Cultural Change*, London and New York: Routledge.

Gilroy, Paul (1987), *'There Ain't No Black in the Union Jack': The Cultural Politics of Race and Nation*, London: Hutchinson.
— ([1991] 1999), 'It's not where you're from, it's where you're at: The dialectics of diasporic identification', in: Steven Vertovec and Robin Cohen (eds), *Migration, Diasporas and Transnationalism*, Cheltenham and Northampton, MA: Elgar Reference Collection, pp. 266–79.
— (1993a), *The Black Atlantic: Modernity and Double Consciousness*, London and New York: Verso.
— (1993b), 'It's a family affair: Black culture and the trope of kinship', in: *Small Acts: Thoughts on the Politics of Black Cultures*, London: Serpent's Tail, pp. 192–207.
— (2004), *After Empire: Melancholia and Convivial Culture*, London and New York: Routledge.
Gledhill, Christine (1987a), 'The melodramatic field: An investigation', in: Christine Gledhill (ed.), *Home is Where the Heart Is: Studies in Melodrama and the Woman's Film*, London: BFI, pp. 5–39.
— (ed.) (1987b), *Home is Where the Heart Is: Studies in Melodrama and the Woman's Film*, London: BFI.
Göktürk, Deniz (2000), 'Turkish women on German streets: Closure and exposure in transnational cinema', in: Myrto Konstantarakos (ed.), *Spaces in European Cinema*, Exeter: Intellect, pp. 64–76.
— (2002), 'Beyond paternalism: Turkish German traffic in cinema', in: Tim Bergfelder, Erica Carter and Deniz Göktürk (eds), *The German Cinema Book*, London: BFI, pp. 248–56.
— (2010a), 'Sound bridges: Transnational mobility as ironic melodrama', Daniela Berghahn and Claudia Sternberg (eds), *European Cinema in Motion: Migrant and Diasporic Film in Contemporary Europe*, Basingstoke: Palgrave Macmillan, pp. 215–34.
— (2010b), 'Mobilität und Stillstand im Weltkino digital', in: Özkan Ezli (ed.), *Kultur als Ereignis: Fatih Akins Film "Auf der anderen Seite" als transkulturelle Narration*, Bielefeld: Transcript, pp. 15–45.
Göktürk, Deniz, David Gramling and Anton Kaes (eds) (2007), *Germany in Transit: Nation and Migration 1995–2005*, Berkeley, Los Angeles and London: University of California Press.
Goody, Jack (1983), *The Development of the Family and Marriage in Europe*, Cambridge: Cambridge University Press.
Gopal, Sangita (2011), *Conjugations: Marriage and Form in New Bollywood Cinema*, Chicago: University of Chicago Press.
Gopinath, Gayatri (2005), *Impossible Desires: Queer Diasporas and South Asian Public Cultures*, Durham, NC, and London: Duke University Press.
Goulbourne, Harry, Tracey Reynolds, John Solomos and Elisabetta Zontini (2010), *Transnational Families: Ethnicities, Identities and Social Capital*, London and New York: Routledge.

Geaves, Ron, Theodore Gabriel, Yvonne Haddad and Jane Idleman Smith (2004), *Islam and the West post 9/11*, Aldershot: Ashgate.
Green, Mary Jean (2011), 'All in the family: Abdellatif Kechiche's *La Graine et le mulet (The Secret of the Grain)*', *South Central Review*, 28:1, pp. 109–23.
Griffiths, Robin (ed.), *Queer Cinema in Europe*, Bristol: Intellect.
Grillo, Ralph (2004), 'Islam and transnationalism', *Journal of Ethnic and Migration Studies*, 30:5, pp. 861–78.
— (2008), 'The family in dispute: Insiders and outsiders', in: Ralph Grillo (ed.), *The Family in Question: Immigrant and Ethnic Minorities in Multicultural Europe*, Amsterdam: Amsterdam University Press, pp. 15–35.
Grossberg, Lawrence (1996), 'Identity and cultural studies: Is that all there is?', in: Stuart Hall and Paul du Gay (eds), *Questions of Cultural Identity*, London, Thousand Oaks and New Delhi: Sage, pp. 87–107.
Grossman, Alan and Áine O'Brien (eds) (2007), *Projecting Migration: Transcultural Documentary Practice*, London: Wallflower.
Hake, Sabine and Barbara Mennel (eds) (2012), *Turkish German Cinema in the New Millennium: Sites, Sounds, and Screens*, Oxford and New York: Berghahn.
Halbwachs, Maurice (1985), *Das Gedächtnis und seine sozialen Bedingungen*, Frankfurt am Main: Suhrkamp.
Hall, Stuart (1993), 'Old and new identities, old and new ethnicities', in: Anthony D. King (ed.), *Culture, Globalization and the World System: Contemporary Conditions for the Representation of Identity*, Basingstoke: Macmillan, pp. 41–68.
— (1996), 'Who needs "identity"?', in: Stuart Hall and Paul du Gay (eds), *Questions of Cultural Identity*, London, Thousand Oaks and New Delhi: Sage, pp. 1–17.
— ([1990] 2003), 'Cultural identity and diaspora', in: Jana Evans Braziel and Anita Mannur (eds), *Theorizing Diaspora: A Reader*, Oxford: Blackwell, pp. 233–46.
Halle, Randall (2008), *German Film after Germany: Toward a Transnational Aesthetic*, Chicago: University of Illinois Press.
Hamm-Ehsani, Karin (2008), 'Intersections: Issues on national, ethnic and sexual identity in Kutluğ Ataman's Berlin film *Lola und Bilidikid*', *Seminar: A Journal of Germanic Studies*, 44:3, pp. 366–81.
Hannerz, Ulf (1996), *Transnational Connections: Culture, People, Places*, London and New York: Routledge.
Hansen, Randall (2000), *Citizenship and Immigration in Post-war Britain: The Institutional Origins of a Multicultural Nation*, Oxford: Oxford University Press.
Hardt, Michael and Antonio Negri (2000), *Empire*, Cambridge, MA, and London: Harvard University Press.
Hargreaves, Alec G. (1997), *Immigration and Identity in Beur Fiction: Voices from the North African Immigrant Community in France*, Oxford: Berg.

— (2000), 'Resuscitating the father: New cinematic representations of the Maghrebi minority in France', *Sites: The Journal of 20th-century / contemporary French Studies*, 4:2, pp. 343–51.

— (2007), *Multi-Ethnic France: Immigration, Politics, Culture and Society* (2nd edn), New York and London: Routledge.

Hargreaves, Alec G. and Mark McKinney (1997), *Postcolonial Cultures in France*, London and New York: Routledge.

Harvey, David (1990), *The Condition of Postmodernity: An Enquiry into the Origins of Cultural Change*, Cambridge, MA: Blackwell.

Harwood, Sarah (1997), *Family Fictions: Representations of the Family in 1980s Hollywood Cinema*, Basingstoke: Palgrave Macmillan.

Heberle, Helge (1978), 'so hat jede ihr schüsselchen zu tragen – "shirins hochzeit"', *frauen und film*, 45:530, pp. 32–4.

Heitmeyer, Wilhelm (1996), 'Für türkische Jugendliche in Deutschland spielt der Islam eine wichtige Rolle', *Die Zeit Online*, 23 August, http://www.zeit.de/1996/35/heitmey.txt.19960823.xml (accessed 2 April 2010).

Higbee, Will (2005), 'The return of the political, or designer visions of exclusion? The case for Mathieu Kassovitz's *fracture sociale* trilogy', *Studies in French Cinema*, 5:2, pp. 123–35.

— (2007), 'Re-presenting the urban periphery: Maghrebi-French filmmaking and the *banlieue* film', *Cineaste*, 33:1, special supplement *Beur is Beautiful*, ed. Carrie Tarr and Richard Porton, pp. 38–43.

— (2011), 'Of spaces and difference in *La Graine et le mulet* (2007): A dialogue with Carrie Tarr', in: Will Higbee and Sarah Leahy (eds), *Studies in French Cinema: UK Perspectives 1985–2010*, Bristol: Intellect, pp. 217–29.

Higbee, William and Song Hwee Lim (2010), 'Concepts of transnational cinema: Towards a critical transnationalism in film studies', *Transnational Cinemas*, 1:1, pp. 7–21.

Higson, Andrew (2003), *English Heritage, English Cinema: Costume Drama Since 1980*, Oxford: Oxford University Press.

Hill, John (1994), 'The future of European cinema: The economics and culture of pan-European strategies', in: John Hill, Martin McLoone and Paul Hainsworth (eds), *Border-Crossing: Film in Ireland, Britain and Europe*, Belfast: University of Ulster and BFI, pp. 53–80.

— (1999), *British Cinema of the 1980s*, Oxford: Clarendon.

— (2009), '"Bonnie Scotland, eh?": Scottish cinema, the working class and the films of Ken Loach', in: Jonathan Murray, Fidelma Farley and Rod Stoneman (eds), *Scottish Cinema Now*, Newcastle: Cambridge Scholars, pp. 88–104.

Hirsch, Marianne (1997), *Family Frames: Photography, Narrative and Postmemory*, Cambridge, MA, and London: Harvard University Press.

— (1999), 'Projected memory: Holocaust photographs in personal and public fantasy', in: Mieke Bal, Jonathan Crew and Leo Spitzer (eds), *Acts*

of Memory: Cultural Recall in the Present, Hanover, NH, and London: University Press of New England, pp. 2–23.
— (2001), 'Surviving images: Holocaust photographs and the work of post-memory', *The Yale Journal of Criticism*, 14:1, pp. 5–37.
Hitchens, Peter (2011), 'Radio silence', *Mail Online*, 11 August, http://hitchensblog.mailonsunday.co.uk/2011/08/radio-silence.html (accessed 10 October 2011).
Hollinger, David A. (2000), *Postethnic America: Beyond Multiculturalism*, New York: Basic.
hooks, bell (1991), *Yearning: Race, Gender, and Cultural Politics*, London: Turnaround.
— (2000), *Feminist Theory: From Margin to Center* (2nd edn), Cambridge, MA: South End.
— (2004), *The Will to Change: Men, Masculinity and Love*, New York: Washington Square Press.
Horrocks, David and Eva Kolinsky (eds) (1996), *Turkish Culture in German Society Today*, Providence, RI, and Oxford: Berghahn.
Huggan, Graham (2001), *The Postcolonial Exotic: Marketing the Margins*, London and New York: Routledge.
Huntington, Samuel P. (1997), *The Clash of Civlizations: And the Remaking of World Order*, London and New York: Simon & Schuster.
Huq, Rupa (2006), 'European youth cultures in a post-colonial world', in: Pam Nilan and Carles Feixa (eds), *Globla Youth? Hybrid Identities, Plural Worlds*, London and New York: Routledge, pp. 14–31.
Huyssen, Andreas (1995), *Twilight Memories: Marking Time in a Culture of Amnesia*, London and New York: Routledge.
— (2003), 'Diaspora and nation: Migrations into other pasts', *New German Critique*, 88, pp. 147–64.
— (2008), 'Nostalgia for ruins', *Grey Room*, Spring, 23, pp. 6–21.
Icarus Films (2007), '*I for India*', http://icarusfilms.com/new2007/i.html (accessed 15 May 2011).
Ingoldsby, Bron B. (2006), 'Family origin and universality', in: Bron B. Ingoldsby and Suzanna Smith (eds), *Families in Global and Multicultural Perspective*, Thousand Oaks, London and New Delhi: Sage, pp. 67–78.
Ingraham, Chrys (1999), *White Weddings: Romancing Heterosexuality in Popular Culture*, London and New York: Routledge.
Ingram, Mark and Florence Martin (2003), 'Voices unveiled: *Mémoires d'immigrés. L'héritage maghrébin*', in: Eva Rueschmann (ed.), *Moving Pictures, Migrating Identities*, Jackson: University of Mississippi Press, pp. 105–20.
Iordanova, Dina (2003), *Cinema of the Other Europe: The Industry and Artistry of East Central European Film*, London and New York: Wallflower.
Jaafar, Ali (2005), '*Le Grand Voyage*', *Sight & Sound*, November, pp. 66–7.
Jäckel, Anne (2010), 'State and other funding for migrant, diasporic and World

Cinemas in Europe', in: Daniela Berghahn and Claudia Sternberg (eds), *European Cinema in Motion: Migrant and Diasporic Film in Contemporary Europe*, Basingstoke: Palgrave Macmillan, pp. 76–95.

Jameson, Frederic (1986), 'On magic realism in film', *Critical Inquiry*, 12.1, pp. 301–25.

— (1991), *Postmodernism, or, the Cultural Logic of Late Capitalism*, Durham, NC: Duke University Press.

Jeffers McDonald, Tamar (2007), *Romantic Comedy: Boy Meets Girl Meets Genre*, London and New York: Wallflower.

Jha, Subhashi (2004), '*Bride and Prejudice* is not a K3G', redriff.com, 30 August, http://in.rediff.com/movies/2004/aug/30finter.htm (accessed 1 August 2010).

Jivani, Alkarim (2004), 'Ten things you need to know about *Bride and Prejudice*', *Time Out*, 22–9 September, p. 24.

Johnston, Cristina (2010), *French Minority Cinema*, Amsterdam: Rodopi.

Julien, Isaac and Kobena Mercer (2002), 'De margin and de centre', in: Graeme Turner (ed.), *The Film Cultures Reader*, London and New York: Routledge, pp. 355–65.

Kaes, Anton (1989), *From Hitler to Heimat: The Return of History as Film*, Cambridge, MA, and London: Harvard University Press.

Kaganski, Serge (2007), '*La Graine et le mulet* d'Abdellatif Keciche', *Les Inrockuptibles*, 11 December.

Kain, Edward L. (1990), *The Myth of Family Decline: Understanding Families in a World of Rapid Social Change*, Toronto: Lexington.

Kalra, Virinder S., Raminder Kaur and John Hutnyk (2005), *Diaspora and Hybridity*. London, Thousand Oaks and New Delhi: Sage.

Kandiyoti, Deniz (1988), 'Bargaining with patriarchy', *Gender & Society*, 2:3, pp. 274–90.

Kantor, Jodi (2009), 'Nation's many faces in extended first family: A portrait of change', *The New York Times*, 20 January.

Kaplan, Ann E. (1992), *Motherhood and Representation: The Mother in Popular Culture and Melodrama*, London and New York: Routledge.

— (1997), *Looking for the Other: Feminism, Film and the Imperial Gaze*, New York and London: Routledge.

Kapur, Jyotsna (2009), 'An "arranged love" marriage: India's neoliberal turn and the Bollywood wedding culture industry', *Communication, Culture and Critique*, 2, pp. 221–33.

Kechiche, Abdellatif (2008), 'Interview with Abellatif Kechiche', bonus material on the DVD release of *Couscous*, Artificial Eye.

Kiliçbay, Baris (2006), 'Impossible crossings: Gender melancholy in *Lola + Bilidikid* and *Auslandstournee*', *New Cinemas*, 4:2, pp. 105–15.

King, Russell (ed.) (1993), *Mass Migrations in Europe: The Legacy and the Future*, London: Belhaven.

King, Russell and Nancy Wood (eds) (2001), *Media and Migration:*

Constructions of Mobility and Difference, London and New York: Routledge.

King, Russell, Mark Thomson, Tony Fielding and Tony Warnesl (2006), 'Time, generations and gender in migration and settlement', in: Rinus Penninx, Maria Berger and Karen Kraal (eds), *The Dynamics of Migration and Settlement in Europe: A State of the Art*, Amsterdam: Amsterdam University Press, pp. 233–68.

Kipling, Rudyard ([1901] 2011), *Kim*, Harmondsworth: Penguin Classics.

Kleinhans, Chuck ([1978] 1991), 'Notes on melodrama and the family under capitalism', in: Marcia Landy (ed.), *Imitations of Life: A Reader on Film and Television Melodrama*, Detroit: Wayne State University Press, pp. 197–204.

Knott, Kim and Seán McLoughlin (eds) (2010), *Diasporas: Concepts, Intersections, Identities*, London and New York: Zed.

Kolinsky, Eva (1996), 'Non-German minorities in contemporary German society', in: David Horrocks and Eva Kolinsky (eds), *Turkish Culture in German Society Today*, Providence, RI, and Oxford: Berghahn, pp. 71–111.

Konstantarakos, Myrto (ed.) (2000), *Spaces in European Cinema*, Exeter: Intellect.

Korte, Barbara and Claudia Sternberg (2004), *Bidding for the Mainstream: Black and Asian British Film since the 1990s*, Amsterdam and New York: Rodopi.

Koschorke, Albrecht, Nacim Ghanbari, Eva Eßlinger, Sebastian Susteck and Michael T. Taylor (2010), *Vor der Familie: Grenzbedingugen einer modernen Institution*, Constance: Konstanz University Press.

Koukoutsaki-Monnier, Angeliki (2004), 'Zoos humains et mises en scène de l'altérité ethnique: *My Big Fat Greek Wedding*', *Canadian Journal of Film Studies*, 13:1, pp. 42–54.

Krutnik, Frank (1998), 'Love lies: Romantic fabrication in contemporary romantic comedy', in: Peter William Evans and Celestino Deleyto (eds), *Terms of Endearment: Hollywood Romantic Comedy of the 1980s and 1990s*, Edinburgh: Edinburgh University Press, pp. 15–36.

Kuhn, Annette (2002), *Family Secrets: Acts of Memory and Imagination*, London and New York: Verso.

Kühn, Heike (1995), '"Mein Türke ist Gemüsehändler": Zur Einverleibung des Fremden in deutschsprachigen Filmen', in: Ernst Karpf, Doren Kiesel and Karsten Visarius (eds), *Getürkte Bilder: Zur Inszenierung von Fremden im Film*, Marburg: Schüren, pp. 41–62.

Lacoste-Dujardin, Camille (2000), 'Maghrebi families in France', in: Jane Freedman and Carrie Tarr (eds), *Women, Immigration and Identities in France*, Oxford: Berg, pp. 57–82.

Laderman, David (2002), *Driving Visions: Exploring the Road Movie*, Austin: University of Texas Press.

Landsberg, Alison (2004), *Prosthetic Memory: The Transformation of*

American Remembrance in the Age of Mass Culture, New York: Columbia University Press.

Landy, Marcia (ed.) (1991), *Imitations of Life: A Reader on Film and Television Melodrama*, Detroit: Wayne State University Press.

Langford, Barry (2005), *Film Genre: Hollywood and Beyond*, Edinburgh: Edinburgh University Press.

Lasch, Christopher (1995), *The Revolt of the Elites and the Betrayal of Democracy*, New York and London: W. W. Norton.

Lau, Jörg (2005), 'Wie eine Deutsche', *Die Zeit Online*, 24 February, http://www.zeit.de/2005/09/Hatin_S_9fr_9fc_9f_09 (accessed 18 September 2008).

Laviosa, Flavia (2010), '"Death is the fairest cover for her shame": Framing honor killings', in: Flavia Laviosa (ed.), *Visions of Struggle in Women's Filmmaking in the Mediterranean*, Basingstoke: Palgrave Macmillan, pp. 185–212.

Lebeau, Vicky (2008), *Childhood and Cinema*, London: Reaktion.

Leibman, Nina C. (1995), *Living Room Lectures: The Fifties Family in Film and Television*, Austin: University of Texas Press.

Levine, Alison J. Murray (2008), 'Mapping *beur* cinema in the new millennium', *Journal of Film and Video*, 60:3–4, pp. 42–59.

Lévi-Strauss, Claude (1996), 'Introduction', in: André Burgière, Christiane Klapisch-Zuber, Martine Segalen, Françoise Zonabend (eds), *A History of the Family: Distant Worlds, Ancient Worlds* (vol. 1), Cambridge: Polity, pp. 1–8.

Linton, Ralph (1959), 'The natural history of the family', in: Ruth Nanda Anshen (ed.), *The Family: Its Function and Destiny*, New York: Harper, pp. 30–52.

Lipsitz, George (1994), *Dangerous Crossroads: Popular Music, Postmodernism and the Poetics of Place*, London: Verso.

Loshitzky, Yosefa (2010), *Screening Strangers: Migration and Diaspora in Contemporary European Cinema*, Bloomington and Indianapolis: Indiana University Press.

Lury, Karen (2010), *The Child in Film: Tears, Fears and Fairy Tales*, London: I. B. Tauris.

MacKinnon, Kenneth (2006), 'Intermingling under controlled conditions: The queerness of *Prick Up Your Ears*', in: Robin Griffiths (ed.), *British Queer Cinema*, London and New York: Routledge, pp. 121–32.

Macnab, Geoffrey (2006), '*Nina's Heavenly Delights*', *Sight & Sound*, October, pp. 74–5.

Malhotra, Sheena and Tavishi Alagh (2010), 'Dreaming the nation: Domestic dramas in Hindi films post-1990', *South Asian Popular Culture*, 2:1, pp. 19–37.

Malik, Sarita (1996), 'Beyond "the cinema of duty"? The pleasures of hybridity: Black British film of the 1980s and 1990s', in: Andrew Higson (ed.),

Dissolving Views: Key Writings on British Cinema, London: Cassell, pp. 202–15.
— (2010), 'The dark side of hybridity: Contemporary Black and Asian British cinema', in: Daniela Berghahn and Claudia Sternberg (eds), *European Cinema in Motion: Migrant and Diasporic Film in Contemporary Europe*, Basingstoke: Palgrave Macmillan, pp. 132–51.
— (2012), 'The Indian family on UK reality television: Convivial culture in salient contexts', *Television & New Media*, http://tvn.sagepub.com/content/early/recent (accessed 1 August 2012).
Manalansan IV, Martin F. (2003), 'In the shadows of Stonewall: Examining gay transnational politics and the diasporic dilemma', in: Jana Evans Braziel and Anita Mannur (eds), *Theorizing Diaspora: A Reader*, Oxford: Blackwell, pp. 207–27.
Mandel, Ruth (2008), *Cosmopolitan Anxieties: Turkish Challenges to Citizenship and Belonging in Germany*, Durham, NC, and London: Duke University Press.
Mannheim, Karl (1952), 'The problem of generations', *Essays on the Sociology of Knowledge*, London: Routledge, Kegan & Paul, pp. 276–320.
Marchetti, Gina (2006), *From Tian'anmen to Times Square: Transnational China and the Chinese Diaspora on Global Screens, 1989–1997*, Philadelphia: Temple University Press.
— (2012), *The Chinese Diaspora on American Screens: Race, Sex, and Cinema*, Philadelphia: Temple University Press.
Marienstras, Richard (1989), 'On the notion of diaspora', in: Gérard Chaliand and Tony Berret (eds), *Minority Peoples in the Age of Nation States*, London: Pluto, pp. 119–25.
Marks, Laura U. (2000), *The Skin of Film: Intercultural Cinema, Embodiment, and the Senses*, Durham, NC, and London: Duke University Press.
Martin, Michael T. (ed.) (1995), *Cinemas of the Black Diaspora: Diversity, Dependence and Oppositionality*, Detroit: Wayne State University Press.
Martin-Jones, David (2009), *Scotland: Global Cinema. Genres, Modes, Identities*, Edinburgh: Edinburgh University Press.
Marx, Lesley and Robin Cohen (2010), 'Cinematic representations of diaspora: Italians and Jews', *Crossings: Journal of Migration and Culture*, 1, pp. 5–23.
Massey, Doreen (1994), *Space, Place, Gender*, Cambridge: Polity.
— (1998), 'The spatial construction of youth cultures', in: Tracey Skelton and Gill Valentine (eds), *Cool Places: Geographies of Youth Culture*, London: Routledge, pp. 121–29.
Massood, Paula J. (2003), *Black City Cinema: African American Urban Experience in Film*, Philadelphia: Temple University Press.
Mather, Nigel (2006), *Tears of Laughter: Comedy-drama in 1990s British Cinema*, Manchester: Manchester University Press.
Matthes, Joachim (1985), 'Karl Mannheims "Das Problem der Generation" neu gelesen', *Zeitschrift für Soziologie*, 14:5, pp. 363–72.

Matussek, Matthias (2006), *Die vaterlose Gesellschaft: Eine Polemik gegen die Abschaffung der Familie*, Frankfurt am Main: Fischer Taschenbuch.

Mazierska, Ewa and Laura Rascaroli (2006), *Crossing New Europe: Postmodern Travel and the European Road Movie*, London and New York: Wallflower.

McClintock, Anne (1995), *Imperial Lather: Race, Gender and Sexuality in the Colonial Context*, New York and London: Routledge.

McFarlane, Brian (2005), 'Something old, something new: *Pride and Prejudice* on screen', *Screen Education*, 40, pp. 6–14.

McLoughlin, Seán (2010), 'Muslim travellers, homing desire, the *umma* and British-Pakistanis', in: Kim Knott and Seán McLoughlin, *Diasporas: Concepts, Intersections, Identities*, London: Zed, pp. 223–9.

McNeill, Isabelle (2010), *Memory and the Moving Image: French Film in the Digital Era*, Edinburgh: Edinburgh University Press.

Meetoo, Veena and Heidi Safia Mirza (2007), '"There is nothing "honourable" about honour killings": Gender, violence and the limits of multiculturalism', *Women's Studies International Forum*, 30, pp. 187–200.

Mehta, Rini Bhattacharya and Rajeshwari Panhariphande (2010), *Bollywood and Globalization: Indian Popular Cinema, Nation and Diaspora*, London: Anthem.

Mennel, Barbara (2002), 'Bruce Lee in Kreuzberg and Scarface in Altona: Transnational auteurism and ghettocentrism in Thomas Arslan's *Brothers and Sisters* and Fatih Akın's *Short Sharp Shock*', *New German Critique*, 87, pp. 133–56.

— (2004), 'Masochism, marginality, and metropolis: Kutluğ Ataman's *Lola and Billy the Kid*', *Studies in Twentieth Century Literature*, 28:1, pp. 289–318.

— (2008), *Cities and Cinema*, London and New York: Routledge.

— (2010), 'Criss-crossing in global space and time: Fatih Akın's *The Edge of Heaven (2007)*', *Transit: A Journal of Travel, Migration and Multiculturalism in the German-Speaking World*, 5:1, http://scholarship.org/uc/item/28x3x9r0 (accessed 10 February 2011).

Mercer, Kobena (1990), 'Black art and the burden of representation', *Third Text*, 4:10, pp. 61–78.

— (1993), 'Dark and lovely too: Gay black men in independent film', in: Martha Gever, John Greyson and Pratibha Parmar (eds), *Queer Looks: Perspectives on Lesbian and Gay Film and Video*, London and New York: Routledge, pp. 238–56.

— (1994), *Welcome to the Jungle: New Positions in Black Cultural Studies*, London and New York: Routledge.

— ([1988] 2003), 'Diaspora culture and the dialogic imagination: The aesthetics of black independent film in Britian', in: Jana Evans Braziel and Anita Mannur (eds), *Theorizing Diaspora: A Reader*, Oxford: Blackwell, pp. 247–60.

Mirzoeff, Nicholas (ed.) (1999), *Diaspora and Visual Culture: Representing Africans and Jews*, London and New York: Routledge.
Mishra, Sudesh (2006), *Diaspora Criticism*, Edinburgh: Edinburgh University Press.
Mishra, Viljay (2002), *Bollywood Cinema: Temples of Desire*, London and New York: Routledge.
Monk, Claire and Amy Sargeant (eds) (2002), *British Historical Cinema: The History, Heritage and Costume Film*, London: BFI.
Moore-Gilbert, Bart (2001), *Hanif Kureishi*, Manchester: Manchester University Press.
Moorti, Sujat (2003), 'Desperately seeking an identity: Diasporic cinema and the articulation of transnational kinship', *International Journal of Cultural Studies* 6:3, pp. 355–76.
Morely, David (2000), *Home Territories: Media, Mobility, Identity*, London and New York: Routledge.
Morely, David and Kevin Roberts (1996), *Spaces of Identity: Global Media Electronic Landscapes and Cultural Boundaries*, London and New York: Routledge.
Mottram, James (2004), 'In the mood for love', *Sight & Sound*, March, pp. 22–3.
Moynihan, D. P. (1965), *The Negro Family: A Case for National Action*, Washington, DC: Government Printing Office, http://www.blackpast.org/?q=primary/moynihan-report-1965 (accessed 15 January 2010).
Muir, John Kenneth (2006), *Mercy in Her Eyes: The Films of Mira Nair*, New York: Applause Cinema and Theatre Books.
Muñoz, Gema Martín (2006), 'Patriarchy and Islam', *Cuadernos del Mediterráneo*, 7, pp. 37–44, http://www.iemed.org/publicacions/quaderns/7/037_Martin (accessed 15 March 2010).
Murdock, George Peter (1949), *Social Structure*, New York: Macmillan.
Naficy, Hamid (ed.) (1999), *Home, Exile, Homeland: Film, Media, and the Politics of Place*, London and New York: Routledge.
— (2001), *An Accented Cinema: Exilic and Diasporic Filmmaking*, Princeton and Oxford: Princeton University Press.
— (2009), 'From accented cinema to multiplex cinema', in: Janet Staiger and Sabine Hake (eds), *Convergence Media History*, London and New York: Routledge, pp. 3–13.
Nagib, Lúcia, Chris Perriam and Rajinder Dudrah (eds) (2012), *Theorizing World Cinema*, London: I. B. Tauris.
Neale, Steve and Frank Krutnik (1990), *Popular Film and Television Comedy*, London and New York: Routledge.
Nederveen Pieterse, Jan (1995), 'Globalisation as hybridization', in: Mike Featherstone, Scott Lash and Roland Robertson (eds), *Global Modernities*, London and New Delhi: Sage, pp. 45–67.
Nilan, Pam and Carles Feixa (2006a), 'Introduction: Youth, hybridity and

plural worlds', in: Pam Nilan and Carles Feixa (eds), *Global Youth? Hybrid Identities, Plural Worlds*, London and New York: Routledge, pp. 1–13.
— (2006b), 'Postscript. Global youth and transnationalism: The next generation', in: Pam Nilan and Carles Feixa (eds), *Global Youth? Hybrid Identities, Plural Worlds*, London and New York: Routledge, pp. 205–12.
Nini, Soraya ([1993] 2000), *Ils disent que je suis une beurette*, Paris: Fixot.
Nora, Pierre (1989), 'Between memory and history: Les lieux de mémoire', *Representations*, 26, pp. 7–24.
Odone, Christina (2011), 'London riots: Absent fathers have a lot to answer for', *The Telegraph*, 9 August, http://blogs.telegraph.co.uk/news/cristinaodone/100100154/london-riots-absent-fathers-have-a-lot-to-answer-for/ (accessed 1 October 2011).
Olden, Mark (1999), 'A quick chat with Ayub Khan-Din', *Kamera.co.uk*, 6 October, http://www.kamera.co.uk/interviews/ayubkhandin.html (accessed 20 October 2011).
Ostria, Vincent (2002), '*La fille de Keltoum*', *Les Inrockuptibles*, 10 April.
Otnes, Cele C. and Elizabeth H. Pleck (2003), *Cinderella Dreams: The Allure of the Lavish Wedding*, Berkeley: University of California Press.
Palriwala, Rajini and Patricia Uberoi (2008), 'Exploring the links: Gender issues in marriage and migration', in: Rajini Palriwala and Patricia Uberoi (eds), *Marriage, Migration and Gender*, Los Angeles and New Delhi: Sage, pp. 23–60.
Parmar, Pratibha (1993), 'The moment of emergence', in: Martha Gever, John Greyson and Pratibha Parmar (eds), *Queer Looks: Perspectives on Lesbian and Gay Film and Video*, London and New York: Routledge, pp. 3–11.
— (n/d), '*Nina's Heavenly Delights*: Interview with director', http://www.ninasheavenlydelights.com/ (accessed 10 April 2011).
Peeren, Esther (2007), 'Through the lens of the chronotope: Suggestions for a spatio-temporal perspective on diaspora', in: Marie-Aude Baronian, Stephan Besser and Yolande Jansen (eds), *Diaspora and Memory: Figures of Displacement in Contemporary Literature, Arts and Politics*, Amsterdam: Rodopi, pp. 67–77.
Penn, Roger and Paul Lambert (2003), *Arranged Marriages in Western Europe: A Comparative Analysis of Britain, France and Germany*, Lancaster: Centre for Applied Statistics.
Perren, Alisa (2004), 'A big fat Indie success story? Press discourses surrounding the making and marketing of a "Hollywood" Movie', *Journal of Film and Video*, 56:2, pp. 18–31.
Peters, John Durham (1999), 'Exile, nomadism and diaspora: The stakes of mobility in the western canon', in: Hamid Naficy (ed.), *Home, Exile, Homeland: Film, Media, and the Politics of Place*, London and New York: Routledge, pp. 17–41.
Petty, Sheila J. (2008), *Contact Zones: Memory, Origin, and Discourses in Black Diasporic Cinema*, Detroit: Wayne State University Press.

Phillips, Alastair and Ginette Vincendeau (eds) (2006), *Journeys of Desire: European Artists in Hollywood*. London: BFI.
Pines, Jim (2001), 'British cinema and black representation', in: Robert Murphy (ed.), *The British Cinema Book*, 2nd edn, London: BFI, pp. 177–83.
Pisters, Patricia (2005), 'Micropolitics of the migrant family in accented cinema: Love and creativity in Empire', in: Patricia Pisters and Wim Staat (eds), *Shooting the Family: Transnational Media and Intercultural Values*, Amsterdam: Amsterdam University Press, pp. 197–212.
Pisters, Patricia and Wim Staat (eds) (2005), *Shooting the Family: Transnational Media and Intercultural Values*, Amsterdam: Amsterdam University Press.
Poirson-Dechonne, Marion (ed.) (2009), *Portraits de famille*, guest-edited issue of *CinémAction*, 132.
Pomerance, Murray (ed.) (2008), *A Family Affair: Cinema Calls Home*, London: Wallflower.
Ponzanesi, Sandra (2012), 'Postcolonial adaptations: Gained and lost in translation', in: Sandra Ponzanesi and Marguerite Waller (eds), *Postcolonial Cinema Studies*, London and New York: Routledge, pp. 172–88.
Powrie, Phil (2007), 'La famille (du cinéma) en désordre: Roudinesco and contemporary French cinema', in: Marie-Claire Barnet and Edward Welch (eds), *Affaires de famille: The Family in Contemporary French Culture and Theory*, Amsterdam: Rodopi, pp. 283–307.
Prasad, Madhava (2003), 'This thing called Bollywood', *Seminar*, vol. 525, May, *Unsettling Cinema: A Symposium on the Place of Cinema in India*, http://www.india-seminar.com/2003/525/525%20madhava%20prasad.htm (accessed 20 December 2011).
Provencher, Denis M. (2007), 'Maghrebi-French sexual citizens: In and out on the big screen', in: Carrie Tarr and Richard Porton (eds), special supplement on *Beur is Beautiful*, *Cineaste*, Winter, pp. 47–51.
Ramachandran, Naman (2004), '*Bride and Prejudice*', *Sight & Sound*, October, pp. 43–4.
Ramdya, Kavita (2010), *Bollywood Weddings: Dating, Engagement, and Marriage in Hindu America*, Lanham: Lexington.
Rand, Nicholas T. (1994), 'Secrets and posterity: The theory of the transgenerational phantom' [editor's preface to part V], in: Nicolas Abraham and Maria Torok, *The Shell and the Kernel: Renewals of Psychoanalysis*, ed., trans. and intro. Nicholas T. Rand, Chicago and London: University of Chicago Press, pp. 165–9.
Rashkin, Esther (1992), *Family Secrets and the Psychoanalysis of Narrative*, Princeton, NJ: Princeton University Press.
Redmond, Sean (2009), 'The healing power of romantic love in popular Indian romantic comedies: Raja Hindustani', in: Stacey Abbott and Deborah Jermyn (eds), *Falling in Love Again: Romantic Comedy in Contemporary Cinema*, London: I. B. Tauris, pp. 65–78.

Reiter, Gershon (2008), *Fathers and Sons in Cinema*, Jefferson, NC: McFarland.
Renov, Michael (1999), 'Domestic ethnography and the construction of the "Other" self', in: Jane M. Gaines and Michael Renov (eds), *Collecting Visible Evidence*, Minneapolis and London: University of Minnesota Press, pp. 140–55.
— (2004), *The Subject of Documentary*, Minneapolis and London: University of Minnesota Press.
— (2008), 'Family secrets: Alan Berliner's *Nobody's Business* and the (American) Jewish autobiographical film', *Framework: The Journal of Cinema and Media*, 49:1, pp. 55–65.
Rings, Guido (2008), 'Blurring or shifting the boundaries? Concepts of culture in Turkish–German migrant cinema', *German as a Foreign Language*, special issue *Cinema and Migration since Unification*, ed. Joanne Leal and Klaus-Dieter Rossade, 1, pp. 6–39.
Rings, Guido and Rikki Morgan-Tamosunas (eds) (2003), *European Cinema Inside Out: Images of the Self and the Other in Postcolonial European Cinema*, Heidelberg: Winter Universitätsverlag.
Robins, Kevin (2007), 'Transnational cultural policy and European cosmopolitanism', *Cultural Politics*, 3:2, pp. 147–74.
Rosello, Mireille (1998), *Declining the Stereotype: Ethnicity and Representation in French Cultures*, Hanover, NH: University Press of New England.
— (2001), *Postcolonial Hospitality: The Immigrant as Guest*, Stanford: Stanford University Press.
Roth, Luanna (2005), 'Beyond communities: Cinematic food events and the negotiation of power, belonging and exclusion', *Western Folklore*, 64: 3–4, pp. 163–88.
Roudinesco, Elisabeth (2002), *La Famille en désordre*, Paris: A. Fayard.
Rowe, Katherine (1995), *The Unruly Woman: Gender and the Genres of Laughter*, Austin: University of Texas Press.
Rubel, Paula and Abraham Rosman (2009), 'The transnational family among urban diaspora populations', in: Giulian B. Prato (ed.), *Beyond Multiculturalism: Views from Anthropology*, Farnham: Ashgate, pp. 57–78.
Rueschmann, Eva (2003a), 'Introduction', in: Eva Rueschmann (ed.), *Moving Pictures, Migrating Identities*, Jackson: University of Mississippi Press, pp. ix–xxx.
— (ed.) (2003b), *Moving Pictures, Migrating Identities*, Jackson: University of Mississippi Press.
Ruhe, Cornelia (2006), *Cinéma beur: Analysen zu einem neuen Genre des französischen Films*, Constance: UVK.
Rushdie, Salman ([1981] 1995), *Midnight's Children*, London: Vintage.
— (1991), *Imaginary Homelands: Essays and Criticism*, London: Granta.
Sadock, Johann (2004), 'L'Origine dévoilée du discours sur la violence et sur les relations interethniques dans le cinéma de Kassovitz', *Contemporary French and Francophone Studies*, 8:1, pp. 63–73.

Safran, William (1991), 'Diasporas in modern societies: Myths of homeland and return', *Diaspora*, 1.1: 83–99.
— (1999), 'Comparing diasporas: A review essay', *Diaspora*, 8:3, pp. 255–91.
Said, W. Edward (1978), *Orientalism*, New York: Vintage.
Samant, Sapna (2005), 'Appropriating Bombay cinema: Why the Western world gets Bollywood so wrong', *Metro*, 145, pp. 82–6.
Sarrazin, Thilo (2010), *Deutschland schafft sich ab: Wie wir unser Land aufs Spiel setzen*, Munich: Deutsche Verlags-Anstalt.
Sassen, Saskia (2002), 'Towards post-national and denationalized citizenship', in: Engin F. Isin and Bryan S. Turner (eds), *Handbook of Citizenship Studies*, London: Sage, pp. 277–91.
Schäffler, Diana (2007), *Deutscher Film mit türkischer Seele: Entwicklungen und Tendenzen der deutsch-türkischen Filme von den 70er Jahren bis zur Gegenwart*, Saarbrücken: VDM.
Schatz, Thomas (1981), *Hollywood Genres: Formulas, Filmmaking, and the Studio System*, Boston, MA: McGraw Hill.
Schiffauer, Werner (2005), 'Deutsche Ausländer: Schlachtfeld Frau', *Süddeutsche Zeitung*, 25 February, http://www.sueddeutsche.de/kultur/deutsche-auslaender-schlachtfeld-frau-1.804443 (accessed 10 September 2011).
Schilt, Thibault (2010), 'Itinerant men, evanescent women: Ismaël Ferroukhi's *Le Grand Voyage*', *The French Review*, 83:4, pp. 786–97.
Schlink, Bernhard (2000), *Heimat als Utopie*, Frankfurt am Main: Suhrkamp.
Schroeder, Erin (2001), 'A multicultural conversation: *La Haine*, *Raï* and *Menace II Society*', *Camera Obscura*, 46, special issue *Marginality and Alterity in Contemporary European Cinema*, ed. Randall Halle and Sharon Willis, 46:16, pp. 143–79.
Schützenberger, Anne Ancelin (1998), *The Ancestor Syndrome: Transgenerational Psychotheraphy and the Hidden Links in the Family Tree*, London and New York: Routledge.
Seeßlen, Georg (2000), 'Das Kino der doppelten Kulturen / Le Cinéma du métissage / The cinema of the inbetween: Erster Streifzug durch ein unbekanntes Kino-Terrain', *epd Film*, 12.
Seidel, Claudius (2010), 'Mitten durchs Herz', *Frankfurter Allgemeine Sonntagszeitung*, 14 February.
Sharpe, Jenny (2005), 'Gender, nation, and globalization in *Monsoon Wedding* and *Dilwale Dulhania Le Jayenge*', *Meridians: Feminism, Race, Transnationalism*, 6:1, pp. 58–81.
Sheffer, Gabriel (ed.) (1986), *Modern Diasporas in International Politics*, London and Sydney: Croom Helm.
Sherzer, Dina (1999), 'Comedy and interracial relationships: *Romuald et Juliette* (Serreau, 1987) and *Métisse* (Kassovitz, 1993)', in: Phil Powrie (ed.), *French Cinema in the 1990s: Continuity and Difference: Essays*, Oxford: Oxford University Press, pp. 148–59.

Shohat, Ella and Robert Stam (1994), *Unthinking Eurocentrism: Multiculturalism and the Media*, London and New York: Routledge.
— (eds) (2003), *Multiculturalism, Postcoloniality, and Transnational Media*, New Brunswick, NJ: Rutgers University Press.
Shumway, David R. (2003), 'Screwball comedies: Constructing romance, mystifying marriage', in: Barry Keith Grant (ed.), *Film Genre Reader III*, Austin: University of Texas Press, pp. 396–416.
Sieg, Katrin (2002), *Ethnic Drag: Performing Race, Nation, Sexuality in West Germany*, Ann Arbor: University of Michigan Press.
Silverman, Max (2007), 'The Empire looks back', The *Caché* Dossier, *Screen*, 48:2, pp. 245–9.
Simpson, Catherine, Renata Murawska and Anthony Lambert (eds) (2009), *Diasporas of Australian Cinema*, Bristol: Intellect.
Sinfield, Alan (2000), 'Diaspora and hybridity: Queer identity and the ethnicity model', in: Nicholas Mirzoeff (ed.), *Diaspora and Visual Culture: Representing Africans and Jews*, London and New York: Routledge, pp. 95–114.
Sollors, Werner (1986), *Beyond Ethnicity: Consent and Descent in American Culture*, New York and Oxford: Oxford University Press.
—— (ed.) (2000), *Interracialism: Black–White Intermarriage in American History, Literature, and Law*, Oxford: Oxford University Press.
Sontag, Susan (1979), *On Photography*, Harmondsworth: Penguin.
Stacey, Judith (1990), *Brave New Families: Stories of Domestic Upheaval in Late Twentieth Century America*, New York: Basic.
Staiger, Janet (2003), 'Hybrid or inbred: The purity hypothesis and Hollywood genre history', in: Barry Keith Grant (ed.), *Film Genre Reader III*, Austin: University of Texas Press, pp. 185–99.
Stam, Robert (1989), *Subversive Pleasures: Bakhtin, Cultural Criticism and Film*, Baltimore and London: Johns Hopkins University Press.
— (2003), 'Beyond Third Cinema: The aesthetics of hybridity', in: Anthony R. Guneratne and Wismal Dissanayake (eds), *Rethinking Third Cinema*, London and New York: Routledge, pp. 31–48.
Starkey, David (2011), 'England riots: "The whites have become black", says David Starkey', *BBC Newsnight*, Emily Maitlis in discussion with David Starkey, Dreda Say Mitchell, Owen Jones, 12 August, http://www.bbc.co.uk/news/uk-14513517 (accessed on 20 September 2011).
Stephens, Gregory (1995), 'Romancing the racial frontier: Mediating symbols in cinematic interracial representation', *Spectator*, 16:1, pp. 58–73.
Sternberg, Claudia (2008), 'Babylon North: British Muslims after 9/11 in *Yasmin* (2004)', in: Lars Eckstein, Barbara Korte, Eva Ulrike Pirker and Christoph Reinfandt (eds), *Multi-Ethnic Britain 2000+: New Perspectives in Literature, Film and the Arts*, Amsterdam and New York: Rodopi, pp. 79–95.
— (2010), 'Migration, diaspora and metacinematic reflection', in: Daniela

Berghahn and Claudia Sternberg (eds), *European Cinema in Motion: Migrant and Diasporic Film in Contemporary Europe*, Basingstoke: Palgrave Macmillan, pp. 256–74.

Sturken, Marita (1999), 'Narratives of recovery: Repressed memory as cultural memory', in: Mieke Bal, Jonathan Crew and Leo Spitzer (eds), *Acts of Memory: Cultural Recall in the Present*, Hanover, NH, and London: University Press of New England, pp. 231–48.

Tapinc, Huseyin (1992), 'Masculinity, feminity and Turkish male homosexuality', in Ken Plummer (ed.), *Modern Homosexualities: Fragments of Lesbian and Gay Experience*, London and New York: Routledge, pp. 39–49.

Tarr, Carrie (2005), *Reframing Difference:* Beur *and* banlieue *filmmaking in France*, Manchester: Manchester University Press.

— (2007), 'Family differences: Immigrant Maghrebi families in contemporary French cinema', in: Marie-Claire Barnet and Edward Welch (eds), *Affaires de famille: The Family in Contemporary French Culture and Theory*, Amsterdam and New York: Rodopi, pp. 209–20.

— (2010), 'Gendering diaspora: The work of diasporic women film-makers in Western Europe', in: Daniela Berghahn and Claudia Sternberg (eds), *European Cinema in Motion: Migrant and Diasporic Film in Contemporary Europe*, Basingstoke: Palgrave Macmillan, pp. 175–95.

— (2011), 'Diasporic families and the rehabilitation of the father in recent French cinema', podcast of a presentation given at The Diasporic Family in Cinema Conference in London on 21 May, http://www.farflungfamilies.net/podcasts/item/diasporic_families_and_the_rehabilitation_of_the_father_figure_in_recent_fr (accessed 1 July 2011).

Tarr, Carrie and Brigitte Rollet (2001), *Cinema and the Second Sex: Women's Filmmaking in France in the 1980s and 1990s*, New York and London: Continuum.

Terkessidis, Mark (1999), 'Globale Kultur in Deutschland, oder: Wie unterdrückte Frauen und Kriminelle die Hybridität retten', *Parapluie*, 6, http://parapluie.de/archiv/generation/hybrid (accessed 14 July 2011).

Thomas, Rosie (1996), 'Melodrama and the negotiation of morality in mainstream Hindi film', in Carol A. Breckenridge (ed.), *Consuming Modernity: Public Culture in Contemporary India*, Delhi: Oxford University Press, pp. 157–82.

Ticknell, Estella (2005), *Mediating the Family: Gender, Culture and Representation*, London: Hodder Arnold.

Tölölyan, Khachig (1991), 'The nation state and its Others: In lieu of a preface', *Diaspora*, 1, pp. 3–7.

Traube, Elizabeth G. (1992), *Dreaming Identities: Class, Gender and Generation in 1980s Hollywood Movies*, San Francisco and Oxford: Westview.

Trémois, Claude-Marie and Mehdi Charef (2002), '*La Fille de Keltoum* de Mehdi Charef', *Esprit*, 3–4, pp. 363–7.

Tudor, Deborah (2008), 'Encounters with Thatcherism: Four women filmmakers', in: Lester D. Friedman (ed.), *Fires Were Started: British Cinema and Thatcherism*, 2nd edn, London and New York: Wallflower, pp. 135–58.

Tunç, Ayça (2011), 'Diasporic Cinema: Turkish–German Filmmakers with Particular Emphasis on Generational Difference', unpublished doctoral dissertation, Royal Holloway, University of London.

Uberoi, Patricia (2006), *Freedom and Destiny: Gender, Family, and Popular Culture in India*, New Delhi: Oxford University Press.

Udwin, Leslee (2011), 'Negotiating between artistic ambitions and the market place: A roundtable discussion with Feo Aladağ, Sandhya Suri, Leslee Udwin, Gareth Jones, Sarita Malik and Daniela Berghahn', podcast of a discussion held at The Diasporic Family in Cinema Conference in London on 21 May, http://www.farflungfamilies.net/podcasts/item/negotiating_between_artistic_ambitions_funding_and_the_market_place (accessed on 1 July 2011).

Urry, John (2002), *The Tourist Gaze*, 2nd edn, London: Sage.

Van Dijck, José (2005), 'Capturing the family: Home video in the age of digital reproduction', in: Patricia Pisters and Wim Staat (eds), *Shooting the Family: Transnational Media and Intercultural Values*, Amsterdam: Amsterdam University Press, pp. 25–40.

Van Every, Jo (1999), 'From modern nuclear households to postmodern diversity? The sociological construction of "families"', in: Caroline Wright and Gill Jagger (eds), *Changing Family Values*, London and New York: Routledge, pp. 165–84.

Van Hear, Nicholas (1998), *New Diasporas: The Mass Exodus, Dispersal and Regrouping of Migrant Communities*, Seattle: University of Washington Press.

Vertovec, Steven (2009), *Transnationalism*, London and New York: Routledge.

Vertovec, Steven and Robin Cohen (1999), 'Introduction', in: Steven Vertovec and Robin Cohen (eds), *Migration, Diasporas and Transnationalism*, Cheltenham and Northampton, MA: Elgar Reference Collection, pp. xxiii–xxviii.

— (2002), 'Introduction', *Conceiving Cosmopolitanism: Theory, Context and Practice*, Oxford: Oxford University Press, pp. 1–22.

Vincendeau, Ginette (1992), 'Family plots', *Sight & Sound*, March, pp. 14–17.

— (2000), 'Designs on the *banlieue*: Mathieu Kassovitz's La Haine (1995)', in: Susan Hayward and Ginette Vincendeau (eds), *French Film: Texts and Contexts*, London: Routledge, pp. 310–27.

— (ed.) (2001), *Film / Literature / Heritage*, London: BFI.

— (2005), *La Haine*, London: I. B. Tauris.

— (2008), 'Southern discomfort', *Sight & Sound*, July, pp. 46–7.

Von Moltke, Johannes (2005), *No Place Like Home: Locations of Heimat in German Cinema*, Berkeley and Los Angeles: University of California Press.

Waites, Matthew (2000), 'Homosexuality and the new right: The legacies

of the 1980s for new delineations of homophobia', *Sociological Research Online*, 5:1, http://www.socresonline.org.uk/5/1/waites.html (accessed 1 April 2011).
Wajid, Sara (2006), 'This isn't just a fantasy world', *The Guardian*, 15 September.
Walby, Sylvia (1990), *Theorizing Patriarchy*, Oxford: Blackwell.
Waldron, Darren (2007), 'From critique to compliance: Images of ethnicity in *Salut cousin* (1997) and *Chouchou* (2003)', *Studies in European Cinema*, 4:1, pp. 35–47.
Walker, Beverly (1991), 'Behind the mountains', *Film Comment*, May / June, p. 2.
Wartenberg, Thomas E. (1999), *Unlikely Couples: Movie Romances as Social Criticism*, Boulder, CO, and Oxford: Westview.
Weeks, Jeffrey, Brian Heaphy and Catherine Donovan (2001), *Same Sex Intimacies: Families of Choice and Other Life Experiments*, New York and London: Routledge.
Webber, Andrew (2008), *Berlin in the Twentieth Century: A Cultural Topography*, Cambridge: Cambridge University Press.
Weigel, Sigrid (2002), '"Generation" as symbolic form: On the genealogical discourse of memory since 1945', *The Germanic Review*, 77:4, pp. 264–77.
Werbner, Pnina (2004), 'Theorising complex diasporas: Purity and hybridity in the South Asian public sphere in Britain', *Journal of Ethnic and Migration Studies*, 30:5, pp. 895–911.
Westdeutscher Rundfunk (ed.) (2011), *Plötzlich so viel Heimat: Identität im Wandel in Film, Kultur und Gesellschaft*, Cologne: Strzelecki.
Weston, Kath (1991), *Families We Choose: Lesbians, Gay, Kinship*, New York: Columbia University Press.
Wexman, Virginia Wright (1993), *Creating the Couple: Love, Marriage, and Hollywood Performance*, Princeton: Princeton University Press.
Wheatley, Catherine (2009), *Michael Haneke's Cinema: The Ethic of the Image*, Oxford and New York: Berghahn.
Wiegman, Robyn (1998), 'Race, ethnicity and film', in: John Hill and Pamela Church Gibson (eds), *The Oxford Guide to Film Studies*, Oxford: Oxford University Press, pp. 158–68.
Williams, James S. (2010), 'Queering the diaspora', in: Daniela Berghahn and Claudia Sternberg (eds), *European Cinema in Motion: Migrant and Diasporic Film in Contemporary Europe*, Basingstoke: Palgrave Macmillan, pp. 196–214.
— (2011), 'Open-sourcing French culture: The politics of métissage and collective re-appropriation in the films of Abdellatif Kechiche', *Journal of Francophone Studies*, 14:3, pp. 391–415.
Williams, Linda ([1984] 1991), 'Something else besides a mother: *Stella Dallas* and the maternal melodrama', in: Marcia Landy (ed.), *Imitations of Life: A*

Reader on Film and Television Melodrama, Detroit: Wayne State University Press, pp. 283–306.

— (2001), *Playing the Race Card: Melodramas of Black and White from Uncle Tom to O. J. Simpson*, Princeton and Oxford: Princeton University Press.

Williams, Tony (1996), *Hearths of Darkness: The Family in the American Horror Film*, Cranbury, NJ: Fairleigh Dickinson University Press.

Wilson, Cheryl A. (2006), '*Bride and Prejudice*: A Bollywood comedy of manners', *Literature Film Quarterly*, October, pp. 323–31.

Wilson, Emma (2003), *Cinema's Missing Children*, London: Wallflower.

Young, Lola (1996), *Fear of the Dark: 'Race', Gender and Sexuality in the Cinema*, London and New York: Routledge.

Yuval-Davis, Nira and Floya Anthias (eds) (1989), *Woman – Nation – State*, Basingstoke: Macmillan.

Zamora, Lois Parkinson and Wendy B. Faris (1995), 'Introduction: Daiquiri birds and Flaubertian parrot(ie)s', in: Lois Parkinson Zamora and Wendy B. Faris (eds), *Magical Realism: Theory, History, Community*, Durham, NC, and London: Duke University Press, pp. 1–11.

Zonabend, Françoise (1996), 'An anthropological perspective on kinship and the family', in: André Burgière, Christiane Klapisch-Zuber, Martine Segalen, Françoise Zonabend (eds), *A History of the Family, Distant Worlds, Ancient Worlds*, vol. 1, Cambridge: Polity, pp. 8–68.

INDEX

9/11, 4, 126, 128, 129, 150n, 167
17, rue Bleue (*17 Blue Street*), 35

Abraham, Nicolas, 13, 101, 108, 117n, 118n
Abschied vom falschen Paradies (*Farewell to a False Paradise*), 69
accented cinema, 32, 51–2
An Accented Cinema (Naficy), 6, 55
The Adventures of Felix (*Drôle de Félix*), 47, 82n
Ae Fond Kiss . . ., 160–1
Affaires de famille (Barnet and Welch), 10
Ahmed, Akbar, 128, 129
Akın, Fatih
  biography, 32
  cultural difference, 8
  The Edge of Heaven, 54–5, 84n
  Head-On, 41, 131, 157
  migratory history, 143
  postmemory, 33, 88–9
  Solino, 55, 56
  We Have Forgotten To Return, 82n, 88–9
Akkus, Sinan, 33, 165
Akomfrah, John, 12, 44
Akyol, Mustafa, 150n
Aladağ, Feo, 48, 52n, 129, 131, 133
Aladağ, Züli, 33, 52n
Alaoui, Amina, 80
Ali, Ayaan Hirsi, 125
Ali, Muhammad, 123
Alice in the Cities (*Alice in den Städten*), 60, 65, 83n
All You Want is Money, All You Need is Love (Dwyer), 178
Allouche, Merzack, 41
Almanya – Welcome to Germany (*Almanya – Willkommen in Deutschland*), 1, 5, 12, 31, 41, 69–75, 81–2
America, America, 82n
Amin, Idi, 101, 102
The Ancestor Syndrome (Schützenberger), 101
Andersen, Erika, 117n
Anita and Me, 33
Another Land (*Pardes*), 150n, 172
Anthias, Floya, 125
Appadurai, Arjun, 13, 23, 27, 28, 120, 136, 141
April Children (*Aprilkinder*), 154, 155
arranged marriage
  diasporic family, 25–6
  East is East, 136, 140

wedding films, 14, 154, 156, 171, 176, 181, 183n
Ashanti, 181
Asian British cinema
  Bend It Like Beckham, 33, 40, 41, 126–8
  Brick Lane, 4, 56
  Bride and Prejudice, 14, 150n, 153, 175–81, 182
  Brothers in Trouble, 136
  diasporic family, 32–3, 39–40
  East is East, 13, 33, 41, 51n, 135–7, 140, 148, 155–6
  I for India, 12, 94–100
  Love + Hate, 159
  Majdhar, 39
  My Beautiful Laundrette, 13, 32–3, 39–40, 103, 109–13, 119n
  Nina's Heavenly Delights, 13, 40, 103, 109, 113–15, 142
  Sammy and Rosie Get Laid, 33
  West is West, 4, 14, 135, 138–40, 142, 148–50
  Yasmin, 4, 126, 156
Assmann, Jan, 89
Ataman, Kutlug, 106
audience, 37, 40, 80, 91, 154, 159, 172–4, 182
Auf der anderen Seite (*The Edge of Heaven*), 41, 54–5, 57, 73, 81, 82n, 84n
Auslandstournee (*Tour Abroad*), 47, 60, 81
Austen, Jane, 176, 177, 178, 179, 180
Austin, J. L., 93
Awaara (*The Vagabond*), 172

Babymother, 4, 15n, 102–3
Bad Faith (*Mauvaise Foi*), 4, 156, 160, 161, 184n
Bademsoy, Aysun, 33
Bakhtin, Mikhail, 12, 55, 63, 64–5
'The Ballad of East and West' (Kipling), 135
banlieue cinema, 34–6, 121–4, 146, 156
Barsaat (*Monsoon*), 179
Barthes, Roland, 91
Başer, Tevfik, 36, 37
Baton Rouge, 34
Bauman, Zygmunt, 84n, 121
Begag, Azouz, 35, 117n
Ben-Davies, Esther, 31
Bend It Like Beckham, 33, 40, 41, 126–8
Benguigui, Yamina
  Aïcha (TV drama), 124
  career, 50n
  cultural difference, 8

Immigrant Memories, 31, 62, 90–4
Inch' Allah Dimanche (*Inch' Allah Sunday*), 35, 62
   migratory history, 143
Benshoff, Harry, 103
beur cinema, 34–7, 93, 122, 124, 143, 146, 156
Bhabha, Homi, 5, 118n, 154
Bidding for the Mainstream (Korte and Sternberg), 40
The Black Atlantic (Gilroy), 23, 60
Black Atlantic chronotope, 23, 56, 60, 61
Black Audio Film Collective, 40
Black British cinema, 4, 14, 15n, 38–40, 52n, 102–3, 122, 156
   Babymother, 4, 15n, 102–3
   Bullet Boy, 4, 15n, 122
   Burning an Illusion, 38
   The Nine Muses, 44
   Pressure, 38, 39, 52n
   Young Soul Rebels, 40
Bloch, Ernst, 59
The Blue Angel, 118n
body, 13, 125, 126, 129, 147
Boehmer, Elleke, 125
Bollywood
   DDLJ, 150n, 162, 172, 179, 180, 185n
   definition, 17n
   Hum Aapke Hain Koun (*Can You Name Our Relationship?*), 14, 154, 162, 169
   in *East is East*, 136
   Pardes (*Another Land*), 150n, 172
   postmemory documentaries, 97, 99
   wedding films, 14, 153–4, 162–3, 169–70, 173, 175–82, 184–5n
Bollywood Weddings (Ramdya), 182
Bondanella, Peter, 4
Bouchareb, Rachid, 61, 62
Boufares, Habib, 145, 150n
Bourdieu, Pierre, 19, 91, 92, 152, 153
Boym, Svetlana, 74
Boys on the Beach (*Le Ciel, les oiseaux . . . et ta mère*), 41
Boyz 'n the Hood, 15n, 122, 147
Bradshaw, Peter, 79
Brah, Avtar, 8, 13, 27, 55, 104, 120
The Brave Heart Will Take the Bride (*Dilwale Dulhaniya Le Jayenge / DDLJ*), 150n, 162, 172, 179, 180, 185n
Brave New Families (Stacey), 20
Brick Lane, 4, 56
Bride and Prejudice, 14, 150n, 153, 182
Bringing Up Daddy (Bruzzi), 10
British cinema, 32–3, 38–40; *see also* Asian British cinema; Black British cinema
Brooks, Peter, 134
Brothers in Trouble, 136
Bruzzi, Stella, 10, 93, 103, 112, 147
Bryceson, Deborah Fahy, 23, 24
Bullet Boy, 4, 15n, 122
Burning an Illusion, 38
Burns, Rob, 37, 68
Burns, Robert, 160

Caché (*Hidden*), 45–6, 47, 52n
Café au lait (*Métisse*), 5, 159–60, 183n
Cameron, David, 2
Il cammino della speranza (*The Road to Hope*), 83n
Can You Name Our Relationship? (*Hum Aapke Hain Koun*), 14, 154, 162, 169
Cassavetes, John, 170

Castles, Stephen, 29–30
Cazalé, Nicolas, 77
Certeau, Michel de, 125
Chadha, Gurinder
   Bend It Like Beckham, 33, 40, 41, 126–7
   Bride and Prejudice, 175–81
   cultural difference, 8
   diasporic family, 32, 33, 40, 41
   What's Cooking?, 142
Chambers, Deborah, 11, 149
Chaplin, Charlie, 71
Charef, Mehdi, 32, 33–4, 35, 36
Chiko, 122
children
   abuse of, 103, 172, 173
   in family, 19, 21, 23
   journeys, 60, 64, 83n
   postmemory documentaries, 90, 93
   trauma, 10
Chouchou, 41, 156
chronotope, 61–6
   Black Atlantic, 23, 56, 60, 61
   definition, 56, 63–4
   family, 56, 65, 66
   homeland, 12, 64
   idyllic, 56, 63, 64–6, 75
   road, 56, 63, 65, 73, 74
   ruin, 74
   ship, 56, 61–3, 83n
   threshold, 63
C. I. D., 170
Le Ciel, les oiseaux . . . et ta mère (*Boys on the Beach*), 41
cinema of duty, 3, 38, 68, 159
cinema of the affected, 37, 68, 69
Cinema Paradiso, 82n
Cinema's Missing Children (Wilson), 10
circumcision, 120, 136, 148, 167
Clifford, James, 25
Cohen, Robin, 22, 50n
comedy
   ethnic, 5, 41, 69, 74, 126, 155
   romantic, 5, 14, 40, 114–15, 142, 149, 152–3, 159, 162, 163–9, 177, 182, 184n
Conn, Shelly, 114
Coontz, Stephanie, 3
Cooper, Darius, 173
Coppola, Francis Ford, 3
Corbett, John, 168
Corrigan, Timothy, 65, 66, 76
Costa-Gavras, Constantin, 34
Couscous (*The Secret of the Grain / La Graine et le mulet*), 14, 35, 142–7, 148, 149
Cowans, Jon, 184n
Creating the Couple (Wexman), 183n
Cunningham, Stuart, 28

Dante Alighieri, 44
The Dark Million (TV show), 95, 97, 98
Das, Vasundhara, 175
daughters, 89, 91, 184n
Davrak, Baki, 55
Day-Lewis, Daniel, 111
DDLJ (*Dilwale Dulhaniya Le Jayenge / The Brave Heart Will Take the Bride*), 150n, 162, 172, 179, 180, 185n
Debré, Michel, 117n
Delorme, Stéphane, 144
Derin, Seyhan, 33, 89, 93, 94
Desai, Jigna, 9, 149n, 173, 182

Deutschland schafft sich ab (Germany is Abolishing Itself) (Sarrazin), 2
Les Deux Papas et la Maman (The Two Dads and One Mom), 41
Dhawan, Sabrina, 169
diaspora
　African, 22, 26, 34, 42, 50n, 61, 122–3
　and cinema, 6–9, 12, 16
　classical, 22
　criticism, 11–12
　definition, 6, 22
　diaspora space, 8–9, 27, 104, 141
　Italian American, 3–4, 15n, 25
　Jewish, 7, 16–17n, 22, 83n
　postcolonial, 6, 43–4
　queer, 13, 40, 103–5, 115–16, 118n
　South Asian, 25–6, 44, 153, 155, 171, 183n
　studies, 18, 85
　victim diasporas, 22
diasporic cinema *see* migrant and diasporic cinema
diasporic optic *see* hybridity, and aesthetics
Dietrich, Marlene, 118n
Dilwale Dulhaniya Le Jayenge (DDLJ / The Brave Heart Will Take the Bride), 150n, 162, 172, 179, 180, 185n
Divine Comedy (Dante Alighieri), 44
Douce France, 156–7
Douglas, Lord Alfred, 118n
dress codes, 13, 23, 25, 125–7, 129
Drôle de Félix (The Adventures of Felix), 47, 82n
Du Bois, W. E. B., 17n
Düğün – The Wedding (Düğün – Die Heirat), 54, 132, 154, 155
Dutt, Geeta, 99
Dwyer, Rachel, 178
Dyer, Richard, 52n, 104, 158, 179–80, 185n

East and West (Purab Aur Pachhim), 179
East is East, 13, 33, 41, 51n, 135–7, 140, 148, 155–6
Eastman, George, 91
The Edge of Heaven (Auf der anderen Seite), 41, 54–5, 57, 73, 81, 82n, 84n
Educating Rita, 184n
Effi Briest (Fontane), 133
Ellis, John, 116
Elsaesser, Thomas, 3, 4, 7
Empire (Hardt and Negri), 9
Erdoğan, Nezih, 84n
Eren, Mine, 94
L'Esquive (Games of Love and Chance), 124
Estaing, Giscard d', 91
ethnic comedies, 5, 41, 69, 74, 126, 155
ethnicity, 183n
European Cinema, 6–8, 14, 16n, 57, 171
Evet, I Do! (Evet, ich will!), 14, 103, 153, 163–9, 182
Exiles (Exils), 82n
extended family, 19, 23, 26, 49n, 73, 74, 100, 136, 138–49, 153, 162, 173
Ezli, Özkan, 84n
Ezra, Elizabeth, 45

family
　of choice, 20, 38, 47, 60, 81, 148–9, 150–1n
　chronotope, 56, 65, 66
　conflict, 13, 76, 121, 128
　definition, 18, 19, 20, 47
　diasporic, 21–9
　diversity, 10, 11, 20, 21, 113

　elective *see* family, of choice
　ethnic minority, 3, 5, 26
　extended, 19, 23, 26, 49n, 73, 74, 100, 136, 138–49, 153, 162, 173
　function of, 19, 20
　hegemonic, 4, 10, 25, 27, 46
　hybrid, 75, 116, 135–42, 149, 157, 159, 161
　immigrant, 2, 9, 10, 21
　joint, 162, 173, 184n; *see also* extended family
　and kinship, 3, 9, 18, 19, 27, 38, 44, 60, 90, 148, 175, 182
　memories, 1, 12, 13, 85–116
　multi-generational, 56, 65, 69, 142
　nuclear, 8, 18, 19, 21, 25, 26
　patchwork, 35, 51n, 142, 148
　and patriarchy, 4, 10, 13, 26, 106, 125, 128–9, 130–41, 146–9
　and photography, 12, 48, 83n, 87, 91–3, 95, 99, 116, 152–3, 162, 174
　reunion, 29–32, 48, 49n, 51n, 93, 96
　secrets, 12, 13, 85–6, 100–6, 115–16, 172
　structure, 10, 12, 14, 18, 20–1, 26, 121, 148–9
　traditional, 3, 26–7, 49n, 65, 113, 158, 163
　transnational, 21, 23, 24, 140–1
　as trope of belonging, 40–7, 105, 106, 113, 116, 118n, 149, 169, 174
　values, 3, 4, 11, 25, 26, 105, 112–14, 121, 126, 133, 146–7, 149, 153, 157–8, 162–4, 171, 174, 178, 185
A Family Affair (Pomerance), 10
Family Affairs (Fröhlich and Visarius), 10
Family Frames (Hirsch), 48, 87, 88, 95
'Family plots' (Vincendeau), 145
Family Secrets (Kuhn), 95, 100
'The Family Spirit' (Bourdieu), 153
Far From Heaven, 10
Farewell to a False Paradise (Abschied vom falschen Paradies), 69
Farrokhzad, Schahrzad, 150n
Fassbinder, Rainer Werner, 118n
father
　absent, 15n, 103
　Bringing Up Daddy, 10
　of choice, 8, 48, 60, 76, 138, 148
　ethnicising patriarchy, 128–9, 130–41, 147–9, 150n, 159
　filiation, 144–5, 150–1
　journeys, 78, 80
　in postmemory documentaries, 89, 90
Father of the Bride, 184n
female body, 125, 126, 129, 147
feminism, 10, 20, 95, 128
Ferroukhi, Ismaël, 75, 76, 79, 80, 81
filiation, 144–5, 150–1
La Fille de Keltoum (Keltoum's Daughter), 54, 57, 59–60, 73, 102, 132
Finnegan's Wake (Joyce), 44
Flame in the Streets, 38
Fontane, Theodor, 133
food, 14, 23, 32, 64, 65, 113, 141–7, 150n
Fortier, Anne-Marie, 86
Forty Square Metres of Germany (Vierzig Quadratmeter Deutschland), 36, 37, 69
Four Weddings and a Funeral, 14, 153, 162, 165, 183n, 184n
Fraser, Laura, 114
Frears, Stephen, 33, 109, 110, 111, 112, 113
Die Fremde (When We Leave), 13, 48, 54, 129–34, 149, 150n
French, Philip, 83n, 179

INDEX

Freud, Sigmund, 100
The Future of Nostalgia (Boym), 74

Gabaccia, Donna, 142
Galt, Rosalind, 16n
Games of Love and Chance (*L'Esquive*), 124
gay identity *see* homosexuality
Geetha, J., 173, 185n
Gegen die Wand (*Head-On*), 41, 131, 150n, 157-8, 183n
gender
  banlieue cinema, 124
  Bend It Like Beckham, 126-7
  Couscous, 146-7
  division of labour, 20, 26, 122
  family trope (motherland, fatherland), 43-4
  female body, 125
  and generation, 13-14, 120-8, 121
  Head-On, 131
  identity, 107, 109, 125, 126
  inequality, 25, 103, 147, 149
  norms, 40, 121, 126, 131, 140, 172, 176
  queerness, 104-5, 108, 109
  When We Leave, 131
generation, 13-14, 36-8, 47, 51n, 121-3, 125-7, 149
genre
  Bollywood family romance, 153-4, 162-3, 169-70, 173, 175-82, 184-5n
  ethnic comedy, 5, 41, 69, 74, 126, 155
  melodrama, 5, 10, 14, 131, 134, 157-8, 161-2, 165, 170, 171, 173, 178, 183n, 184n
  road movie, 5, 12, 65, 66, 73-8, 80, 83n
  romantic comedy, 5, 14, 40, 114-15, 142, 149, 152-3, 159, 162, 163-9, 177, 182, 184n
  wedding film, 14, 49, 152-85
Geraghty, Christine, 110
Germany is Abolishing Itself (*Deutschland schafft sich ab*) (Sarrazin), 2
Giddens, Anthony, 3, 20, 26-7
Gillespie, Marie, 150n
Gilroy, Paul
  Black Atlantic chronotope, 12, 23, 56, 60, 61
  conviviality, 28, 160, 183n
  diasporic family, 23, 28, 44, 49n
  double consciousness, 17n
  hip hop, 123
  'It's a family affair', 44
  journeys, 55, 60, 61
  There Ain't No Black in the Union Jack, 112, 118n
Glenaan, Kenneth, 126
globalisation, 1-2, 9, 24, 43, 129
The Godfather Trilogy, 3-4
Gogh, Theo van, 125
Göktürk, Deniz, 131
Golden Door (*Nuovomondo*), 83n
Golden Youth (*Jeunesse dorée*), 82n
Le Gone du Chaâba (*The Kid from Chaaba / Shantytown Kid*), 35, 117n
Goodness Gracious Me (TV show), 33, 179
Gopal, Sangita, 162, 184n
Gopinath, Gayatri, 104
The Graduate, 184n
La Graine et le mulet (*Couscous / The Secret of the Grain*), 14, 35, 142-7, 148, 149
The Grand Tour (*Le Grand Voyage*), 12, 75-80, 81, 84n, 138, 148
The Grapes of Wrath, 55
Grease, 179

The Great Dictator, 71
Grillo, Ralph, 25, 49n
Guess Who's Coming to Dinner, 158-9

habitats of meaning, 13, 120, 121, 124, 132
La Haine (*Hate*), 5, 47, 122, 123, 159
Halbwachs, Maurice, 89
Hall, Stuart, 28, 44, 59, 105, 127
Hamlet (Shakespeare), 101, 118n, 119n
Haneke, Michael, 45-6, 47
Hannerz, Ulf, 13, 24, 50n, 120, 124, 132
Hardt, Michael, 9
Hargreaves, Alec, 78
Harvey, David, 82n
Hate (*La Haine*), 5, 47, 122, 123, 159
Hatoum, Mona, 149n
Le Havre, 84n
Haynes, Todd, 10
Head-On (*Gegen die Wand*), 41, 131, 150n, 157-8, 183n
Hear, Nicholas van, 50n
Heimat, 43, 58-9, 72-3, 75, 82n
Heimat (TV show), 59
Heitmeyer, Wilhelm, 150n
Henderson, Martin, 178
Henriques, Julian, 103, 110
Hepburn, Katharine, 158
Herzl, Hafsia, 145
Hidden (*Caché*), 45-6, 47, 52n
Higbee, William, 144, 147
hip hop, 122, 123
Hirsch, Marianne, 12, 48, 83n, 87, 91, 94-5
Hirschfeld, Magnus, 105
Hitchens, Peter, 15n
Hitler, Adolf, 106
Hollinger, David, 28, 151
Hollywood, 7-10, 183n, 185n
homeland, 12, 58-60, 64, 81, 103, 104, 138-40
Homer, 44
homophobia, 106, 108
homosexuality, 20, 103, 106-9, 118n, 157, 184n
honour
  family, 26, 125, 128-9, 131, 150n, 155, 158, 173
  killings, 2, 13, 25, 128-31, 133, 134, 150n
hooks, bell, 128
How to Do Things with Words (Austin), 93
Huggan, Graham, 8
Hum Aapke Hain Koun (*Can You Name Our Relationship?*), 14, 154, 162, 169
Huntington, Samuel, 167
hybridity
  and aesthetics, 8, 32, 40, 70, 115, 122-3, 170-1, 184n
  cultural, 13, 29, 38, 104-5, 115, 118n, 122-3, 141-2, 144, 149, 169, 185n
  and genre, 14, 163, 175, 179, 182
  and family, 75, 116, 135-42, 149, 157, 159, 161
  and identity, 8, 13, 28, 40, 75, 101, 104-5, 109, 116, 127, 135, 137, 144, 149, 157, 159, 168, 179

I Am My Mother's Daughter (*Ich bin Tochter meiner Mutter*), 89, 93, 94
I for India, 12, 94-100
identity
  collective, 22, 25, 86
  diasporic, 11-12, 40, 22, 28, 57, 103-5, 127
  ethnic, 22, 142
  formation, 2, 60, 86

219

identity (cont.)
  gender, 107, 109, 125, 126
  hybrid, 8, 13, 28, 40, 75, 101, 104–5, 109, 116, 127, 135, 137, 144, 157, 159, 168, 179
  hyphenated, 8, 11, 44
  politics, 8, 95
  queer, 13, 40, 60, 83n, 85, 103–5
Idir (Hamid Cheriet), 83n
idyllic chronotope, 56, 63, 64–6, 75
Im Juli (*In July*), 82n
Imaginary Homelands (Rushdie), 185n
Immigrant Memories (*Mémoires d'immigrés – L'héritage maghrébin*), 12, 30–1, 62–3, 90–4
immigration, 2, 9, 11, 29–31, 94, 95, 97
Impossible Desires (Gopinath), 104
In July (*Im Juli*), 82n
Inch' Allah Sunday (*Sunday God Willing / Inch' Allah Dimanche*), 35, 62, 150n
Ingoldsby, Bron, 20, 49n
intercultural cinema, 13, 141
Intercultural Cinema (Marks), 141
interethnic romance, 14, 158–61, 164–5, 182–4
interracial romance, 10, 40, 101–2, 158–9, 183n
Iordanova, Dina, 16n
Islam
  and female dress codes, 25, 91, 124–5, 128, 130
  fundamentalism, 4, 82, 82n, 167
  Hajj, 75–80
  and patriarchy, 4, 13, 128–9, 130–41, 147–9, 150n
  Sufism, 76, 78, 84n, 138–9, 148
Islam under Siege (Ahmed), 128
It Happened One Night, 164, 165
'It's a family affair' (Gilroy), 44

Jamal, Ahmed Alauddin, 39
James, Oscar, 39
Jameson, Frederic, 83n, 179, 181
Jeunesse dorée (*Golden Youth*), 82n
Jewish diaspora, 7, 16–17n, 22, 83n
Johar, Karan, 170
John, Elton, 162
joint family, 162, 173, 184n; *see also* extended family
Journey of Hope (*Reise der Hoffnung*), 12, 48, 53, 57, 65, 66–9, 81
journeys
  Almanya, 69–75
  attachment to homeland, 46, 58–60
  chronotopes of diaspora, 61–6
  Le Grand Voyage, 75–80
  homebound, 12, 57–9, 80, 138–9
  Journey of Hope, 66–9
  of migration, 12, 53–84
  Monsieur Ibrahim and the Flowers of Koran, 77–8
  outbound, 12, 55–7, 66–9, 69–75
  overview, 53–8, 80–2
  of quest, 46, 59, 75
  road movie, 5, 12, 55, 65, 66, 73–8, 80, 83n
Joyce, James, 44
Julien, Isaac, 40, 81

Kaagaz Ke Phool (*Paper Flowers*), 99
Kaes, Anton, 59
Kaganski, Serge, 144
Kaplan, Anne E., 117n
Kapoor, Rajaat, 175
Kassovitz, Mathieu, 124, 149n, 159

Kechiche, Abdellatif
  biography, 32
  Couscous, 35, 142, 143, 145, 146, 150n
  cultural difference, 8
  cultural métissage, 51n
  diasporic family, 32, 35
  gender, 124
Kekilli, Sibel, 130, 133
Keltoum's Daughter (*La Fille de Keltoum*), 54, 57, 59–60, 73, 102, 132
Khan, Aqib, 137
Khan, Saroj, 177
Khan, Shah Rukh, 150n, 172
Khan-Din, Ayub, 32, 33, 135, 140, 143
The Kid from Chaaba (*Shantytown Kid / Le Gone du Chaâba*), 35, 117n
Kim (Kipling), 139
Kipling, Rudyard, 135, 139
Kiss Me Kismet (*My Crazy Turkish Wedding / Meine verrückte türkische Hochzeit*), 163
Koller, Xavier, 48, 53, 66, 69
Korte, Barbara, 40, 135
Koyuncu, Kazım, 54, 82n
Kuhn, Annette, 12, 91, 95, 100
Kureishi, Hanif, 32–3, 110–13

labour migration, 6, 23–5, 29, 30, 83n
Lambert, Paul, 183n
Landsberg, Alison, 12, 48, 88
Laverty, Paul, 160
Lebeau, Vicky, 10
Lee, Ang, 157
Lee, Bruce, 123
lesbianism, 20, 103, 104, 113–15
Lévi-Strauss, Claude, 19
lieux de mémoires, 86
Little Miss Sunshine, 83n
Little Senegal, 61–2, 68
Living in Paradise (*Vivre au paradis*), 35
Loach, Ken, 160
Lola, 118n
Lola and Bilidkid (*Lola und Bilidikid*), 5, 13, 103, 106–9, 183n
Lola rennt (*Run, Lola, Run*), 118n
Loshitzky, Yosefa, 67, 83n
Loulou, 145
Love + Hate, 159
Lury, Karen, 10, 83n

McClintock, Anne, 42, 125
McNeill, Isabelle, 86
Maghrebi French cinema, 14, 34–7, 41, 47, 61–3, 122
  17 Blue Street, 35
  Bad Faith, 156, 160, 161, 184n
  Baton Rouge, 34
  Boys on the Beach, 41
  Café au lait, 5, 159–60, 183n
  Chouchou, 41, 156
  Couscous, 14, 35, 142–7, 148, 149
  Games of Love and Chance, 124
  Golden Youth, 82n
  Immigrant Memories, 12, 30–1, 62–3, 90–4
  Keltoum's Daughter, 54, 57, 59–60, 73, 102, 132
  The Kid from Chaaba, 35, 117n
  Living in Paradise, 35
  Pierre and Djemila, 159, 184n
  The Race, 41
  Raï, 124
  Samia, 124, 144

Sous les pieds des femmes, 35
Tea in the Harem, 33–7, 122, 144, 146
see also beur cinema
magical realism, 70, 71, 74, 82–4
Majd, Mohamed, 77
Majdhar, 39
Make Yourself at Home (TV show), 95, 97
Malik, Sarita, 38, 40, 68, 156
Mama, There's a Man in Your Bed (*Romuald et Juliette*), 184n
Mandel, Ruth, 118n
Mangeshkar, Lata, 99
Mannheim, Karl, 36, 37, 51n
Marienstras, Richard, 22
Marks, Laura, 13, 141, 144, 149n
Martin-Jones, David, 113
Massey, Doreen, 32, 169
Matthes, Joachim, 37, 51n
Matussek, Matthias, 21
Mauvaise Foi (*Bad Faith*), 4, 156, 160, 161, 184n
Measures of Distance (Hatoum), 149n
Mediating the Family (Ticknell), 10
Mein Vater, der Gastarbeiter (*My Father, the Guest Worker*), 12, 30, 89, 93
Meine verrückte türkische Hochzeit (*My Crazy Turkish Wedding / Kiss Me Kismet*), 163
melodrama, 5, 10, 14, 131, 134, 157–8, 161–2, 165, 170, 171, 173, 178, 183n, 184n
Mémoires d'immigrés – L'héritage maghrébin (*Immigrant Memories*), 12, 30–1, 62–3, 90–4
Memorial (*Samadhi*), 170
memory, 85–116
  collective, 12, 22, 25, 45, 48, 57, 86, 89, 95
  definition, 117n
  diasporic family, 33, 37, 86
  family secrets, 100–6
  journeys into the past, 58, 64, 83–4n
  of migration, 1, 25, 33, 64
  overview, 85–6
  phantoms, 101, 106, 108–9, 117n, 118n
  postmemory, 12, 37, 48, 86–94, 117n
  prosthetic memory, 48, 87–8, 99
  transgenerational transmission, 13, 94–100, 108
Memory and the Moving Image (McNeill), 86
Menace II Society, 122
Mennel, Barbara, 82n, 84n
Mercer, Kobena, 81
Métisse (*Café au lait*), 5, 159–60, 183n
Midnight's Children (Rushdie), 70, 71, 74, 84n
migrant and diasporic cinema
  aesthetics, 6, 40, 141, 144, 171, 175; *see also* hybridity, and aesthetics; hybridity, and genre
  Asian British: *Bend It Like Beckham*, 33, 40, 41, 126–8; *Brick Lane*, 4, 56; *Bride and Prejudice*, 14, 150n, 153, 175–81, 182; *Brothers in Trouble*, 136; diasporic family, 32–3, 39–40; *East is East*, 13, 33, 41, 51n, 135–7, 140, 148, 155–6; *I for India*, 12, 94–100; *Love + Hate*, 159; *Majdhar*, 39; *My Beautiful Laundrette*, 13, 32–3, 39–40, 103, 109–13, 119n; *Nina's Heavenly Nights*, 13, 40, 103, 109, 113–15, 142; *Sammy and Rosie Get Laid*, 33; *West is West*, 4, 14, 41, 135, 138–40, 142, 148–50; *Yasmin*, 4, 126, 156
  banlieue cinema, 34–6, 121–4, 146, 156
  beur cinema, 34–7, 93, 122, 124, 143, 146, 156
  Black British, 4, 14, 15n, 38–40, 52n, 102–3, 122, 156; *Babymother*, 4, 15n, 102–3; *Bullet Boy*, 4, 15n, 122; *Burning an Illusion*, 38; *The Nine Muses*, 44; *Pressure*, 38, 39, 52n; *Young Soul Rebels*, 40
  definition, 6–9, 37
  diasporic family, 32–41
  Maghrebi French, 14, 34–7, 41, 47, 61–3, 122; *Bad Faith*, 156, 160, 161, 184n; *Baton Rouge*, 34; *Boys on the Beach*, 41; *Café au lait*, 5, 159–60, 183n; *Chouchou*, 41, 156; *Couscous*, 14, 35, 142–7, 148, 149; *Games of Love and Chance*, 124; *Golden Youth*, 82n; *Immigrant Memories*, 12, 30–1, 62–3, 90–4; *Keltoum's Daughter*, 54, 57, 59–60, 73, 102, 132; *The Kid from Chaaba*, 35, 117n; *Living in Paradise*, 35; *Pierre and Djemila*, 159, 184n; *The Race*, 41; *Raï*, 124; *Samia*, 124, 144; *17 Blue Street*, 35; *Sous les pieds des femmes*, 35; *Tea in the Harem*, 33–7, 122, 144, 146; *see also beur* cinema
  memory, 86–116
  music, 40, 54, 62, 83n, 122, 136, 146, 160, 169, 170, 181, 184n
  postmemory, 12, 33, 37, 48, 87–8
  transnational cinema, 37, 49, 64
  Turkish German, 7, 14, 33, 41, 48, 60, 88–9, 156; *Almanya*, 1, 5, 12, 31, 41, 69–75, 81–2; *April Children*, 154, 155; *Chiko*, 122; diasporic film culture, 7; *Düğün – The Wedding*, 54, 132, 154, 155; *Evet, I Do!*, 14, 103, 153, 163–9, 182; *Farewell to a False Paradise*, 69; *Forty Square Metres of Germany*, 36, 37, 69; *Head-On*, 41, 131, 150n, 157–8, 183n; *I Am My Mother's Daughter*, 89, 93, 94; *Lola and Bilidikid*, 5, 13, 103, 106–9, 183n; *My Crazy Turkish Wedding*, 163; *My Father, the Guest Worker*, 12, 30, 89, 93; *Tour Abroad*, 47, 60, 81; *We Have Forgotten To Return*, 82n, 88–9; *When We Leave*, 13, 48, 54, 129–34, 149, 150n; *Winter Flowers*, 82n; *Yasemin*, 126, 131, 150n, 155
  and World Cinema, 6, 8, 10, 11
migration
  diasporic family, 21–3, 29–31, 33, 49
  labour, 6, 23–5, 29–30, 83n
  memory of, 1, 12, 23, 25, 37, 56, 64, 88
  postcolonial, 6, 43–4
  postwar, 7, 23–5, 29, 44, 48, 50n
  transnational, 2, 9, 16n, 21–3, 72, 80
Miller, Mark J., 29–30
Mississippi Masala, 101–2, 169
Monsieur Ibrahim and the Flowers of Koran (*Monsieur Ibrahim ou les fleurs du Coran*), 77, 81, 84n, 148
Monsoon (*Barsaat*), 179
Monsoon Wedding, 14, 49, 103, 153, 162, 182, 184–5
Moonstruck, 3, 152, 184n
Moore-Gilbert, Bart, 110
Moorti, Sujat, 169, 175
Morely, David, 58
mother, 4, 10, 15n, 42–3, 44, 46, 48, 59, 60, 89, 90, 93, 102, 113, 126, 135–6, 146, 149n, 158, 184n
Moynihan Report, 50n
Mukli, Gandi, 107
Multi-Ethnic France (Hargreaves), 78
multiplex, 6
Murdock, George Peter, 19, 20, 49n
Müren, Zeki, 83n
music, 40, 54, 62, 83n, 122, 136, 146, 160, 169, 170, 181, 184n

221

My Beautiful Laundrette, 13, 32–3, 39–40, 103, 105, 109, 115, 119n
My Best Friend's Wedding, 153
My Big Fat Greek Wedding, 14, 142, 150n, 153, 163–4, 167–8, 182–3
My Crazy Turkish Wedding (*Kiss Me Kismet / Meine verrückte türkische Hochzeit*), 163
My Fair Lady, 184n
My Father, the Guest Worker (*Mein Vater, der Gastarbeiter*), 12, 30, 89, 93

Naficy, Hamid
  accented cinema, 6, 32, 51–2, 55
  chronotope, 12, 64
  daughter text, 89
  diasporic family, 32, 51n, 52n
  doubling, 84n
  extended family, 149n
  homeland, 140
  Jewish diaspora, 16–17n
  journeys, 55, 57–8, 64, 67, 84n
  multiplex, 6
Nagra, Parminder, 127
Nair, Mira, 8, 101, 169, 170, 172, 173, 175, 180, 184n
The Namesake, 56, 81, 169
National Socialism, 106, 108, 118n
Negri, Antonio, 9
Nietzsche, Friedrich, 44
Nina's Heavenly Delights, 13, 40, 103, 105, 109, 113–15, 142, 149
The Nine Muses, 44
Nini, Soraya, 124
No Place Like Home (Von Moltke), 58
Nölle, Stefan, 84n
Nora, Pierre, 12, 86, 117n
Norville, Herbert, 39
nostalgia, 3, 22, 23, 48, 49n, 74–5, 81, 182
Nostalgia (*Nostalghia*), 74
nuclear family, 8, 18, 19, 21, 25, 26
Nuovomondo (*Golden Door*), 83n

Obama, Barack, 43
Obama, Michelle, 42, 43
Odone, Christina, 15n
Olympia, 106
Orientalism (Said), 5
Otnes, Cele, 162
Ové, Horace, 52n

Pacino, Al, 123
paedophilia, 103, 172, 173
Pagnol, Marcel, 145
Pakeezah, 136
Paper Flowers (*Kaagaz Ke Phool*), 99
Pardes (*Another Land*), 150n, 172
Paris, Texas, 65, 83n
Parmar, Pratibha, 109, 113, 118n
parody, 179, 181
pastiche, 179–80, 181, 185n
patchwork family, 35, 51n, 142, 148
patriarchy, 4, 10, 13, 26, 106, 125, 128–9, 130–41, 146–9
Pencha, Madhorma, 170
Penn, Roger, 183n
Pennebaker, D. A., 170
phantoms, 101, 106, 108–9, 117n, 118n
photography
  and family, 12, 48, 83n, 86, 87, 91–3, 95, 99, 116, 152–3, 162, 174
  and wedding, 92–3, 152–3, 174

Pialat, Maurice, 145
Pierre and Djemila (*Pierre et Djemila*), 159, 184n
Pines, Jim, 38, 39
Pisters, Patrica, 9
Playing the Race Card (Williams), 10
Pleck, Elizabeth, 162
Poitier, Sidney, 159
Polat, Ayşe, 33, 47
Pomerance, Murray, 10
The Postcolonial Exotic (Huggan), 8
Postcolonial Hospitality (Rosello), 36
postcolonial urban conviviality, 160, 183n
postmemory, 12, 37, 48, 87–8, 117n
postmemory documentaries, 12, 33, 85, 86–94, 116
Powell, Enoch, 136
Pressure, 38, 39, 52n
Pretty Woman, 164, 184n
Pride and Prejudice, 176, 180
The Principle of Hope (*Das Prinzip Hoffnung*) (Bloch), 59
A Private Enterprise, 136
production of locality
  in *Couscous*, 141–7
  definition, 120–1
  in diasporic family, 13, 23
  in *East is East* and *West is West*, 135–41
  gender and generation, 120, 121, 147–9
  rites of institution, 153
prosthetic memory, 48, 87–8, 99
psychoanalytic framework, 11, 13
Purab Aur Pachhim (*East and West*), 179
Puri, Om, 137
Pyaasa (*Thirst*), 172
Pygmalion (Shaw), 184n

queerness
  definition, 104
  diasporic identities, 13, 40, 103–5, 115–16, 188n
  family secrets, 13, 103–5, 116
  Lola and Bilidkid, 106–9
  My Beautiful Laundrette, 109–13
  Nina's Heavenly Delights, 113–15
  The Wedding Banquet, 157–8

The Race (*Le Raïd*), 41
Raging Bull, 123
Raï, 124
Rai, Aishwarya, 176, 178
Le Raïd (*The Race*), 41
Raising Arizona, 83n
Ramdya, Kavita, 182
rap music, 122
Ray-Gavras, Michèle, 34
reggae music, 40
Reise der Hoffnung (*Journey of Hope*), 12, 48, 53, 57, 65, 66–9, 81
Reiss, Ira, 20
Reitz, Edgar, 59
Renoir, Jean, 145
Renov, Michael, 89–90, 95
Representing the Family (Chambers), 10
Retake Film and Video Collective, 39, 40
Riefenstahl, Leni, 106
road chronotope, 56, 63, 65, 73, 74
road movie, 5, 12, 55, 65, 66, 73–8, 80, 83n
The Road to Hope (*Il cammino della speranza*), 83n
Roberts, Kevin, 58
Robeson, Paul, 44

Rocco and his Brothers (*Rocco e i suoi fratelli*), 55
romance, 152–85
  Bride and Prejudice, 175–81
  interethnic, 14, 158–61, 164–5, 182–4
  interracial, 10, 40, 101–2, 158–9, 183n
  Monsoon Wedding, 169–75
  overview, 152–4, 181–3
  romantic comedy, 163–9
  variations on the wedding theme, 154–63
romantic comedy
  Bride and Prejudice, 175–81
  Evet, I Do!, 14, 103, 153, 163–9, 182
  generic conventions, 5, 14, 40, 142, 149, 152–3, 163–9, 176–7, 184n
  My Big Fat Greek Wedding, 163, 164, 167–8
  Nina's Heavenly Delights, 114–15
  romance and weddings, 5, 14, 40, 159, 162, 163–9, 182
Romuald et Juliette (*Mama, There's a Man in Your Bed*), 184n
Rosello, Mireille, 36, 150n
Rosman, Abraham, 24
Roudinesco, Elisabeth, 21
Rowe, Katherine, 184n
Rubel, Paula, 24
Rueschmann, Eva, 111
Run, Lola, Run (*Lola rennt*), 118n
Runaway Bride, 153
Rushdie, Salman, 70, 71, 73, 74, 83–4n, 118n, 185n

Safran, William, 22, 50n
Said, Edward, 5
Salaam Bombay, 169
Samadhi (*Memorial*), 170
Samant, Sapna, 178
Samdereli, Nesrin, 33
Samdereli, Yasemin, 31, 33
Samia, 124, 144
Sammy and Rosie Get Laid, 33
Sanders-Brahms, Helma, 154, 155
Sankofa Film and Video Collective, 40
Sapphire, 38
Sarrazin, Thilo, 2, 15n
Sawalha, Nadim, 137
Scarface, 123, 149n
Schafmeister, Heinrich, 166
Schatz, Thomas, 5
Schiller, Nizam, 133
Schilt, Thibaut, 80
Schlink, Bernard, 58
Schützenberger, Anne Ancelin, 101
'Screen Memories' (Freud), 100
second-wave feminism, 20, 95
The Secret of the Grain (*Couscous* / *La Graine et le mulet*), 14, 35, 142–7, 148, 149
secrets, 12, 13, 85–6, 100–6, 115–16
Seeßlen, Georg, 37, 38
sexuality, 10, 19, 40, 103, 109, 147, 167, 171
Shah, Naseeruddin, 175
Shakespeare, William, 44, 118n
Shantytown Kid (*The Kid from Chaaba* / *Le Gone du chaâba*), 35, 117n
Sharpe, Jenny, 172
Shaw, George Bernard, 184n
Sheffer, Gabriel, 25
The Shell and the Kernel (Abraham and Torok), 101
ship chronotope, 56, 61–3, 83n
Shirin's Wedding (*Shirin's Hochzeit*), 154–5

Shohat, Ella, 27, 169
Shooting the Family (Pisters and Staat), 9
Shor, 99
Short Sharp Shock, 47, 122, 123
Sillars, Jane, 45
Sinclair, John, 28
Sinfield, Alan, 103
Singleton, John, 15n
The Slave Ship (Turner), 61
slavery, 23, 61, 62, 159
Soetoro-Ng, Maya, 43
Solino, 55
son, 15n, 77–8, 122, 144
Sontag, Susan, 91, 92
soul music, 40
The Souls of Black Folk (Du Bois), 17n
Sous les pieds des femmes, 35
The Squale (*La Squale*), 124
Staat, Wim, 9
Stacey, Judith, 20
Staiger, Janet, 14, 175, 185n
Stam, Robert, 27, 63–4, 169
Starkey, David, 15n
Steinbeck, John, 55
stereotypes, 5, 16n, 110, 128, 139–40, 147, 154, 167, 179
Sternberg, Claudia, 40, 135, 136
Sternberg, Josef von, 118n
Submission, 125, 149n
Sufism, 76, 78, 84n, 138–9, 148
Sunday God Willing (*Inch' Allah Sunday* / *Inch' Allah Dimanche*), 35, 62, 150n
Suri, Sandhya, 33, 94–6, 98–100, 117n, 143
Suri, Yash Pal, 95–100
Sürücü, Hatun, 130
'Surviving Images' (Hirsch), 88
Suzie Gold, 163
Syal, Meera, 33

Tarkovsky, Andrei, 74
Tarr, Carrie, 34, 35, 156
Taxi Driver, 123
Tea in the Harem (*Le Thé au harem d'Archimède*), 33–7, 122, 144, 146
Thatcher, Margaret, 110, 112, 113, 119n
Le Thé au harem d'Archimède (*Tea in the Harem*), 33–7, 122, 144, 146
There Ain't No Black in the Union Jack (Gilroy), 112, 118n
Thirst (*Pyaasa*), 172
Thomas, Rosie, 171
Thus Spake Zarathustra (Nietzsche), 44
Tölölyan, Khachig, 1, 44
Toni, 145
Torok, Maria, 13, 101, 108, 118n
A Touch of Pink, 40, 103
Tour Abroad (*Auslandstournee*), 47, 60, 81
tourism, 180, 181
Tracy, Spencer, 158
traditional family, 3, 26–7, 49n, 65, 113, 158, 163
transnational family, 21, 23, 24, 140–1
transnational migration, 2, 9, 16n, 21–3, 72, 80
Tunç, Ayça, 51n
Turkish German cinema, 7, 14, 33, 41, 48, 60, 88–9, 156
  Almanya, 1, 5, 12, 31, 41, 69–75, 81–2
  April Children, 154, 155
  Chiko, 122
  Düğün – The Wedding, 54, 132, 154, 155
  Evet, I Do!, 14, 103, 153, 163–9, 182

Turkish German cinema (cont.)
  Farewell to a False Paradise, 69
  Forty Square Metres of Germany, 36, 37, 69
  Head-On, 41, 131, 150n, 157–8, 183n
  I Am My Mother's Daughter, 89, 93, 94
  Lola and Bilidkid, 5, 13, 103, 106–9, 183n
  My Crazy Turkish Wedding, 163
  My Father, the Guest Worker, 12, 30, 89, 93
  Tour Abroad, 47, 60, 81
  We Have Forgotten To Return, 82n, 88–9
  When We Leave, 13, 48, 54, 129–34, 149, 150n
  Winter Flowers, 82n
  Yasemin, 126, 131, 150n, 155
Turner, William, 61
The Two Dads and One Mom (Les Deux Papas et la Maman), 41

Uberoi, Patricia, 174
Udwin, Leslie, 41
Unthinking Eurocentrism (Shohat and Stam), 27
Urry, John, 180

The Vagabond (Awaara), 172
Vanity Fair, 169
Vardalos, Nia, 164, 168
Vertovec, Steven, 50n
Vierzig Quadratmeter Deutschland (Forty Square Metres of Germany), 36, 37, 69
Vincendeau, Ginette, 145, 149n
Visconti, Luchino, 55
Vivre au paradis (Living in Paradise), 35
von Miller, Julia, 84n
Von Moltke, Johannes, 58, 59
Vuorela, Ulla, 23, 24

Walker, Beverly, 66
Warnecke, Gordon, 111
Wartenberg, Thomas, 164
The Way We Never Were (Coontz), 3
We Are What We Eat (Gabaccia), 142
We Have Forgotten To Return (Wir haben vergessen zurückzukehren), 82n, 88–9
A Wedding, 184n
The Wedding Banquet, 103, 157, 158
The Wedding Planner, 153
The Wedding Singer, 153
weddings, 152–85
  April Children, 154, 155
  Bride and Prejudice, 175–81

Douce France, 156–7
Düğün – The Wedding, 154–5
East is East, 156–7
Four Weddings and a Funeral, 153, 162, 165
Head-On, 157–8
Monsoon Wedding, 169–75
Moonstruck, 152
My Big Fat Greek Wedding, 153, 163–4, 167–8, 182–3
overview, 14, 152–4, 181–3
photography, 92–3, 152–3, 174
rituals, 140
romantic comedy, 163–9
sham weddings, 14, 153, 157, 158
Shirin's Wedding, 154–5
variations on wedding theme, 154–63
The Wedding Banquet, 103, 157, 158
Weigel, Sigrid, 51n
Wenders, Wim, 60, 65
Werbner, Pnina, 49n
West is West, 4, 14, 135, 138–40, 142, 148–50
West Side Story, 179
western films, 65
Weston, Kath, 151
Wexman, Virginia Wright, 183n
What's Cooking?, 142
When We Leave (Die Fremde), 13, 48, 54, 129–34, 149, 150n
White (Dyer), 52n
Wilde, Oscar, 103, 118n
Williams, James, 51n
Williams, Linda, 10
Winter Flowers (Winterblume), 82n
Wir haben vergessen zurückzukehren (We Have Forgotten To Return), 82n, 88–9
Wolfe, Thomas, 60
women's role, 10, 20, 95, 125–6, 129
Wondrous Oblivion, 183–4n
World Cinema, 6, 8, 10, 11

Yara (The Wound), 82n
Yasemin, 126, 131, 150n, 155
Yasmin, 4, 126, 156
Yavuz, Yüksel, 33, 51n, 89, 93, 143, 155
Yıldız, Erdal, 107
Young Soul Rebels, 40
Yuval-Davis, Nira, 125

Zem, Roschdy, 161
Zwick, Joel, 165